MUSIC AND HUMAN EXPERIENCE

To my children—
Ned, Nicholas, and Oliver

Schirmer Books
A Division of Macmillan Publishing Co., Inc.
866 Third Avenue, New York, N.Y. 10022

Collier Macmillan Canada, Ltd.

Library of Congress Catalog Card Number: 79-7479

Printed in the United States of America

printing number

1   2   3   4   5   6   7   8   9   10

Library of Congress Cataloging in Publication Data

Komar, Arthur
   Music and human experience.
   1. Music—Analysis, appreciation.   I. Title.
MT6.K812M9   780'.15   79-7479
ISBN 0-02-871070-3

MUSIC AND HUMAN EXPERIENCE

ARTHUR KOMAR

SCHIRMER BOOKS
A Division of Macmillan Publishing Co., Inc.
NEW YORK

CHAPTERS:

Unit III ▪ Music and Society 139

x

CONTENTS

CHAPTERS:

Unit II ▪ The Music of Lands and Peoples 57

CHAPTERS:

Unit VI ▪ Music and Emotion   **343**

Unit VII ▪ Music and Death   **395**

CHAPTERS:

INDEX OF COMPOSERS
AND COMPOSITIONS

(Boldface type indicates works featured in the text; boldface page numbers indicate listening guides. All vocal works—including anonymous popular, folk, and patriotic songs—and instrumental works identifiable by unique titles—such as *Art of the Fugue* and *Don Quixote*—are listed in the General Index starting on page 495.)

Index of Composers and Compositions

Index of Composers and Compositions

Index of Composers and Compositions

Index of Composers and Compositions

Index of Composers and Compositions

Index of Composers and Compositions

INTRODUCTION

Music communicates!

Poets interpret the world in verbal configurations; painters depict the world in color, line, and texture. Composers are aural—rather than verbal or visual—artists who express the vast range of human experience in combinations of sounds. Instrumental and vocal tones comprise composers' palettes, the interrelation of these tones their syntax. A piece of music can be likened to an abstract poem or a nonobjective painting, for in none of these is everyday language the medium of expression. Limiting the discussion to music, its very abstraction constitutes a serious problem. Composers may "say" a-lot, but what do they mean? Sending and receiving messages inexpressible in words, musicians appear to be isolated from the world surrounding them. I, the author of this book, am communicating with you, its reader, and you comprehend my meaning. If I had tried to express myself by composing tones instead of writing words, could you still understand me? Or would my music erect a communications barrier between us?

This suggests a certain remoteness in music. What is the purpose of purely musical expression? Wherein lies its value?

Think for a moment about the act of speaking. Try talking with words alone, with no facial expressions, hand gestures, or changes of voice pitch. The result? You sound and look like a zombie, more dead than alive. Words by themselves do not suffice. To get your ideas across you must inflect your words, speak with feeling. Right now, as you read these words, you are automatically adding inflective nuances to help me get my ideas across. Moreover, words cannot always be found to fit every situation; whole areas of human experience escape them. The more elusive the right word, the more reliant the speaker on visual gestures and oral inflections. Musical expression is related to these inflections and finds a way into cracks not penetrable by concrete words. A special virtue of music is to convey feelings—feelings that we often cannot identify or otherwise delineate verbally. Music remote? Certainly not!

But, if music is basic to the human experience, why do so many people find it hard to enjoy? Of course, folk and popular styles demand little of the listener, but *classical music* is something else again. Undoubtedly, it was of classical music Romain Rolland was thinking when he wrote: "Music perplexes those who have no feeling for it; it seems to them an incomprehensible art, beyond reasoning and having no connection with reality."[1] For much of the general populace classical music is more than perplexing; it is downright unpopular. Most people are content to leave the pleasure of music to the ears of a small band of musical connoisseurs. In so doing, they are depriving themselves of a rich and rewarding facet of human existence.

The aim of an introductory music course should be to remove the barriers preventing the musical newcomer from entering the world of classical music, to help direct the student toward an appreciation of masterpieces past and present. The approach presented in *Music and Human Experience* is to seek out and exploit a bond inherent in teacher, student, performer, and composer alike. All four share a single indisputable attribute: their common humanity. Each of them is born to enjoy and suffer, to work and play. Each knows the rewards and frustrations of love. Everyone has been exposed to, or is at least aware of, some form of religion. Great social, moral, and ethical issues confront us. We are sensitive to nature, and we fantasize about travel to foreign lands. Each of us has thought about death and has known someone who has died. Listener, performer, and composer, we are all intensely human and can share our humanity with one another. In this respect composers are especially important. As creative artists, they write down more than notes: they inscribe their experiences as human beings, for all to hear.

How did Beethoven deal with human experience in a piece like his *Symphony No. 5*? This is a tough question, one that aestheticians have long pondered with inconclusive results. It is one thing to argue that music sounds purposeful, that it seems to be *about* something, and another to specify precisely what that something is. On the other hand, we know what Beethoven's *Symphony No. 6* is about. Known as the *Pastoral,* this symphony was created with the explicit intention of registering, in artistic terms, the composer's observations and feelings about country scenes. (Note the qualification, *in artistic terms;* merely identifying the subject of a musical piece is not the same as being able to translate the music into words.) In the realm of orchestral music, Beethoven's "program symphony" was a novelty, establishing a precedent which composers enthusiastically adopted immediately after Beethoven's death (1827). Hector Berlioz' *Symphonie fantastique* (1830) portrays an unrequited opium-sated lover; Franz Liszt wrote a symphony about the philosopher Faust (1854); and Richard Strauss drew on German folklore for his tone poem, *Till Eulenspiegel's Merry Pranks* (1895). The trend continued unabated into the twentieth century, with programmatic masterpieces such as Claude Debussy's *La Mer* (The Sea). Nor is descriptive music limited to orchestral works. Composers in the sixteenth through eighteenth centuries produced an abundance of program pieces for keyboard (William Byrd, François Couperin) and chamber ensembles (Antonio Vivaldi). The nineteenth century, with its *Scenes from Childhood* by Robert Schumann and *Songs Without Words* by Felix Mendelssohn, was a heyday of small-scale character pieces for piano. And in the twentieth century we have witnessed the unveiling of works like Charles Ives's *Concord Sonata* for piano and Arnold Schoenberg's *Transfigured Night* for strings. With all this instrumental music, one can respond to the extramusical content first, the purely musical elements second. In other words, one can first absorb oneself in the subjects of death, love, religion, society, and politics, and so on, as a transition to experiencing the music for its own sake.

An enormous quantity of Western music, ancient and modern, is based on verbal texts. Solo vocal music may tell about anything under the sun. There are love songs, both happy and sad; songs about war and about peace; songs on nature, work, and adventure. Liturgical music is represented in anthems and motets for small vocal ensembles and in cantatas and oratorios for large groups. And then there is the form that Samuel Johnson once described as "an extravagant and irrational entertainment" — opera. Many of the world's greatest plays, myths, and national epics have been transformed into monumental grand operas. The Broadway musical is a special kind of modernized, popular opera. It derives from the nineteenth-century comic opera tradition of Gilbert and Sullivan, as well as from the operettas of Sullivan's continental counterparts, Jacques Offenbach and Johann Strauss, Jr. The operetta form itself is a direct offshoot of grand opera. Still another genre, bridging vocal and symphonic music, is the vocal symphony, the progenitor of which is Beethoven's *Symphony No. 9,* with its magnificent setting of Schiller's *Ode to Joy.* In all these vocal genres, the composer communicates to us verbally as well as by purely musical means. We need not rely solely on the music to find out what the composer had in mind.

In the final analysis, the perception of extramusical content has little to do with appreciating great music, but it can facilitate one's initial exposure to the masterworks. The key word here is *exposure.* The idea is for students to overcome their reluctance to discover the sounds of classical music, to sample a wide range of musical styles and genres. To this end, *Music and Human Experience* surveys a multitude of vocal and instrumental works relating to various aspects of the human condition. The general procedure is to combine assigned listening with just enough explanatory comment to allow the student to perceive the historical/structural content of the music. For example, in dealing with the nationalist movement in European music, the student first listens to relevant works by Smetana, Sibelius, Bartók, and Falla (Chapter 6) and then reads three interconnected general essays on this subject (Chapter 7). The acquiring of historical and technical information remains consistently subsidiary to the primary goal of intensive listening.

The book is divided into seven basic units and is further subdivided into thirty-three smaller chapters. Each unit deals with music associated with a single broad topic: (1) nature, (2) nationalism and foreign travel, (3) society, (4) philosophy, (5) worship, (6) emotion, and (7) death. The units are segmented into from three to seven chapters, providing descriptions of individual pieces and supplementary background readings. Some chapters consist exclusively of guides to specific compositions, with each assigned piece accompanied by a discussion of its expressive/humanistic content, and a mixture of biographical, historical, and stylistic data. Other chapters contain readings designed to clarify the assigned pieces, discuss particular issues, and/or broaden the student's general understanding of music. Numerous chapters combine listening guides and brief background readings. Earlier units are longer than later ones, due to the necessity of introducing essential historical and technical information at an early stage.

From the outset the student is exposed to a variety of different styles. For example, in Unit 1 the listening assignments of Chapters 1 and 4 represent six major composers and four historical periods. The readings of Chapter 2 serve mainly to supplement the music of Chapter 1, introducing matters of general importance which will be amplified further in subsequent units. Chapter 3 comprises practical guides applicable to all listenings and readings. The supplementary essays of Chapter 5 are of lesser importance, relating to issues raised for the most part only in Unit 1. Nevertheless, these optional readings may prove useful as a stimulus to extra listening. Of course, the final determination of essential and optional readings rests with the teacher.

The six remaining units alternate listening guides with a mixture of primary and secondary readings. Each unit covers limited material, but the totality of all seven units approaches comprehensiveness. Every historical period is touched on, each important Western nation is visited, the three major religions are examined, and so on. Aspects of theory are explored, genres surveyed, and terms defined. Most important, nearly all major composers (and some minor ones as well) are featured in at least one unit, if not in several units. To cite only the four composers represented in Chapter 1, the student encounters Beethoven's *Pastoral Symphony* in Unit 1, his *Eroica Symphony* in Unit 3, *Symphony No. 9* in Unit 4, and the *String Quartet in A Minor,* Op. 132, in Unit 6. Debussy's music appears in Unit 1 (*La Mer*) and Unit 3 (*Children's Corner*). Vivaldi and Mendelssohn are featured in Unit 1 alone, although occasional references to their music crop up elsewhere in the text as well. This arrangement approximates the cumulative learning experience of the commited music student. For example, budding young pianists do not limit themselves to studying one composer at a time, taking up Mozart first, then dropping him in favor of Beethoven, and finally proceeding to Chopin to the exclusion of both Mozart and Beethoven. Rather, easier works by all three masters are selected at first, giving way gradually to more difficult works by these and other composers. Musicians switch continually from one composer to another, one period to another, and one genre to another, accumulating experience and knowledge little by little. The framework of *Music and Human Experience* follows the same line of approach. At the end of a semester's work, students will have encountered a large body of music and will have acquired much information concerning that music. Having absorbed the music in the meaningful associative context of extramusical topics of universal interest, they will have a good chance of enjoying and remembering a substantial amount of this voluminous material.

Music and Human Experience offers a number of helpful learning tools. Definitions and dates are stated and repeated frequently throughout the text. A list of concepts and terms is found at the conclusion of each unit, and a Glossary of Terms is provided in Appendix II. Thought-provoking and memory-stimulating questionnaires follow Units 2, 4, 6, and 7, and Unit 7 concludes with some general advice to the reader. Following the Table of Contents is an Index of Composers and Compositions, with works featured in listening guides listed in boldface print. Numerous musical examples illustrate the discussions. Although no previous musical training is expected of the reader, much useful information can be gleaned from these examples; to that end a brief guide to music notation is presented in Chapter 3. Chapter 3 also offers pointers in understanding titles and subheadings, using recordings for homework and independent research, and preparing listening reports.

A novelty of this book is its focus on literature. Our educational system introduces reading to the very young but postpones listening to serious music until much later, if not indefinitely. Literary references to music, drawn from fiction, nonfiction, poetry, and drama, help bring the student into closer contact with the world of music.

Introduction

Some of this literary material deals with subject matter covered in selected musical works, while other items deal directly with music and musicians themselves. The student who enjoys modern fiction may develop a special feeling for Beethoven's "Holy Song of Thanks" (from the *String Quartet in A Minor*) in the context of Aldous Huxley's novel, *Point Counter Point* (see Chapter 27). Thomas Mann's stories help the reader to enjoy Wagner's music dramas (Chapters 29 and 33), whereas Mann's novel, *Doctor Faustus*, serves as an intriguing introduction to twelve-tone music (Chapter 22). An annotated version of Whit Burnett's charming story, "The Everlasting Quartet" (first published in the *Atlantic Monthly*), invites us into the intimate world of chamber music (Chapter 17). Poetry by Keats, Donne, and Shelley; prose excerpts by George Bernard Shaw, H. L. Mencken, and Elmer Davis; and fiction by Kleist, Hesse, Gide, Cather, Updike, and others—all are quoted or cited in connection with specific pieces or with music generally. Furthermore, many of the musical works considered are interpretations of outstanding poems and plays. For example, Shakespeare's *Romeo and Juliet* is the subject of compositions by Berlioz, Tchaikovsky, Prokofiev, and Bernstein (Chapter 29). An appreciation of Shakespeare can greatly enhance one's enjoyment of the musical achievements of these four diverse composers.

Illustrations appearing throughout the book include original photographs and line drawings and reproductions of world-famous paintings. A folio of instruments and instrumentalists appears between Units 3 and 4.

Appendix I offers suggestions for student assignments outside the scope of daily homework. These projects range from short oral or written reports to extensive term papers, providing the teacher with ample material from which to judge the student's overall effort and accomplishment. The teacher can base course grades exclusively on these independent projects or on a combination of independent work and traditional written and/or listening exams. Most of the projects involve responding to live or recorded performances in connection with research into a particular aspect of music. The wide selection should allow every student the opportunity to pursue special interests that may arise during the semester. Many of the projects permit joint participation by a small group or even the entire class.

Music and Human Experience combines the innovative with the tried and true. It emphasizes texted and program music without sacrificing concrete historical/technical information as found in more traditional textbooks. The teacher may explore new pedagogical pathways; the student can become acclimated to classical music within a humanistic framework. Together, student and teacher can investigate music in a setting that underscores their mutual sharing of the human experience.

NOTE TO THE STUDENT

Society disperses laurels among its top creative artists, raising them up on pedestals, real or figurative. In the case of the great composers, many of us feel that we should love their music without reservation, but realistically no one can live up to this expectation at all times. In this regard, I wish to share a personal experience with the reader. One of Bach's best known cantatas is No. 106, "God's Time Is the Best Time." I originally encountered this music some twenty-five years ago, and it quickly became a favorite with me. Then somehow I did not hear the piece again until I began preparing this book. In the meantime, however, my love for Bach's choral music grew stronger and stronger. So, when I recently acquired a recording of *Cantata No. 106,* I looked forward to hearing it as one looks forward to meeting an old friend. This pleasurable feeling was heightened by praise from many outstanding musicians, who regard the work as one of Bach's finest. But, after placing the needle on the record, I was disappointed to find that the music was irritatingly unfamiliar. It seemed as if I had never heard it before, and my attention wandered instead of holding fast. It then occurred to me that I was experiencing what students might often experience in the course of studying this book; they too might find reputed masterpieces annoyingly strange and inaccessible. This was a sobering thought. In researching and writing this book I was drawing upon an enthusiasm stemming from years of studying, teaching, playing, and simply listening to music. How should I expect the musically inexperienced reader to keep pace?

Now in fact I do not expect you to delve into all the music discussed in this book. A voluminous amount of music is included, to offer flexibility of choice to both teacher and student; in all probability you will sample only a fraction of the pieces. In any case, I want to address myself to the problem of familiarizing oneself with individual pieces of music. Let us say that a work, such as *Cantata No. 106,* is universally admired by all who know it well. That means that the music must be beautiful, doesn't it? But, if, as the proverb says, beauty lies in the eye of the beholder, may it not also sometimes rest in the ear of the listener? A piece that one person loves may fall on the dead ears of another. If you are unfamiliar with a particular period, a particular composer, a particular genre, you may be incapable of enjoying a particular musical selection. Of course, this kind of standoff may only be temporary. After listening to a piece several times in succession, the beauty that others detect in it may begin to emerge for you as well. (But a warning: Overfamiliarity may spoil a piece, too.) Incidentally, it may not be necessary—or even desirable—to concentrate on a piece of music the first few times you hear it through; it may sink in more easily if you absorb it first as background.

This brings to mind an interesting essay, entitled *Bach,* by the noted writer, Gilbert Highet. Highet tells us that for the first twenty years of his musical lifetime he thought that Bach "was a dry old stick who had written some peculiarly difficult puzzles for the piano and organ, and some tediously monotonous religious utterances for the choir. Now I think he was the greatest composer who ever lived."[2] What an extraordinary about-face! These words come from the pen of a noted Columbia University professor, the author of many books, and an outstanding radio lecturer on the arts, including music. If at first Highet could not succeed in liking Bach, then it is little wonder that others have those same feelings. Highet's essay suggests ways of approaching Bach by learning to understand three ideals of Baroque music: tradition, symmetry, and control. Reading Highet, one may gain a better appreciation for Bach's music, but there is no guarantee of loving it. In and of itself, no expository writing (and that includes the essays in this book) will convince you to love a piece of music. As I have indicated, many works can be appreciated from successive hearings, especially if your listening is separated by time intervals. If you find that you cannot initially respond positively to a particular piece, try another part of it or a different one, or go back to another you have enjoyed in the past. Later, give the difficult piece a second chance. Like Highet, you may eventually experience a change of heart about a work by Bach or some other master.

It is time to proceed. Think of the upcoming semester as an opportunity to meld your own life's experiences with those of a broad spectrum of composers. Here is an opportunity to examine music mixed with humanity, to listen to music as the earnest and wonderful expression of mankind.

A.K.

ACKNOWLEDGMENTS

I wish to thank my friends and colleagues for their help during the writing of *Music and Human Experience*. Steven Haflich and Joseph Dyer read substantial portions of the manuscript and offered many useful suggestions. Jeanne Bamberger, John Buttrick, Roland Hutchinson, Mimi Kagan, Mary Lewis, Elizabeth McCrae, Gerald Romanow, Norman Rubin, Robert W. Smith, and Ella Zonis gave advice on several points. Leo Snyder gave assistance with regard to the title. Photographs were provided by Geoff Brewer, Caldwell Colt, David Komar, Eric Levenson, and the publicity offices of Massachusetts Institute of Technology and the New England Conservatory of Music. Nicholas Altenbernd, Arlene Siegel, and Linda Solow assisted with illustrative materials, and Elizabeth Shapiro contributed line drawings of composers and members of the Thoreau Circle. Yale Marshall, Gerald Romanow, and Alberto Sadun supplied translations from the German and Italian.

I am especially indebted to several hundred M.I.T. students who over a period of three years tested this book in its formative stages. Many of these students were uninhibitedly direct in telling me what parts they liked and what parts they thought should be changed. Wherever feasible I have followed their advice. Finally, a word of gratitude to Steve Dydo for the musical autography, and to my ever-helpful editors, Ken Stuart, Abbie Meyer, and William Martin.

MUSIC AND NATURE

NATURE IN ORCHESTRAL SETTINGS

A composer may respond to nature by painting her in musical images. The wind, the sea, or a birdcall may be projected, even without the composer's conscious intent. Consider the orchestral music of Jean Sibelius, the Finnish master who was active during the period 1890–1925. Sibelius's music often suggests winds blowing over the countryside, as string instruments play smooth rising and falling scales, sometimes without stopping on particular pitches (*glissando*).* Yet many of Sibelius's orchestral works bear neutral titles such as *Symphony No. 1*, which reveal nothing at all of their extramusical content. In this same connection, Peter G. Davis, referring to "the profound mystery of natural forces [which] came to pervade all of [his] music," has cited nature as the "source of spiritual inspiration" for Frederick Delius, an English contemporary of Sibelius.[1] And the French writer André Gide has described selected pages of Chopin's† piano music as "shot through with the play of light, with the murmur of water, with wind and foliage," likening certain flowing passages to the "discrete purling of a stream."[2]

Aside from ostensibly nonrepresentational (*absolute*) music, such as Sibelius's symphonies and Chopin's piano pieces, many compositions depict various aspects of nature openly. Four examples of explicit nature music are presented in Chapter 1.

Washington Allston, *The Rising of a Thunderstorm at Sea*. Combining the vocabularies of the visual artist and the composer, Debussy assigned *La Mer* the subtitle, "Three Symphonic Sketches."

Courtesy Museum of Fine Arts, Boston

DEBUSSY, LA MER (THE SEA)

Claude Debussy (1862–1918) was a French composer who eventually became the leading exponent of the compositional style known as *Impressionism*. Paris in the 1870s and 1880s was a hotbed of artistic ferment. Poets, painters, and musicians intermingled

---

*The term *scale* means a succession of ascending or descending adjacent pitches, while *glissando* refers to sliding scales without articulation of individual pitches. For further clarification of technical terms (often printed in italics), check the Glossary in Appendix II.

†Frédéric Chopin was an early nineteenth-century Polish/French composer. Gide (1869–1951) received the Nobel Prize in Literature for his accomplishments as novelist, essayist, and diarist.

their personal and professional lives, striving to discover and develop new modes of expression. Young Debussy lived in direct contact with some of the great minds of the time—Symbolist poets and Impressionist painters in particular—and studied piano under a former student of Chopin. *La Mer* (1905) is a *tone poem* (descriptive work) for large orchestra. Its shimmering sounds reflect the delicacy, vagueness, and ambiguous shapes of the Impressionist school of painting, represented by Monet, Degas, Pissarro, and Renoir, among others. *La Mer* stands as a first-rate example of Impressionist music.

Combining the vocabularies of the visual artist and the composer, Debussy assigned *La Mer* the subtitle *Three Symphonic Sketches*—three sketches for orchestra. The first of these is called "From Dawn to Noontime on the Sea." The music starts very softly, indeed so softly that on a recording you may not be able to determine precisely when the music commences. This softness may be presumed to picture the first breaking through of streaks of light from below the horizon. Only string basses, cellos, violas, harps, and tympani are heard.* Then the violins enter, playing very soft (*pianissimo*) high notes with their bows trembling very fast on the strings (*tremolo*). An atmosphere of expectation is created as the low strings replace the violins with a soft tremolo background underneath a brief tune played in a low register by trumpet and English horn (a deeper member of the oboe family). The sense of expectation is rewarded as the speed (*tempo*) picks up, and the volume grows slightly, suggesting swelling waves along with increasing light. Next comes a rippling figure in the strings, serving as accompaniment to a melody in the French horns. Shortly thereafter a striking passage is played by the oboe and cello. Other instruments are featured as the rolling music reaches its first climax. The music intensifies continually, reflecting water, wind, and sky. By the end of the first sketch, the sun has reached its zenith, and the full orchestra shouts a loud salute to the brightness of the day. Debussy's biographer, Edward Lockspeiser, has described this ending as "amazing in its grandeur . . . surely the greatest evocation of nature in a work for orchestra. . . . Here is not merely a great pantheistic drama of the sea; it is also the musical equivalent of a Proustian drama of mankind."[3][†]

Pierre Auguste Renoir, *Two Young Girls at the Piano.* Renoir (1841–1919) was one of the most important exponents of Impressionism, the school of painting from which Debussy's compositional style drew its name.

*The instruments of the orchestra are listed and discussed in Chapter 2.

†*Pantheism* refers to the worship of nature as God. Marcel Proust, a contemporary compatriot of Debussy, wrote a panoramic set of novels, *Remembrance of Things Past* (1913–1927).

Music and Nature

Listen to the first sketch (*movement*) of *La Mer*. You may also want to hear the remaining two sketches, "Play of the Waves" and "Dialogue Between the Wind and the Sea." Debussy loved the sea from childhood and at one time even considered taking up a maritime career. "You perhaps do not know that I was destined for the fine life of a sailor and that it was only by chance that I was led away from it. But I still have a great passion for the sea."[4] As a composer, Debussy produced orchestral effects corresponding to different combinations of color; indeed, Debussy was as clever with the pen as Monet with the brush. At the same time, the music is intensely human in its portrayal of the sea. In connection with the second sketch Lockspeiser recounts a passage

> where the nasal *cor anglais* [English horn] picks its way through a maze of chattering trills,* lightened by the sparkling glockenspiel and triangle. . . . Such a teasing, nervous portrayal can only be symbolical of all that human emotion knows of agility, malice, and vivacity.[5]

However, not all writers share Lockspeiser's sense of Debussy's humanity. Referring to *Fêtes* (*Festivals*) and *Sirens* from Debussy's *Nocturnes* for orchestra, Constant Lambert has written of the former that its "wild exhilaration . . . is the exhilarating bustle of wind and rain, with nothing in it of human gaiety. And the icy waves that lap the siren's rock are disturbed by no Ulysses and his seamen."[6]

For more information on Impressionist music, see Chapter 5, p. 48ff.

Caricature of Antonio Vivaldi by Pier Leone Ghezzi. Drawn in 1723, it is the only authenticated portrait.

VIVALDI, THE SEASONS, "SPRING"

Debussy was far from the first major composer to paint orchestral pictures of nature. We cannot identify with precision the earliest tonal scene composers, but we do know that about two hundred years before *La Mer*, Antonio Vivaldi (1678–1741) composed *The Seasons,* a set of four orchestral works subtitled "Spring," "Summer," "Autumn," and "Winter." Vivaldi was a colorful figure (quite literally so, for he sported a headful of bright hair) who resided in the important commercial and cultural center of Venice, Italy. Trained early as a violinist, he subsequently entered the priesthood; however, a heart defect made it difficult for him to recite Mass, and he soon gave up his clerical duties. Vivaldi now led the life of a professional musician, composing an abundance of

*A *trill* is a rapid alternation of adjacent pitches.

music for the violin, an instrument which he played with great agility. *The Seasons* consists of four *concertos* (i.e., works scored for one or more soloists accompanied by orchestra).* The orchestra is made up exclusively of strings and harpsichord, the latter being a forerunner of the piano. Each concerto is prefaced by a sonnet describing a particular season. The sonnet is then illustrated in the music, line by line. The "Spring" concerto consists of three short movements featuring a violin soloist.† Listen for the chirping of different bird species, the rustling of breezes, and other nature effects. The first movement is held together by a recurring section (*refrain*) scored for the entire complement of strings. Between refrains we hear nonrepeated sections (*episodes*) for the solo violin, sometimes with extra solo parts played by members of the orchestra.

Example 1

VIVALDI, *Spring*, 1st Mvt., Solo Episode

---

*For more on concertos, see Chapter 10. The four concertos of *The Seasons* are actually part of a set of twelve. Composers of Vivaldi's time were characteristically prolific and often combined otherwise independent pieces, like these concertos, into sets. For some reason, the numbers that composers favored for these sets were multiples of six. Thus, Handel composed twelve concerti grossi for strings (1739), and Bach composed six *Brandenburg Concerti* for orchestra. Bach also composed a variety of keyboard sets: six *French Suites*, six *English Suites*, and two separate sets of twenty-four preludes and fugues (*The Well-Tempered Clavier*).

†A movement is a principal subdivision of a concerto, symphony, or other large work. For further amplification regarding these forms, see Chapter 2, p. 23.

Music and Nature

The subdued second movement is scored for violins and violas alone—no cellos or basses are heard. It pictures a murmuring wind (violins) punctuated by the barking of a shepherd's watchdog (violas). The last movement is a pastoral dance for nymphs and shepherds as they celebrate the arrival of spring.

Listen to the complete concerto. Afterward, you may also wish to hear the natural effects Vivaldi concocted for the remaining three concertos of *The Seasons*. Here is Vivaldi's preface to the *Spring* Concerto.

SPRING

Movement I: Spring has arrived and the birds merrily greet it with their joyful song. And the brooks meanwhile murmur sweetly, driven by the blowing breath of the soft zephyr. Lightning and thunder, chosen to announce Spring, arrive, covering the air with a black mantle. Then, as the roar quiets down, the birds return to enchant with their song.

Movement II: Later, on the delightful field abounding in flowers, the shepherd sleeps with his loyal dog beside him amidst the whispering of leafy branches and other plants dear to him.

Movement III: Nymphs and shepherds dance to the rejoicing sound of the pastoral bagpipe on the beloved roof created by the shiny appearance of Spring.

Anonymous
(translated from the Italian by Alberto Sadun)

BEETHOVEN, PASTORAL SYMPHONY

Ludwig van Beethoven's *Symphony No. 6* (the *Pastoral*) is perhaps the most famous of all orchestral representations of nature. Beethoven (1770–1827) was born in the small northern German city of Bonn (now the capital of West Germany), but as a young adult he relocated in the great Austrian capital of Vienna. Vienna at this time was already a noble city of impressive cultural attainment. By dint of his extraordinary musical ability, Beethoven carved for himself a niche among the upper echelons of Viennese society: he rarely lacked for wealthy and cultivated admirers. Secure in his position, Beethoven enjoyed getting away periodically into the bucolic countryside beyond the outskirts of the Austrian metropolis. The *Pastoral Symphony* stands as testimony to the composer's delight in the simple innocence of country folkways. Composed in 1808, it follows the pattern of other Beethoven symphonies as a large orchestral work divided into several contrasting movements but it stands apart from all other symphonic creations of the *Classical* period (roughly 1740–1825—see Chapter 2, Historical Periods) by portraying various aspects of nature. Each movement bears a title signifying some element of a rural scene. Thus, the first movement, one of the most genial of Classical symphonic movements, is entitled "Awakening of Pleasant Feelings upon Arriving in the Country." Beethoven was somewhat ambivalent about attaching these titles to his music. In one of his sketch books he wrote, "Anyone with a notion of country life will imagine the composer's intentions without the help of titles or headings."[7] Beethoven was undoubtedly right in this case, but in the end he assigned a title to each movement anyway.

In the second movement of the *Pastoral*, the charming "Scene at the Brook," you can hear a string figure imitating the gentle babbling of a brook.

Beethoven Composing the "Pastoral Symphony" (1834 Swiss lithograph). In the second movement of the *Pastoral* you can hear a string figure imitating the gentle babbling of a brook.

Music and Nature

Example 2

BEETHOVEN, *Pastoral Symphony*, 2nd Mvt.

Nature in Orchestral Settings

In his novella, *The Pastoral Symphony*, André Gide tells of a prelate (pastor) who takes his blind ward Gertrude to a concert featuring Beethoven's *Symphony No. 6.* After the concert, Gertrude is very thoughtful.

> For a long time after we had left the concertroom, Gertrude remained silent, as though lost in ecstasy.
> "Is what you see really as beautiful as that?" she asked at last.
> "As beautiful as what, dear child?"
> "As that 'scene on the bank of a stream'?" I did not answer at once, for I was reflecting that those ineffable harmonies painted the world as it might have been, as it would be without evil and without sin, rather than the world as it really was.[8]

"A world without evil," an escape from the cares of modern life—that is what the "Scene at the Brook" portrays, Gide suggests. Do you agree with this interpretation—does the music have the same peaceful effect on you?

At the end of the second movement are heard the calls of the nightingale (flute), quail (oboe), and cuckoo (clarinet). For an extended discussion of these and other imitations of bird song, see Chapter 5, Bird Song.

The last three movements of the *Pastoral* run together; that is, there is no pause between movements after the third movement commences. First you will hear a cheerful peasant dance, the "Happy Gathering of the Peasants," in a fast tempo and with pulses organized into groups (*measures*) of three beats (i.e., in *triple meter*). Later the movement changes to a heavy-footed duple meter (i.e., two beats per measure), slower than the preceding section, with a bagpipe drone and lots of strong accents. Then the first part of the dance recurs. Suddenly the tempo quickens into a frenzy, leading directly into the fourth movement, "The Downpour, Storm." The realism here is striking. At first there is merely a sense of distant foreboding, like a waft of cooler air which warns of an ensuing thunderstorm. Suddenly loud thunder peals through the entire orchestra. The music alternates between streaks of lightning accompanied by crashes of thunder, with soft but tense interludes as the storm gathers fresh momentum. The wind increases, the thunder claps, and at last the storm reaches its climax. Now Beethoven becomes even more masterful as he scores the waning of the storm—not gradually, but fitfully, with recurring outbursts among ever softer signs of the storm moving on.

The oboe now introduces a simple but lovely melody which ushers in the last movement (*finale*), "The Shepherd's Song— Happy Thankful Feelings After the Storm." The clarinet follows with a shepherd's piping call, which is immediately taken up by the French horn. The violins extend this figure into the principal theme of the movement. There are some grand moments during the course of the finale, but for the most part it restores the quiet geniality of the opening movement. The horn concludes the symphony with a final repetition of the shepherd's call.

Example 3
Pastoral Symphony, Finale

Music and Nature

MENDELSSOHN, FINGAL'S CAVE OVERTURE

As just noted, Beethoven's *Pastoral Symphony* represents an idealized recollection of the composer's occasional excursions into the neighboring countryside. Composers have also been known to undertake much more extensive travels and then recall them musically. As a case in point, consider Felix Mendelssohn (1809–1847). Mendelssohn was raised in a prosperous German home in which culture and the amenities of life were appreciated in equal measure. The name Felix means "happy," which is appropriate enough, for Mendelssohn's music is known for its cheerful, bright character. Felix traveled widely and in the summer of 1829 visited Scotland. Several works resulted from this trip, including the *Scottish Symphony* (No. 3) and the orchestral piece, *Fingal's Cave Overture* (also known as *The Hebrides*). The term *overture* usually signifies a prelude to an opera or other large-scale musical/dramatic work, but in this case it simply means a tone poem in one movement (see Chapter 2 for further discussion of this term).

Felix Mendelssohn. He traveled widely, and in the summer of 1829 visited Scotland. Several works resulted from this trip, including *Fingal's Cave Overture.*

Fingal's Cave, located on the island of Staffa, has long stood as one of the great tourist attractions of Scotland. Some ten years before Mendelssohn's visit, a renowned poet, John Keats, recorded his own reaction to the spot.

I am puzzled how to give you an Idea of Staffa. It can only be represented by a first rate drawing. One may compare the surface of the island to a roof—the roof is supported by grand pillars of Basalt standing together as thick as honey combs. The finest thing is Fingal's cave: it is entirely a breaking away of basalt pillars. Suppose now the Giants, who came down to the daughters of Men, had taken a whole mass of these Columns and bound them together like Bunches of Matches; and then with immense axes had made a Cavern in the body of these Columns. Such is Fingal's cave except that the sea has done this work of excavation and is continually dashing there. So that we walk along the sides of the Cave on the heads of the shortest pillars which are left as for convenient stairs—The roof is arch'd somewhat gothic wise, and the length of some of the entire pillars is 50 feet. About the island you might seat an army of men one man on the extremity of each pillar snapped off at different heights. The length of the Cave is 120 feet, and from its extremity the View of the Sea through the large Arch at the Entrance is very grand. The colour of the columns is a sort of black with a lurking gloom of purple therein. For solemnity and grandeur it far surpasses the finest Cathedral. As we approached in the Boat there was such a fine swell of the sea that the columns seem'd rising immediatly out of the waves—it is impossible to describe it. . . .[9]

At the end of the letter Keats appended his new poem, *Staffa*, containing such evocative images as

This was architected thus
By the great Oceanus:
Here his mighty waters play
Hollow organs all the day.

Fingal's Cave. Having jotted down some of the musical ideas which he was to use later, Mendelssohn wrote to a friend, "You will excuse a short note. . . . What I can best tell you is contained in the music."

Music and Nature

Mendelssohn's response to Fingal's Cave was no less ecstatic than Keats' and he too appears to have felt that the marvel of the place could not adequately be registered in ordinary prose. Having jotted down some of the musical ideas which were later to be incorporated into *Fingal's Cave Overture*, Mendelssohn wrote to a friend, "In order to make you understand how extraordinarily the Hebrides affected me, the following came into my mind there.... You will excuse a short note, the more as what I can best tell you is contained in the music."[10] Many writers have accorded the composer high praise for the success of his musical pictorializing.

> Of all the distinguished visitors to Staffa, none has caught the wild atmosphere of its Atlantic setting more vividly than Mendelssohn in his *Hebrides Overture*.... Anyone who has entered the Cave and walked on Staffa will at once realize that it exactly corresponds to the mood of the place....[11]

Apparently Mendelssohn found it harder to please himself, for he wrote, "The middle section in D major is very stupid, and the whole so-called development [section] smells more of counterpoint* than of blubber, gulls, and salted cod."[12]

For another writer, however, the musical sketching of *Fingal's Cave Overture* is an unqualified success, even with respect to the gulls which the composer claims to have slighted. W. Gilles Whitaker describes Mendelssohn's music as a continuous "sea picture," with the restless Atlantic sometimes fierce, then suddenly docile, its playful waves glittering in the bright sunlight. And he particularly mentions the loud cries of gulls and the chirping of smaller birds.[13]

You may find it interesting to compare Mendelssohn's Scottish "water music" with Beethoven's musical brook as depicted in the second movement of his *Pastoral Symphony*. This is what one critic has said about the matter:

> Both ... suggest the sound made by moving water, but here the resemblance ceases. Beethoven, dealing with a brook, wanted a soft, unobtrusive, continuous sound, and the constant murmur of accompaniment throughout the brook scene is ideal for this purpose. But Mendelssohn, portraying the stormy northern seas, required the separate noise of individual waves, each with its own breaking and ebbing. His wave-figure is ideally designed for this purpose. It is first played by bassoons and cellos in unison, with the violas doubling an octave higher.

Example 4
MENDELSSOHN, *Fingal's Cave Overture*, Wave Figure

*By the term *development* Mendelssohn meant subjecting a theme to motivic treatment—that is, playing a short part of a theme (*motive*) in various versions, keys, instrumental combinations, and the like, sometimes interwoven with other such motives. The term *counterpoint* signifies a mixture of two or more melodic lines, wherein the individuality of each is maintained, while at the same time a vertical element is added, namely, *harmony*. In Mendelssohn's usage, *counterpoint* stands for dry, academic musical writing, as opposed to descriptive, emotional, or evocative music.

The one-bar phrase keeps the separate wave-effects from running together . . . [allowing] for that endless repetition [with] which Beethoven gives the effect of the sounds of nature. Furthermore, it can be combined into larger units, as in bars 37–38, where the gathering and breaking of a huge wave is very clearly suggested.[14]*

*Incidentally, despite its title, Handel's famous *Water Music* is not germane to the discussion here, for the music is nondescriptive. The title originated in the fact that the music was written to be performed for the edification of King George I on a barge in the Thames River.

Music and Nature

BASICS:
MUSIC HISTORY AND FORM

2

THE ORCHESTRA

The orchestra as we know it today consists of about one hundred members, somewhat more than half of whom play string instruments. The remaining instruments belong to the woodwind, brass, and percussion families. In the following list, numbers in parentheses indicate the typical size of each family and instrumental section.

The String Family (68)
violin (32, divided equally into firsts and seconds—the second violins play the same instrument but different music from the firsts)
viola (12)
violoncello (cello) (12)
string bass (double bass, bass viol) (10)
harp (not ordinarily classed with the other strings) (2)

The Woodwind Family (Winds) (16)
flute (3)   clarinet (3)
piccolo (high flute) (1)   bass clarinet (1)
oboe (3)   bassoon (3)
English horn (low oboe) (1)   contrabassoon (low bassoon) (1)

The Brass Family (11)
trumpet (3)
French horn (4)
trombone (3)
tuba (1)

The Percussion Family (5)*
tympani (kettle drums)
bass drum
cymbals
triangle
snare drums
glockenspiel (bells)
xylophone
piano (considered a percussion instrument in modern scores other than piano concertos)
celesta (a small keyboard instrument creating the effect of soft pitched bells)
et al.

*One percussionist usually specializes in tympani and one keyboard player in piano and celesta, while the other section members play the remaining instruments more or less interchangeably.

This list represents the instruments required in a modern work like Debussy's *La Mer*. By contrast, Vivaldi's orchestra, preceding Debussy's by two hundred years, consisted mainly of strings and of a much smaller complement at that. Most Vivaldi concertos call for no more than twenty players. One of these, a harpsichordist, plays a *continuo* part the purpose of which is to fill in chords outlined by the bass and soprano instruments. (The organ replaces the harpsichord in music intended for church performance.) Vivaldi, Bach, Handel, and their contemporaries occasionally included winds and brass in their orchestral scores, but not in predictable combinations. For example, Bach's *Brandenburg Concerto No. 1* calls for three oboes, two French horns, and one bassoon, in addition to strings; Bach's *Brandenburg Concerto No. 2* is scored for just single oboe, trumpet, flute, and strings; and the *Brandenburg Concerto No. 6* is scored exclusively for violas and cellos (and continuo).* Only toward the end of the eighteenth century—in the orchestral music of Haydn and Mozart—did there arise a standardized combination of strings, winds (including the newly invented clarinet), brass, and tympani. With its more varied instrumental forces, the enlarged late eighteenth-century orchestra no longer needed the harpsichord to fill in the texture. By the beginning of the nineteenth century, Beethoven was writing for a regular mixture of pairs of flutes, oboes, clarinets, bassoons, and trumpets, two to four French horns, tympani, and occasionally for piccolo, trombone, and such relatively exotic (for that time) percussion instruments as cymbals and triangle.

The larger the complement of winds, brass, and percussion, the greater the number of strings that were required to achieve a proper acoustical balance. So, whereas an early Mozart or Haydn symphony might need twenty-five to thirty players, a Beethoven symphony would call for forty-five to sixty. The size of Mendelssohn's orchestra approximates that of Beethoven's, but the orchestra grew steadily throughout the nineteenth century, prodded especially by Hector Berlioz and Richard Wagner, who introduced the English horn, harp, bass clarinet, tuba, and a variety of percussion instruments into their scores. By the end of the nineteenth century some composers were calling for mammoth combinations, including especially heavy concentrations of brass. In this connection one thinks of Richard Strauss, Gustav Mahler, and especially Arnold Schoenberg, whose *Gurrelieder* (1900–1913) is scored for no less than four flutes, four piccolos, five oboes, seven clarinets, three bassoons, two contrabassoons, ten French horns, seven trumpets, seven trombones, celesta, four harps, and eleven percussion instruments, as well, of course, as an enormous horde of strings to counterbalance them. Limitations in the size of concert hall stages and restrictions in orchestra budgets eventually put a stop to this fantastic growth. Only the percussion section of the orchestra has developed extensively during the twentieth century; some recent works call for as many as twenty to thirty percussion instruments to be played by half a dozen or more percussionists. At the same time, many modern composers have adapted to the realities of contemporary economics (and aesthetics) by writing for chamber orchestra, equivalent in size to the ensemble Mozart worked with two centuries ago.

---

*Bach composed six orchestral works (concertos) under commission from his aristocratic patron, Christian Ludwig of Brandenburg. For further information see the discussion of concertos in Chapter 10.

Music and Nature

Gunther Schuller conducts the New England Conservatory Orchestra at the Old State House, Boston, Massachusetts. The orchestra as we know it today consists of about one hundred members, somewhat more than half of whom play string instruments.

HISTORICAL PERIODS

The works discussed in Chapter 1 represent four distinct musical/historical periods.

Vivaldi, *The Seasons*	Baroque period
Beethoven, *Pastoral Symphony*	Classical period
Mendelssohn, *Fingal's Cave*	Romantic period
Debussy, *La Mer*	Modern period

To place each of these periods within a general historical framework, we shall highlight developments in science, accomplishments in the other fine arts, and power struggles both national and international. Then we shall compare a variety of purely musical factors, to aid aural differentiation from one period to another.

The **Baroque** period commenced roughly in 1600 and ended with the deaths of Bach (1750) and Handel (1759). In America this was the early colonial period; in Europe it was a period of great courtly splendor, with kings and princes vying to outdo one another in their cultivation of learning and the fine arts. Painting, architecture, sculpture, ballet, drama, and music all thrived. The early Baroque coincided with the plays of Shakespeare, Rembrandt's paintings, the building of the Louvre in Paris, and the theories of Isaac Newton. But this was also a period of internecine warfare between entrenched Catholic authorities and rebellious Protestant reformers (The Thirty Years' War—see Chapter 24). The late Baroque saw the rise of a new period of enlightenment, highlighted by Swift's *Gulliver's Travels* and Voltaire's writings on free thinking.

The **Classical** period overlapped the end of the Baroque, beginning in about 1730 and continuing until about 1820. (The dates given here are necessarily ambiguous, because periods of music history tend to merge gradually from one to the next instead of beginning and ending abruptly.) The first part of the Classical period is called Rococo. In the second half of the eighteenth century, the aristocratic establishment began to give ground to newer orders, as royalty could no longer maintain its supremacy (see Chapter 13). This was the era of Benjamin Franklin and Thomas Jefferson, American independence, the French Revolution, and the rise of Napoleon. Watt's steam engine and the building of the first factories signaled the commencement of the Industrial Revolution. As for the fine arts the achievements of Haydn, Mozart, Beethoven, and Schubert in the field of music paralleled those of Kant, Goethe, Schiller, Jane Austen, Shelley, and Goya in the fields of philosophy, belles lettres, and painting.

The **Romantic** period runs from about 1815 to 1910. (Beethoven represents a bridge between the Classical and Romantic periods; the *Pastoral Symphony* is a manifestation of both periods, although it is perhaps more Classical than Romantic.) With the invention of the railroad, the steamship, the telegraph, electric lights, and so on, the Romantic period witnessed the full-fledged development of industrialism. Political fer-

Richard Wagner (1813–1883), a late Romantic composer. The Romantic period witnessed in the arts a new celebration of the individual.

Music and Nature

ment raged throughout Europe, the power of the British monarchy diminished, Karl Marx wrote the *Communist Manifesto*, and the women's rights movement was born. The burgeoning United States gradually assumed control of the entire North American continent (below Canada). Lincoln led us through the trauma of the Civil War, and at the same time the serfs were freed in Russia. The telephone and phonograph were invented, X-rays were discovered, and the Eiffel Tower was built. Pasteur developed principles of modern hygiene.

During the Romantic period the arts focused on a new celebration of the individual. In music it was a time of powerful emotional expression (see, for example, Chapter 28, *Music of Mania and Despair*). The outpourings of an impressive array of writers, artists, and philosophers paralleled an astonishing flowering of musical creativity. The novels of Dickens and George Eliot in England, of Melville, Hawthorne, and Mark Twain in the United States, of Balzac, Hugo, and Dumas in France, and of Tolstoy and Dostoyevsky in Russia; the poetry of Heine, Baudelaire, Verlaine, Browning, Tennyson, Whitman, and Longfellow; the theoretical writings of Thoreau, Kierkegaard, and Nietzsche; the paintings of Delacroix, Degas, Turner, Whistler, and Van Gogh; the plays of Ibsen, Pushkin, Strindberg; Rodin's sculptures—all stand alongside the superb musical achievements of Berlioz, Liszt, Wagner, Verdi, Schumann, Chopin, Mendelssohn, Bruckner, Brahms, Mussorgsky, Tchaikovsky, Dvořák, and (representing the last vestiges of Romanticism) Sibelius, Mahler, and Richard Strauss.

Paul Rosenberg Collection, Paris

Igor Stravinsky (1882–1971). Drawings by Pablo Picasso, 1920. Stravinsky was one of the most important composers of the Modern period (see p. 20).

Basics: Music History and Form

The **Modern** period starts roughly at the turn of the century and extends to the present. The choice of the term *modern* for music originating as far back as 1900 may seem strange from our present standpoint, yet many compositions from those early years still sound remarkably fresh and challenging. Debussy's *La Mer* represents the early modern idiom known as Impressionism (1890–1925). Impressionism was only one of several important styles and techniques (including *Expressionism, Neoclassicism,* and *Serialism*) developing at this time. Music written since the end of World War II is generally differentiated from earlier modern music by the label *contemporary.*

During the Modern period we have seen the rise of the new technology, far surpassing the scientific accomplishments of the nineteenth century. The automobile, airplane, radio, cinema, television, and computer are among the most prominent of the new inventions. Isaac Newton has given way to Albert Einstein, and trans-Atlantic travel has become secondary to round-the-world flights and journeys into outer space. The world has been shaken by violent upheavals, beginning with World War I and continuing with the Russian Revolution of 1917, the Spanish Civil War during the 1930s, World War II, the Korean and Vietnamese conflicts, and countless outbreaks in other places. Sophisticated military technology and the harnessing of nuclear energy have created a need for world government, as exemplified by the League of Nations and the United Nations. American power threatens and is threatened by Soviet power, with China, India, and many Arab/African nations constituting a powerful Third World counterbalance. The fine arts—music foremost among them—have undergone wrenching changes not unlike those seen in the political/social/scientific realms. A yawning chasm separates the new music from the old. The sounds of hard rock and electronic synthesizers represent the extremes of a musical revolution, whisking us away into outer musical space, far from the comfortable traditions of the "three Bs"—Bach, Beethoven, and Brahms.

One of the challenges confronting the beginning music student is to perceive differences in musical styles from one historical period to another. In some cases, this kind of observation is easy. For example, it would be hard to confuse the innocent simplicity of Vivaldi's *Seasons* (Baroque) with the full-blown sophistication of Debussy's *La Mer* (early Modern). On the other hand, close stylistic resemblances often inhere in music originating in adjacent periods, as in the case of Beethoven's *Pastoral* (late Classical) and Mendelssohn's *Fingal's Cave* (early Romantic). Furthermore, composers vary individually within the *same* historical period. Thus, Bach and Handel, although exact Baroque contemporaries, differ significantly, as with other paired contemporaries, such as Haydn and Mozart (Classical), Berlioz and Liszt (Romantic), and Debussy and Ravel (Impressionist). For that matter, stylistic variants occur even within the oeuvre of a single composer—for example, the chamber music of Schubert (1797–1828) sounds quite Classical, whereas his songs are distinctly Romantic.

A good way to learn about styles is to notice carefully the period of every piece you listen to (finding the information in this book, on record jackets, in music dictionaries, etc.), gradually storing up knowledge of characteristic similarities and differences. Of course, you will need much listening experience before being able to recognize historical periods easily. The four works of Chapter 1 offer you an initial comparison, from which you can build as you listen to the music encountered in the remaining

Music and Nature

chapters of this book. In addition, consideration of the factors discussed in the following paragraphs will help make you more familiar with historical styles.

To begin, notice the size of the performing forces required by a given piece. Baroque orchestral music calls for small ensembles, often limited to strings and harpsichord, and therefore is not ordinary fare for a large symphony orchestra. An orchestral work featuring a large brass section is probably Romantic or Modern. A diverse percussion section almost certainly indicates the Modern period.

Another factor is duration. Individual movements in the music of the Baroque and early Classical periods (through Mozart and Haydn) tend to be considerably briefer than movements of the late Classical and Romantic periods. And the size of late Romantic movements is often nothing less than gargantuan! Duration is not a useful guide to the recognition of Modern works, which vary from extremely short to very long, but there is another feature that serves well for this purpose—the use of dissonance. *Dissonance* is the harmonic effect of two or more tones which clash. Without going into an extensive discussion of dissonance and its opposite effect, *consonance*, we can observe that in much twentieth-century music dissonance is emancipated—which is to say that harsh, jarring, even ugly sounds are not only permitted but emphasized. Dissonant sounds are commonly heard in earlier styles as well, but here they are generally understood in terms of an overall consonant harmonic framework which effects a sense of mitigation or *resolution* of dissonance. Modern dissonance, on the other hand, is typically allowed to stand on its own, without—as it were—musical apology. Many listeners find it difficult to overcome their initial shock and dismay upon encountering "nonbeautiful" sounds and consequently refuse to hear enough of this century's classics to realize that beauty comes in many shapes and styles. (Debussy's *La Mer*, representing the modern period in Chapter 1, does not exemplify the kind of emancipated dissonance being discussed here; in fact the Impressionist style is just barely more dissonant than that of late Romanticism.) In subsequent chapters you will be introduced to a variety of modern styles, giving you an opportunity to discover that modern trends in music—as in painting, sculpture, poetry, and dance—are highly characteristic of more general trends in twentieth-century culture. Modern life is hectic, unstable, exciting, frightening—in a word, dissonant! To the extent that unresolved dissonance inheres in contemporary life, it is only appropriate that it characterize modern music as well.

Of the four historical periods listed earlier, the connection from Classical to Romantic was smoothest, for the Romantic era represented a big change in composers' attitudes but little change in compositional techniques. At the beginning of the Romantic period, the construction of sonatas, symphonies, songs, and oratorios remained essentially unaltered, and even the operas of the early Romantic Carl Maria von Weber (1786–1826) are not greatly dissimilar from those of his elder Classical relative, Wolfgang Amadeus Mozart (1756–1791). Eventually there were to be many important innovations in Romantic music, but these developed only slowly throughout the nineteenth century. This is not to deny a sharp change in what even early Romantic composers put of themselves into their music, as compared with their Classical predecessors. Mozart, Haydn, and the young Beethoven all employed a fairly consistent compositional style which tended to submerge individualistic traits. By contrast, the Romantic com-

Basics: Music History and Form

poser was self-assertive and not seldom idiosyncratic. While there was no absence of stylistic similarities among Romantic composers, the best of them—Berlioz, Chopin, Schumann, Wagner, Verdi, Mussorgsky, and Brahms—seem quite distinct and original with respect to one another. The Romantic composer's music often reflected a desire for self-expression. Earlier historical periods managed to combine expressiveness with a generality of style (as conveyed by the term *classical*). At the risk of overstatement, the Classical composer was restrained, the Romantic composer effusive.

From the Baroque period to the Classical, there was a greater cleavage than between Classical and Romantic. One of the most significant differences hinged on the practice of continuo in instrumental ensemble music. As noted, the Baroque orchestra—indeed almost all Baroque instrumental music—used a keyboard instrument as chord-filling support for the rest of the group. A common Baroque ensemble consisted of two violins, a cello, and a harpsichord. The harpsichordist would "realize" chords and motivic figures above a bass line played also by the cello, as accompaniment to the solo lines played by the violins.* An oboe or flute might replace the violins, and a string bass or bassoon might substitute for the cello, but a harpsichord or organ was always present in Baroque ensemble music. This all changed in the Classical period. Con-

Johann Sebastian Bach (1685-1750) and Carl Philipp Emanuel Bach (1714-1788). Portraits by Samuel Anton Bach, 1732/33. J. S. Bach represented the culmination of the Baroque, and his eldest son, Carl Philipp Emanuel, conceived many of the innovations which were to become hallmarks of the new Classical style.

*This combination of bass line and keyboard part is known as *continuo* or *figured bass*. One speaks of a *trio* sonata for two violins and continuo, albeit a quartet of players is required to perform it.

tinuo practice died out as the harpsichord all but disappeared from the musical scene. The piano took over as the principal keyboard instrument, and the newly developed orchestra omitted keyboard parts altogether.

Perhaps the most important distinction between the Baroque and Classical periods lay in their treatment of musical forms. Baroque composers went in heavily for collections of dance forms (*suites*) based on characteristic court dances handed down from earlier times—the sarabande, gavotte, gigue, and so on—while Classical composers preferred more highly integrated forms—sonatas, symphonies, and the like.* The new Classical forms survived throughout the nineteenth century and even into the twentieth century. When it comes to modern music, however, many composers have abandoned traditional forms; in fact, during this century form has withstood as much emancipation as harmony (see the preceding discussion of dissonance). You will be told more about the interrelation of style and structure (i.e., *form*) in the discussion of the music of Chapter 1 immediately below.

The music prior to 1600 falls into two main periods: the *Medieval* (circa 800–1400) and the *Renaissance* (1400–1600). The music of these early periods is taken up in Chapters 23, 25, and 32.

FORMS

The music discussed in Chapter 1 represents four differing types of formal organization. Vivaldi's *Spring Concerto* consists of three brief movements. Debussy's *La Mer* is also tripartite, but each movement is longer and more elaborate than the corresponding Vivaldi movement. Mendelssohn's *Fingal's Cave*, an early example of *symphonic poem* (i.e., an orchestral tone poem which depicts visual imagery, recounts a story, conveys a philosophical idea, etc.), is in a single relatively lengthy movement. Beethoven's *Pastoral Symphony* contains five movements, one more than normal for late Classical symphonies (in turn exceeding by one the number of movements usually found in early Classical symphonies). Its fast outer movements typify Classical/Romantic symphonic structure, although some first movements and an occasional finale commence with a short, slow introduction. The second movement ("Scene at the Brook") is slow and lyrical, as is always the case with one of the middle movements of a symphony. The "Peasant Dance" is basically a *scherzo,* a fast rambunctious version of the *minuet,* a Classical symphonic holdover from the Baroque dance suite. Minuets and scherzos generally evidence triple meter (three beats to a measure) and follow a large-scale three-part pattern, A–B–A. The B part is known as the *trio,* which is usually lighter and gentler than the A part, but the "Peasant Dance" is exceptional in that its trio is heavier than the opening and switches to duple meter. We have now accounted for four of the *Pastoral's* five movements, so it seems that the "extra" movement must be the fourth, coming directly on the heels of the "Peasant Dance." The depiction of a storm makes it proper to designate the fourth movement as a tone poem. That is, its form is not determined as much by Classical constraints or formulae (such as *sonata form, theme and*

---

*From the Classical period on, the term sonata signifies the equivalent of a symphony scored for just one or two instruments, as in *piano sonatas* and *sonatas for violin and piano.*

variations, minuet and trio, or rondo*), as by the quasi-dramatic requirements of a musical thunder-and-lightning storm. All the aforementioned forms achieve balance through the repetition of previous sections; for example, A–B–A is a general Classical scheme (inherited from the Renaissance and Baroque periods) in which an exact or varied replica of the first section rounds out the form after an intervening contrasting section. Storms, however, do not end the way they start; so the *Pastoral's* fourth movement helped to set a structural precedent with an ending which is considerably different from its beginning.

The other movements of the *Pastoral* show that the utilization of traditional forms is not antithetical to musical depiction, in that each follows a more or less traditional structural procedure despite its programmatic content. Similarly, Vivaldi's three movements in the *Spring Concerto* are much like those of most Baroque orchestral works (*concerti grossi*). Interestingly enough, even a Romantic tone poem may betray Classical form, as in the case of Mendelssohn's *Fingal's Cave Overture,* which structurally resembles the first movement of the *Pastoral*. Of the four works of Chapter 1, only *La Mer* exhibits formal freedom throughout its entirety. You will recall that the first sketch (movement) progresses from dawn to noon (see p. 4).† It should come as no surprise that Debussy chose not to repeat the dawn music as the movement approaches noon; a traditional construction—like the A-B-A pattern already discussed—would hardly seem appropriate. This is not totally to deny the existence of melodic repetition in *La Mer*, any more than in Beethoven's storm music. The point is simply that neither of these examples offers an entire final section closely modeled after an earlier part, as in the A-B-A and A-B-A' Classical prototypes.

In comparing the formal plans of these four works, one should take note of their interaction with musical/historical developments. During the Romantic period, program music took hold of composers' imaginations as never before, with a resulting weakening of Classical ideals of form. By the middle of the nineteenth century, two opposing groups of composers were emerging: those who adhered to Classical models (one thinks in particular of Brahms) versus those who rejected past constraints in favor of the necessarily freer conditions inherent in illustrative music (as in the music dramas of Wagner and the tone poems of Liszt, Mussorgsky, and Richard Strauss).‡ However, one should take care not to exaggerate the differences between these two compositional "schools," for they both made use of essentially the same vocabulary and syntax. It was mainly the shell—the external shape—of the works which differed.

*For amplification of some of these terms, see Chapter 12 (sonata form), Chapter 18 (theme and variations), and Chapter 30 (rondo, in the finale of Stravinsky's *The Rite of Spring*).

†Erik Satie (1866–1925), a composer friend of Debussy's who enjoyed poking fun at himself and others, once remarked that he particularly liked the first sketch when it reaches 10:45 A.M.!

‡Further information about this conflict is presented in Chapter 19.

Music and Nature

BASICS:
RESEARCH AND NOTATION

3

The following information is intended to assist the reader in pursuing various aspects of music study. To start, there are three brief research guides. The first deals with titles of compositions and their subdivisions and includes basic tempo and expression terms. The second guide explains how to make use of a record library catalog as well as how to interpret the information provided on record jackets and album liners. This part also suggests how to recognize where one movement ends and the next begins. The third guide gives general hints on preparing concert reviews and other accounts of one's listening experiences. This is followed by a survey of the fundamentals of music notation—which are introduced to help the reader decode the musical examples spread throughout the text. The principal subsections of this notation guide deal with pitch designation (including key signatures), durational values (including time signatures), and interpretive markings (including gradations in dynamics).

RESEARCH AIDS

Titles and Subheadings

Music titles often appear in foreign languages, which usually correspond to the original or adopted nationality of the composer. Some works are known both in English (e.g., Mozart's *The Magic Flute* and Stravinsky's *The Rite of Spring*) as well as in their original languages (*Die Zauberflöte* [German] and *Le Sacre du printemps* [French]).* Other titles are left untranslated, as in Debussy's *La Mer*, which is never referred to as *The Sea*. Look directly after or below an original foreign title for its English equivalent; if you do not find it there, check the accompanying program notes.

The principal subdivisions of a work, such as movements of a sonata or symphony, are generally listed according to their tempo and/or expression markings. For example, the full title of Beethoven's *Symphony No. 1* as it would appear in a concert program or on a record jacket reads as follows:

Beethoven, *Symphony No. 1 in C Major,* Op. 21

Adagio molto—Allegro con brio
Andante cantabile con molto
Menuetto. Allegro molto e vivace
Adagio—Allegro molto e vivace

These subheadings tell us that the symphony is divided into four separate movements. Despite his German heritage, Beethoven provided subheadings in Italian, as he

---

*Mozart, an Austrian, spoke German as his mother tongue. Stravinsky was born in Russia but was living more or less permanently in France at the time he composed *Le Sacre*.

generally did in all his music. In and of itself this is not remarkable, for by common consent Italian has long been the international language of tempo and expression markings. Certain key Italian terms recur again and again. Once you secure a knowledge of these terms, you will be able to wend your way through the maze of traditional movement subheadings. (Subheadings sometimes also appear in French or German, and much more rarely in English and other languages.)

Some common Italian tempo terms include

allegro	fast
allegretto	medium fast
andante (an-<u>dan</u>-tay)	medium slow
lento	slow
largo	very slow, solemn
adagio (a-<u>dah</u>-jo)	very slow
vivace (vi-<u>vah</u>-chay)	very fast
presto	extremely fast

It will also help to know the meanings of a few small modifiers and conjunctions:

poco	a little
molto	much, very
meno	less
più	more
non troppo	not too much
e	and
ma	but
con	with

Expressive character in music is denoted by adjectival and adverbial qualifiers, many of which can be recognized by virtue of their English cognates:

moderato	moderately
animato (ah-nee-<u>mah</u>-to)	animated
dolce (<u>dol</u>-chay)	sweet, gently
agitato (ah-jee-<u>tah</u>-to)	agitated
cantabile (cahn-<u>tah</u>-bi-lay)	lyrical, singing
marcato	marked, accented
appassionato	passionate
maestoso (my-e-<u>sto</u>-zo)	majestic
simplice (<u>sim</u>-plee-chay)	simply

Look back at the subheadings for Beethoven's *Symphony No. 1* and consulting the above vocabulary lists, try translating Beethoven's terminology. In the first movement there seems to be a paradox, as *adagio molto* means very slow, whereas *allegro con brio* means fast with verve. No actual contradiction exists, however, for the movement simply has two sections, the first slow, the second fast. (Fast movements often begin with slow introductions.) Sometimes the composer indicates the form of the movement first (e.g., minuet, scherzo, theme and variations, or rondo), and only then gives

Music and Nature

the tempo/expression markings (as in the third subheading of Beethoven's *Symphony No. 1*).

Now try figuring out the movement subheadings of another work, Brahms's *Symphony No. 1 in C Minor*, Op. 68. Again the terms are in Italian. Although you may not recognize all the terms, try to guess them anyway.

Un poco sostenuto—Allegro
Andante sostenuto
Un poco allegretto e grazioso
Adagio—Allegro non troppo ma con brio

How did you do?* Do not be discouraged if you did not get all the right answers. You will pick up expertise as you go along.

Examining once again the full title of Beethoven's *Symphony No. 1 in C major*, Op. 21, two items remain unclarified. The term *C Major* refers to the overall key of the symphony. Consideration of the important concept of keys and key relationships will be deferred until Chapters 9 and 12 in Unit 2. Regarding Op. (Opus) 21, this signifies that the *Symphony No. 1* is Beethoven's twenty-first musical publication. (However, this is not his twenty-first composition, as prior to Op. 1 he composed numerous works which he did not publish; moreover some of his opuses comprise more than one work—e.g., Op. 2, which is a collection of three separate piano sonatas). Opus numbers often but not invariably reflect chronological order of composition. However, the belated printing of youthful efforts sometimes results in composers' early works carrying higher opus numbers than their mature works. Opus numbers are often revised or replaced as musicologists refine their knowledge of older composers' chronologies. An early leader in this field was Ludwig Ritter von Köchel, whose catalog of the complete works of Mozart first appeared in 1862. Köchel expended Herculean energy in overcoming the chaotic situation at Mozart's death, for Mozart left more than 600 unnumbered or incorrectly numbered works. Köchel's pioneering efforts are now acknowledged in all Mozart titles, with K numbers designated in place of traditional opus numbers—for example, Mozart's *Piano Concerto in C Major*, K. 503.

Records and Tapes

Locating recordings of works of foreign origin can pose a serious challenge to the beginning music student. Record library catalogs list these works in two ways. (1) Descriptive titles are presented in the original language, sometimes with a separate English cross-reference as well. Thus, while you may be able to find *The Rite of Spring* under *r* for *rite*, you are certain to find it under *s* for *sacre* according to its original title, *Le Sacre du printemps*. (2) Generic titles, such as *sonata*, *concerto*, and *symphony*, are

---

*A little sustained: [then] fast
Medium slow, sustained
A bit fast and gracefully
Very slow; [then] fast, but not too much
   so, and with verve

listed in English regardless of their original titles. Thus, a piano concerto by Mozart is listed under *concerto*, rather than the German equivalent, *Konzert*. Note that one looks up "concerto for piano" or "sonata for violin and piano" rather than "piano concerto" or "violin sonata." Other genres are less clear; you may have to look twice before finding a string quartet under *q* or *s*. Ignore initial articles, such as the English *a, an, the*; the French *le, la, les*; and the German *der, die, das*. Thus, *La Mer* is listed under *m*, and *Die Zauberflöte* under *z*. Ordinarily, when using the catalog you should check first under composer, then title, but, in the case of prolific composers, it may be quicker to look up the title directly, especially if it is a descriptive one. Excerpts from large works are listed only if recorded apart from the complete work; to find a listing for Bach's "Crucifixus" (see Chapter 23), check under the parent title, *Mass in B Minor*. When looking for German composers, beware the umlaut (¨) over the vowels *a, o,* and *u*. Some catalogs ignore the umlaut, while others add an e after the vowel in question. Thus, *Schütz* may be treated either as *Schutz* or as *Schuetz*. (Arnold Schoenberg, the twentieth-century Austrian composer, emigrated to the United States in the mid-1930s, after which he officially changed the spelling of his last name from *ö* to *oe*.)

Once you have a desired recording in hand, you will find that many record jackets are designed more with an eye for catchy graphics than for imparting clear information—making it hard to distinguish the names of the piece, the composer, and the performer(s). When in doubt, look at the label on the record itself; here there is rarely any obfuscation. When an album contains two or more disks, sides 1 and 2 are not ordinarily found back to back. Thus, in the case of four disks, the sequence of sides is ordinarily 1–8, 2–7, 3–6, and 4–5. But check carefully, for some record companies follow a 1–2, 3–4 policy.

Recordings which are intended for international sale sometimes provide titles and/or program notes in several languages, in which case you may have to search a bit before finding what you are looking for in English. If there is a text in a foreign language—as is likely in vocal genres such as opera, oratorio, and songs—the recording may include an accompanying English translation. (However, sometimes only an English synopsis is provided.) When following vocal texts, bear in mind that text repetitions, though common, are rarely written out in full. Instead they are usually indicated by dotted lines or *etc*. Ensemble scenes are indicated by vertical brackets.

A movement or other section of a work which does not commence at the beginning of a disk is ordinarily preceded by a silent band on the disk. For example, most recordings of Brahms's *Symphony No. 1* present Movements 1 and 2 on Side 1 (separated by a band) and Movements 3 and 4 on Side 2 (another band). The visibility of such bands is one advantage of records over tapes (but of course tapes do not wear out as quickly). Warning: A composer may require the end of one movement to run directly into the beginning of the next. (This is indicated in the score by the word *attacca*.) In this situation there will be no separating band to help you isolate the movements. For example, Beethoven's *Symphony No. 5* has no pause between the third and fourth movements, and the *Pastoral Symphony* (see Chapter 1) runs its final three movements together. In outward appearance, a disk containing these three *Pastoral* movements looks like one very large movement, but in listening you will be able to detect distinct contrasts in theme, tempo, and mood from one movement to the next.

Music and Nature

Listening Reports

In preparing listening reports you will find much potentially useful information in concert programs and album liner notes. However, if you are not familiar with this style of discourse you may find this kind of material quite confusing. After reading it, sort out what you do understand from what you do not. Look up new terms in the glossary of this book or in a music dictionary. Make a summary of the commentary, but never copy it word for word. Although presumably intended for the layperson, program notes often abound in technical jargon, and nothing is gained from repeating verbatim terms and ideas which you do not actually understand. Never put yourself in the position of defending a report you have written with the remark, "I don't know what it means, but that's what the record notes said." Make the reports truly *yours* by using your own natural style of expression. A spontaneous informal response is much to be preferred over cribbed technical gibberish. Remember, no one expects you to turn into a musical authority overnight!

When jotting down information about pieces, observe carefully the spelling of names, many of which may be foreign and unfamiliar. Check on the pronunciation of difficult names in a music encyclopedia or dictionary. You will produce more effective results if the terms in your papers are properly spelled and your oral reports correctly delivered.

INTRODUCTION TO MUSIC NOTATION

For the untrained reader, the numerous musical examples in this book may at first seem unintelligible. But the basics of music notation are not difficult to learn. Even if you do not follow every musical detail, you can nevertheless glean from the examples much useful information.

Pitch Notation

The Staff   A music *staff* consists of lines and spaces. The lines of the staff are analogous to the rungs of a ladder. Each "rung" and intervening space represents a different pitch. Let us say that the bottom line represents E above middle C. (On a piano, middle C is located approximately in the center of the keyboard. The first letter of the maker's name—for example, S of Steinway—is usually placed directly over middle C.) In that case, the next line up is G, and the space in between is F. Once you identify the pitch of any one of the lines or spaces, you can determine the others by counting up or down from the starting point.

Clefs   A *clef* tells you the identity of the lines and spaces on a staff. The *bass clef* 𝄢 is used for low sounds. The line between the two dots 𝄢 is F below middle C. The *treble clef* 𝄞 is used for high sounds. The second bottom line of the treble staff 𝄞 is G above middle C. The bass and treble clefs are used in piano music, and most orchestral instruments use one or both of them as well. Other clefs include the *alto* 𝄡, with the middle line signifying middle C, and the *tenor* 𝄡, with middle C on the second line from the top. These "C clefs" are found in scores played by middle-register instruments such as the viola, cello, and bassoon.

Leger Lines.　If on the treble staff the second bottom line is G above middle C, where then is middle C itself? Proceeding down the "ladder," the bottom space is F and the bottom line is E. 🎼 There seems to be no room for middle C on the treble staff, so let's try the bass staff. F below middle C is located on the second top line. Moving up, the top space is G, and the top line is A. 🎼 Again there is no apparent location for middle C. The solution is to extend the staff up or down, as the need may be, with leger lines. A *leger line* below the treble staff represents a sixth line, giving us middle C at last. 🎼 Middle C is also signified by a leger line added above the bass staff. Leger lines can be added in any number to provide required extra note locations. For example, in Mozart's *The Magic Flute,* the Queen of the Night sings all the way up to "high F," seven notes above the top line of the treble staff. The passage looks like this:

F A C F C D Bb C

Accidentals.　The notes indicated by the lines and spaces of a staff coincide with the white keys of a piano. The notes corresponding to the black keys of a piano are indicated by *flats* (♭) and *sharps* (♯), which are collectively known as *accidentals*. A sharp raises a pitch by a half step, and a flat lowers a pitch the same distance. For example, the black note above middle C is called C♯ but since the same black note is located directly below D, it may also be notated as D♭. 🎼 A double sharp (×) raises a pitch by two helf-steps, and a double flat (♭♭) lowers it by two half steps.

Key Signatures.　*Key signatures* consist of flats or sharps notated at the commencement of a piece and repeated at the beginning of each subsequent staff. The accidentals of a key signature remain in effect until the piece concludes, unless a different key signature is introduced. The titles of many works are based on their keys—for example, Chopin's *Waltz in C♯ Minor* and Brahms's *Clarinet Sonata in E♭ Major.* The key signature of C♯ minor calls for four sharps: F♯, C♯, G♯, and D♯. E♭ major requires three flats: B♭, E♭, and A♭. The apparent omission of a key signature in a piece—the absence of any sharps or flats— indicates C major or A minor (or no key at all, as in atonal music).

C# Minor: Eb Major:

Flats and sharps not included in a given key signature can be added at any point in a piece. In this case the accidental is placed directly before the notehead in question; and it controls all other noteheads on that line or space for the remainder of the measure—that is, until the next bar line—unless subsequently cancelled by a natural sign. A *natural sign* (♮) is an accidental which cancels a previously indicated sharp or flat. Like added sharps or flats, a natural sign applies only until the end of the measure. (Bar lines and measures are explained in the next section).

D   A   G#   G#   G♮   F   G#   G♮   E

Other Aspects of Pitch Notation.   Certain instruments sound an *octave* (span of eight notes) higher or lower than notated. The piccolo (small flute) sounds an octave higher than written, and the string bass and contrabassoon sound an octave lower than written. (This saves overuse of leger lines.) Other instruments are known as transposing instruments—for example, the clarinet in A and the trumpet in B♭. In the case of a B♭ instrument, a notated C *sounds* B♭; where the key of a piece is B♭ major (normally requiring a signature of two flats, B♭ and E♭), the key signature for a B♭ instrument is blank (corresponding to the signature of C major for nontransposing instruments). In other words, as played by a B♭ trumpet, a notated C major scale sounds like a B♭ major scale played on a nontransposing instrument like the piano.

Rythmic Notation

Beats and Measures.   Musical pulses are known as *beats*. A grouping of alternating strong and weak beats is called a *measure*. A *bar line* is the boundary between one measure and the next.

Durations.   Note durations are signified by a variety of notational symbols.

symbol	name	duration
o	whole note	four quarter-note beats
𝅗𝅥	half note	two quarter-note beats
♩	quarter note	one quarter-note beat
♪	eighth note	1/2 quarter-note beat
♬	sixteenth note	1/4 quarter-note beat

Musical notation is the composer's means of communicating with the performer. Composers' personal notational styles vary from the extremely neat and elegant to the messy and almost indecipherable. Above, a page from one of Bach's manuscripts and across a page from one of Beethoven's sketch books.

Two or more flagged notes in succession can be beamed. Thus, ♪♪♪ is equivalent to ♫♩. The number of beams corresponds to the number of flags on the single notes. (The up or down direction of stems and flags is unrelated to duration. Noteheads on or above the third line of a staff normally receive downstems, and lower noteheads receive upstems. A variety of other considerations may effect exceptions to this rule, however.)

A *dot* (.) extends the duration of a note by half.

♩.	dotted half note	three quarter-note beats
♩.	dotted quarter note	three eighth-note beats

Double dots work on the same principle. The second dot extends the duration of a note by half the first dot.

♩..	*double-dotted half note*	three and one-half quarter-note beats

A *tie* (⌣ or ⌢) extends the duration of a note where the use of a dot is impractical: ♩ ♪.

A triplet sign (⌐3⌐) indicates triple subdivision of a beat or other time span where duple subdivision would normally be assumed. For example, ♫♩₃ indicates three equal subdivisions of a quarter-note beat. The duration of each eighth note subsumed

Music and Nature

by the triplet sign is two-thirds that of a regularly notated eighth note. In $\frac{2}{4}$ meter (see the following discussion of time signatures), $\underset{3}{\flat\flat\flat}$ represents one complete measure subdivided into three equal time spans.

A *fermata* (⌢) over a note signifies the extension of its duration for an indefinite time.

A series of noteheads appearing one after the other from left to right indicates a melody or other succession of individually sounding pitches. On the other hand, vertically aligned noteheads represent pitches sounding simultaneously, as in a *block chord*.

Rests. For each note value, there is an equivalent rest, or silence value.

Basics: Research and Notation

Time Signatures. The *meter* of a musical composition—that is, the number and type of beats in successive measures—is ordinarily specified by a *time signature*, expressed as two vertically aligned numerals occurring at the beginning of a piece and remaining in force throughout (unless replaced by a different time signature). The upper numeral signifies the number of beats per measure. For example, a waltz or minuet, both of which are organized in measures of three beats, would normally bear a time signature of ¾. (The lower numeral is explained below.)

There are four essential categories of beat groupings: (1) duple: two, four, or eight beats per measure; (2) triple: three beats per measure; (3) compound: six, nine, or twelve beats per measure with each measure breaking down into two, three, or four subdivisions of three beats each; and (4) irregular compound: five, seven, eleven, and other prime numbers of beats per measure. The latter are variants of regular compound groupings: $2+3$, $2+2+3$, and so on. For that matter, more conventional beat groupings may also subdivide irregularly; for example, eight beats per measure can break down into $3+2+3$ instead of the usual $4+4$; similarly, nine as the upper numeral of a time signature ordinarily represents $3+3+3$, but may also divide into $2+2+2+3$.

The lower numeral in a time signature specifies the notation of a single beat. ¼, ²⁄₄, and ³⁄₄ signify different numbers of beats per measure, but in each case a quarter note (♩) specifies one beat. ¾ and ⅜ both signify triple meter; in the former a quarter note gets one beat, whereas in the latter an eighth note gets one beat and a quarter note two beats.

Tempo Indications. The actualized duration of a single beat is, necessarily, a function of the *tempo* of a given piece. Tempo markings are rarely found in music composed before the Classical period; in those early days, performers were expected to infer proper tempos from the general character of the music. Starting with Classicism, composers indicated tempos with words (such as *allegro*, *andante*, etc.) and/or metronome markings. The metronome was a device invented by Maelzel, a contemporary of Beethoven, the first major composer to supply metronome markings in his scores. The notation ♩=88 specifies the correct tempo as eighty-eight quarter-note beats per minute. The notation ♩=120 means that each beat lasts half a second. This notation appears much more precise than it really is. Composers have always found it hard to select accurate metronome markings, in part because they conceive of tempos in their imaginations, whereas under actual performing conditions specific tempo indications may turn out impractical—that is, unsuitably fast or slow. For this reason the more generalized tempo terms as discussed earlier are more useful than metronome markings, giving the performer a certain interpretive leeway in determining precise tempo inflections. Often metronome markings serve merely as a supplement to traditional verbal tempo terms.

The term *ritardando* means to get gradually slower; *accelerando* means to get faster. A composer wishing that the tempo become instantaneously slower or faster simply introduces the Italian words for these concepts. Thus, *più mosso* means abruptly to play faster, without the gradual change suggested by *accelerando*. The terms *a tempo* and *Tempo I* mean to return to the main tempo previously in effect.

Music and Nature

Interpretive Markings

Articulation Signs.

⌒ = *legato*: smooth
♩ ♩ ♩ = *staccato*: short, clipped
pizz. = *pizzicato* (pit-si-<u>ka</u>-to): plucked
arco = bowed (as opposed to pizzicato)
8 - - - ⌐, 8 - - - ⌐ = an octave higher or lower

Dynamics.

p (piano) = soft
pp (pianissimo) = very soft
ppp (triple piano) = extremely soft
mp (mezzo[<u>met</u>-zo] *piano)* = medium soft
mf (mezzo forte [<u>for</u>-tay]) = medium loud
f (forte) = loud
ff (fortissimo) = very loud
fff (triple forte) = extremely loud
∧ or > or *sf (sforzando* [sfort-<u>san</u>-do]) = accented
◁ or *cresc(endo)* [cre-<u>shen</u>-do] = get louder
▷ or *dim*(in-u-<u>en</u>-do) = get softer
con sordino (con sor-<u>dee</u>-no) = with mute

4   NATURE IN VOCAL MUSIC

In Chapter 1 we focused our attention exclusively on music composed for instruments. Turning now to the voice, we find numerous compositions based on nature-related texts. We shall consider two important examples: Haydn's *The Creation* and Ravel's *Histoires naturelles*.

HAYDN, THE CREATION

Haydn's oratorio, *The Creation* (1798), is perhaps the most impressive of all vocal interpretations of nature. Franz Joseph Haydn was an Austrian composer who lived a long and fruitful life (1732–1809), producing bountiful quantities of cheerful and expressive sonatas, quartets, symphonies, etc., while serving the great Esterhazy family in Hungary. Toward the end of his life Haydn resettled in Vienna, where he was accorded a position of esteem and reverence. He enjoyed Mozart's friendship and briefly taught the young Beethoven—which is to say that he lived at the very hub of Viennese musical activity.

An *oratorio* is a large work for vocal soloists, chorus, and orchestra. (See also page 42 below.) The text of *The Creation* is based on German translations of the Old Testament (*The Book of Genesis*) and John Milton's epic poem, *Paradise Lost* (1667). The work is divided into three main parts, which break down further into more than thirty individual subsections. The fourth subsection of Part I opens with an exclamation which applies as well to this culminating opus of the 66-year-old Classical master: "Look with wonder upon the marvelous achievement!" *The Creation* describes a wide variety of nature scenes with truly marvelous vigor and imagination. The orchestral introduction, "Chaos," conveys all the terror of nothingness, albeit within the strict framework of Classical stylistic constraints (see Chapter 2, p. 21). As the bass soloist introduces the age-old words, "In the beginning God created heaven and earth," the listener experiences a surge of relief as order gradually replaces chaos. The initial choral pronouncement is bathed in great warmth: "And the spirit of God moved upon the face of the water, and God said, 'Let there be light.'" At this point the whole orchestra lights up in blaring C major triads—the C major triad being especially apt here in view of its general acceptance as the most fundamental of chords*—and the bass concludes: "And God saw the light, that it was good, and divided the light from the darkness."

*The C major triad is regarded as fundamental by analogy with the primeness of the *key* of C major. The key of C major is fundamental, because it is the only major key without sharps or flats in its signature. The first, third, and fifth notes of the C major scale (C, E, and G) comprise the C major triad, with the principal note of the key (i.e., C) serving as its *root*.

Joseph Haydn with the score of his "Surprise" Symphony. Portrait by Johann Zitterer.

The remainder of *The Creation* is sung alternately by the three soloists (soprano, tenor, and bass) and chorus, accompanied by the orchestra. Many of the subsections commence in the solo vocal style known as *recitative*. In a recitative passage, unlike a song or aria, neither the melody nor the form is determined by purely musical considerations. Rather, recitatives represent a declamatory singing style in which the melodic lines and rhythmic values approximate those of ordinary speech. Recitative passages usually serve as introductions or transitions to arias or other formal numbers. In *The Creation* the recitatives consist typically of pronouncements such as "And God said" or "And God created," which lead into arias and ensembles that amplify these pronouncements. For example, after the recitative announcing that God created the earth and the sea, the bass soloist continues by singing a formal aria describing the billowing waves, the mountains and rocks, the plains, the rivers, and little brooks. We then hear another recitative concerning the bringing forth of grass, herbs, and fruits, followed directly by the lovely soprano aria, "With Verdure Clad,"

The Creation contains some breathtaking choral work. Few choral anthems surpass the mixture of excitement and enthusiasm projected by the conclusion of Part I, "The Heavens are Telling the Glory of God."

Example 5
HAYDN, *The Creation,* **Part 1**

Part II opens with a soprano aria listing a variety of birds: eagles, the lark, cooing doves, and the nightingale. Here, as throughout the rest of the work, the vocal part is only mildly pictorial, the descriptive burden being carried mainly by the verbal text. Indeed, much of the music is less obviously imitative than the instrumental nature music of Chapter 1; for with words at his disposal, Haydn was not restricted to getting the message across by purely musical means. The representations of the cooing doves and the nightingale can hardly be considered even casual imitations of birdsong. By comparison, Beethoven really hit the mark with his bird calls in the *Pastoral Symphony* (see Chapter 5, p. 44).

Part II is mainly concerned with the characters of Adam and Eve—as impersonated by the bass and soprano soloists. The serpent and the apple are ignored, and the text is all rosy and serene. The oratorio ends in a cloud of fantasy, as the human couple live happily ever after in earthly paradise.

Listen to a thirty-minute segment drawn from Parts I or II of *The Creation*. Since most, if not all, recordings of this work are sung in the original German, you should attempt to follow the portion you select in English translation.*

*You will find that modern recordings of oratorios (and other vocal works with foreign texts) normally include a printed English translation side by side with the original text.

Music and Nature

Etching of the creation. Haydn's *Creation* text is derived from Genesis and Milton's *Paradise Lost*.

Nature in Vocal Music

We now turn to a collection of songs for solo voice and piano by the French Impressionist composer, Maurice Ravel (1875–1937). In Chapter 1 we encountered the Impressionist style of Claude Debussy's *La Mer*. The young Ravel, thirteen years Debussy's junior, was held by many to be derivative from his elder colleague, a view that Ravel resented with some bitterness. It is true that there was much similarity between the two composers' styles, but in many respects Ravel's was as original as Debussy's. Indeed, the younger composer matured so quickly that the two were regarded as peers—and even rivals—as early as the turn of the century.

Ravel composed several fine sets of songs (*song cycles*). The five songs of *Histoires naturelles* are drawn from charming prose poems of Jules Renard. (Several of the stories in the original publication were illustrated by the great artist, Toulouse-Lautrec.) The first song is called "The Peacock." The piano introduction sets the mock-solemn tone for the song's opening line, "He will surely be getting married today." In the middle we hear the peacock's diabolical cry, "Léon! Léon!" The second song tells of the cricket, whose delicate chirpings are deftly caught in the piano accompaniment.*

Example 6
RAVEL, "The Cricket"

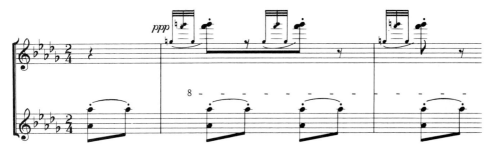

Ravel turns next to "The Swan," which "glides upon the pool like a snow-white sleigh." The piano provides a suitably shimmery accompaniment, to be played (according to the composer's directions) "very gently, enveloped in pedal." (This refers to the *sustaining pedal*, the rightmost pedal as viewed by a person sitting at a piano.) At the beginning of the song Ravel uses only the *penatonic scale*, a five-note scale represented by the five different black notes of the piano keyboard. Sit down at a piano and try playing the pentatonic scale back and forth very softly, "enveloped in pedal"—that is, with the sustaining pedal held down. This will give you a firsthand taste of

*This imitation can be compared to Bartók's delightful piano piece, "From the Diary of a Fly," *Mikrokosmos,* Vol. 6.

what Ravel's accompaniment is like.* (Ravel's "Swan" is not to be confused with another swan piece, the famous cello solo from *Carnival of the Animals,* by Camille Saint-Saëns, see Chapter 16.)

The fourth song of *Histoires naturelles* concerns the kingfisher, a bird resembling a blue jay which is often seen hovering and diving for fish. The calm and languorous song recounts how the kingfisher mistook a fisherman's rod for a tree branch. The fifth and last song of the cycle depicts the nasty guinea hen. The piano introduction cleverly recreates her crotchety personality.

Example 7
RAVEL, "The Guinea Hen"

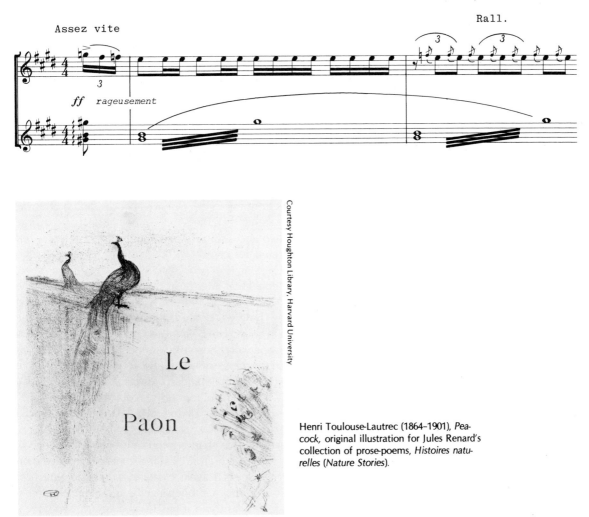

Henri Toulouse-Lautrec (1864–1901), *Peacock,* original illustration for Jules Renard's collection of prose-poems, *Histoires naturelles (Nature Stories).*

Courtesy Houghton Library, Harvard University

*See also Chapter 5, Reading 2, on whole-tone and pentatonic music.

Listen to the entire cycle, matching to the best of your ability the English translation accompanying the recording with the original performing text in French.

BASICS: VOCAL GENRES

A musical *genre* is a category or type of music. Genres are conceived according to the instruments and/or voices required for performing individual works, and other factors such as their form, duration, and intended function. An example of an instrumental genre is a tone poem. In the case of vocal music, we have the genre of the solo song, most often accompanied by piano, but sometimes by lute, guitar, harpsichord, or orchestra. Songs are usually short, rarely lasting more than a few minutes apiece. At the opposite extreme, the vocal genre *opera* may last as long as several hours, depending on the complexity of the original drama and the composer's treatment thereof. Most operas are composites of many smaller genres, such as *arias* (solo songs), *duets, trios,* larger *ensembles,* and *choruses.* These set pieces are separated either by sparsely accompanied monologues or dialogues (*recitatives*) or else by scenes of musically unaccompanied spoken drama.* A light, or comic, opera is sometimes called an *operetta,* which in turn is the model for the modern Broadway *musical.*

An *oratorio* resembles an opera in that it unfolds a plot, but it is performed without costumes, scenery, or staging; moreover, the soloists often merely narrate or comment on the story, rather than overtly enact it. An oratorio based on the events connected with the crucifixion of Christ is known as a *passion* (see Chapter 25, p. 318). The most famous of all oratorios is Handel's *Messiah,* which recounts the birth, life, and death of Christ (see Chapter 25, p. 320). The term *cantata* often signifies a short oratorio, utilizing the same combination of performing forces (soloists, chorus, and orchestra), but lasting thirty to forty-five minutes rather than the two to three hours of an oratorio. Some cantatas involve only one or two vocal soloists (accompanied by orchestra but without chorus), while others are scored for chorus without soloists. (Two of Bach's cantatas are illustrated in Chapter 24.)

Renaissance composers exhibited a great interest in short vocal genres involving just a handful of performers. Examples of these small forms are the French *chanson* and the English and Italian *madrigal.* These works are ordinarily sung without instrumental accompaniment (*a cappella*). In church we hear *motets* and *anthems,* which are short works for choir. Many hymns, especially those of German origin, are known as *chorales.* Catholicism provides us with the *mass,* a kind of oratorio when judged from a purely musical standpoint but using as text the standard liturgical Latin High Mass. Other parts of Catholic liturgy supply the texts and format for *requiems, te deums,* and *vespers,* genres dating as far back as the Medieval period, 800–1400 (see Chapters 23 and 32).

The compositions analyzed earlier in this chapter represent two contrasting vocal genres. Haydn's *The Creation* is a full-scale oratorio, calling for large choral and orchestral forces, along with three vocal soloists. Ravel's *Histoires naturelles,* a musical setting of five poems, is a song cycle requiring just one singer and a piano accompanist. Song cycles may contain from as few as three songs to as many as two dozen.

*For more on opera structure, see Chapter 13 and Mozart's *The Marriage of Figaro.*

Music and Nature

A Chorus of Singers, etching by William Hogarth (1697–1764), satirizes a rehearsal of an oratorio in eighteenth-century England. The oratorio reached its high-point in the works of Handel.

While the best known song cycles are designed for solo voice and piano, others are scored for voice accompanied by orchestra. Other combinations are possible as well; for example, Brahms's *Liebeslieder (Lovesong) Waltzes* is a cycle for vocal quartet accompanied by two pianists at one keyboard (a combination known as *piano four hands*). Typically, all the poems of a song cycle derive from a single author and not uncommonly from just one collection of the author's poetry. In such cases there may be a narrative—as in Schumann's *Frauenliebe und Leben (A Woman's Love and Life)* based on poems by Chamisso—but it is also not unusual for a cycle to exhibit texts similar in content and style but otherwise unconnected—as in Ravel's *Histoires naturelles.*

Haydn and Ravel represent two distinct periods of music history. *The Creation* is a late Classical conception composed just before the beginning of the nineteenth century. Ravel's song cycle, dating from about one hundred years later than Haydn's oratorio, represents Impressionism, one of the important movements associated with the beginning of the modern period.

THE COMPOSER AS IMITATOR

BIRD SONG

At the end of the second movement of the *Pastoral Symphony* Beethoven introduced three birds: the nightingale, the quail, and the cuckoo. An engaging view of this passage is presented by Calvin S. Brown:

> This . . . brings us to one of the most hotly disputed points in all music—the bird imitations just before the end of the movement. After a pause, the nightingale (flute) begins with a repeated F, which then begins to alternate more and more rapidly with a G until it leads into a trill. Just before the trill begins, however, the quail (oboe) comes in with a repeated figure consisting of a dotted sixteenth, a thirty-second, and an eighth note, all on the same D. Before the conclusion of this figure the cuckoo (clarinet) joins the other two birds with the literal imitation of a descending major third. The first violins then come in for half a bar, after which the entire performance is repeated; and then three more bars form the conclusion of the movement. This is a bare statement of what happens, and many critics have unequivocally condemned it as a puerile trick cheapening the entire movement. Beethoven himself wanted the imitation recognized, for he wrote the names of the birds into the score. He might well have spared himself the trouble, for they are so obviously bird-calls and are so strange from a purely musical point of view that there was little chance of their failing of recognition. A few critics have objected . . . to the birds. . . . Another group contends that this passage, far from being a silly stunt, is one of the greatest beauties of the symphony. . . .[See Example 8.]
>
> Personally, . . . I wish that Beethoven had left the ornithology alone. The birds always produce in me that very unpleasant sort of embarrassment which comes when one sees a loved and revered friend mildly but publicly making a fool of himself.[1]

In view of the reverence accorded Beethoven by the music lovers of our time, Brown's blunt criticism of the birdcalls is certainly unusual. What is your opinion in this matter? Listen again to the passage in question (see Chapter 1) and decide for yourself. Are the birdcalls a "silly stunt" or "one of the greatest beauties of the symphony"?

As we know from Vivaldi's bird song imitations in the *Spring Concerto* (see Example 1), Beethoven was by no means the first composer to portray birds. A sampling of Renaissance, Baroque, and Classical vocal and instrumental bird music, culled from the *Oxford Companion to Music,* includes the following:

Jannequin: *Song of the Birds*
Frescobaldi: *Capriccio on the Cuckoo*
Handel: "Cuckoo and the Nightingale" (*Concerto*) for Organ
Haydn: *String Quartet in C,* Opus 33, No. 3, "Bird Quartet"
Boccherini: *"Aviary" String Quartet*
Vivaldi: *"Cuckoo" Concerto*[2]

Example 8

BEETHOVEN, *Pastoral Symphony*, 2nd Mvt., Conclusion

Numbered among works composed in the twentieth century are Ottorino Respighi's tone poem, *The Birds*, Ravel's piano solo *Oiseaux tristes (Sad Birds)*, and Delius's *On Hearing the First Cuckoo of Spring*. The contemporary French master, Olivier Messiaen, has written several bird compositions, including *Blackbird*, for flute and piano, *Catalogue of the Birds* for solo piano, and *Exotic Birds*, a large work for piano and orchestra based on upward of forty different bird calls. Nicolas Slonimsky has described the latter as "conjuring up in sophisticated idealization the tweets, chirps, warbles, twitters, and trills of polychromatic birds of Asia and America."[3] Messiaen has made an extensive study of ornithology and justifiably boasts an encyclopedic knowledge of birdcalls.

Another example of bird song is found in the music of Béla Bartók (1881–1945), who several years before his death emigrated from Hungary to the United States. Here is a description of his escape from the noise of New York City to the quiet of Asheville, North Carolina:

> ... the constantly tormenting screams of auto horns and police sirens were drowned in memory by the concert of the birds. Their cries and calls can be heard in the second movement of Bartók's *Third Piano Concerto.* ... He had returned to the sources of nature. In the last pages he ever wrote, the Hungarian, the European, the great citizen of the world set a small, lovely monument to the birds of North Carolina.[4]

Not all bird music involves human representations of birds. One eighteenth-century vogue had English musicians playing recorders as a means of training caged birds to imitate human melodies.* One such collection is entitled *The Bird Fancier's Delight.* And current musically oriented ornithologists have recorded bird songs and even written them out in music notation, ostensibly demonstrating the decided compositional prowess of various bird species. Incidentally, Respighi was probably the first composer to use a recording of actual bird song, a nightingale's, in his orchestral work, *The Pines of Rome* (1924).

Bird music can be found in several operas. One of the principal characters in Mozart's *Die Zauberflöte (The Magic Flute)* is Papageno, the bird catcher. In his first aria, describing his professional activities, he imitates a generalized bird call by means of a five-note panpipe (flute). Richard Wagner, famous for the monumental size of his music dramas, calls for singers endowed with monumental voices, but in *Seigfried*, the third music drama of the *Nibelungen* series (see Chapter 14), the atypical role of the Forest Bird calls for a *lyric coloratura* — a light, high soprano voice. In Ravel's delightful children's opera, *L'Enfant et les sortilèges (The Child and the Sorceries)*, a nightingale, an owl, and a bat are among the various creatures that populate the child's hallucinatory dreams.

Example 9

MOZART, *The Magic Flute,* Papageno's Aria

*The recorder was a Baroque precursor of the transverse flute used today.

Music and Nature

While representations of birds are comparatively rare in operas composed during the past two hundred years, bird arias were quite common in many of the now-neglected operas of the Baroque period. A recent Handel revival has occasioned recollection of a contemporary review by Joseph Addison, the noted essayist of *The Spectator*. It seems that at the original London performances of *Rinaldo* (1711), flocks of sparrows were released during the singing of its bird aria. Addison had a rather tart opinion of Handel's sparrows:

> There have been so many flights of them let loose that it is feared the house will never get rid of them; and that in other plays they make their entrance in very wrong and improper scenes; besides the inconveniences which the heads of the audience may sometimes suffer from.[5]

BASICS: PENTATONIC AND WHOLE-TONE SCALES

The scales which underlie the music of the sixteenth through nineteenth centuries (and much of the twentieth) are represented by the white notes of the piano keyboard. Ascending from C, you pass through seven different white notes, C D E F G A B, before reaching C again. This is the *major scale*, otherwise known by the syllables *do re mi fa sol la ti do*. Similarly, you can create the *natural minor scale* by starting on A and proceeding through seven white notes to the next A.

Example 10
Major Scale

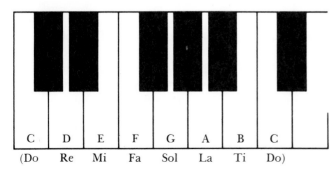

C D E F G A B C
(Do Re Mi Fa Sol La Ti Do)

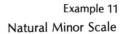
Example 11
Natural Minor Scale

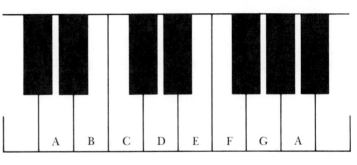

A B C D E F G A

The major and minor scales are the foundation of much of the music you will listen to in connection with this book. But two other scales are prominent in the Impressionist style of Debussy and Ravel, discussed in Chapters 1 and 4.

The Pentatonic Scale

This scale is represented by the five black notes of the piano keyboard (as well as by various other combinations of five white or five white and black notes). You encountered this scale in Ravel's "The Swan," the third song of *Nature Stories* (see Chapter 4). The pentatonic scale is sometimes described as a gapped scale, since it is identical to the major scale with its fourth and seventh degrees omitted. For example, if you take the C major scale and eliminate F and B, you are left with the pentatonic C D E G A.

Example 12
Pentatonic Scale

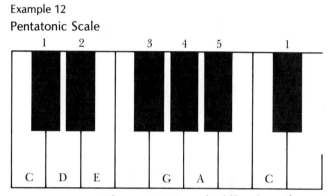

The pentatonic scale differs from the major and minor scales in that if you play all five notes simultaneously you get a pleasingly lush harmonic effect (in contradistinction to the harsh dissonance which results from sounding all seven notes of the major or minor scales together). The pentatonic scale figures prominently in our Western conception of Oriental music and its presence in the music of Ravel and Debussy is a portent of their interest in the music and culture of the Orient. Debussy used the pentatonic scale in his piano piece, "Pagodas," from *Estampes,* while Ravel used it in "Little Ugly One, Empress of the Pagodas," from his *Mother Goose Suite.* The pentatonic scale is also found in Debussy's piano prelude, "The Sunken Cathedral" and in "Jimbo's Lullaby" from his *Children's Corner* for piano.

Example 13
RAVEL, Mother Goose Suite

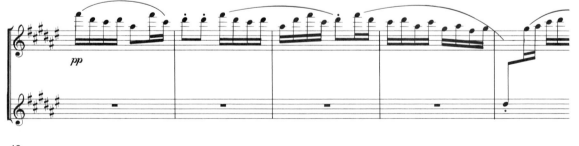

Music and Nature

The Whole-Tone Scale

This is another important scale in Impressionist music. You can easily derive it from the *chromatic scale*, as represented by the succession of all twelve different black and white notes on the piano keyboard. The space (*interval*) between adjacent notes of the chromatic scale is called a *half step* or *semitone*. Omitting every other note leaves a scale of six different notes in which each is separated from its neighbor by an interval of two half steps, or one *whole step* or *whole tone*. Since the sole interval now found between adjacent scale notes is the whole tone, the scale is appropriately called the *whole-tone scale*.

You can experiment with making some "primitive" Impressionist music of your own in the following way: At a piano keyboard select a group of three black notes (as opposed to a group of just two black notes)—see Example 14. The first of these three notes is G♭. Lying a whole tone above G♭ is the next black note, A♭, and still another whole tone up is the third black note, B♭. If you continue ascending by whole tones, you will next reach a white note, C. The fifth and sixth notes will also be white (D and E) and then, as you reach the next higher group of three black notes, you will hit G♭ again. (If your seventh note is *not* G♭, check back to make sure you have consistently omitted exactly one semitone as you proceeded from one scale degree to the next.)

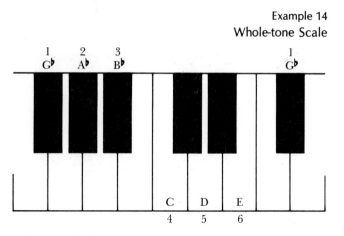

Example 14
Whole-tone Scale

Having found the six notes of the whole-tone scale, play all of them successively and then simultaneously. Experiment with holding down three of the notes while playing the remaining three one at a time and in another area of the keyboard. Perhaps you can construct a brief melody, made up exclusively of these six members of the whole-tone scale. Notice that when you play some or even all of the notes together, the resulting chord is only mildly severe or dissonant; in fact the effect can be lush and pleasing, as with the pentatonic scale. Now switch to the remaining six notes of the chromatic scale. These notes also comprise a whole-tone scale, for they represent an exact duplication (*transposition*) of the first six notes. (A transposed note collection is internally constructed like the original collection, but starts on a different note.) As you alternate back and forth between the two six-note whole-tone scales, you will produce

The Composer as Imitator

an Impressionist texture not unlike what you sometimes hear in the music of Debussy, Ravel, and their contemporaries.

You should think of your whole-tone experiment as being in the nature of an improvisation. Now it is one thing to improvise, and quite another to compose, and the simple explorations suggested will hardly enable you to compose a full-fledged Impressionist piece. Most Impressionist music combines the whole-tone scale with other scales, both traditional and modern, and in any case even a relatively straightforward whole-tone piece like Debussy's *Voiles (Sails)* employs motives, tone painting, and harmonies in intricate and subtle ways. But at least you now know, at first hand, about the shimmery, naturelike quality of the whole-tone scale.

Vaslav Nijinsky in his original role as the faun in Debussy's ballet *The Afternoon of a Faun*.

The Impressionists appear to have created a musical style suggestive of nature even when that was not their announced intent. Thus, much of Debussy's music matches the naturelike quality of *La Mer* (see Chapter 1) without corresponding to its programmatic content. For example, his *Prelude to the Afternoon of a Faun* (a musical interpretation of an erotic poem by Stefan Mallarmé) starts with a flute solo based on a modified whole-tone scale. This solo is repeated a little later over a soft tremolo background similar to the opening sonorities of *La Mer*. We may imagine a wooded scene for the faun's dreamy monologue, but certainly not in an oceanic setting! This

Music and Nature

suggests that to some extent—it is hard to say how much—reflections of nature, and other things as well, are projected from inside our heads. That is, in the first movement of *La Mer* Debussy's title prepares us to hear a musical description of the sea between dawn and noon. We respond to this combination of verbal information and aural input by associating the latter with our notion of what the "music of the sea" might actually sound like; Debussy instructs us to hear sea music, and we do our best to comply. But, in another work, he directs our attention to an entirely different subject—a mythical faun—and we no longer think of the sea, despite the similarity of compositional style. This is not to denigrate Debussy's achievements, for with his titles and subheadings he has communicated what interested him when he was creating his music. "I was thinking of the ocean," Debussy has informed us, and we have the option of thinking about it too. It is important to realize, however, that we also have the choice of ignoring the program of *La Mer* and listening to it as purely nonpictorial music.

FURTHER LISTENING FOR UNIT I

In this section we shall survey a variety of compositions featuring the subject of nature. The works are arranged in four categories: (1) piano pieces, (2) orchestral music, (3) ballet music, and (4) vocal music.

Piano Pieces

Much nature music has been written for the piano. Following in the footsteps of Bach (early eighteenth century) and Chopin (early nineteenth century), Debussy (early twentieth century) composed a set of twenty-four piano preludes; unlike his musical forefathers, however, he added a title to each prelude. Curiously, the titles come at the end of each prelude rather than at the beginning, as if Debussy wanted to acknowledge their programmatic content but at the same time to emphasize their purely musical function, irrespective of extramusical content. Several of the preludes describe nature: "What the West Wind Saw," "The Wind in the Plain," "Dead Leaves," and "Footsteps in the Snow." In other piano collections Debussy wrote "Reflections in the Water" and "Garden in the Rain." The prelude "The Sunken Cathedral" suggests an ancient edifice lying beneath water, gradually emerging into view, and then sinking back again into obscurity. (This piece features the pentatonic scale, as discussed above.) Another atmospheric piece by Debussy is "Claire de lune" ("Moonlight") from his *Suite Bergamasque*. (With regard to Debussy's music we are reminded here of Gide's comments on Chopin, quoted in the introduction to Chapter 1.)

An American contemporary of Debussy, Edward MacDowell (1861–1908) composed a set of piano pieces, *Woodland Sketches*. Among these are "To a Wild Rose," "To a Water Lily," and "Told at Sunset." The British pianist, Clive Lythgoe, has written the following commentary on MacDowell and his music:

> On a recent visit to MacDowell's house near Peterboro, New Hampshire, I came face to face with what was the very essence of his inspiration—Nature. Here today at what is now the MacDowell colony, composers, painters, sculptors, writers, and poets come to create their works free from worldly cares. . . . In this refuge amid nature, MacDowell escaped into his own private world of forests, elves, spirits, knights in armour, deserted farms, and wild flowers.[6]

The Composer as Imitator

Compare the blurred outlines of Claude Monet's (1840–1926) *Rouen Cathedral* with the explicit photograph of the same subject. The visual effect of Monet's painting is similar to the aural effect of Debussy's piano piece, "The Sunken Cathedral," which suggests an ancient edifice, gradually emerging into view and then sinking back again into obscurity. With its vague outlines and shimmery details, Impressionist painting paved the way for musical Impressionism.

Other instances of nature as a subject of piano music include "The White Peacock," one of four *Roman Sketches* by the American Impressionist, Charles Griffes (1884–1920), and the *Out of Doors* suite (1926) by the Hungarian composer, Béla Bartók. The latter contains "With Drums and Pipes," "Barcarolla," "Musettes," "Musiques nocturnes," and "The Chase."

Orchestral Music

Prior to *La Mer* (see Chapter 1), Debussy produced two other orchestral works associated with nature: *Printemps* (Spring) and *Nocturnes*. The former is said to have been inspired by Botticelli's painting *Primavera*. In *Printemps* Debussy wanted to suggest "the slow and miserable birth of beings and things in Nature, their gradual blossoming and finally the joy of being born into some new life."[7] *Nocturnes*, first performed in 1901, contains two nature-related sections, *Nuages* (Clouds) and *Sirens*. In *Sirens*, the delineation of the sea anticipates the later Impressionist style of *La Mer*. Debussy also composed *Images pour Orchestre*, which includes a section entitled "Spring Rounds" (1909).

Music and Nature

The English composer Ralph Vaughan Williams (1872–1958) wrote a *Sea Symphony* for vocal soloists, chorus, and orchestra. The four movements are named "A Song for All Seas, All Ships," "On the Beach at Night Alone," "The Waves," and "The Explorers." Richard Wagner (1813–1883) had earlier painted a sea picture in the overture to his music drama, *The Flying Dutchman*, concerning a mythical figure cursed to living six of every seven years at sea. This music contains a memorable depiction of a storm, as does also *En Saga*, a tone poem by Jean Sibelius (1865–1957).

A significant American work is Ferde Grofé's *Grand Canyon Suite*, composed in 1931 for the Paul Whiteman Orchestra. (Grofé had orchestrated George Gershwin's *Rhapsody in Blue* for its premiere by Whiteman's group several years before—see Chapter 10.) The *Grand Canyon Suite* belongs to that nebulous category, *semiclassical music*—that is, music which fits somewhere between the extremes of outright popular music and classical genres. The suite consists of five pictorial settings: "Sunrise," "Painted Desert," "On the Trail," "Sunset," and "Cloudburst." You may wish to compare Grofé's "Sunrise" with Debussy's "From Dawn to Noontime on the Sea" (*La Mer*) and also Grofé's "Cloudburst" with Beethoven's storm in the fourth movement of the *Pastoral Symphony* (see Chapter 1). Incidentally, the theme of "On the Trail" is familiar to millions of older Americans from its years of use in a Philip Morris cigarette commercial.*

Ballet Music

Any music which is used to accompany staged ballet dancing belongs to the category of *ballet music*. Some ballet music is simply adapted from the concert literature (even if the composer had no such intent) but many original scores have been commissioned specifically for ballet accompaniment. Often the composer of a lengthy ballet will later reduce the complete score to a suite geared for orchestral concerts, and in some cases an entire ballet score becomes accepted as a concert work. Igor Stravinsky's *Le Sacre du printemps* (*The Rite of Spring*), subtitled "Pictures of Pagan Russia," is frequently heard in concert performance, but it is only rarely performed as a ballet. The music evokes the bursting of bonds and surging of fertility, in connection with pagan spring rites. Part I, "The Adoration of the Earth," includes "Spring Rounds" and "Dance of the Earth." (This work is discussed in greater detail in Chapter 30.) Stravinsky also wrote *Renard*, a humorous ballet based on the traditional farmyard offensive-defensive strategy of fox and rooster: and in 1962 the octegenarian Stravinsky composed the television ballet, *Noah and the Flood*.

---

*Beethoven, who when it came to money matters was nobody's fool, might no doubt be making a bundle writing commercials if he were alive today. And à propos of earning money, a film commentator has recently written:

> Purists protest at the thought of Bach or any great master writing for films but it is more than likely that had they lived in the twentieth century they would have been thus engaged. A little investigation reveals Mozart and Haydn writing music for patrons even less appreciative than film producers.

See Tony Thomas, *Music for the Movies*, New York, 1973, p. 19.

53

Vocal Music

A song cycle comparable to Ravel's *Histoires naturelles* (see Chapter 4) is *Le Bestiaire*, a set of animal songs based on poems of Guillaume Apollinaire and composed by Ravel's younger compatriot, Francis Poulenc (1899–1963). The menagerie which populates this song cycle includes a dromedary, Tibetan goat, locust, dolphin, crab, and carp. Stravinsky's *Three Tales for Children* (1915–1917), based on Russian folk texts, deals with a cat, goat, rooster, ducks, swans, geese, fleas, and a bear. The American composer Aaron Copland wrote an unaccompanied choral setting, *In the Beginning* (1947), founded—like Haydn's *The Creation* (see Chapter 4)—on opening verses of *The Book of Genesis*. Nature and its seasons are sometimes featured in popular music, as in such diverse songs as "June Is Bustin' Out All Over," from Rodgers and Hammerstein's *Carousel,* and—at the opposite end of the calendar—Irving Berlin's sentimental "I'm Dreaming of a White Christmas."

Nature scenes abound in opera. Wagner's *Die Walküre* and Verdi's *Otello* both open with storm music, and we have already cited the tossing sea music of *The Flying Dutchman* overture. The beginning of Wagner's *Das Rheingold* depicts the flowing undulations of the Rhine River, and later the opera boasts a marvelously orchestrated rainbow scene (see Chapter 14). Debussy's *Pelléas et Mélisande* commences with a beautiful orchestral painting of a forest, while later a ship setting sail in the distance recalls the music of *La Mer*.

CHECKLIST: CONCEPTS AND TERMS IN UNIT 1

The following terms are ones you should check for review. They are of general importance, and many of them recur frequently throughout subsequent chapters. The numbers in parentheses after each term refer to the pages where it is first and/or principally used and/or explained. In many cases the explanation suffices to clarify the term only for the particular context in which it is used, and in some cases no separate explanation is provided at all, as the meaning of the term is clear from the context alone. In either case, a more general and complete definition may usually be found in the Glossary (Appendix II).

General Terms

absolute music (1)
finale (10)
genre (42)
motive (13n)
movement (6n)
opus (27)
program music (241-45)
semiclassical (53)
tempo (4, 26, 34)
theme (10)
transposition (49)
trill (5n)

Historical Periods

Baroque (17, 20-23)
Classical (18, 20-23)
Contemporary (20)
Impressionism (3, 48-51)
Modern (20-23)
Romantic (18-23)

Instruments: Forms, Techniques, etc.

ballet suite (53)
chamber orchestra (16)
concerto (6)
concerto grosso (6n, 24)
continuo (16, 22-23)
development (13n)
episode (6)
glissando (3)
minuet (23)
orchestra (15-16)
overture (11)
refrain (6)
scherzo (23)
slow introduction (26)
sonata (23)
suite (23)
symphony (7)
tone poem (4)
tremolo (4)

The Composer as Imitator

Vocal Music

aria (42)
bass (37)
oratorio (36, 42)
recitative (37)
song cycle (40)
soprano (37)
tenor (37)

Theory

beat (31)
block chord (33)
chromatic scale (49)
counterpoint (13n)
dissonance (21)
figured bass (22n)
half step (49)
harmony (13n)
interval (49)
major scale (47)
measure (10, 31)
meter (10, 34)
minor scale (47)
octave (31)
pentatonic scale (40, 48)
scale (3)
whole step (49)
whole-tone scale (49–50)

Notation

Pitch (29–31)
clef (treble, bass, etc.)
flat
key signature
leger line
middle C
natural (sign)
sharp
staff

Rhythm (31–34)
accelerando
bar line
compound meter
dot
duple meter (triple, etc.)
fermata
metronome marking
quarter note (half note, etc.)
rest
ritard
tie
time signature
triplet sign

Articulation (35)
arco
legato
pizzicato
staccato

Dynamics (35)
con sordino
crescendo
diminuendo
forte
fortissimo
mezzo forte
mezzo piano
piano
pianissimo
sforzando

THE MUSIC OF LANDS AND PEOPLES

In Unit 1 we examined a variety of composers' responses to their natural surroundings. Some of these works emphasize raw nature (Debussy's *La Mer*, Mendelssohn's *Fingal's Cave Overture*); others stress birds, insects, and animals (Vivaldi's *The Seasons*, Haydn's *The Creation*, and Ravel's *Histoires naturelles*); and some include human beings as well (*The Seasons; The Creation*, Part III; and Beethoven's *Pastoral Symphony*). From the music of nature it is but a short step to music which describes specific peoples in specific locales. *Fingal's Cave Overture* itself describes an actual place, but the music lacks a sense of human presence. A considerably different picture is painted in *Ma Vlast (My Native Land)*, by the nineteenth-century Czech composer, Bedrich Smetana. *Ma Vlast* is a composite of six interdependent orchestral tone poems which recount the historical traditions of Bohemia. The first of these compositions is entitled "Vysehrad," after the great rock outside Prague in whose castle (now ruined) lived Czech princes of yore. Undoubtedly this rock is an impressive natural wonder, but our interest is focused rather on its *historical* importance. Smetana's music attempts not only to convey an image of this great rock, but also to project its status as a national shrine in the heritage of the people presently living around it.

The second and best known part of *Ma Vlast* is "The Moldau," named for a river which flows through the Bohemian countryside. Here again we have music which describes more than pure nature, for it includes an element not present in Mendelssohn's *Fingal's Cave*: national pride. "From Bohemia's Meadows and Forests," the fourth tone poem of the series, has been likened to Beethoven's *Pastoral Symphony* as a composer's response to his natural environment. But again there is an important difference: for, although Beethoven was inspired by his wanderings in the Austrian provinces, his music is instilled with little in the way of nationalistic features. Smetana's music, on the other hand, informs us about country life in *Bohemia*, not just about country life in general.

Ma Vlast represents the compositional trend known as *nationalism*, a movement which spread to various European musical outposts — Spain, Norway, Finland, Hungary, Russia, and elsewhere, eventually reaching America. Chapter 6 offers in-depth exposure to nationalistic music originating in four different corners of Europe. After you have familiarized yourself with these pieces, you may move on to the fuller account of nationalism presented in Chapter 7. Chapters 8 and 10 deal with American music. In between, Chapter 9 introduces several important theoretical concepts relating to the tonal system (scales, intervals, chords, and so on). Chapter 10 also explains concerto form, as a follow-up to Gershwin's one-movement concerto, *Rhapsody in Blue*. Chapter 11 consists of another brief reading about musical nationalism, followed by a longer essay on musical souvenirs. Finally, Chapter 12 presents an outstanding example of musical Americana, Dvořák's symphony, *From the New World*. This chapter also includes important information on symphonic structure and the special form known as *sonata form*.

The Music of Lands and Peoples

THE MUSIC OF
EUROPEAN NATIONALISM

SMETANA, THE MOLDAU

"Bedrich Smetana has rightly been called the founder of Czech music," according to a recent study of this important nineteenth-century nationalistic composer.[1] Born in 1824, just three years prior to the death of Beethoven, Smetana received his musical education during the exciting early years of the Romantic period. Later he earned the admiration of one of the most influential of the early Romantics, Franz Liszt. But Smetana's life was dogged by frustration. Determined to ground his music in Czech history and culture, he was nevertheless looked on as a musical conservative by many of his musical compatriots. Of his numerous operas, only *The Bartered Bride* succeeded in arousing serious interest. Like Beethoven, Smetana turned deaf in middle life; like Schumann, mental illness marred his last years. All the same, Smetana created his most important works during this last period. (He died in 1884.) *Ma Vlast* (*My Native Land*) is a set of six tone poems written over a seven-year period starting in 1872. Having recently completed *Libuse*, an opera concerning the founding of the first Czech dynasty, Smetana conceived of *Ma Vlast* as a musical portrayal of the subsequent history of the Czechoslovakian peoples.

Bědrich Smetana (1824–1884).

Despite his personal difficulties Smetana's late music is wonderfully bright and hopeful. This is especially true of the second tone poem, "The Moldau," a musical celebration of the integrity of the Czech nation. The work depicts several scenes of life along the Moldau River. As the music starts, we hear the confluence of two mountain streams, the first represented by an undulating figure in the flutes, the second by a complementary figure in the clarinets. The entrance of the oboes (joined by the first violins) signals the principal theme of the work—a magnificent, broadly scored melody depicting the fully formed Moldau River. In its first appearance the melody is set in the *minor mode*, but following a contrasting middle section it returns even more majestically, now partially in the *major mode*. (For the present the reader is invited to listen to the music, taking note of the terms *minor mode* and *major mode*, with the understanding that they are explained in Chapter 9.)

Example 15
SMETANA, *The Moldau*, Main Theme

a) 1st Statement in Minor

b) 2nd Statement, Partially Major

c) Final Version—All Major

Più moto (Faster)

The prominence of French horns and other brass instruments now suggests a hunt along the Moldau's banks. Another episode occurs as peasant wedding festivities resound to the bouncing rhythms of a polka. Next we hear an enchanting Water Nymphs' Dance. A gentle mood of moonlight is created by muted strings, accompanied by rippling figures in the flutes and clarinets. After this, the Moldau theme is fully restated in all of its three parts.

The river now passes through the turbulent St. John's Rapids, indicated by *fortissimo* outpourings from the entire orchestra. After a quiet interlude the full orchestra once again presents the Moldau theme, somewhat faster than before and now completely in major (see Example 15c). Then, as the river passes the mighty fortress Vysehrad, we hear the principal theme of the first tone poem of *Ma Vlast* (discussed in the introduction to this unit).

The Music of Lands and Peoples

Example 16

The Moldau, Finale, *Vysehrad* Theme

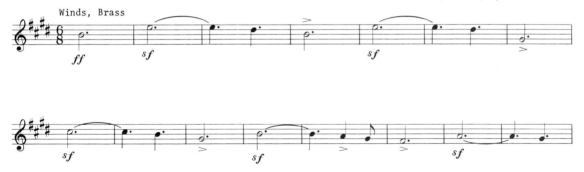

The Moldau concludes, according to the testimony of the composer himself, as the river passes through the capital city of Prague and finally empties into the Elbe River.

Jean Sibelius, photograph by Alvin Langdon Coburn. Sibelius composed *Finlandia* to honor the new spirit of Finnish nationalism which was on the upsurge as the Finns tried to cast off the fetters of Russian domination.

SIBELIUS, FINLANDIA

All during the second half of the nineteenth century, when musical nationalism was developing in Czechoslovakia and other European locales, the nation of Finland lay somnolent—Russian by political affiliation, Swedish by language and culture (due to previous Swedish political domination in the eighteenth century). A sense of Finnish national identity remained latent and untapped. Like the English and French tongues in Eastern Canada, the Swedish and Finnish languages had clashed in eighteenth-century Finland, with Swedish gaining the upper hand. At the beginning of the nineteenth century there was barely a hint of the nationalism that was to assert itself in Finland during the next hundred years.

Jean Sibelius was born in 1865 in the Finnish hamlet of Hämeenlinna. Swedish by family background, the young Sibelius nevertheless took a great interest in Finnish culture. As a student in Berlin he was strongly impressed by a symphony (composed by another Finn) based on the *Kalevala*, the Finnish national epic (which was later to be a source for many of his own works). Having distinguished himself as a notable musical talent, Sibelius was granted a lifetime pension at the age of 29; thereafter he devoted himself to composing full time. By 1889 the rising tide of nationalism was causing widespread unrest in Finland—which in turn provoked repressive measures on the part of her Russian rulers. Sibelius responded to this crisis by composing a variety of patriotic works, among them the tone poem *Finland Awakes*, later renamed *Finlandia*.

Finlandia opens with a slow and somber introduction, first featuring brass instruments and later continuing with "choirs" of winds and strings. A faster section introduces an insistent *tattoo* (rhythmic motive) in the brass. The thematic material of the preceding slow section is heard again, but with a new sense of patriotic fervor. Finally, the main part of the work commences at a quick stride, presenting an important new theme accompanied by the brass tattoo. After two complete statements of this fast section, the winds introduce a solemn theme accompanied by soft tremolo strings. (The hymnlike character of this theme had led to its adaptation as a choral work with added verbal text.) The hymn theme is heard twice, the second time played principally by the strings assisted by clarinets, bassoons, and a soft rumbling in the bass drum. The final section (*coda*) consists of the earlier fast main theme followed by a final brass statement of the hymn theme played by the entire orchestra with "all stops out."

Example 17
SIBELIUS, *Finlandia*, Main Theme

The Music of Lands and Peoples

Finlandia is just one of many orchestral works which demonstrate Sibelius's interest in the Finnish nationalist cause.

> The symphonic poem has throughout the nineteenth century acted as a convenient outlet for composers discovering their national folklore. Probably the most important function of the symphonic poem was to serve as a vehicle for Sibelius's interest in Finnish mythology. . . . The *Kalevala* exercised a fascination over him throughout his life, and this found its most natural (though not its only) outlet in the symphonic poem.[2]

Readers who wish to further acquaint themselves with Sibelius's orchestral interpretations of the *Kalevala* can choose from among the following:

En Saga, 1892	*Lemminkäinen in Tuonela*, 1895
The Swan of Tuonela, 1893	*Lemminkäinen's Homeward Journey*, 1895
Lemminkäinen and the	*Pohjola's Daughter*, 1906
Maidens of Saari, 1895	*Tapiola*, 1926

Many musicians regard *Tapiola* as one of Sibelius's finest compositions. Its title refers to Tapio, the god of the forest, and the music attempts to convey a sense of the primeval northern woodlands, with its "wood-sprites [which] in the gloom wave magic secrets."[3] In its evocation of nature, *Tapiola* has been favorably compared to Debussy's *La Mer*:

> One does not have to have experienced the vast forests of Scandinavia with all their variety of moods, colours and sounds, their immense loneliness, their magic, terror and majesty, for Sibelius's vision in *Tapiola* to make its impact . . . it is as perfect an evocation of the forest as *La Mer* is of the sea.[4]

BARTÓK, FIFTEEN HUNGARIAN PEASANT SONGS

Béla Bartók was born in 1881 in a region of Hungary which, what with the vagaries of Eastern European borders during the first half of the twentieth century, now happens to belong to Rumania. Just as the young Sibelius's Finland was controlled by a civil service elite of Swedish extraction, Bartók's homeland in his youth was dominated by a German upper class. The first internationally famous Hungarian composer, Franz Liszt (1811–1886), was more German than Hungarian in his cultural orientation; indeed, the very name "Franz" is the German equivalent of the Hungarian "Ferenc." Liszt composed a number of Hungarian rhapsodies, but these were based on gypsy musical styles rather than on the genuine folk themes of the Hungarian (Magyar) peasantry. It awaited Bartók, and his colleague Zoltán Kodály, to kindle an interest in peasant music as an expression of the new Hungarian cultural nationalism.

> The pronounced nationalism of Bartók and Kodály led them early to seek means of national expression in music, and when they came into contact with Hungarian peasant music, ignored as corrupt by their predecessors, they found in it elements which, once assimilated, were to lead them to the production of an art music as Hungarian as its sources and yet international in its communication.[5]

63

Bartók first started music lessons at the age of five, and he was composing by the age of nine. One of his first major works was *Kossuth*, a tone poem of ten tableaux picturing the unsuccessful Hungarian revolt of 1848–1849 (led by Lajos Kossuth). Until the age of twenty-three Bartók was unaware of genuine Magyar, as opposed to gypsy, music. Having once encountered the real thing, he set out to scour the hills and dales of his native land and the countries adjoining it, digging up and notating a vast treasure of folk materials. The fruits of Bartók's researches are evident in his folk music arrangements—for example, the *Rumanian Folk Dances* for piano and *Four Slovak Songs* for chorus—as well as in his idiomatic *absolute* style, as represented by the six string quartets and the *Concerto for Orchestra*.

Bartók composed his collection of *Fifteen Hungarian Peasant Songs* between 1914 and 1917. Most of the tunes can be traced to his ethnic expeditions and studies. The fifteen songs are grouped into four large sections. The first section consists of "four old tunes." You can imagine these tunes as folk songs, albeit now textless and scored for piano, their free rhythmic style matching the accent and flow of the omitted

Béla Bartók with the pianist Gyorgy Sandor. Bartok's folk-oriented piano work, "Dance Suite," can be seen on the piano.

The Music of Lands and Peoples

Hungarian words. The tunes are accompanied by mildly dissonant chords. Paradoxically, these transformed vocal pieces come across highly pianistic; Bartók has coined a delightful piano/vocal idiom.

The second section consists of a single piece (No. 5) entitled "Scherzo." A *scherzo* is a jocular piece, and this one is based on a lusty tune which seems even a bit drunken. After its first throaty statement, the tune is repeated an *octave* higher, then presented a little slower in the style of harp music. The song closes with a final repetition of the tune in the opening low register, accompanied by a few extra "growls" and "hiccups."

Section 3, entitled "Ballad," is again a single piece (No. 6) consisting of a theme followed by a brief set of variations. The theme, which is first presented in octave doublings (illustrated in Example 18), is striking for its irregular pulse groupings (*meter*) of seven beats per measure. Each measure is broken up into three subgroupings of two, three, and two beats, respectively, resulting in a strange effect of regular irregularity! (Meter and time signatures are explained in Chapter 3.)

Example 18

BARTÓK, *Fifteen Hungarian Peasant Songs*, "Ballad"

After its first statement, the theme then appears three times in succession in the right hand, accompanied by flowing linear motions in the left hand. Next comes a severe dramatic variation punctuated by loud chords which seem quite "thick" compared with the versions heard before. A harplike strumming variation—soft and gentle, and much slower—leads to an interlude not based on the theme. The piece ends with two final variations in the loud style of variation 4, but now even louder and more imposing, with the theme projected successively in two, three, and four octaves.

Section 4 consists of several succinct dance tunes. No. 9 produces a drone or bagpipe effect. No. 11 imitates a harp even more closely than the strumming variations of the "Scherzo" and the "Ballad." No. 12 is a jocular tune alternating between triple and duple meter: each measure of three beats is followed by a measure of two beats.

The last section (*finale*), No. 15, once again effects a drone. The piece continuously builds in excitement until it quiets down just before the end—as if the frenetic dancers had run out of steam. But they are quickly restored to their senses by two jolting final chords.

Although in the last years of his life Bartók turned away from folk music transcriptions, devoting himself mainly to absolute works for chamber ensembles and orchestra, the influence of folk music never entirely abated. For example, the fourth movement of his *Concerto for Orchestra,* "Interrupted Intermezzo," presents two themes that bear the unmistakable stamp of Eastern Europe. The first of these sounds Oriental, with its small range and irregular meter. The second theme recalls in its broadness the "Ballad" from Bartók's *Fifteen Hungarian Peasant Songs* (see Example 18).

Example 19
BARTÓK, *Concerto for Orchestra,* 4th Mvt., 2nd Theme

Even the third non-Hungarian theme of this movement, the "interruption," bears witness to the composer's intense patriotism. It seems that Bartók composed the *Concerto for Orchestra* in 1943 shortly after taking up permanent residence in the United States. At this time Dmitri Shostakovich's *Leningrad Symphony* (No. 7) was frequently being aired in the United States as American tribute to her Russian ally fighting valiantly against German invaders. (The symphony had been composed in recognition of the defense of Leningrad, Russia's second largest city, which lay under extended German

The Music of Lands and Peoples

Folk dancers executing the czardas, a popular Hungarian dance. Many of the melodies heard in Bartok's music can be traced to his ethnic expeditions and studies.

siege during the winter of 1941–1942.) To signify the immorality of the Germans, Shostakovich had introduced an irreverent variant of a theme from *The Merry Widow*, an operetta composed by the Austrian Franz Lehar. While sharing Shostakovich's anti-German bias (for Hungary had been swallowed whole in the course of Hitler's eastern onslaught), Bartók nevertheless developed an intense distaste for the overplayed Lehar-Shostakovich melody, and so he chose to burlesque it as the third theme of his "Intermezzo." Bartók's dislike for Shostakovich's music was indeed prophetic, in view of the subsequent Russian take-over of Hungary (following the Nazi collapse). With one stroke of his musical pen, Bartók struck at two of the major Hungarian oppressors of modern times, Germany and Russia.

67

Manuel de Falla was born in 1876 in Cadiz, a city located in the Spanish region known as Andalusia. As a young man Falla won an important prize for his opera, *La Vida Breve* (*Life Is Short*). After this he headed for Paris, intending to stay for seven days, but remaining instead for seven years! Falla easily fitted in with his Parisian contemporaries (Chabrier, Debussy, Ravel, et al), many of whom were fascinated by Spanish musical idioms. Most of Falla's music is grounded in the native music of Spain. Although he rarely quoted actual folk themes, the *Spanish Folk Songs* cycle is an exception, for here one finds several genuine folk melodies. Since Spanish folk music blends early Byzantine chant, Moslem and Hebraic elements, and gypsy tunes, Falla's songs represent an engaging mixture of diverse musical ideas.

The first song is a delightful ditty about a "A Moorish Cloth." The piano introduction establishes the unmistakable Spanish character of the song. Throughout we hear the scintillating irregular alternation of a lively 3/8 with a slower 3/4, a combination found in the traditional *seguiriya gitana,* or gypsy lament. The vocal line here is notable for its restricted range (seven notes, G♯ to F♯) and melodic ornamentation (see Example 20, measure 3).

Example 20

FALLA, "A Moorish Cloth"

The music of the second song originated in the province of Murcia, in the eastern part of the country. In its fast and spirited Flamenco style, the song warns people in glass houses not to throw stones and also to observe other time-tested maxims. The third song moves north to Asturias, a region bounded on three sides by mountains, with the ocean situated on the fourth. "Asturiana," sad yet peaceful, tells of the comfort provided by a pine tree to one in need of solace. The music is extraordinarily touching, its simplicity notwithstanding.

Song 4 is a colorful *jota,* a bright, lively triple-meter dance from the ancient province of Aragon. The extended piano introduction exhibits typical jota figuration, including characteristic triplet note groupings. "Jota" is longer than the first three songs, breaking down into five distinct sections (fast, slow, fast, slow, fast) followed by a brief, slow coda. The piano plays alone in the fast sections and accompanies the voice in the contrasting slow sections. The text embodies a declaration of love from a man who must temporarily bid farewell to his beloved.

Example 21
FALLA, "Jota"

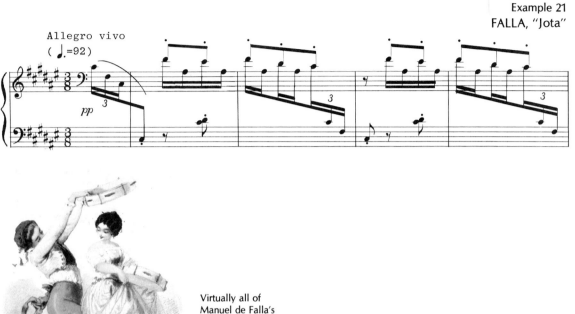

Virtually all of Manuel de Falla's music is grounded in the native music of Spain.

Song 5, "Nana," is a lullaby. The accompaniment rocks gently underneath a highly stylized, ornamental melody. The sixth song, "Canción," is the lament of a disappointed lover. The meter is a relaxed 6/8, with gentle *syncopated* (offbeat) chords on the second of each grouping of three beats.

Example 22
FALLA, "Canción"

Por trai- do-res, tus o - jos, Voy á en-te - rrar - los;
(Shame on your eyes, those traitors, let me dispatch them!)

The last song is a brilliant *polo*, a form derived from the seguiriya gitana (see Song 1)—thereby giving the cycle a sense of unity based on the resemblance of its first and last songs. The tempo marking here is *vivo*. The song is a throaty lament on the cruelty of love. After the quick piano opening, the singer exclaims a long "Ay!" as the piano thumps out guitarlike two- and three-beat figuration. The wailing voice part soon becomes high and florid, as the singer curses the love which has caused so much pain. The song ends with one final "Ay!"—a veritable shriek, accompanied by explosive piano triplets.

Falla once explained that his collection of Spanish folk songs should not be regarded as "a literal transcription of folk tunes, but a subtle artistic transmutation of their essential values."[6] According to Gilbert Chase, an expert on Spanish music, a folk song for Falla was not "a simple tune to be arbitrarily adorned. Each folk song [Falla believed] . . . conceals a deep musical meaning, a latent wealth of expression, that the arranger should endeavor to fathom and extract."[7] In his collection of *Seven Spanish Folk Songs*, Falla in exemplary manner practiced compositionally what he preached theoretically.

The Music of Lands and Peoples

BASICS: NINETEENTH-CENTURY MUSIC HISTORY

FIRST EFFORTS IN MUSICAL NATIONALISM

During the past thousand years two conditions have prevailed in the Western musical world. At certain times musical activity has been more or less evenly distributed among numerous national centers (as exemplified by the musical scene in Europe and the United States today); at other times a single country has musically dominated all the others. During the seventeenth century Italian composers were preeminent in almost every musical genre: religious music, chamber music (music for small ensembles), and, perhaps most significantly, opera. This is not to say that music was dormant in other major European powers, such as England, France, and Germany, but rather that Italy was the leader—and where Italian composers led, others followed.*

Gradually, however, during the late Baroque period of ·Bach and his contemporaries (roughly 1700–1750), musical leadership swung toward Central Europe. At this juncture in history, Germany, Austria, and many of the lands lying to their east and south (comprising the sprawling Austro-Hungarian empire) were united through the common heritage of the German language. Of course, Hungarian and the various Slavic tongues of Eastern Europe were spoken by the peasantry, but German was the tongue associated with commerce, education, government, and the arts. By the end of the eighteenth century all the great Classical composers were either German or Austrian—Haydn, Gluck, Mozart, Beethoven, and Schubert; and Vienna, the Austrian capital, had assumed dominance in the musical world. Not that there were no important musical centers in other countries, notably the French capital of Paris. But with the exception of Berlioz, Chopin, and the Italian opera composer Rossini—all of whom dwelt for the greater part of their lives in Paris—the outstanding composers of the first part of the nineteenth century were once again German or Austrian—Weber, Mendelssohn, Schumann, and Wagner. By midcentury still another generation of important German-speaking composers was maturing—Bruckner, Brahms, and the operetta king, Johann Strauss, Jr. Still later came Mahler, Wolf, Richard Strauss (unrelated to Johann), and Schoenberg. So the period 1700–1900 witnessed the rise and stabilization of German dominion in the world of music.

At first, composers from other countries and ethnic traditions could do little to resist the onslaught of German musical culture. Edvard Grieg (1843–1907), a Norwe-

---

*Johann Kuhnau (1660–1772), a German composer renowned for his *Biblical Sonatas* for keyboard, published in 1700 an amusing novel, *Der Musicalische Quack-Salber (The Musical Charlatan)*, about the ease with which any musical fake could make a fortune in Germany, provided only that he sport an Italian name and accent. The novel is unavailable in English translation, but an extensive summary of it can be found in Romain Rolland's essay, "A Humorous Novel by an Eighteenth-Century Composer," in *A ·Musical Tour Through the Land of the Past,* New York, 1922, pp. 1–20.

Edvard Grieg (1843–1907). With Grieg's music as illustration, we can define musical nationalism as a composer's defiance of internationally accepted modes of composition in favor of styles reflecting native musical elements.

gian, was one of the first composers to arrive at a non-Germanic style. As a young man he studied in Leipzig, a stronghold of midnineteenth-century German musical romanticism. Grieg dutifully learned all the correct German styles and forms, yet all the while developing a musical individuality suggestive of his Nordic homeland. If you listen to his incidental music for Ibsen's drama, *Peer Gynt*, or to the famous *Piano Concerto in A Minor*, you may discover a certain Scandinavian touch. This quality is hard to explain, but its presence undoubtedly contributes to Grieg's staying power nearly seventy-five years after his death. For while Grieg's reputation does not rank very high compared with many of the German-Austrian "greats", it thrives on Grieg's being one of the earliest non-German nationalistic composers.

Although Grieg was already well known to Americans from some of his *Peer Gynt* music ("Hall of the Mountain Kings," "Anitra's Dance," etc.) and the *Piano Concerto*, his popularity reached a new high with the opening in 1944 of the Broadway musical, *Song of Norway*. This work was put together by two experienced Broadway craftsmen, George Forrest and Robert Wright. Matching original lyrics with Grieg's music, they came up with a score which carried an unimpressive biographical plot (about the composer) through a long Broadway run. Later, *Song of Norway* was converted into a splendid Hollywood spectacular. An example of Forrest and Wright's ingenuity is their transformation of two Grieg piano pieces, *Nocturne* and *Wedding Day at Trollhaugen*, into the lovely song, "Strange Music in My Ears." (For an enjoyable listening challenge, listen to Grieg's *Piano Concerto* in its original form and then try to pick it out from the sound track of *Song of Norway*.)

With Grieg's music as illustration, we can define musical nationalism as a composer's defiance of internationally accepted modes of composition in favor of styles reflecting native musical elements. Composers may achieve nationalistic effects by incorporating genuine folk themes into their music or else may write completely original music that merely imitates native folk styles.

A case in point is the music of Frédéric Chopin (1810–1849). While still a young man, Chopin emigrated to France and remained there for most of the rest of his life.

The Music of Lands and Peoples

His output consists primarily of short pieces for piano—nocturnes, waltzes, preludes, etudes, and the like—as well as a few extended sonatas and concertos. As token of patriotic feelings for his homeland, Chopin composed two sets of piano pieces derived from national dances of Poland: the *mazurka* and the *polonaise.* There are no folk tunes in these collections, but their exploitation of traditional dance rhythms infuses the music with a definite Polish flavor.

Frédéric Chopin (1810–1849) shortly before his death in Paris.

Example 23

Polonaise Rhythmic Pattern

The polonaise is a slow dance in triple meter characterized by the subdivision of its beats into crisp duple military figures. In their principal themes both of Chopin's best known polonaises follow this rhythmic procedure.

Example 24

a) CHOPIN, *Polonaise in A Major,* "Military"

b) CHOPIN, *Polonaise in A♭ Major*

As the nineteenth century progressed, nationalistic music became more and more fashionable. Chopin's friend, Franz Liszt, famous both as composer and virtuoso pianist, was Hungarian by birth. While much of his music cannot be differentiated from the mainstream of German Romantic music, some of it reflects Hungarian styles—as in his *Hungarian Rhapsodies* for piano. Liszt apparently knew little of genuine folk music (see the discussion of Bartók in the preceding chapter), preferring instead the melodic and rhythmic patterns of gypsy styles. (Eastern European gypsy styles are occasionally also reflected in the music of non-Hungarian composers such as Schubert and Brahms.) The *Hungarian Rhapsody No. 15* is a setting of a traditional Hungarian tune, the "Rakoczi March." This stirring tune is named for Prince Ferenc Rakoczi, leader of a Hungarian revolt against Austria in the early eighteenth century. (The same tune was also orchestrated by Berlioz as an interlude in his opera, *The Damnation of Faust.*)

THE RUSSIAN SCENE

During the remainder of the nineteenth century, significant nationalistic movements were to develop in Czechoslovakia, Spain, and Finland (see Chapter 6), but undoubtedly the strongest nationalistic effort arose in Russia starting in the 1860s. Russia's musical nationalism came at a critical stage of the country's social history. The country was just beginning to break out of semifeudalistic somnolence. The freeing of the serfs, the industrial revolution, the awakening of the intelligentsia—*vide* the powerful novels of Tolstoy, Turgenev, and Dostoyevsky—all began fermenting at this time, during which there was also an upsurge in musical creativity. The year 1855 was a landmark in this "Russian Renaissance" movement, coinciding with the death of the reactionary and repressive Czar Nicholas I.

The first important Russian composer was Mikhail Glinka (1804–1857). Previous Russian musicians had composed in traditional German styles, whereas Glinka's music—particularly his opera *Ruslan and Ludmila*—is prophetic of the "Russianized" music to come. In the year of Glinka's death Mili Balakirev, barely twenty years old himself, took under his wing four poorly trained musical amateurs: César Cui and Modest Mussorgsky, both military officers; Nicolai Rimsky-Korsakov, a midshipman at the Naval Academy, and Alexandr Borodin, a scientist at the Academy of Medicine. The newly formed group was known as The Mighty Handful, or simply The Five. Balakirev had received little formal training in music theory, but this was all to the good, since at that time the term "music theory" meant restrictive German formalism. Balakirev, abetted by Glinka's younger sister, inspired his friends with Glinka's vision of a truly national Russian musical style. Many Russian musicians disagreed with this novel approach, and a vicious antagonism developed between "conservatives" and "radicals." To counterbalance the new German-oriented conservatory in St. Petersburg (now Leningrad), Balakirev organized a Free Music School—free in tuition as well as in musical ethic—something like the free schools which sprang up in the United States during the war in Vietnam. Balakirev's new music school, initially a great success, was offset in turn by the founding of the Western-oriented Moscow Conservatory. Musicians from both camps shared a love for the German masters of the eighteenth and nineteenth centuries, but differed acutely in drawing inspiration from them. All this musical infighting exemplified the more general conflict in Russian intellectual circles between the Slavophiles (i.e., cultural nationalists) and the cosmopolites (appreciators of the cultural achievements of the West). From our twentieth-century vantage point we now find little intrinsic conflict between these two schools of musical thought. We can enjoy the music of Beethoven *and* Mussorgsky, rather than just one to the exclusion of the other. But for nineteenth-century Russians an appreciation of both kinds of music seemed out of the question.

The Music of Lands and Peoples

Modest Mussorgsky (1839–1881).

Mussorgsky and Boris Godunov

Of all the composers in the "mighty handful" of Russian nationalist rebels, Modest Mussorgsky (1839–1881) stands out as a great artist, one whose music transcends time and place. He started out as a piano student and, at the age of eighteen, took an interest in studying composition. Balakirev, Mussorgsky's senior by only two years, and little more than a novice himself, served as his mentor. The freeing of the serfs in the early 1860's led to the impoverishment of the Mussorgsky family, with the consequence that the young composer was forced to accept a menial clerical job in a government office. Mussorgsky remained in this stultifying position for most of the rest of his life. Thus, it is an ironic fact that one of the principal factors in the modernization of the Russian nation, the freeing of the serfs, served to hinder the career of her greatest nationalistic composer.

At about this time Mussorgsky moved into a communal apartment with five other young intellectuals. He was terribly undisciplined as a composer; for example, he started a huge opera based on *Salammbo*, a novel by the French writer Gustave Flaubert, only to work on parts of three different acts without completing any of them. After three years he finally gave up the project. However, it was not to be a total loss, for Mussorgsky later used some of the music in his masterpiece, *Boris Godunov*.

During the season of 1868–1869, Mussorgsky made the acquaintance of one V. V. Nikolsky, an expert on the works of the revered Russian poet and playwright, Alexandr Pushkin (1799–1837). Nikolski broached the idea of devising an opera based on Pushkin's *Boris Godunov*, a dramatization of the career of a seventeenth-century Russian czar. Mussorgsky was immediately won over and plunged into the project as best he could while still holding down his full-time clerical position. By the beginning of 1870 the opera was completed, but the musical authorities rejected it. One of their main objections was the absence of a heroine (no one had ever heard of an opera without at least one major female role), so the composer added a new act centering around a Polish princess and her ambition to marry the pretender to Boris's throne. After numerous other alterations the opera was eventually produced. It achieved a *succès d'estime*, receiving fifteen performances during Mussorgsky's remaining nine years of life. It was then put aside and forgotten until Mussorgsky's old friend and fellow Handful member, Rimsky-Korsakov, revised the opera. By this time Rimsky-Korsakov had become a successful opera composer himself and was especially adept in the art of orchestration —an area in which Mussorgsky had been uneven. Rimsky-Korsakov's efforts brought *Boris Godunov* back to life; the work has become one of the mainstays of the modern operatic repertoire and is performed regularly throughout the world. (Curiously, none of Rimsky-Korsakov's own operas has achieved the universal recognition accorded his version of Mussorgsky's masterpiece.)

The music of *Boris* was and is still strikingly unique and original, which may explain its relative lack of success during the composer's lifetime. Rimsky-Korsakov's editing and recomposing robbed the work of some of its individuality, and many prefer the music in its original form. But the work was in no way emasculated; Mussorgsky's genius shines through, loud and clear. Considering the obscurity of the work at the time of Mussorgsky's death, one can only be grateful that Rimsky-Korsakov got his hands on it. Until recently only the "revised" version has been available on records, but one or another of Mussorgsky's original versions is mounted occasionally at major opera houses around the world.

As a character, Boris Godunov manifests paranoid tendencies not unlike Shakespeare's Macbeth. Indeed, Boris's death at the end of the opera is due more to inner turmoil than to any external causes. In any case, our interest here lies in the opera as an expression of the new Russian musical spirit. Based as it is on a realistic episode in Russian history (Boris having been the successor to no less than Czar Ivan the Terrible), Pushkin's drama represented a perfect vehicle for Mussorgsky's nationalistic enthusiasm. In some ways the opera unfolds like a historical novel, featuring real people and real events. The chorus consists of Russian peasants, townspeople, and noblemen. In the first scene a large and varied group is milling around the Kremlin walls, waiting for word of a new czar. Several of the themes resemble Russian folk tunes, particularly in the limited range between their highest and lowest tones, and in their imploring, lamenting nature. The harmonies are colorful in a style more consistent with the later Impressionism (see Chapter 1) than the then current German mainstream of Wagner and Brahms. The scene ends with a procession of pilgrims, indicative of the monumental power of Russian piety and religious pomp.

Example 25
MUSSORGSKY, *Boris Godunov*, Prologue

a) Opening Theme

b) People's Lament

Why dost thou a - ban - don us, thy folk, O fa — ther!

The Music of Lands and Peoples

The second scene presents the coronation of Boris. It begins with the sonorous clanging of Kremlin bells, with two rich chords alternating in an insistent *ostinato*. Then Mussorgsky introduces a genuine Russian folk theme ("Glory to God in Heaven"), as the people shout, "Glory to Boris, our new Czar!" (Beethoven had used this same theme in the third movement of his *String Quartet in E Minor*, Op. 59, No. 2, in tribute to his Russian patron, Count Rasumovsky.)

Example 26

Boris Godunov, Coronation Scene

Hail to sun-light out-pour - ing, shin-ing up - on us, glor - y!

Saint Basil's Cathedral, Moscow. The clanging bells of the Kremlin churches highlight the ceremonial character of the "Coronation Scene" in Mussorgsky's nationalistic opera *Boris Godunov*.

As Boris enters, the people are stilled, and he sings a solemn monologue acknowledging the crushing weight of the crown he is about to accept. But Boris's somber mood restrains the enthusiasm of his subjects only temporarily, and soon they launch again into their paean of praise and glory.

The remainder of *Boris Godunov* is a panorama taking us from the monastery cell of an aged monk to an inn on the Lithuanian border, from a family gathering in Boris's private apartments to scenes of palace intrigue and Polish conspiracies, from

77

the Duma (parliament) of the Russian boyars (noblemen) to a violent rural uprising. Throughout the opera the music is heavy with the Russian spirit which seems to pervade all of Mussorgsky's music. The opera's sweep is extraordinary, a marvelous cross between historical realism and the grandeur of a Cecil B. De Mille Hollywood spectacular.

Other Russian Composers

Another work which evokes the spirit of Russian life is Alexandr Borodin's *From the Steppes of Russia*. Borodin, like Mussorgsky, was one of the five composers who attempted to nationalize Russian music during the second half of the nineteenth century. This work, along with other Borodin compositions, formed the musical core of the successful Broadway musical, *Kismet* (1953). It was assembled by the same collaborators who had fashioned *Song of Norway* a decade earlier (see the preceding discussion of Grieg). The hit song of the show, "Stranger in Paradise," remains popular to this day.

Peter Ilich Tchaikovsky (1840–1893) is by and large the most popular Russian Romantic composer today. Although he did not ally himself with The Five, Tchaikovsky's music nevertheless betrays a definite Russian flavor. As already indicated, Russian folk songs are notable for their limited vocal range. The "Song of the Volga Boatmen" is fairly typical of Russian folk melodies, what with its brief grunting phrases, small distances from one note to another (*intervals*), and modal quality (more minor than major)—altogether very similar to the opening themes of *Boris Godunov* shown in Example 25. If you listen to Tchaikovsky's *Symphony No. 4 in F Minor*, you will discover that many of its themes display these same Russian stylistic features.

Once under way in the nineteenth century, the nationalist movement in music was by no means short lived. It was taken up by many early twentieth-century composers, and still remains a potent force even today. Igor Stravinsky (1882–1971) is one of the great names in twentieth-century music. Born in Russia, he based his early ballets, *Firebird, Petrouchka* and *The Rite of Spring*, as well as the one-act opera, *Mavra*, on Russian folk legends. During the difficult days of World War I Stravinsky lived in Switzerland, where he consoled himself by reading various collections of Russian folk poetry.

> My profound emotion on reading the news of war, which aroused patriotic feelings and a sense of sadness at being so distant from my country, found some alleviation in the delight with which I steeped myself in Russian folk poems.
>
> What fascinated me in this verse was not so much the stories, which were often crude, or the pictures and metaphors, always so deliciously unexpected, as the sequence of words and syllables, and the cadence they create, which produces an effect on one's sensibilities very closely akin to that of music. . . . I culled a bouquet from among them all, which I distributed in three different compositions that I wrote after the other, elaborating my material for *Les Noces*.[1]

Les Noces (The Wedding) is an unusual ballet in which the dancers are accompanied by vocal soloists, four pianos, and percussion (and no other instruments). Stravinsky's aim in this complex work was to transmit the special qualities of Russian nuptial customs. Claiming that "a knowledge not only of the cultural customs, but also of the language of *Les Noces* is necessary to anyone aspiring to a true appreciation of the work," Stravinsky has explained the sources and nature of the music in considerable

The Music of Lands and Peoples

detail.[2] Yet for all his early use of Russian themes and folkways, Stravinsky later grew averse to the use of genuine folk themes in music. Speaking of Bartók, he wrote, "I never could share his lifelong gusto for his native folklore. This devotion was certainly real and touching, but I couldn't help regretting it in the great musician."[3]

SOUNDS OF SPAIN

In no country has musical nationalism been so all pervasive as in Spain during the past one hundred years. One of the most important Spanish composers was Isaac Albéniz, born in 1860. At a tender age, Albéniz struck out on his own, under the spell of the early science fiction writer, Jules Verne (*Twenty Thousand Leagues Under the Sea*, etc.). After traveling about Spain for awhile, Albéniz stowed away on a ship heading for Puerto Rico, was put ashore in Argentina, raised enough money to get to Cuba (having by now reached the advanced age of thirteen), and eventually wound up in San Francisco playing the piano backwards with his hands upside down! After this unseemly beginning, Albéniz returned to Europe where he took up serious music study. Almost all of his music reflects his native land.

> Taking the guitar as his instrumental mode, and drawing his inspiration largely from the peculiar traits of Andalusian folk music—but without using actual folk themes—Albéniz achieves a stylization of Spanish traditional idioms that, while thoroughly artistic, gives a captivating impression of spontaneous improvisation.[4]

Albéniz's great musical achievement is *Iberia*, a collection of twelve impressions of the Iberian peninsula (Spain and Portugal) and especially of the Spanish region of Andalusia. The titles themselves are evocative of Spain: "El Puerto" (The Port), "Triana" (a section of Seville), "Rondeña" (a fandango-like dance), "Almería" (a Mediterranean seaport), and "El Albaicín" (the gypsy quarter of Granada), among others. National dance rhythms prevail throughout Albéniz's music. Debussy, a Frenchman who himself composed an orchestral work entitled *Iberia*, declared that "Never has music achieved such diversified, such colorful impressions"—a powerful expression of enthusiasm from one of the principal exponents of Impressionism (see Chapter 1).[5]

Francisco de Goya (1746–1828), *The Bullfight*. Enrique Granados composed both a piano suite and an opera based on Goya's depictions of life in Madrid.

79

Another important Spanish nationalist composer was Enrique Granados (1867–1916). Granados greatly admired the paintings of the Spanish master Francisco Goya (1746–1828) and composed a piano suite and an opera based on Goya's depictions of life in Madrid. Both works are called *Goyescas*.

Along with Albéniz and Granados, the third important composer associated with Spanish nationalism in the early twentieth century was Manuel de Falla. His collection of *Seven Spanish Folk Songs* is featured in Chapter 6.

In Chapter 7 we have examined musical nationalism emanating from several European locales. In Chapter 8 we shall explore the development of musical nationalism on the American side of the Atlantic.

AMERICAN MUSIC

For Americans living at the end of the twentieth century it is hard to realize the magnitude of our pioneer culture up until about one hundred years ago. The successive waves of settlers and immigrants reaching our shores in the seventeenth, eighteenth, and early nineteenth centuries had little time or use for "Culture" with a capital C. Museums, research libraries, opera houses, symphony orchestras, and music conservatories were all well and good back in the European homeland, for there Western civilization had been developing steadily for more than a thousand years. But what the American colonies needed was hard labor, commerce, and industry; the fine arts could wait until later. And wait they did, for the better part of 250 years, before European culture began to take firm root in American soil. The multiplicity of cultural institutions currently available to the average American is fundamentally a novelty in our society, a modernism akin to the recent rapid growth of science and technology.*

Just as an appreciation of European arts came belatedly to America, musical nationalism was slow in asserting itself here. In the nineteenth century the paucity of local college music departments and conservatories forced budding composers into traveling abroad to further their musical studies. Edward MacDowell (1861–1908), one of the first American composers to make a mark for himself, studied in Germany and wrote music which Virgil Thomson has described as "a pale copy of its continental models."[1] Himself an honored American composer now in his eighties, Thomson has pointed out that when MacDowell and other early Americans wished to depict their homeland in music, "they did so as European travelers might have done and no whit more convincingly than Dvořák, who during the 1890s spent three years in America, in his *New World Symphony* actually did do."[2] (See Chapter 12 for an extended discussion of this work.) Thomson has also stated that in the absence of indigenous master composers (there being no American Bach, Mozart, or Beethoven), American composers at the turn of the twentieth century had to face the issue of nationalism; in American folk sources lay virtually the only hope for the foundation of a new and genuinely American musical tradition. The Negro spiritual, cowboy songs, blues—these were the wellsprings for American musicians to draw upon. Much of the story of American music in this century is of young hopefuls going off to Europe to study compositional technique and then returning home to establish their identity as *American* composers.

---

*This is not to deny the presence of significant pockets of musical activity in early American society. In the mid-eighteenth century, the Moravians were performing full cantatas with chorus and orchestra in Pennsylvania and North Carolina. By the 1790s, Philadelphia (and, to a lesser extent, Boston and New York) had a flourishing musical life, quite sufficient to attract European musicians to immigrate and settle there.

Chapter 8 will introduce you to two twentieth-century composers who have placed a distinctly American stamp on their music: Aaron Copland and Charles Ives.

COPLAND, LINCOLN PORTRAIT

Aaron Copland, born in Brooklyn, New York in 1900, was a "first generation" offspring of parents who had recently emigrated from Eastern Europe. The Coplands belonged to the huge wave of Jewish humanity which reached America in the late nineteenth and early twentieth centuries. The world in which young Copland grew up was subdivided into strict ethnic units: Irish, Germans, Italians, Jews, each group keeping to itself as if still living in the old country. However, Copland's music gives no hint of his old world heritage; it shows him rather to belong to the vanguard of those striving to write native American music instead of imitations of European models. (Copland's music falls into two categories—the "Americanistic" works and those with a more international flavor.) His numerous American works include the music for five Hollywood films and the ballets, *Billy the Kid, Rodeo,* and *Appalachian Spring.* The "Hoedown" from *Rodeo* is an exciting concert adaptation of an old-fashioned square dance tune.

Martha Graham, leading American choreographer who revolutionized dance in America, in *Appalachian Spring*, music by Aaron Copland.

Appalachian Spring, named after a Hart Crane poem, incorporates the lovely Shaker hymn, "Simple Gifts." Copland ingeniously devised imitative counterpoint for this melody, in the style of a round (*canon*)—that is, one set of instruments begins the melody, with another set starting out soon thereafter. This treatment lends a dignified "classical" touch to the simple folk melody.

Example 27
"Simple Gifts" Canon

The Music of Lands and Peoples

Copland's most patriotic work is his *Lincoln Portrait*, composed during World War II. Arnold Dobrin has explained the genesis of the work:

> By 1942 the war had begun to dominate most aspects of American life. Along with other workers everywhere, artists wanted to serve their country. In the interests of national morale, André Kostelanetz, the symphony conductor, commissioned Aaron Copland and several other composers to write musical portraits of great Americans.
>
> Because Copland had always been fascinated by the work of Walt Whitman, this seemed like the perfect moment to write a work based on this poet's grand vision of life. But Jerome Kern . . . had chosen Mark Twain and Kostelanetz did not want to have two literary men in the series.
>
> Copland's next choice was Abraham Lincoln . . .[3]

Copland's tribute to Lincoln consists of excerpts from the Great Emancipator's speeches recited against an orchestral backdrop. The work has been performed by all manner of public speakers, actors, and politicans, among them Gregory Peck and the late Democratic Party presidential candidate, Adlai Stevenson. (Stevenson's great-grandfather, Jesse Fell, was Lincoln's campaign manager.) As the music begins, one hears a solemn orchestral introduction which grows into a stirring fortissimo climax. Then the clarinet plays the American folksong, "Springfield Mountain."

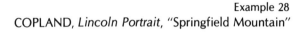

Example 28
COPLAND, *Lincoln Portrait*, "Springfield Mountain"

Arthur Berger has pointed out that, with a slight change in the rhythmic structure of this tune, Copland has converted a "saucy ditty" into one which "expresses majesty."[4] And here again we find the canonic treatment Copland earlier incorporated in *Appalachian Spring* (see Example 27).

Next comes an exciting barn dance tune, the familiar "Camptown Races," which undergoes extensive development. The volume and intensity of the music increase as we again hear the first few notes of "Springfield Mountain." Finally, in a quieter vein, the winds and brass sing out "Springfield Mountain" in conjunction with lively quotes from "Camptown Races" played by the strings.

We now hear the speaker's first words: "Fellow citizens, we cannot escape history." "Springfield Mountain" provides a gentle accompaniment. A brief reminder of the solemn orchestral introduction precedes a recitation of the facts concerning Lincoln's early years. The orchestra serves alternately as support for the recited text and as "commentator" in the breaks between successive text sections. Much of the text spells out important principles of American democracy, for example, "As I would not be a slave, so I would not be a master. This expresses my idea of democracy." These inspiring words are accompanied by the "democratic justice" motive heard at the beginning of the piece. The work concludes with these immemorial lines from the Gettysburg Address:

> We here highly resolve that these dead shall not have died in vain; that this nation, under God, shall have a new birth of freedom; and that government of the people, by the people, for the people, shall not perish from the earth.

The music supports these words with a final dignified passage scored for the entire orchestra.

THE MUSIC OF CHARLES IVES

During the past fifty years American composers have earned their livelihoods mainly through university and conservatory affiliations. Copland is an exception to this rule, in that as a prosperous "serious" composer he has never had to depend on teaching for financial security. Charles Ives, who preceded Copland in the field of "Americanized" concert music, was also financially successful, but he pocketed little from his music. Ives led two professional lives, one as a highly innovative and well-rewarded insurance broker, the other as a little-understood experimental composer. At first no one paid any attention to Ives the composer; later, as the belated winner of many honors, Ives deflected royalties and other musical earnings in the direction of less fortunate composers. (When at the age of seventy-two Ives was informed that he had won the Pulitzer Prize, his response was, "Prizes are for boys—I'm grown up.")

Ives was born in Danbury, Connecticut in 1874. Just as Leopold Mozart, a professional violinist, molded the genius of his prodigy son, Wolfgang Amadeus, the musical development of the young Charles Ives was deeply influenced by his father, George Ives.

> Behind Charles Ives there was another powerfully imaginative and experimental mind, the mind of his father, George Ives. The germ of every new type of musical behavior that Charles Ives developed or organized can be found in the suggestions and experiments of his father, the busy bandmaster of Danbury, Connecticut. At the same time, it was due to his father's insistence that Charles Ives as a boy was trained in all the conventional ways of treating music too.[5]

The senior Ives played piano for local dances, was a church organist, led a marching band, taught several instruments, and arranged music for all kinds of vocal and instrumental combinations—in short he was a musical pillar of Danbury society. But George Ives was not a composer; it was left to his son Charles to *originate* music. According to Henry and Sidney Cowell, "it is not too much to say that the son has written his father's music for him"[6] Chapter 2 of the Cowells's book, "George Ives and His Son Charlie," tells the fascinating story of the education of an American composer, our first genuinely native product. Charlie was exposed to all kinds of nontraditional sounds that were nothing short of revolutionary in the context of other European and American music of the 1880s. For example, frustrated by the limitations of the piano and wishing to elicit sounds from the cracks *between* the keys, George Ives attempted to construct a keyboard for playing *quarter tones*, which are half the size of the smallest interval on a standard piano. He embraced dissonances of all sorts with enthusiasm, and experimented freely with water-filled glasses, new combinations of human voices,

The Music of Lands and Peoples

Charles Ives (1874–1954), a true musical prophet, regarded by many as the father of twentieth-century avant-garde and experimental traditions.

and accompaniments to familiar songs in different keys from those of the vocal lines. (The latter is an example of *polytonality*, as illustrated in Example 30.) In addition to all this, Charlie heard the music of the European classics as played by George and his cronies, albeit usually in instrumental combinations far removed from those originally specified by the composers.

Here is a polytonal experiment that you and your fellow students can perform by way of imitating some of Charles Ives's early musical experiences. First, the entire class should sing "Frère Jacques" in unison. Now repeat the song while your instructor or another student plays it simultaneously on the piano *in a different key*. The pianist and the class can start at exactly the same time or treat the song traditionally as a round. Next the class should divide into two groups, singing "Frère Jacques" as a round in two different keys. One way of managing this is to have group 2 start out on the pitch sung by group 1 at the beginning of the second phrase ("Dormez-vous?")—as in Example 30. Once the class has mastered singing this *bitonal* version of "Frère Jacques," the pianist can make it "tritonal" by playing in still another key. And, because the song is a four-part round, there are obviously many other ways of producing polytonal versions. Some of these will be more felicitous than others, but all of them will give you an amusing glimpse into the musical environment of the young Charles Ives.

Example 29
"Frère Jacques"

Frè - re   Jac - ques   Frè - re   Jac - ques,   Dor - mez   vous?   Dor - mez   vous?

Son-nent les ma-tin- es,   Son-nent les ma-tin- es,   Ding-dong-ding,   ding-dong-ding.

Example 30
"Frère Jacques" — Bi-Tonal Round

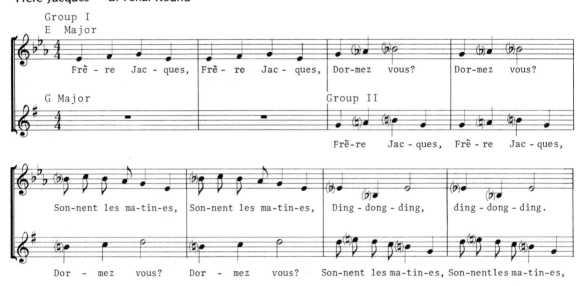

Group I
E Major

Frè - re   Jac - ques,   Frè - re   Jac - ques,   Dor-mez   vous?   Dor-mez   vous?

G Major   Group II

Frè - re   Jac - ques,   Frè - re   Jac - ques,

Son-nent les ma-tin- es,   Son-nent les ma-tin- es,   Ding - dong - ding,   ding - dong - ding.

Dor - mez   vous?   Dor - mez   vous?   Son-nent les ma-tin-es, Son-nent les ma-tin-es,

One other element in Ives's early years was paramount in the formation of the musical mind of the future composer: his exposure to the indigenous hymn music, band music, patriotic songs, and dance tunes of New England. Ives often attended religious camp meetings held in nearby Redding, Ct. for farmers, field hands, visiting friends, and families, and he also observed parades, square dances, and conventional church services. "Columbia, the Gem of the Ocean," "When Johnny Comes Marching Home," "The Battle Hymn of the Republic," "Nearer, My God, to Thee," "Yankee Doodle," "Turkey in the Straw" — Ives heard, sang, and played all of these songs, absorbing them into his bloodstream. Many of these songs appear in his music, sometimes just as a brief allusion, at other times full blown. They also influenced the kind of melodies and harmonies that Ives devised from his own talent and imagination. True, he unhesitatingly experimented with crashing and clashing dissonances, unusual instrumental combinations, multiple simultaneous melodies, and polytonality (sometimes imitating the effect of several parade bands playing different tunes in different keys at the same time). Yet at the bottom of Ives's often complex textures one finds an absorption and fascination in simple "people's music" — consisting of folk music of undetermined

The Music of Lands and Peoples

origin and composed music of universal popularity—which he knew as a youth. For Ives, the thousand-year heritage of European classicism was not a jot more important than his own heritage of local folk and popular music.

Charles Ives was a true musical prophet, "whether he knew it or not, the father of us all," according to Virgil Thomson.* As with all artistic prophets (those who shake up the world of art through their daring and innovation), the question of whether Ives's compositional expertise matches his experimental cunning remains to be tested by time. For years no one would play his music; it was so purely American and boldly modern that its shock value to the conservative audiences of the post-Romantic period can scarcely be overstated. Only recently have Ives's works begun to be played and recorded in sufficient measure to allow for meaningful criticism, and for many interested observers of the American musical scene the ultimate value of Ives's music remains moot. In any event, Ives will always be honored as the founder of the American movement in modern music.

Augustus Saint-Gaudens (1848–1907), *The Robert Gould Shaw Memorial* in the Boston Common. Ives chose Saint-Gaudens's sculpture as one of the subjects of his *Three Places in New England.*

*Thomson, *American Music Since 1910*; see photo caption following p. 78. Thomson indulges here in a play on words, inasmuch as he had once collaborated with the avant garde writer, Gertrude Stein, on an opera entitled *The Mother of Us All.*

Several of Ives's works deserve mention here. Many of his songs are pithy and humorous. Some of them are written in a folk or hymn style, as in the engaging "By the River." "Charlie Rutlage" is a delightful cowboy song (discussed further in Chapter 31). Notable among the works for instruments are *Variations on America* for organ (based on "My Country, 'Tis of Thee" with bitonal interludes between the variations), *Three Places in New England* for orchestra, the *Second Piano Sonata*, "Concord, Mass. 1840–1860" (discussed in Chapter 20), and *New England Holidays*. Also known by the title *Holidays Symphony*, the last-mentioned work is more a loose collection (*suite*) of tone poems than a symphony; Ives himself said that the work's four parts could be played either separately or "lumped together as a symphony." The work is subtitled "Recollections of a Boy's Holidays in a Connecticut Town" and celebrates four major American holidays: Washington's Birthday, Decoration (Memorial) Day, the Fourth of July, and Thanksgiving. Among the variety of marches and hymns heard in "Decoration Day" are "Adestes Fideles" and "Taps." "Fourth of July" features "Columbia, the Gem of the Ocean," "The Battle Hymn of the Republic," and the bugle call "Reveille" ("It's time to get up, it's time to get up in the morning"). The music climaxes with the deafening roar of several different marching tunes being played simultaneously, only to be followed immediately by a comically soft two-measure finale.

An interesting view of Ives's music has been recorded by the Hollywood composer Bernard Herrmann (*Citizen Kane*, etc.):

> Ives's music doesn't go on in time and space. His music is a photographic replica in sound of a happening. His *Fourth of July* is a replica not of all Fourth of Julys, but of one. *Washington's Birthday* is the same. . . . Everything in him is something that he heard happen which he transferred and caught at a moment in time like a photograph.[7]

The problem with listening to Ives is that his inclination to interweave simple tunes with complex harmonic, rhythmic, and melodic configurations often produces a mind-boggling "stream-of-consciousness" effect which is likely to discourage all but the most adventurous music lovers. "Washington's Birthday" has been chosen as an introduction to Ives's compositional style just because the piece is both short (9–10 minutes) and relatively simple compared to many other Ives compositions.

WASHINGTON'S BIRTHDAY

The score calls for flute, piccolo, French horn, and strings (violins, violas, cellos, and basses), plus optional bells and jew's harp. (As defined in the *American Heritage Dictionary*, the jew's harp is "a small musical instrument with a lyre-shaped metal frame and a projecting steel tongue that is held between the teeth when played.") According to Ives's detailed notes, the music is divided into three parts.[8] Part I depicts "the dismal, bleak, cold weather of a February night." The tempo is very slow. Listen near the beginning (measure 5) for a hint of "The Old Folks at Home" played by French horn. This section continues for several minutes. The remaining two parts mix "barn-dance tunes and songs of the day 'half humorous, half sentimental, and half serious.'" (Apparently there are three halves in Ives's conception of a whole!) Part II starts with an old-fashioned quadrille, a square dance of French origin. The second violins play the perky tune:

The Music of Lands and Peoples

Example 31
IVES, *Washington's Birthday*, Quadrille Tune

Throughout this section one hears a variety of familiar melodies, such as the "Sailor's Hornpipe," played by flute with quirky second violins following a step behind in canon. Flute and horn play a variant of "Camptown Races" (heard also in Copland's *Lincoln Portrait*), and later the flute presents a snatch of "For He's a Jolly Good Fellow."

Example 32
Washington's Birthday, "Sailor's Hornpipe"

The unusual sound of the jew's harp is now heard, as the strings play a fairly straightforward version of "The White Cockade." "Turkey in the Straw" soon follows (flute), with "The Campbells Are Coming" soon after (horn and jew's harp). Why did Ives amalgamate so many different tunes into his ever increasingly louder fabric? Here is Ives's explanation:

> As I remember some of these dances as a boy . . . a group would be dancing a polka . . . another a waltz, with perhaps a quadrille or lancers going on in the middle. Some of the players in the band would, in an impromptu way, pick up with the polka, and some with the waltz or march. Often the piccolo or cornet would throw in "asides." Sometimes the change in tempo and mixed rhythms would be caused by a fiddler who, after playing three or four hours steadily, was getting a little sleepy—or by another player who had been seated too near the hard cider barrel. Whatever the reason for these changing and sometimes simultaneous playings of different things, I remember distinctly catching a kind of music that was natural and interesting. . . . The allegro part of *Washington's Birthday* aims to reflect this, as well as to depict some of the old breakdown tunes and backwoods fun and comedy and conviviality that are gradually being forgotten.[9]

Example 33
Washington's Birthday, "The White Cockade"

After a final loud bang in Part II, Part III starts out in a completely different style. The strings now play alone, very softly and somewhat slower than before. One still hears several tunes combined, but in a gentler, more relaxed mood. The effect is of an evening's festivities coming sentimentally to an end (listen for a hint of Schubert's "Ave Maria"), with some of the participants half dozing in the corner. We hear a gentle phrase of "Good Night, Ladies," and then the piece fizzles out with quiet murmurings in the strings.

"Washington's Birthday," a delightful example of musical Americana, was completed in 1913 but was not to receive its first full-fledged public performance until eighteen years later—and even this was presented not in the United States, but in Europe, by a touring orchestra funded by Ives himself. Ives's music began to be performed only in the 1940's and was not played with any kind of regularity until after his death in 1954. Today, with the progress of time, Ives is gradually being accepted as the first master of American music.

The Music of Lands and Peoples

BASICS:
THE CONCEPT OF TONIC

A common bond underlies most of the music composed between about 1500 and the present: the structural principle of *tonality*. Medieval composers conceived of their music in terms of scale formations known as *modes*, of which there were many in common use. Gradually, during the fifteenth and sixteenth centuries, two modes assumed preeminence, the *major* and the *minor*. (Other modes are discussed in Chapter 27.) The first note of the major and minor scales, the *tonic*, is the chief melodic note as well as the main harmonic note of a tonal piece. Despite the extraordinary stylistic changes that were to occur in music during the Baroque, Classical, and Romantic periods, the concept of tonic held absolute sway until the first years of the twentieth century. And although many of the most important composers of the early modern period abandoned tonality in favor of various forms of *atonality*,* others retained tonality in a limited way (Debussy, Ravel, Stravinsky, etc.), or remained uninhibitedly tonal (Sibelius, Richard Strauss) as did all variety of popular and semipopular composers. Even today much of the new music exemplifies tonality as did the music of the Baroque Bach, the Classical Beethoven, and the Romantic Brahms.

SCALES

How does a specific note assert itself as the principal note of a musical fabric—as its tonic? When we speak of Beethoven's *Symphony No. 2* as being in the key of D Major, we mean that the tonic note of that work is *D*. But what makes D, as opposed to the other members of the D major scale (or for that matter the remaining five notes of the chromatic scale), sound like the tonic note? Two elements are required: a scale and a chord. Consider the scale of D major. Something in the structure of this scale (D, E, F♯, G, A, B, C♯, D) makes D "stronger" than the other notes. Is it simply that the scale starts and ends on the same note, D? No, for if we start on any other note of the scale, D still emerges as preeminent. Thus, the succession F♯, G, A, B, C♯, D, E, F♯ still sounds like the scale of D major, rather than F♯ major. It is the internal structure of the major scale, regardless of which of the twelve major scales we select (one can build one starting on any note of the chromatic scale) which makes the tonic note sound special.

All of this talk about scales should not create the false impression that tonal pieces consist mainly of scalelike melodies. This happens only occasionally. The familiar Christmas carol, "Joy to the World," is a good example of a scale melody:

---

*See, for example, the discussions of Schoenberg's *Phantasy for Violin* in Chapter 22, Berg's *Violin Concerto* in Chapter 33, and the striking compositional innovations described in Chapter 20.

Example 34

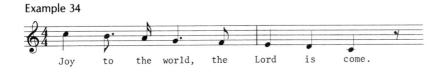

Joy to the world, the Lord is come.

But most melodies do not contain complete scales, and in fact many melodies totally lack scale formations. Nevertheless, all tonal melodies are based on the major and minor scales (see Chapter 5, Examples 10 and 11). This is how it works: Consider the well-known theme from Mozart's *Piano Sonata in C Major, K. 545.* Although the melody is not overtly scalar, every one of its pitches is drawn from the major scale of its tonic note, C. That is, all the notes of the C major scale are present, although not in scalar order from 1 through 8. (The scale degree "1" usually refers to the tonic note when located at the bottom of the scale, and "8" signifies the same note at the top of the scale.) Similarly the first theme of Beethoven's *Symphony No. 5* draws exclusively on scale notes associated with C Minor.

Example 35
MOZART, *Piano Sonata in C Major, K. 545, 1st Mvt.*

Example 36
BEETHOVEN, *Symphony No. 5 in C Minor, 1st Mvt.*

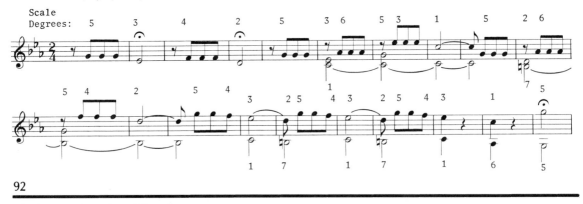

The Music of Lands and Peoples

The chords which support tonal melodies also consist of notes of the major and minor scales. In fact, some pieces emphasize harmonic progressions almost to the exclusion of melody, as in Example 37. Here there are no scale formations yet every note of each measure belongs to the C major scale. In fact, every note of the C major scale is represented in the first three measures (see Example 37a).

Example 37

BACH, *The Well-Tempered Clavier*, Vol. 1, Prelude No. 1 in C Major

Example 37a
Chordal Reduction of Example 37

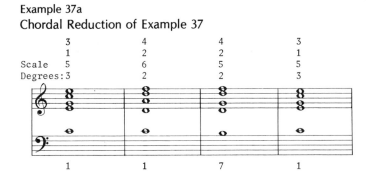

Basics: The Concept of Tonic

TRIADS

A *triad* is a chord containing three notes separated by intervening scale notes: for example, in C major, C–E–G, D–F–A, E–G–B, and so on. In the major mode, three of the triads are *major*: 1–3–5, 4–6–8, and 5–7–2; three are *minor*: 2–4–6, 3–5–7, and 6–1–3; and one is *diminished*; 7–2–4. In a minor key there is the same distribution of major, minor, and diminished triads, but they are constituted from different combinations of scale degrees. Triads are often identified by Roman numerals, signifying their *roots* or lowest notes. The principal chord of a tonal piece is the *tonic triad*, the triad built on the first scale degree.

Example 38
Triads of the Major and Minor Modes

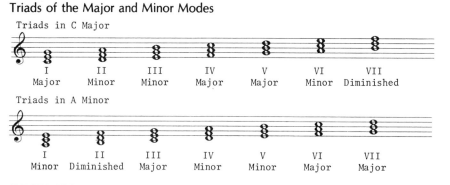

INTERVALS

One can differentiate the sound of major, minor, and diminished triads—and for that matter all other chords—according to their *intervals*, that is, the distances separating their constituent members. Thus, in the major triad the bottom two notes are separated by an interval of four half steps, whereas the bottom two notes of the minor triad are separated by only three half steps. Correspondingly, the upper third of the major triad is an interval of three half steps, of the minor triad, four half steps. Both intervals of a diminished triad are three half steps. The interval between outer notes of both major and minor triads is seven half steps, while the outer interval of a diminished triad is six half steps.

Example 39
Interval Sizes of Triads (in Half Steps)

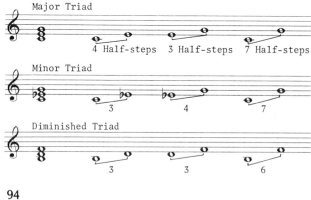

94

Observe that the major and minor triads contain the same internal intervals, but in reverse order, while both triads contain the same outer interval. The two triads sound different because of the different ordering of internal intervals. Any two chords which contain the same ordering of identical intervals will sound alike, for example, the three major triads of the major mode, I, IV, and V. The notes of each of these triads are different (1–3–5, 4–6–8, 5–7–2), but in each case the intervalic ordering is constant. Each of these triads is a *transposition* of the other two.

Example 40
The Three Major Triads of the Major Mode:
Different Notes, Same Intervals (in the Same Order).

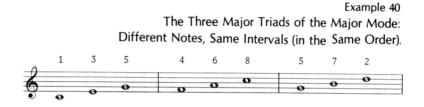

CONSONANCE AND DISSONANCE

One of the most important characteristics of chords is their consonance or dissonance. The most stable or consonant tonal chord is the tonic triad, be it major or minor. Any interval belonging to either of these triads is defined as *consonant*; all other intervals are considered unstable or *dissonant*.

Consonant and Dissonant Intervals in the Major and Minor Scales

Scale Degrees	Interval	Chromatic Measurement in Half Steps
3–4, 7–8	Minor Second (Diss.)	1
1–2, 2–3, 4–5, 5–6, 6–7	Major Second (Diss.)	2
2–4, 3–5, 6–8, 7–2	Minor Third (Cons.)	3
1–3, 4–6, 5–7	Major Third (Cons.)	4
1–4, 2–5, 3–6, 5–8, 6–2, 7–3	Perfect Fourth (Cons.)	5
4–7	Augmented Fourth (Diss.)	6

Each of these intervals can be turned upside down (*inverted*) as follows:

Minor Second inverts to Major Seventh (Diss.)
Major Second inverts to Minor Seventh (Diss.)
Minor Third inverts to Major Sixth (Cons.)
Major Third inverts to Minor Sixth (Cons.)
Perfect Fourth inverts to Perfect Fifth (Cons.)
Augmented Fourth inverts to Diminished Fifth (Diss.)

Basics: The Concept of Tonic

The chromatic measurement of an inverted interval is calculated as 12 minus the chromatic size of the given interval; for example, a perfect fourth of five half steps inverts to a perfect fifth of seven half steps.

Example 41
Intervals and Their Inversions

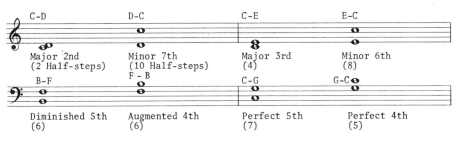

Chords are generally characterized as consonant or dissonant according to the presence or absence of dissonant intervals therein. A single dissonant interval makes an entire chord dissonant even if a majority of its intervals are consonant. For example, if to the consonant major triad (consisting of three consonant intervals, 1–3, 3–5, and 1–5) is added a fourth scale degree, 7, the result is a total of five consonant intervals (1–3, 1–5, 3–5, 3–7, 5–7), yet the entire combination is a dissonance by virtue of the single dissonant interval, 1–7.

Example 42
Intervallic Make-Up of Consonant and Dissonant Chords

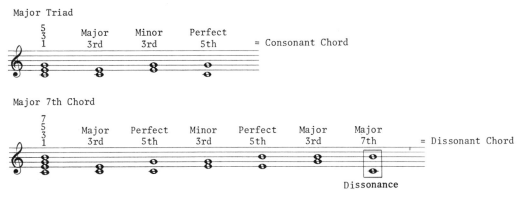

Contextual relationships influence the consonance–dissonance effect of a given chord, so that a chord containing nothing but consonant intervals may nevertheless sound dissonant. In Example 43a, the middle chord is dissonant by virtue of the intervals b–f and f–g, respectively a diminished fifth and a major second. No dissonant intervals are present in the middle chord of Example 43b, and therefore taken on its own

The Music of Lands and Peoples

merits the chord is consonant. Yet within this entire three-chord context the notes D and B function as dissonances with respect to the tonic note C; following the initial I chord, the second chord (V) sounds unstable and requires *resolution* to the concluding stable tonic chord.

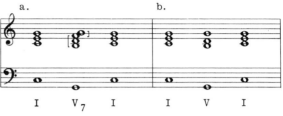

Example 43
Overt and Contextual Dissonance—Both V Chords Are Dissonant Within a Total I-V-I Context.

HARMONIC MINOR

Pieces in the minor mode typically involve a special scale in which the seventh degree is raised by one half step. (See the C minor scale as enumerated in Example 36: one finds B♮ as the seventh degree in place of the regular minor seventh degree, B♭.) This scale is known as the *harmonic minor*, as distinguished from the unaltered *natural minor*. The harmonic minor scale contains two intervals (and their inversions) not found in the natural minor scale: 3–7, an augmented fifth (8 half steps), and 6–7, an augmented second (3 half steps). Their inversions are 7–3, a diminished fourth, and 7–6, a diminished seventh. Observe that the chromatic size of the augmented fifth is the same as that of the minor sixth (8 half-steps) and that the augmented second similarly matches the minor third (3 half-steps). For example, 3–7 of the A harmonic minor scale is the dissonant interval C–G♯, while 1–6 of C minor is the consonant interval C–A♭. On the piano one depresses the same pair of keys to effect the sound of these two intervals, yet they sound entirely different in the context of their respective scales. Such intervals are known as *enharmonically equivalent*, referring to the assignment of more than one alphabetical name to a given note—thus, G♯ is the enharmonic equivalent of A♭.

Another scale formation found in the minor mode is the *melodic minor*, consisting of both raised sixth and seventh degrees. This scale is identical with the major scale except for its third degree, the single note which characterizes the scale as minor.

Example 44
The Three Minor Scales

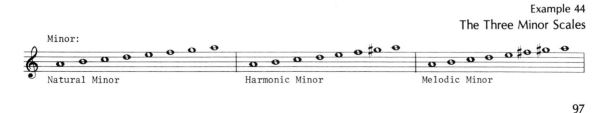

Natural Minor   Harmonic Minor   Melodic Minor

Basics: The Concept of Tonic

Although ordinarily only one note functions as tonic for a complete piece, other notes may serve as temporary tonics within that piece. The most common secondary tonic is the fifth scale degree, the *dominant*; it becomes a temporary tonic when the fourth scale degree of the basic tonic scale is raised a half step, which converts it into the seventh scale degree of the dominant:

Example 45a
Conversion of E Major into a Secondary Tonic Through the Raising of D♮ to D♯.
See Example 45b.

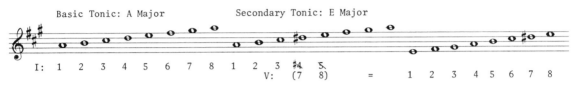

If a secondary tonic is merely alluded to, one speaks of the compositional process as a *tonicization*; if the secondary tonic appears to replace the tonic, the process is known as a *modulation*. No matter how strong the modulation, however, the basic tonic is eventually reasserted (in most examples of tonality drawn from the seventeenth through nineteenth centuries). Example 45b presents an example of a tonicized dominant in the opening phrase of a sonata movement by Beethoven. D♯ is introduced in measure 3, suggesting the scale of E major (see Example 45a). The introduction of D♮ in measure 5, and its repetition in measures 6–8, reaffirms A major as tonic.

Example 45b
BEETHOVEN, *Piano Sonata in A Major*, Opus 2, No. 2, 3rd Mvt.

Separate movements of sonatas, symphonies, and other large-scale works often manifest different keys from the overall tonic of the work. For example, the overall key of Mozart's *Symphony No. 41, The Jupiter,* is C major, but the second movement is in F major. The note F functions as tonic throughout that movement, yet in the context of the entire symphony it functions only as a secondary tonic. The keys of Beethoven's *Symphony No. 3, The Eroica,* are Eb major, C minor, Eb major, and Eb major. Brahms's *Symphony No. 3* starts in F major, proceeds to inner movements in C major and C minor, and ends with a movement that commences in F minor but eventually switches to F major. The movements of Beethoven's *Symphony No. 5* are in C minor, Ab major, C minor, and C major. The overall key of a large-scale work is almost always determined by that of the opening movement of the work.

Aside from key changes from one movement to another, a variety of keys are ordinarily traversed in the course of a single movement. Some of these keys reign just briefly, while others last a comparatively long time. The longer the duration of a secondary key, the longer usually the reaffirmation of the tonic resolving it.

NON-TONIC CHORDS

Within a given principal or secondary key, harmonic variety is achieved through the introduction of all kinds of nontonic chords. Also, any chord can be inverted so that the same notes are retained, but the bass note changes from root to other members of the chord. Seventh chords include an extra third above a triad and likewise may be presented either in root or inverted positions.

Example 46

Root Position and Inversions of a Tonic Triad and Dominant Seventh Chord.

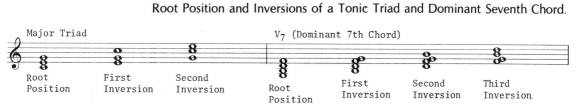

Chromatic chords arise from substitutions of notes from alternate modes or keys. One of the most important of these is the *diminished seventh chord*, consisting of the seventh, second, fourth, and sixth scale degrees of the harmonic minor scale. The chord can be used interchangeably in major and minor keys. Another widely used chromatic formation is the *German sixth chord*, consisting of the VI triad in minor (scale degrees 6, 8, 3) with the addition of the seventh degree (*leading tone*) of the major scale of the dominant (i.e., raised 4). This chord is distinctive for containing a pair of notes forming the interval of the *augmented sixth*.

Example 47

Chromatic Chords—Diminished 7th and Augmented 6th.

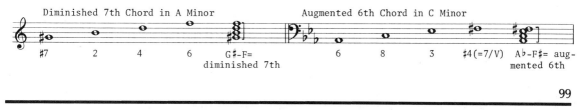

Basics: The Concept of Tonic

Still other chords arise from rhythmic manipulations of single notes, known as *anticipations* and *suspensions*. The presence of an anticipation or suspension in a chord often results in a scintillating, if temporary, dissonance.

Example 48
Anticipations and Suspensions.

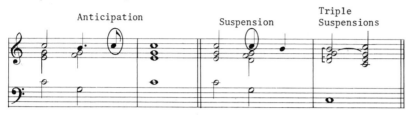

In addition, unusual chords can be formed by combining ornamental neighbor and passing notes with one another and or with more stable chord notes. In the following example, each of the notes of a dominant seventh chord is preceded by a neighbor note. Two of these notes belong to the tonic key of G minor (G and Eb), while two of the neighbor notes are chromatic (B♮ and G♯). The neighbor chord is shockingly dissonant in the context of a Classical symphony.

Example 49

Chromatic Neighbor Chord from Mozart's *Symphony in G Minor* (No. 40), 1st Mvt. Unusual Chords Like This One Receive No Verbal or Numeric Designation.

POPULAR MUSIC IN THE AMERICAN CONCERT HALL

62011

Most of the music discussed in this book belongs to the category known as "classical music"—music that is neither folk nor "pop." Included also are a small number of nonclassical works, as well as others which bridge the gap between serious/classical and folk/pop. *Rhythm*, a story by Ring Lardner, tells about a successful pop song composer who secretly borrows melodies from little known or forgotten nineteenth-century operas. Lardner well knew that many pop tunes have been adapted straight from classical sources, particularly from music of the Romantic period. (One of the best known examples is "Tonight We Love," derived from the first movement of Tchaikovsky's *Piano Concerto in Bb Minor*.) In recent years electronic synthesizers have been used to transcribe older music; in fact, Bach has become quite popular with the synthesizer set. Twentieth-century composers like George Gershwin, Kurt Weill, and Leonard Bernstein have worked successfully in both camps. (Bernstein's *Mass* can be labeled neither classical nor popular—it is a unique mixture of both.) For that matter, classical composers have been integrating authentic or imitation folk music into their own works since the dawn of Western music many centuries ago. And popular (secular) music of the Medieval and Renaissance periods sounds much like the classical (religious) products of the same remote past.

One aim of this book is to encourage students to listen to music of every kind without worrying about labels or pidgeonholes. With few exceptions, successful pop composers have been classically trained, and many serious composers have acquired experience in some aspect of popular music. So let us not make undue fuss over distinctions between classical and popular categories!

In the meantime, however, we need not hesitate to acknowledge two basic types of "American" music—the serious sort performed in the concert hall and the opera house and the other sort, consisting of folk music, jazz, Broadway musicals, popular songs, and rock & roll. In Chapter 8 we encountered folk, religious, and patriotic music at the core of works by the serious American composers, Aaron Copland and Charles Ives. Now we shall consider the works of two composers whose principal artistic residence was Tin Pan Alley and the Broadway musical theater. In Kurt Weill's case we shall examine *Down in the Valley*, an opera unlike any that has ever graced the stage of the Metropolitan Opera. And then we shall proceed to *Rhapsody in Blue*, a unique concerto for piano and orchestra which George Gershwin composed to prove that a viable art work could be derived from popular tunes and the blues.

Chapter 10 concludes with an essay on concerto form.

What is American music? Is it simply music composed on American soil? If so, then what about late-in-life scores by European emigrés, such as Schoenberg and Stravinsky, which betray little evidence of transatlantic resettlement? Or is American music simply music by native-born Americans? If so, what about the European character of the music produced by most nineteenth-century American composers? And how shall we account for the international style of much of the American music composed since the end of World War II? The fact is that "American music" is an umbrella term covering many different types and styles of music, and it is hard to rule precisely what does or does not belong in this category. Perhaps we can agree that American musical nationalism is represented by styles which openly ignore traditional European models in favor of those grounded in native folk and/or popular sources. Admittedly much of our supposedly indigenous folk music itself originated in songs and dances brought here from Africa and Europe during the past 350 years or so. Still, most of this music underwent a quick Americanization which rendered it uniquely American.

All of this is by way of introducing an outstanding example of "American music" by a German composer. Born in Dessau at the beginning of this century, Kurt Weill's early music took root in the post-Romantic styles of Mahler, Strauss, and Schoenberg. Before he was thirty Weill had carved a niche for himself in Germany with *Die Dreigroschenoper* (*The Threepenny Opera*), an updated version of John Gay's eighteenth-century social satire, *The Beggar's Opera* (see Chapter 15). Up until this time Weill's music had been aimed at the "serious" concertgoer, but now it assumed a semipopular, jazzy style. With the advent of Hitler, Weill emigrated to the United States. Here he turned to the field of popular music, composing several Broadway hits, including *Lady in the Dark* (with Danny Kaye making his acting debut) and *Lost in the Stars*. If Weill picked up the craft of Broadway musicals with apparent ease, he was soon to demonstrate a corresponding sensitivity to American folk styles as well. Indeed, his folk opera *Down in the Valley* is as thoroughly American as any music discussed in this unit, whether by the first-generation Copland and Gershwin or by the old Yankee Charles Ives.

Weill's opera originated in the mid-1940s as a pilot for a radio series on folk music (which never got off the ground). Then, in 1947, a member of the prestigious publishing firm of G. Schirmer & Sons conceived the idea of a stage work that could be performed easily by amateur college and community groups throughout the country.

> During the summer of 1947 I had given a few lectures on various aspects of musical life. After one of them, in a small community, a man got up. He explained that all the big and important things I had been talking about meant little to them. The Metropolitan Opera would never bring its stars to their little town in Tennessee. Was there an opera they could perform themselves, with their own forces, with local singers, a local chorus, a little ballet they had formed, with homemade costumes and self-painted scenery, to be sung in English in a high school auditorium that had no pit, no elaborate lighting, few technical facilities?[1]

As the composer of *The Threepenny Opera* and other "proletariat" offerings, Weill seemed the perfect choice to meet this challenge; collaborating with his librettist, Arnold Sundgaard, he quickly expanded the discarded radio pilot into a one-act opera. Following its successful premiere at the University of Indiana, the work was mounted during the next twenty years in roughly 3,000 productions with a total of more than 15,000 performances.

The plot of *Down in the Valley* concerns a pair of young lovers, Jennie and Brack, and the obstacles preventing the fulfillment of their love for each other. Jennie's father dislikes Brack and instead promotes an older man, the mean moneylender, Thomas Bouché. Brack and Bouché get into a fight, and Brack kills Bouché in self-defense. Brack is sentenced to death, but escapes to spend his last night with Jennie. Up to now the plot of *Down in the Valley* resembles many of the melodramas underpinning nineteenth-century French and Italian grand opera, but the similarity goes no farther. For one thing, Weill's opera is the opposite of grand; if anything it is simplistic. Most important, the bulk of Weill's music is drawn from American folk sources. In addition to the title song, four other folk songs are used: "The Lonesome Dove," "The Little Black Train," "Hop up, My Ladies," and "Sourwood Mountain."

The curtain rises after a brief orchestral introduction. The chorus is arranged in a semicircle within which the action of the show takes place. The role of the chorus shifts back and forth from commentator to participant. Against a mellow humming background, the Leader of the chorus sings the opening verse of "Down in the Valley":

Example 50
WEILL, Arrangement of "Down in the Valley"

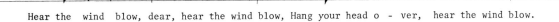

Down in the val-ley, val-ley so low, Hang your head o-ver, hear the wind blow.

Hear the wind blow, dear, hear the wind blow, Hang your head o-ver, hear the wind blow.

The chorus then takes up the second verse, with the sopranos singing the melody and the other voices contributing a rich and varied accompaniment. The Leader now sings the outlines of Jennie and Brack's story (to a new tune), followed by a third verse of the theme song rendered by the tenors with lush assistance from the rest of the chorus. (Weill made good use of his experience as Broadway show composer!)

The story unfolds, sometimes narrated by the Leader, sometimes enacted by the protagonists. After singing a touching song from his jail cell, Brack discusses with another prisoner a plan to break out that night—his last night. The risk is great but Brack has nothing to lose. The escape succeeds.

The scene changes to Jennie's home later that night. Standing on her front porch, she sings a verse of the theme song:

Roses love sunshine, violets love dew,
Angels in heaven know I love you.

Charles Hoffmann, *View of the Montgomery County Almshouse Buildings.* Hoffmann was a self-taught nineteenth-century folk artist. Through its emphasis on folk songs, Kurt Weill's *Down in the Valley* captures the simple essence of scenes like Hoffmann's.

Jennie's father tries to talk her into going to bed, but she insists on maintaining her lonely vigil. Brack's arrival sparks a tender reunion. Jennie sings "The Lonesome Dove":

> O don't you see that lonesome dove
> That flies from vine to vine?
> She's mourning for her own true love
> Like I will mourn for mine.

The lovers reminisce about how they first met at a prayer meeting ("There's a Little Black Train A-Comin' "). Against an orchestral background of "Down in the Valley," the two reenact their plan of attending the upcoming dance on Saturday night. Brack then sings, "Hop up, My Ladies." ("All the folks are goin' dancin', won't you go, won't you go?") Other flashbacks depict a nasty confrontation between Jennie's father and Mr. Bouché, the dance itself ("I Got a Gal at the Head of the Holler"), Brack's declaration of love for Jennie, and the fatal fight between Brack and Mr. Bouché. Final verses of "The Lonesome Dove" and "Down in the Valley" bring the folk opera to an inspiring conclusion: "Angels in heaven know I love you."

GERSHWIN, RHAPSODY IN BLUE

Two years before Aaron Copland was born (see Chapter 8), another Brooklyn family of recent Jewish immigrants was blessed by the birth of a son, George. The year was 1898. These two composers developed in virtually opposite directions. Copland at first became a "serious" composer who later turned for inspiration to folk music and jazz. George Gershwin started right out in popular music, and by the age of 21 his fame was established by Al Jolson's rendition of "Swanee, How I Love you, How I Love You." Starting in 1918 Gershwin annually provided music for one or more Broadway shows, with titles like *Half-Past Eight, La La Lucille,* and *George White's Scandals of 1920 (1921,*

The Music of Lands and Peoples

1922, etc.). At the same time Gershwin was nursing ambitions directed at the field of serious music. David Ewen tells of interviewing Gershwin in 1923, when the composer was just twenty-five:

> Gershwin told me of his hopes to become an *important* popular composer, as distinguished from a *successful* one; that the idiom of American popular music was a significant one, even for a serious composer; that a popular song written by a creator who had a full command of the tools of composition could become important music.[2]

A year later Gershwin made his first stab at serious music with *Rhapsody in Blue*, a one-movement concerto for piano and orchestra, followed in 1925 by his full-fledged *Piano Concerto in F*. The latter was commissioned by the New York Symphony Society and was premiered at New York's prestigious Carnegie Hall with Gershwin as soloist under the baton of Walter Damrosch. Several years later Gershwin composed *Porgy and Bess*, an opera about blacks living in the South. Yet just as Copland has never become a "popular" composer, it would be unjustifiable pretense to regard Gershwin as a "serious" composer (like his contemporaries Copland, Ravel, Stravinsky, etc.). This

A scene from George Gershwin's *Porgy and Bess*, a folk opera about blacks living in the South.

statement is not meant to denigrate Gershwin's musical contribution, for he achieved a unique position in the history of American music—albeit one that defies simple neat classification. Perhaps he should be described as a "serious popular" composer who succeeded in writing in a highly personal style which blends the spirited enthusiasm of Broadway show tunes in classical formats. Where Gershwin's special talent would eventually have led him no one can say, for he was struck down by a brain tumor just ten weeks before his thirty-ninth birthday.

The circumstances leading to the first performance of *Rhapsody in Blue* are as follows: In 1918 Paul Whiteman founded a popular orchestra, with the assistance of the brilliant arranger, Ferde Grofé. (Grofé's *Grand Canyon Suite* is discussed in Chapter 5.) Whiteman's orchestra soon reached stardom, with its attendant financial rewards, but Whiteman was still not content. He was determined to prove that popular music and high artistic goals need not be incompatible. To that end he undertook a concert to show the musical world just how much could be achieved in jazz and pop styles. Meanwhile, Gershwin took time out from his busy theater schedule to compose a jazz-style work for Whiteman's proposed concert. George's brother and lyricist Ira suggested the title *Rhapsody in Blue* after seeing a painting entitled *Nocturne in Blue and Green* by the nineteenth-century American painter, James Whistler. As word of the concerto got out, skeptics were quick to mock Gershwin's move to enter the serious music field and labeled the concert "Whiteman's Folly."

The concert took place in Aeolian Hall, New York City, in February 1924. Many famous classical musicians attended the event, including such luminaries as the violinist Jascha Heifetz, the composer Sergei Rachmaninoff, and the conductor Leopold Stokowski. The program was overly ambitious and dragged on too long, but, coming almost at the end, *Rhapsody in Blue* created a sensation, and the whole concert was judged a success. (Gershwin's performance was greeted by an ovation lasting several minutes. The single remaining work on the program—an arrangement of *Pomp and Circumstance* by the British composer Edward Elgar—must have come as an absurd anti-climax after the Gershwin work.) Thereafter *Rhapsody in Blue* was discussed heatedly in the press—not all the critics shared the audience's enthusiasm—and the work was launched as possibly the most popular concert work ever written. David Ewen reports that Gershwin earned more than $250,000 in performance fees and royalties during the first decade following the premiere. (Ironically, Whiteman lost about $7,000 on the concert.)

The term *rhapsody* first entered the vocabulary of music during the nineteenth century, largely in connection with piano works by Liszt and Brahms. The term suggests a free form in the rhapsodic style of gypsy music. A rhapsody may be scored for a single instrument, a small ensemble, or a large group of performers. Gershwin's work is a piano concerto. In its original form the soloist was accompanied by jazz band, but a couple years later a revised version was issued for full orchestra. Both versions were scored by Grofé, not Gershwin, based on the latter's two-piano version. (One is reminded of Maurice Ravel's imaginative orchestration of Mussorgsky's piano suite, *Pictures at an Exhibition*. In both cases a notable composition for piano achieved fame through an orchestral adaptation by another composer.) Grofé's involvement followed established procedure in popular music circles: one person composes the music, another arranges it. (Thus, many of Richard Rodger's songs from *South Pacific, Sound of*

Music, etc., are known to us through orchestrations by Robert Russell Bennett.) In later years, Gershwin made his own orchestral scores (*Piano Concerto in F, An American in Paris*), demonstrating that he could take full responsibility for his own music from start to finish.

Rhapsody in Blue contains five themes—four principals and one secondary. Although the work is not divided into discrete subsections, one can nevertheless perceive it in four parts, identified by the successive entrances of the four main themes. The piece starts out with the clarinet playing Theme 1, which is then further stated in six successive keys:

trumpet	A♭ major	piano solo	C Minor
tutti (all)	G♭ major	tutti	A major (twice)
piano solo	A major (twice)	tutti	C minor

Despite the frequency of repetition, Gershwin achieved a varied effect by juggling two important elements, instrumentation and key—equivalent to a painter's duplication of a single object in varying colors and textures. (Keys are specified throughout this analysis, giving the student an opportunity to consider the effect of key changes in a work in which thematic repetition is easily recognizable.)

Beginning with its second statement, Theme 1 is "answered" by a traditional blues figure:

Example 51

GERSHWIN, *Rhapsody in Blue*, Blues Motive

An unaccompanied piano episode expands on this motive, ending with Theme 1 in A major. The blues motive is also heard prominently in the next solo piano passage, just after the presentation of theme 1 in C minor.

Following the final statement of Theme 1, we hear a transitional passage featuring a saucy new theme played by two trumpets in octaves. This theme is analyzed as secondary because it appears only this once in the piece.

A vibrant Theme 2, loud and brash, is now introduced by the full orchestra. The piano provides off-beat "punctuation." The key is now C major. (If Theme 2 seems fa-

Example 52

Rhapsody in Blue, Theme 2

107

George Gershwin (1898–1937). Photograph by Nickolas Muray.

The Music of Lands and Peoples

miliar, go back and listen to the opening of the rhapsody, where it was played briefly by a handful of wind and brass instruments between the first two statements of Theme 1.) After a very short time the key changes again, and we hear Theme 3 in G major. (Up to this point the treatment of Theme 2 has been unimposing, but it will come back in a big way later in the piece.) Theme 3 may best be described as a jaunty march. After

Example 53
Theme 3

two further brief statements in G major and Bb major, Theme 3 breaks out at a faster clip (*animato*) in Db major. Later it moves on to E major and back to the original G major. At this juncture the piano plays a short bravura solo passage (*cadenza*) and then quietly reintroduces Theme 2. The key is still G major. Accompanied only by a single French horn, the piano repeats Theme 2 up a scale degree in A major. The horn drops out, the key of G major returns, and the piano loudly proclaims Theme 1. Oboe and bassoon immediately take up the same theme while the piano plays dashing sixteenth notes and grace notes. (A *grace note* lasts momentarily, leaning into an ensuing more powerful note. The notation of a grace note involves a miniscule notehead and a tiny stem. The temporal attack point of a grace note virtually coincides with the note which follows it.)

Meanwhile, where are we in terms of the four discrete sections of *Rhapsody in Blue*? We have passed the onset of Theme 3 and have heard recapitulations of Themes 2 and 1 (in that order), but we have not yet reached Theme 4. During the solo piano passage now coming up we will again hear Theme 3. This admixture of different themes resembles the *development section* of classical *sonata form* (a full discussion of which is to be found in Chapter 12).

Section 4 commences with the mellow "hit tune" of the rhapsody, played by strings and winds, with a *countersubject* (paired second theme or motive) in the French horns. The piano is silent throughout the first statement of Theme 4. Then we hear this theme again, played fortissimo by the full orchestra, with the horns' countersubject now taken up by the piano. An ensuing solo passage gives the piano a crack at Theme

4 by itself. Interestingly, in contrast to the frequent key changes of the earlier themes, Gershwin chose to stay in just one key (E major) for all three of these statements of Theme 4.

Example 54
Rhapsody in Blue, Theme 4

The solo piano writing continues with an episode marked *agitato e misterioso.* This is one of Gershwin's most inspired moments—original, idiomatic, and full of bouncy accents.

The rhapsody is heading for its last few minutes. The horn and trombone bring in a peppery version of Theme 4 as counterpoint to the piano's continued agitation. A big climax is followed by a suspenseful pause and then a loud dissonant crash. The piano deftly brings back the blues motive associated with Theme 1 (see Example 51). Another build-up leads to a wild and joyous rerun of Theme 2, the piano playing in loud octaves supported by orchestral "oom-pahs." Finally, returning to the initial key of B♭ major, Gershwin gives us Theme 1, with the entire ensemble playing its loudest. With the orchestra holding a final B♭ major triad, the piano resounds with the characteristic blue-note seventh of the blues motive (Example 51).

For a final comment on *Rhapsody in Blue*, read these words of Gershwin's biographer, David Ewen:

> The form . . . came from the Hungarian Liszt; the main slow section was derived from the Russian Tchaikovsky; and the harmony sometimes suggests the French Debussy or the Polish Chopin. Yet, like the melting pot that is America, the *Rhapsody* fused the various foreign elements into a personality wholly American. The *Rhapsody* is American music in its youth, brashness, restlessness, optimism. . . . The work as a whole never loses its ability to excite the listener.[3]

The Music of Lands and Peoples

A performance of a Baroque chamber concerto (eighteenth-century Swiss engraving). Among the small accompanying ensemble are two flutists, two horn, and three string players.

BASICS: THE CONCERTO

Gershwin's *Rhapsody in Blue* is a short piano concerto in one movement. It is an exceptional work, for concertos are normally subdivided into three or four movements. There are two basic types of concerto, the *modern concerto* which had its inception during the Classical period, and its forerunner, the *Baroque concerto*. In essence the modern concerto is a symphony featuring one or more soloists. These genres differ mainly in that whereas a symphony offers occasional brief solos for the orchestral personnel, a concerto features a specific soloist (or soloists) throughout the entire work. Symphonic solo passages are performed from the players' normal seats; whereas a concerto soloist, usually a guest artist rather than a member of the orchestra, is always positioned in front of the orchestra, nearest to the audience.

The concerto genre arose in the Baroque period and is therefore somewhat older than the symphony. (The term *symphony* was already in use at that time but rarely signified an extended orchestral work, as in its modern sense. It was sometimes equivalent to a modern-day overture, or even a short prelude for keyboard.) Unlike its modern counterpart, the Baroque concerto seldom emphasized soloistic independence and virtuosity (as, for example, in *Rhapsody in Blue*). The older form is quintessentially a chamber work which balances a small solo group against an accompanying force of about twenty players, usually limited to strings and harpsichord. The soloists often are not even seated apart from the other members of the ensemble. Arnold Schering has aptly characterized the Baroque concerto as a

> contrasting of heterogeneous ensembles, rather like quarreling individuals forced to discuss their troubles with one another. The ideas of *tutti* and *solo*, peculiar to the concerto form . . . signify nuances of the argument . . .[4]

So, whereas the term *concerto*, in its modern sense, implies the assertion of the individual, its Baroque sense suggests a sharing of the limelight. Beginnings and endings of solo passages are often blurred because the soloists play along during the tutti sections, and the dramatic solo entrances associated with the modern concerto are seldom experienced. Moreover, even in Baroque concertos for just one soloist, orchestra members may be assigned solos similar to those of the "official" soloist. For example, Vivaldi's *Spring Concerto* (Chapter 1) is billed as a concerto for one violinist, yet presents several (soloistic) violin duets.

Soloistic flair varies in degree from one Baroque concerto to another. Some provide little chance for the soloist(s) to display brilliance and dexterity, as in Handel's *Concerto Grosso in D Minor*, Op. 6, No. 10. (The term *concerto grosso* signifies a work for relatively many players, as opposed to a lesser sized chamber work scored for a mere handful.) The piece features solos for two violins and one cello, along with the usual complement of subsidiary strings and harpsichord. Its six brief movements all bear the same key signature, with the exception of the D major finale. The solo passages barely differ in character from the orchestral material; the soloists play throughout, and contrast arises mainly from fluctuations in volume as the accompanying group "enters" and "exits." The solo parts demand little genuine virtuosity from the featured players.

Bach's *Brandenburg Concerto No. 5 in D Major* is another matter. Featuring harpsichord, flute, and violin, it offers many exciting passages requiring considerable agility of the three soloists. The first movement is a cheerful *allegro* that bounces along with unrestrained energy. The form of the movement is hard to plot. There is little thematic contrast, and sectionings occur mainly in terms of solo passages versus *tuttis*. The harpsichord plays throughout, functioning as solo instrument as well as *continuo* backup for the accompanying strings. (For the tutti sections Bach followed the practice of *figured bass*, providing merely a bass line with numerical indications of the notes to be filled in above. In the solo sections, he generally wrote out the complete harpsichord part.) See Example 55.

Toward the end of the movement, the other instruments gradually fade as the harpsichord plays cascading scales and arpeggios. Finally, the harpsichord is left alone to play a long and challenging solo passage (*cadenza*). The movement then concludes with a repetition of the brief tutti passage which opened the movement.

The Music of Lands and Peoples

Example 55
BACH, *Brandenburg Concerto No. 5*, 1st Mvt., Mm. 137–141

Popular Music in the American Concert Hall

Next comes a lyrical slow movement in the key of B minor, the *relative minor* of the original key of D major. (Both keys manifest the same key signature of two sharps.) This movement is played exclusively by the three soloists, thereby temporarily converting the piece from a concerto into a *trio sonata*, a familiar Baroque chamber music genre. The finale restores the tutti along with the key, tempo, and cheery good humor of the first movement.

With the rise of symphonic music during the Classical period, the concerto assumed its modern form as a symphony with featured soloist. (A detailed examination of symphonic form is presented in Chapter 12.) The "chamber concerto" of the Baroque now disappeared in favor of the individualistic solo concerto. Mozart, the most important concerto composer of the Classical period, wrote all but three of this thirty-seven concertos for a single soloist. (Numbers do not entirely differentiate Baroque and Classical concerti, however, for some Baroque examples feature a single soloist, while some later examples feature several.) Another important factor is that the Classical concerto soloist rarely plays during orchestral tuttis, resulting therefore in a much greater differentiation between solo and accompanying material. Virtuoso display is now the norm rather than the exception. Cadenzas, invariable in first movements and not uncommon in other movements, are usually preceded by a big orchestral build-up, as if to herald the importance of the event. Unlike Bach's cadenzas in the fifth *Brandenburg Concerto*, Classical cadenzas were usually left to the performer to improvise freely during actual performances. (There was already some precedent for this procedure in solo Baroque concertos.) Audiences thrilled to the spontaneous improvisations of Mozart, Beethoven, and other Classical composer/virtuosi, as they skillfully wove complex musical fabrics from the principal thematic strands of a given movement. Part of the fun of concert going lay in anticipating and observing the compositional/performing derring-do of the cadenzas. (Publishers now provide us with cadenzas as they were written out by the composers or subsequently by outstanding performers. A few daring contemporary musicians still prepare their own cadenzas, although they rarely improvise them "on the spot" in actual performances.)

Classical concertos gradually assumed larger dimensions, and the orchestra expanded to include winds, brass, and percussion. The newly invented piano came into its own, replacing the harpsichord, and the piano concerto became an especially popular genre. In these works the keyboard no longer consistently provided continuo support for the rest of the orchestra; indeed, at about this time (1780–1810) the practice of continuo began to die out in all types of music.

Romantic composers of the nineteenth century adopted the Classical concerto more or less intact. Outstanding piano concertos were composed by Schumann, Chopin, Liszt, Brahms, and Tchaikovsky. Beethoven composed a superb violin concerto, and so in turn did Mendelssohn, Tchaikovsky, and Brahms. A few composers introduced one-movement concertos, much like tone poems—for example, Liszt's *Totentanz* (*Dance of Death*) (see Chapter 30). Note that some Romantic and Modern concertos are not factually called concertos, as in the Liszt work just mentioned and Gershwin's *Rhapsody in Blue*.

In the twentieth century the concerto remains substantially unchanged. Rachmaninoff composed four standard piano concertos, plus his delightful *Rhapsody on a Theme of Paganini*. His Russian compatriot, Sergei Prokofiev, composed five piano

Niccolo Paganini (1782–1840), whose stupendous technique, power, tone control, energy, and virtuosity epitomized the demands placed on the solo virtuoso player in the Romantic concerto.

concertos, Bartók three, and Ravel two, including one for the left hand alone (dedicated to a pianist who lost his right arm in World War I). Important modern violin concertos have been composed by Sibelius, Bartók, Prokofiev, Berg (Chapter 33), Schoenberg, and Stravinsky. One can also find a scattering of concertos for other instruments: Haydn composed trumpet concertos, Mozart composed concertos for bassoon, horn, and clarinet, Schumann and Saint-Saëns each wrote a cello concerto, and Bartók left an almost completed viola concerto.

Some modern composers have tried to revive the spirit of the Baroque concerto grosso. Ernest Bloch's *Concerto Grosso No. 1* (1924), scored for piano and strings, and Stravinsky's *Concerto in D* for strings (1946) represent this movement. Both works manifest the stylistic/formal return to the past known as *Neoclassicism* (discussed further in connection with Stravinsky's opera, *The Rake's Progress*, see Chapter 31). One of the most widely admired orchestral works of this century is Bartók's *Concerto for Orchestra*, a paradoxical title which nevertheless implies the presence of soloistic passages for virtually every instrument of the orchestra. Bartók's approach is most easily observed in the second movement, subtitled "Game of Pairs" and consisting of successive duets for bassoons, oboes, clarinets, flutes, and trumpets. For each duet Bartók selected a different vertical interval with which to separate the two solo instruments. Thus, the bassoons play in *parallel sixths*, which is to say that the lower line imitates the upper

Example 56

BARTÓK, *Concerto For Orchestra*, 2nd Mvt., "Game of Pairs." Mm. 9–12 (Bassoons in Parallel 6ths—String & Percussion Parts Omitted)

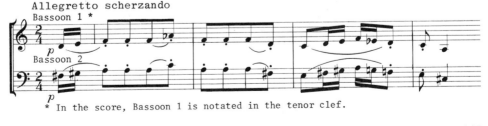

* In the score, Bassoon 1 is notated in the tenor clef.

115

line six scale degrees lower. The oboes play in thirds (minor or major), the clarinets in sevenths, the flutes in fifths, and the trumpets in seconds (usually major seconds). (These intervals are explained in Chapter 9.) After a quiet brass interlude, the game begins again, but the first duet now becomes a trio of bassoons, the oboes and clarinets combine, the flutes join them, and the trumpets are accompanied by harp *glissandi*.

The contemporary Polish composer, Witold Lutoslawski (b. 1913), an admirer of Bartók's music, also composed a *Concerto for Orchestra* (in 1954) in homage to the great Hungarian master.

The Music of Lands and Peoples

PATRIOTISM

Although all nationalistic music implies an element of patriotism, one can listen to Chopin's polonaises and Smetana's tone poems without feeling compelled to salute the flag. There is, however, a body of music which openly seeks to arouse patriotic sentiments. The choral anthem, "This Is My Country," which is widely sung in public schools throughout the United States, is one such work. Another example is Irving Berlin's "God Bless America." Having composed this song in 1918 for a now-forgotten musical, Berlin withdrew it before the premiere. Twenty years later he undusted it for an Armistice Day (November 11) broadcast. The song became an instant hit and virtually achieved the status of a second national anthem in the ensuing years of World War II. Other patriotic American hymns include the perennial "Battle Hymn of the Republic," "America," and "America the Beautiful." A fine patriotic "folk song" much heard in this country is Woody Guthrie's stirring "This Land Is Your Land, This Land Is My Land." And in this category one must include Jerome Kern's beautiful "Ol' Man River," from the musical, *Showboat.* This song, despite its regional emphasis, appeals to Americans from all parts of the country.

Sheet music cover for a nineteenth-century American patriotic hymn.

The precedent for including patriotic songs in concert works goes back at least as far as the Classical period, when Haydn was commissioned to compose an Austrian national anthem. In 1797 the Imperial High Chancellor decided that the Austrian peoples needed a national hymn equivalent to the British peoples' "God Save the King." Haydn based his theme on an old Croatian (Yugoslavian) folk tune, and the music took hold immediately. (Later it was adopted as the German national anthem, "Deutschland über Alles.") Haydn worked this theme into his *"Emperor" String Quartet*, Op. 76, No. 3, as the foundation of a lovely set of variations. Beethoven composed two sets of piano variations based on "God Save the King" and "Rule Britannia." And Tchaikovsky included both the Russian and French national anthems—the latter is the well-known "Marseillaise"—in his famous *1812 Overture*, which celebrates the head-on collision between the armies of Napoleon and the Czar in that fateful year.

In his piano prelude *Hommage à S. Pickwick, Esq., P.P.M.P.C.*, Debussy inserted strains of "God Save the King" in deference to the nationality of Dickens's comic hero. You can hear the tune very clearly in the bass part of the opening measures, and bits and pieces of it also turn up at various points later in the piece. In this regard, an unintentionally funny incident occurred in 1944 in connection with a Boston Symphony Orchestra concert. It seems that Igor Stravinsky, wishing to express his pleasure and gratitude at attaining American citizenship, made a special arrangement of "The Star Spangled Banner." According to Nicolas Slonimsky, the inveterate music encyclopedist and anecdote collector, Stravinsky's version

> adheres generally to the established tonality, but there are some contrapuntal countersubjects and toward the end a modulatory digression into the subdominant is introduced by means of a passing seventh, commonly known as a blue note.[1]

In other words, Stravinsky jazzed up our national anthem! Someone at the first performance complained to the authorities, who discovered an old Boston ordinance which, among other things, prohibited performing "The Star Spangled Banner" with any sort of extraneous embellishment. Twelve policemen appeared at the second scheduled rendition, but Stravinsky, forewarned, had revised the arrangement and the occasion passed without further incident. Thus one of the earliest experiences of the great Russian as an American citizen was to learn at first hand the meaning of the expression, "Banned in Boston."*

An excellent patriotic composition of greater length is Sergei Prokofiev's cantata, *Alexandr Nevsky,* commissioned as the sound track for the film of that name by the great Russian producer, Sergei Eisenstein. The film, which honors Nevsky's defense of thirteenth-century Russia against the invading Knights of the Teutonic Order (Crusaders), was made in 1938—at a time when Russians once again feared the eastward gaze of German armed might. The music contains several rousing choral passages, with the "German army" singing in Latin (the language of the Holy Roman Empire) and the defenders responding in their native Russian. The Russian text lends a special national flavor to the music, whereas the Latin portions sound more like ecclesiastical chant. (See Chapter 23 for music of the Roman Catholic liturgy.)

An entirely different musical treatment of patriotism is found in Gilbert and Sullivan's operetta *H.M.S. Pinafore*. The story concerns a romance between Josephine, the elevated daughter of the Captain of the *Pinafore*, and Ralph, a lowly seaman. Their elopement is foiled at the last moment by Josephine's haughty father and the crippled tattle-tale, Dick Deadeye. When the Captain insinuates that Ralph's social position is

---

*This incident raises the question of whether Bostonians have ever objected to local performances of Puccini's opera, *Madame Butterfly*. It offers a richly harmonized version of the first phrase of "The Star Spangled Banner" as a motive associated with the role of B. F. Pinkerton, a lieutenant in the United States Navy. Puccini's use of this phrase is an appropriate reflection of Pinkerton's nineteenth-century American imperialistic bravado.

The Music of Lands and Peoples

no match for his daughter's high station, Ralph cries out, "I am an Englishman, behold me!" The Boatswain then carries the idea to its logical conclusion:

> For he himself has said it,
> And it's greatly to his credit,
> That he is an Englishman!
> For he might have been a Roosian,
> A French, or Turk, or Proosian,
> Or perhaps Eye-talian!
> But in spite of all temptations
> To belong to other nations,
> He remains an Englishman!

Sullivan's music, a grandiose hymn, perfectly fits the Boatswain's noble outburst. Laughable as it may be, the scene inevitably arouses English national pride (if only vicariously) in the hearts of its audience.

MUSIC AND TRAVEL

Alongside nationalism in music, there is a parallel category which might well be called musical internationalism—the response of composers to the world lying outside their own homeland. This kind of music is exemplified by Mendelssohn's *Fingal's Cave Overture* (Chapter 1), as well as his Scottish and Italian symphonies. But as a composer Mendelssohn belonged to the German tradition of Schütz, Bach, and Handel dating from the Baroque period, and Haydn, Mozart, Beethoven, and Schubert from the Classical period, and his music never abandoned the traditional sounds and structures associ-

James McNeil Whistler (1834–1903), *Nocturne.* Whistler, a native American, recorded his impressions of Venice in a series of etchings entitled *Nocturnes*—a term usually associated with musical compositions. Another of Whistler's paintings, *Nocturne in Blue and Green,* suggested the title of Gershwin's *Rhapsody in Blue.*

Home and Abroad

ated with that heritage. *Fingal's Cave* is successful as nature music but exhibits little that can be regarded as genuinely Scottish. On the other hand, there are many examples of "musical souvenirs" which ably communicate the spirit of the visited land. For instance, the American composer Aaron Copland (Chapter 8) composed *El Salon Mexico* following a Mexican sojourn in 1932. The piece is named for a popular dance hall in Mexico City and is resplendent with the energy and bounce of native Mexican folk music. Here is what Copland himself has said about the music:

> All that I could hope to do was to reflect the Mexico City of the tourists, and that is why I thought of *Salon Mexico.* Because in that "hot spot," one felt, in a very natural and unaffected way, a close contact with the Mexican people. It wasn't the music I heard, but the spirit I felt there, which attracted me. Something of that spirit is what I hope I have put into my music.[2]

Copland's musical recollections belong in a category that includes Rimsky-Korsakov's *Capriccio Espagnol,* Hugo Wolf's *Italian Serenade,* Tchaikovsky's *Capriccio Italien,* Debussy's *Iberia,* Ravel's *Rhapsodie espagnole,* and Gershwin's *An American in Paris.* In his autobiography, Stravinsky tells of a visit he made to Spain.

> Many of the musicians who had preceded me in visiting Spain had, on their return, put their impressions on record in works devoted to the music they had heard there, Glinka having far outshone the rest with his incomparable *La Jota aragonaise* and *Une Nuit à Madrid.* It was probably in order to conform to this custom that I, too, paid tribute to it. The whimsicalities of the unexpected melodies of the mechanical pianos and rattletrap orchestrinas of the Madrid streets and the little night taverns served as theme for this piece, which I wrote expressly for the pianola. . . . Subsequently, I orchestrated the piece, which was called *Madrid,* [and] formed part of my *Quartre Etudes pour Orchestre* . . .[3]

In most of these musical travelogues it is the native spirit, as Copland suggests, rather than actual folk melodies which are incorporated into the compositions. But there are exceptions to this rule. Richard Strauss introduced the popular Neapolitan song, "Funiculi' Funicula'" into his tone poem *Aus Italien (From Italy)* and Tchaikovsky's *Capriccio Italien* is based on a genuine Italian folk song. Regarding the origin of this "rollicking little tune", (see Example 57), Vincent Sheehan has written

> It is known more or less all over Italy, but its birthplace is, I think, somewhere up in the northern region. There is a village on Lake Maggiore where . . . the song is . . . regarded as a local product, almost as a folk song. Any calm evening on the lake you can hear boys singing it from their boats. They may not have the precise version Tchaikovsky heard and noted down. . . . Somewhere, somehow, Tchaikovsky, in his wanderings with his brother Modest, came upon this tune and wrote it down. No doubt it got in his head and stuck there, as the way of such insidious little tunes, until the only thing he could do with it was develop it into a sort of album-leaf, a souvenir of Italy.[4]

A musician need not actually visit a foreign land to find the materials with which to make a musical picture. Folk music has long been published and made available for home study. The nineteenth-century Frenchman Georges Bizet never so much as set

The Music of Lands and Peoples

Example 57

foot on Spanish soil, yet from assiduous visits to Parisian libraries he learned enough to compose one of the most successful musical portrayals of Spain, the opera *Carmen*. The work is full of characteristic Spanish tunes, such as the seductive "Seguidilla," with its clicking castenets, and the famous "Habeñera."

We also have musical remembrances in which composers avoid explicit folkloristic elements, neither quoting folk themes nor imitating them. Such is the case in Hector Berlioz's symphonic work, *Harold in Italy*. Berlioz (1803–1869) once won a prize which enabled him to live for an extended time in Rome. As we learn from his detailed memoirs, he made an extensive walking trip into the Abruzzi region, not far from Rome. Subsequently, when the violin virtuoso, Paganini, commissioned Berlioz to compose a viola concerto, the latter turned to his experiences in the Abruzzi.

> My idea was to write a series of orchestral scenes in which the solo viola would be involved, to a greater or lesser extent, like an actual person, retaining the same character throughout. I decided to give it as a setting the poetic impressions recollected from my wanderings in the Abruzzi, and to make it a kind of melancholy dreamer in the style of Byron's *Childe Harold*.[5]

Each of the four movements is a musical vignette, as the titles indicate:

I   "Harold in the Mountains"
II "Procession of Pilgrims Singing the Evening Prayer"
III "Serenade of an Abruzzi Mountaineer to His Sweetheart"
IV "Orgy of the Brigands"

As in other Berlioz works (such as the *Symphonie fantastique*—see chapter 28), a central theme (representing the protagonist, Harold) is heard in each movement. With the exception of the delightful scherzo melody of the third movement, most of *Harold in Italy* cannot be described as "Italian"; the music is simply typical of Berlioz's unique compositional style.

The two parts of the world that have most strongly appealed to the European composer's taste for the exotic are the American continent and the Orient. The French composer Darius Milhaud (1892–1974) was deeply affected by visits he paid to both South and North America. He lived for a time in Brazil, where he served as private secretary to the French ambassador. On returning to France, Milhaud's "head [was] filled with the sounds of the Brazilian forest and the rhythms of the tango."[6] We have his charming suite for piano, *Saudades do Brasil*, as musical testimony of that visit. Another twentiety-century composer, Ottorino Respighi, also visited Brazil and left us his orchestral suite *Brazilian Impressions* (1927).

A delightful inversion of the musical travelogue is found in music of the native Brazilian composer, Heitor Villa-Lobos (1887–1959). An admirer of the music of J. S. Bach, he composed several short works under the title *Bachianas brasileiras,* combining Bachian styles with South American musical idioms. The fifth work in this series, a vocalise for soprano accompanied by eight cellos, is especially attractive.

During a visit to New York, Milhaud was fascinated by the music he encountered in Harlem night spots. Later he returned to France carrying a large collection of popular song and dance records. His ballet, *The Creation of the World* (1923), anticipated by a year some of the jazz effects of Gershwin's *Rhapsody in Blue* (see Chapter 10).

> *La Création du monde* gave Milhaud the chance he had been seeking of using jazz techniques for an extended work. He modelled his orchestra on those he had seen in Harlem, and wrote his score for seventeen soloists including piano. . . . Milhaud's achievement lies in his genuine synthesis of jazz elements with classic western procedures. . . . The jazz fugato is a brilliant exercise where Milhaud convincingly shows that he has fulfilled his original ambition. The blend is perfect and the idiom absolutely right.[7]*

The fugato occurs in the second section of the ballet. It is based on a subject similar to the blues motive in *Rhapsody in Blue* (Example 51). A solo string bass starts things off, against a rhythmically complex accompaniment of piano and percussion.

Example 58
MILHAUD, *The Creation of the World,* Jazz Fugue Subject

The Orient and its sounds have held a special interest for French composers, stimulated in part by the international exposition held in Paris in 1889. It was on this occasion that the twenty-seven-year-old Debussy encountered the fascinating timbres of the Balinese gamelan—a kind of percussion orchestra. In Debussy's piano piece, "Pagodas" (from the suite *Estampes*), you can detect a distinctly Oriental flavor, due to his use of the *pentatonic scale* (Chapter 5). Ravel was just fifteen at this time, but he had other opportunities to learn the sounds and spirit of the East. By 1903 he had composed *Shéhérazade,* a cycle of three songs for mezzo-soprano and orchestra. (This work should not be confused with the famous tone poem of the same title by Rimsky-Korsa-

*The term *fugato* refers to a passage of fugue in a work that is not primarily fugal. See the essay on fugue in Chapter 16.

The Music of Lands and Peoples

Javanese performers at the Paris Exposition of 1889. The
twenty-seven year old Claude Debussy was among
French composers who were impressed by the unique
flavor of Javanese music.

kov.) The first and longest of the songs, "Asie," consists of a detailed list of the wonders
to be found in the magical lands of Asia. Line after line commences, "Je voudrais voir
. . ." ("I would like to see . . ."). One can enjoy the sumptuous vocal and orchestral writing in a purely musical way, without reference to the words; but for a full appreciation
of the music you should follow an English translation (normally provided as a supplement to the recording), making an effort to keep pace with the French vocal text. At
first you may find it hard to coordinate the English with the French, but the poetic/
musical reward will amply justify your efforts.

Ravel also composed the sultry *Madagascan Songs* for soprano, flute, cello, and
piano. His friend and student, Maurice Delage, composed an interesting set of songs
for soprano and chamber ensemble, *Hindu Poems*. Other examples of "Oriental" music are Puccini's operas, *Madama Butterfly* (set in Japan) and *Turandot* (set in China), as
well as the Gilbert and Sullivan operetta masterpiece, *Mikado*. This work is more English than Japanese, just as Puccini's operas are essentially Italian despite occasional
sounds of gongs and other Oriental effects. But the *Mikado* overture does begin with a
melody based on the pentatonic scale, which is strongly, although by no means exclusively, associated with Oriental music (see Chapter 5).

For most Americans the ultimate musical souvenir is Gershwin's *An American in Paris*. He started work on this tone poem during a visit to Paris in 1928. The piece consists of a variety of musical episodes depicting a brash American as he walks down the Champs-Elysées, crosses over to the Left Bank, gazes at the Eiffel Tower, runs across a fellow American, and so on. In *An American in Paris* Gershwin added a novel instrument to the ever-increasing percussion battery of the twentieth-century orchestra — the taxi horn! The work has been a great hit ever since its New York premiere during the 1928 season. And its fame reached a new peak in the movie based on it, starring Gene Kelly as the transplanted American.

The Music of Lands and Peoples

THE OLD WORLD LOOKS AT THE NEW

DVOŘÁK, SYMPHONY NO. 9 IN E MINOR

One of the most popular works in the orchestral repertoire is Antonin Dvořák's *Symphony No. 9 in E Minor*, subtitled "From the New World." Like Smetana, Dvořák was a Czech composer of the Romantic period, and their compositional styles correspond closely. (Smetana's *The Moldau* is discussed in Chapter 6.) In 1892 Dvořák agreed to come to New York City to direct the National Conservatory of Music. While in the United States, Dvořák composed several works, including the *"American" String Quartet* and the *New World Symphony*. Many hailed the latter as Dvořák's salute to his American hosts. Several of the themes were taken to be imitations of American Indian tunes, while other melodies—particularly the largo theme of the second movement— were attributed to Negro sources. Among his students Dvořák numbered several blacks, including H. T. Burleigh, who subsequently became noted for his arrangements of black music. Burleigh sang spirituals for Dvořák's edification and pleasure, and Dvořák went on record stating that American composers were neglecting the rich indigenous musical resources available to them. However, back in the composer's homeland people thought the new symphony sounded Czech just like Dvořák's other works. (He frequently introduced Czech dances into his symphonies—the furiant, polka, skocná [reel], and sauseda [slow waltz].) Certainly the third movement (scherzo) of the *New World*, and especially its lovely theme in E major, sounds as genial and Czech as anything in Smetana's *The Moldau*. Dvořák himself denied any explicit connection between authentic Indian or Negro folk tunes and his own melodies. Nevertheless, one of the first movement themes bears an unmistakable resemblance to the spiritual, "Swing Low, Sweet Chariot" (see Example 62).

Czech composer, Antonin
Dvořák (1841–1904).

The *New World Symphony* is organized along traditional Classical/Romantic lines—that is, it consists of four contrasting movements. The first movement begins with an *adagio* (very slow) introduction, followed by the main fast section. The second movement is slow and lyrical throughout, and the next movement is a traditional *scherzo*. The *finale* provides a boisterous, exciting climax to the entire work. In this chapter the student is asked for the first time to study the structure of a complete symphony.

Movement 1

The first melodic idea is offered by the cellos, very slow and accompanied pianissimo by violas and string basses. The same idea is then played by a trio of one flute and two oboes, followed by violent fortissimo outbursts in the whole orchestra. Throughout this introduction and indeed the rest of the movement, Dvořák makes much use of the rhythmic effect known as *syncopation*. (See later in this chapter for more on syncopation.) The composer seems to have particularly enjoyed alternations of long-short and short-long note pairs, the metrical accent falling in each case on the first note of the pair (see Examples 59 and 60a). A highly accented, assertive minor-mode theme commences the principal fast portion of the movement (Example 60 a and b).

Example 59
DVOŘÁK, *New World Symphony*, 1st Mvt., Slow Introduction, M. 16

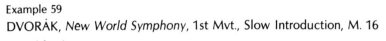

*=metrical accents

Example 60
1st Mvt., Theme 1

a) 1st Phrase

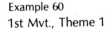

* =metrical accents

b) 2nd Phrase

The Music of Lands and Peoples

A second theme, also minor, even more strongly suggests a flavor of American Indian music. If you examine Example 61, you will find that the fourth note of measure 4 (i.e., the nineteenth note counting from the beginning of the excerpt) is preceded by a *natural sign* (♮), indicating the pitch F♮. This F♮ is the seventh degree of the G *natural minor* scale. Based on the vast majority of minor melodies that we hear, we would normally expect to hear F♯, as the seventh degree of the *harmonic minor* scale. The presence of the F♮ accounts for the ethnic or "Indian" inflection of the melody. (Go back to Chapter 9 and review the natural and harmonic minor scales.)

Example 61
New World Symphony, 1st Mvt., Theme 2

Next Dvořák gives us a genial theme that seems characteristically Czech but that actually duplicates many of the notes of the American spiritual, "Swing Low, Sweet Chariot," starting on the word *chariot*. The first two measures of this theme (Example 62b) exhibit the long-short, short-long rhythmic pattern of Example 60a. Successive statements of this new theme by solo flute, then violins, and finally low strings and trombones, complete the first section of the movement. Dvořák's performance instructions require a verbatim repetition of the fast portion of the movement which we have heard so far, but many recordings ignore these directions and press right on to the next section of the movement.

Example 62a
"Swing Low, Sweet Chariot"

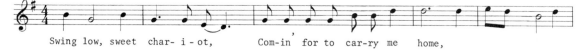

Swing low, sweet char- i - ot,   Com-in' for to car-ry me   home,

Example 62b
New World Symphony, 1st Mvt., Theme 3

The second section is based on the themes shown in Examples 60 and 62b. You are now invited to follow a "play-by-play" description of how these three themes recur in this section. As you listen, try to identify the various orchestral instruments, singly and in combinations.

1. The basses and cellos play an altered version of measures 3–4 of Theme 3 (Example 62b).
2. The French horn plays the same theme from its beginning.
3. The flute immediately repeats Theme 3, with
4. The trombone soon echoing the last measures thereof.
5. The oboes answer with the second half of Theme 1 (Example 60b).
6. Cellos and flutes immediately present Theme 3 four times in a row at double its normal speed. The first two times are in major, the last two in minor.
7. The violins play measure 1 of Theme 3 fast, while the trumpet plays the same theme at its regular tempo.
8. The basses immediately respond with the first half of Theme 1 (Example 60a), alternating simultaneously with slow and fast versions of Theme 3.
9. Shortly thereafter the whole orchestra blurts out the first phrase of Theme 1, oboes and trumpets answering with the fast variant of Theme 3.
10. The oboes take a turn at Theme 1, punctuated fast but softly by Theme 3 in the strings.
11. The flute then imitates the oboe with Theme 1, with *pizzicato* (plucked) string basses not far behind.

The third section of the movement begins with horns playing Theme 1. The succession of the themes now approximates that of the first allegro section of the movement.

The *coda*, or final section, gives us a *fff* tutti, starting with the first half of Theme 3 in the trumpets combined with the main theme (i.e., Theme 1) in the trombones. The violins take up Theme 1, first at regular tempo, later twice as fast. The coda ends with low strings and brass playing Theme 1.

(The foregoing analysis constitutes an in-depth exposure to one of the principal forms of Classical/Romantic music, *sonata allegro form*, or simply *sonata form*. It is discussed in greater detail later in this chapter.)

Spillville, Iowa, in which Dvořák found a Czech community where he could feel at home away from home. He spent his first summer in America there, rather than make the long trip home to Czechoslovakia. During his sojourn in Iowa, Dvořák composed his *"American"* String Quartet.

The Music of Lands and Peoples

Movement 2

The English horn solo which starts the slow movement of the *New World Symphony* is undoubtedly one of the best known themes in the symphonic literature. This theme is associated with the idea of homesick blacks longing for their native Africa. In reality it was Dvořák who was homesick for his native Czechoslovakia, where several of his children remained behind during his first year in New York. The notion of this theme as a black folk lament became fixed in the public mind only after 1922, when a white man, William Arms Fisher, transformed it into the song, "Goin' Home." Fisher wrote the words, adapting them to Dvořák's thirty-year-old melody.

Example 63

New World Symphony, 2nd Mvt., English Horn Solo

*The English Horn normally sounds a perfect fifth lower than written. In the score, the actual key signature contains just four flats, and the first note is C, not F.

The remaining themes of the largo seem more characteristically Slavic than American. First a gentle theme is played by flute and oboe, followed by a sumptuous theme for two clarinets. Both themes are repeated by the strings. Then a new and lively theme is introduced in the winds, quickly building to a climactic tutti which includes elements of Themes 1 and 3 of the first movement. Just as suddenly quiet is restored, and the English horn once again begins its lament. The movement then comes to a peaceful close.

Movement 3

The scherzo alternates a spritely minor theme with a lyrical major theme. Later, after a return of the first theme, a third theme—also major—is introduced. The opening section of the scherzo returns, after which there is a short coda. Once again Theme 1 of the first movement is briefly heard, played *ff* by French horns, but it is quickly displaced by the main scherzo theme.

Movement 4

After a fanfare opening, the brass play the principal theme of this final movement (*finale*). As in Theme 2 of the first movement (Example 61), the flatted seventh of the natural minor scale is prominently displayed—listen for the eighth note of the

The Old World Looks at the New

theme. Several other new themes are introduced during the course of the movement, but more noteworthy is the reprise of melodies from all three of the preceding movements. At one point the first phrase of the principal largo theme (second movement, Example 63) is hooked onto the first phrase of the principal finale theme, accompanied by a hint of the main scherzo theme. At another point, the main first movement theme is answered by the main finale theme. The last pages of the finale bring back the largo and scherzo themes as preparation for a final statement of the main finale theme. We hear a final reference to the first movement, and the symphony closes with a Dixieland figure in the basses—giving us one last glimpse of Dvořák's interest in native American folk material.

Example 64
New World Symphony, Combinations of Thematic Material from 2nd, 3rd, & 4th Movements

The Music of Lands and Peoples

Syncopation

The term *syncopation* refers to off-beat accents and particularly to notes which start on a weak beat and continue through and beyond the next strong beat. This rhythmic condition can easily be illustrated with the familiar nursery rhyme, "Twinkle, Twinkle, Little Star." When you say (not sing) "twinkle" and "little" in normal conversational fashion, you accent the first syllable of each word but dwell longer on the second syllable:

```
Twink-le,      twink-le      litt-le      star
```

If we were to notate this combination of accents and durations, it might look like this:

```
Twink-le,      twink-le      litt-le      star
```

Notice that each second syllable lasts three times longer than each preceding syllable. A more efficient notation of the same pattern is

```
Twink-le,     twink-le     litt-le     star
```

(See the explanation of rhythmic notation in Chapter 3.) At a slow tempo, try beating time with your hands as you say these four words. Start by tapping your desk or knee, coordinating your left hand with the first syllable of each word. As you alternate tapping your two hands at the same speed, you will find yourself beating once for each first syllable, and three times for each second syllable:

```
Twink-le,    twink-le    litt-le    star
  L    R-L-R   L   R-L-R   L   R-L-R  L-R-L-R
```

(The last word, *star*, which gets four taps, is unsyncopated.) Now in beating time, each odd-numbered left-hand beat is "strong" (S), and each even-numbered right-hand beat is "weak" (W). (Test this yourself by marking time, left-right-left-right.)

1 2 3 4	1 2 3 4	1 2 3 4
L R L R	L R L R	L R L R
S W S W	S W S W	S W S W

So you can see that each second syllable of the first three words starts on a weak beat and *continues* through the ensuing strong beat.

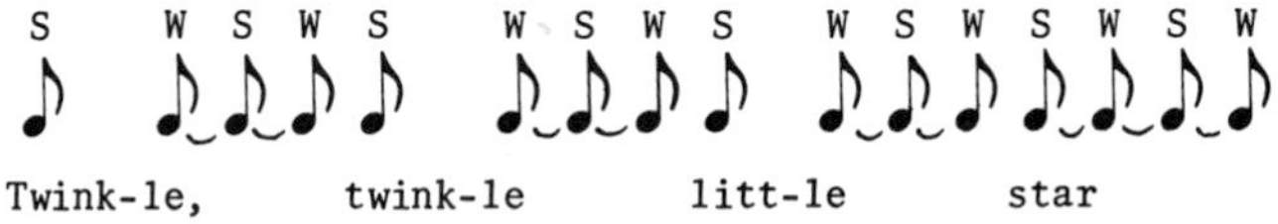

This is what is meant by *syncopation*.

Turning back to Example 59 you can observe syncopation in the introduction to Dvořák's *New World Symphony*. The tempo is very slow, giving a feeling of four beats per measure, each lasting an eighth note. (The time signature of 2/4 might better read 4/8.) There are two notes to each of these four beats. In the first beat, the first note is three times longer than the second—that is, a dotted sixteenth versus a thirty-second.

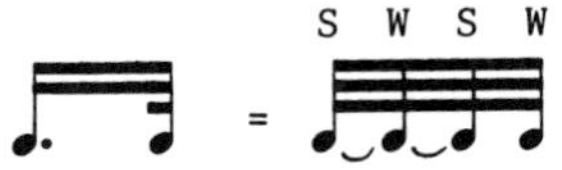

Does this pattern exhibit syncopation? No, for the long note starts on a strong pulse, the first pulse of the metric grouping. But now move on to the second eighth-note beat:

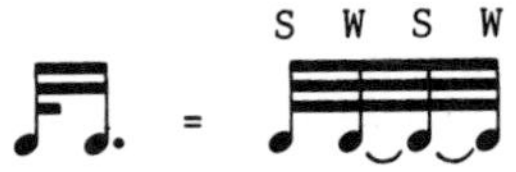

Here we have syncopation, since the second note starts on the weak second pulse and continues through the next stronger third pulse. The fourth eighth-note beat of Example 59 is also syncopated, and one finds this effect again in the second and fourth measures of Example 60a. There is no syncopation in Examples 60b and 61, but one finds it in the second and sixth measures of Example 62b. It is also a feature of measures 1, 2, and 5 of "Swing Low, Sweet Chariot," Example 62a.

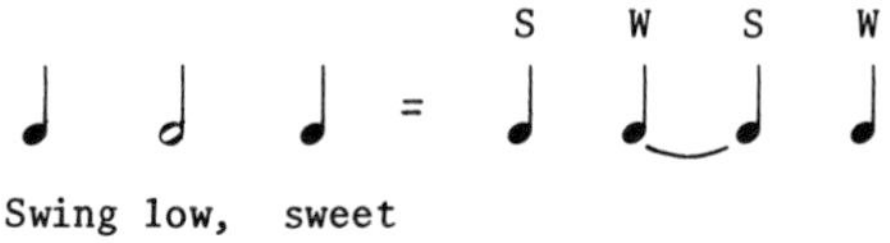

Curiously enough, in the sung version of "Twinkle, Twinkle" strong and weak syllables last equal durations, thereby eliminating the syncopation inherent in the conversational version.

Twink-le,   twink-le   litt - le   star

If you speak these words in the same even rhythmic pattern of the sung version, you get the stilted effect known as "sing-song"; which is to say that you substitute an unsyncopated musical pattern for the conventional syncopated spoken pattern.

Sonata Form

Based on our observations of the first movement of the *New World Symphony*, we can make the following statements about *sonata form*:

1. It starts with a slow introduction. (But this is optional. For example, the outer movements of Beethoven's *Pastoral* are in sonata form but do not commence with slow introductions.)

2. The first principal section, the *exposition*, presents the themes which are to be subjected to further treatment later in the movement. After the presentation of the first theme, the key changes from tonic to dominant or some other secondary key. The exposition is usually supposed to be repeated but often is not in actual performances.

3. Some or all of these themes are taken up in the *development section*, which follows the exposition. They are presented in a variety of keys, instrumental combinations, moods, and textures. Moreover, themes are often cut up into smaller constituent parts, known as *motives*, and typically a single motive is developed extensively, while others are merely touched upon or ignored.

4. Section 3, the *recapitulation*, is modeled after the exposition but is not an exact repetition. Most, if not all, of the themes are presented exclusively in the tonic key.

5. The *coda* comes last, and is something like a second development, although usually shorter than the development section itself.

Bear in mind that not all examples of sonata form follow a strict pattern, and deviations from the norm are not at all uncommon. Thus, some developments introduce new themes, some recapitulations disregard the precedents established in the exposition, and some codas are quite long. (In one extreme case, the finale of Beethoven's *Symphony No. 8*, the coda exceeds in length the entire preceding part of the movement.) And the greatest area of divergence—key relationships—is one that we have barely touched upon. (Key relationships are extremely difficult to explain without the aid of aural illustrations. Your instructor may wish to explain the key relationships of sonata form in class.)

Two more points regarding sonata form: This term arose because many examples of this kind of formal organization occur in solo and duo sonatas, but the term applies also to genres scored for larger combinations, such as trios, quartets, quintents, and all the way up to symphonies. Thus, a quartet is equivalent to a sonata for four instruments, a symphony is a sonata for orchestra, and so on.

Most first movements of sonata-like genres are fast sonata forms, therefore the term *sonata allegro form*. But, since other movements, including slow movements, may also be constructed in the same way, the more widely applicable term *sonata form* has become more generally accepted.

Cyclic Form

The *New World Symphony* represents an example of *cyclic form*. This simply means that themes from one or more movements recur in later movements. In his *Symphony No. 5*, Beethoven hinted at cyclic form by reintroducing the principal theme of the third movement scherzo in the middle of the Finale, and in his *Symphony No. 9* he went so far as to commence the last movement with brief reminders of all three preceding movements (Chapter 18). Berlioz made cyclic form a feature of his precedent-setting *Symphonie fantastique* (1830) by employing a single general theme for all five of its movements (Chapter 28), and he did the same thing later in his *Harold in Italy* (Chapter 11). Brahms and Tchaikovsky also resorted to cyclic form in some of their symphonies, and César Franck, the late nineteenth-century French composer, used it prominently in his *Symphony in D Minor*. Thus, Dvořák's cyclic treatment in the *New World Symphony* is thoroughly in keeping with nineteenth-century practice.

What are the virtues of cyclic form? In program symphonies, such as the Berlioz works mentioned, the repetition of a principal cyclic theme provides a sense of narrative continuity. In absolute (i.e., nonprogram) works, cyclic technique serves the structural function of integrating several movements into a unified whole. (This purely musical consideration is also of no small importance in program works, the success of which ultimately depends more on musical than extramusical considerations.) Listeners are treated to unexpected recurrences of themes from earlier movements—themes thought to be over and done with but turn out only to have been temporarily laid aside. Variety gives way to unity, and the listener can indulge in the pleasure of recognizing a familiar theme in an unexpected new context. Furthermore, as we noted in the analysis of the *New World* finale, a "new" theme can be devised by linking part of one movement's theme with part of a theme from another movement (Example 64). Of course, this technique is available for the several themes of a single movement (most appropriately in a development section), but cyclic form makes the process even more complex and fascinating. To put it another way, cyclic form offers the composer an extra challenge in musical construction and the listener an extra challenge in musical perception.

CHECKLIST: CONCEPTS AND TERMS IN UNIT 2

As at the end of Unit 1, the numbers in parentheses indicate the pages where each term is first and/or principally used. (Unlike in Unit 1, however, many of these terms are not given explicit definitions; rather, the student is expected to infer their meanings from the contexts in which they occur and/or look them up in the Glossary.) Terms preceded by (•) are included in the list of Concepts and Terms from Unit 1.

General and Historical

Austro-Hungarian Empire (71)
- Baroque period (71, 112)
- Classical period (71, 112)
- finale (65, 129)
The Five (74)
Flamenco (68)
- Impressionism (76)
Mighty Handful, The (74)
nationalism (57, 72)
- Romantic period (59)

Instrumental Music

cadenza (109, 112)
cyclic form (134)
- concerto (111–116)
- concerto grosso (112)
- continuo (112)
- development (133)
exposition (133)
- glissando (116)
jew's harp (88)
mazurka (73)
- pizzicato (128)
polonaise (73)
recapitulation (133)
rhapsody (106)
- scherzo (65, 129)
sonata form (133–34)
- suite (88)
symphonic poem (63)
- symphony (88, 126–30)
- tone poem (57)
- tremolo (62)
variations (65)

Vocal Music

- song cycle (68)
vocal range (68, 76)

Theory

bitonal (85)
blue note, blues (107, 110, 118)
canon (82)
chords (99–100)
coda (62, 133)
consonance (95)
- counterpoint (82, 110)
countersubject (109)
- dissonance (95)
dominant (98)
enharmonic equivalent (97)
grace note (109)
- half step (94)
harmonic minor (97)
- intervals (78, 94)
inversion (95)
- irregular meter (65)
keys (91, 98)
leading tone (99)
melodic minor (97)
- modes (major, minor) (59, 91)
modulation (98)
- motive (133)
- natural minor (97, 127)
- octave (65)
ornamentation (68)
ostinato (77)
- pentatonic scale (122, 123)
quarter tone (84)
register (65)
relative minor (114)
scale degree (92)
- scales (91)
suspension (100)
syncopation (69, 131–33)
tonality (91)
tonic (91ff)
tonicization (98)
- transposition (95)
triad (94)
- triplets (68)
tutti (107, 112)

The Old World Looks at the New

REVIEW: UNITS I AND II

Despite having been confronted with just two general subject areas so far—nature and lands and peoples—you have nevertheless encountered a wide variety of musical styles, with intensive exposure to part or all of sixteen pieces and a passing introduction to numerous other works. Several important aspects of music have been discussed, including instruments and the orchestra, genres and forms, history and chronology, and technical rudiments. And you have been introduced to a sizable musical vocabulary—all told, a formidable amount of musical information. This information can be categorized according to three levels of importance. In the first category are facts and concepts which you should actively retain if you are to handle forthcoming material with competence. The second category includes background information to make your music study more interesting, as well as to provide perspective for interpreting the information in category 1. Much historical and biographical material falls into category 2. Finally, category 3 includes optional material—for example, the essay on bird music in Chapter 5. To try to memorize the information in all three categories would not only be extremely impractical, but unnecessary to boot. With this thought in mind the lists of concepts and terms for Units 1 and 2 have been pared down to cover the first two categories alone. Thus, a variety of vocal genres are mentioned in Chapter 4 without being included in the Unit 1 terms list (especially as there will be ample opportunity to focus on some of these terms when you encounter specific examples of these genres in later units).

The following exercises are designed to help you remember information from categories 1 and 2. *Note*: If your teacher has opted to omit certain chapters and assigned listenings, adapt each exercise accordingly.

1. Name the four historical periods discussed so far, and give their approximate dates.

2. Just as it is helpful to know that Shakespeare was an Englishman who lived in the Elizabethan period, it is often useful to know composers' nationalities and historical periods. The composers of the sixteen pieces assigned for listening in Units 1 and 2 are presented here in the order in which they appear in the chapters.

a. Indicate the nationality of each of these composers.

b. Using the letters *b, c, r,* and *m,* indicate the historical period in which each composer belongs. Do not depend too literally on birth and death dates in making your decisions. For example, Ravel was born in 1875, near the end of the Romantic period, but his music belongs to the Impressionist (early modern) period. Therefore, Ravel rates an *m*, not an *r.* By the same token, Richard Strauss (not featured yet) died in 1949, but the tone poems which established his reputation were all composed well before 1900 in a decidedly Romantic style. In cases of this sort, where a composer may be thought of as straddling two periods, you may use two letters—for example, Sibelius rates an *r* for his early works, *m* for his late symphonies. (As far as *Finlandia* is concerned, *r* suffices.)

Claude Debussy	Béla Bartók
Antonio Vivaldi	Manuel de Falla
Ludwig van Beethoven	Modest Mussorgsky
Felix Mendelssohn	Aaron Copland
Franz Joseph Haydn	Charles Ives
Maurice Ravel	Kurt Weill
Bedrich Smetana	George Gershwin
Jean Sibelius	Antonin Dvořák

3. Which of these composers' music had you heard before? Do you remember any of the titles? Did you find the pieces you knew from before similar or different with respect to the assigned works by the same composers? Are there composers outside the sixteen listed above whose music you would like to hear and know more of?

4. Indicate your personal preferences with regard to the listening assignments. Rate each of the composers from 1 to 16 (with 1 signifying your favorite). Or you may prefer to group them into three or four categories of favorite, enjoyable, indifferent, and/or unpleasant. Do you find your preferences influenced by composers' nationalities (and/or your own ethnic heritage)? their historical periods? genres? instrumentation or vocal scoring? other considerations?

5. The following genres, listed alphabetically, are represented in the sixteen pieces assigned for listening in Units 1 and 2. Define each genre and link with the composers listed in Exercise 2. After completing this question, compare your answers with the definitions found in the Glossary (see Appendix II).

concerto	song cycle
opera	suite
oratorio	symphony
rhapsody	tone poem

6. Explain the following technical terms as best you can *in your own words*. Then compare your answers with the definitions found in the Glossary. (Your instructor may wish to delete some of these terms and possibly add others culled from the Lists of Concepts and Terms at the ends of Units 1 and 2.)

four family groupings	opus
of the modern orchestra	pentatonic scale
half step	polytonality
movement	sonata form
musical souvenir	syncopation
natural minor	tremolo
octave	whole-tone music

7. Write a brief essay describing your reaction to nationalism in music. Bear in mind the following questions:

a. Do you like hearing and identifying folk themes in concert works, or do you prefer a more general kind of ethnic music—as exemplified by Grieg's nonfolkloristic Norwegian music?

b. As an American do you respond to Americanistic music (by Copland, Ives, etc.) differently from examples of European musical nationalism?

c. Do you regard it as significant that both works in Chapter 8 are celebrations of American political leaders as opposed to the nonpolitical/heroic content of most of the European examples?

d. Do you detect differences between nationalistic music on the one hand and musical souvenirs on the other—for example, between the American music of Copland and Ives versus Dvořák's *New World Symphony*?

e. Similarly, what about "French" Spanish music (Bizet, Ravel, etc.) versus nationalistic music by Spaniards (Albéniz, Granados, etc.), and how much significance do you attach to these differences?

(*Note:* To answer these questions thoroughly you should listen again to several of the examples from Unit II, possibly supplementing them with other relevant pieces.)

8. Concoct two or three questions that would be useful for your fellow classmates to consider.

9. Which aspects of Units I and II have interested you the most? Looking ahead in the Table of Contents, which of the forthcoming chapters do you expect most to engage your interest?

MUSIC AND SOCIETY

Unit 1 deals with musical representations of nature, and Unit 2 takes up musical characteristics of countries and peoples. In Unit 3 we shall consider music pertaining to various aspects of people living together in society. Chapters 13–15 deal with social tensions as interpreted primarily in the realm of music theater—opera and its derivative, operetta. You will meet a servant couple deflecting the amatory pursuits of their aristocratic employer, a poor sailor striving for the love of his rich captain's daughter, an overambitious family group seeking "upward mobility," the cut-throat world of beggars and pimps, and an impoverished half-crazy soldier beset by the machinations of his sadistic superior officers. The composers represent the Classical, Romantic, and Modern periods: Mozart, Sullivan, Wagner, Weill, and Berg. Some of the music is serious and grand, some is comic and light, but all of it gives one a sense of societal struggles, past and present.

The emphasis on musical theater in these three chapters makes appropriate the inclusion of brief historical essays on the development of opera and related forms. There is also a consideration of a major nonoperatic work, Beethoven's *Eroica Symphony*, in relation to democratic aspirations in early nineteenth century Europe.

Following the musical confrontation of social issues offered in Chapters 13–15, the last two chapters of Unit 3 move on to less weighty material. Chapter 16 takes up a special aspect of society—its children and the music composed for their edification and pleasure. The joy radiated by children's music comes as welcome contrast to the heavy atmosphere of some of the earlier music of this unit. Here, as perhaps in no other section of the book, we encounter music designed to help us relax and forget about the burdens we shoulder in the adult world.

Finally, Chapter 17 introduces us to the cooperative side of music making, the world of chamber music. This chapter is based on a short story about a quartet of musicians for whom literally nothing on earth is as important as playing string quartets together. There is much humor in this chapter, although it arises not from the music itself (as in some of the examples of "Music and Children") but from a fictional account of amateur musicians "doing their thing."

Music and Society

MARRIAGE AND SOCIAL CLASS 13

The primary social unit of humankind is the family. Of course before a family can be started, a couple must meet, mate, and be married (in some order thereof). But social obstacles often harass young lovers, and many musical works portray hapless couples pitted against their families and society as a whole. We encountered this kind of conflict in the folk opera *Down in the Valley* (Chapter 10), where Jennie's father opposes her love for Brack Weaver. Shakespeare's idealized lovers, Romeo and Juliet, doomed by the hatred of the Capulet and Montague clans, are captured in numerous musical settings of their drama (Chapter 29). And the list goes on and on, of musical portrayals of couples denied happiness and fulfillment due to interfering social pressures.

MOZART, THE MARRIAGE OF FIGARO

Romance as it relates to social position is the subject of Mozart's comic opera, *The Marriage of Figaro*. Based on the second of three related plays by the eighteenth-century dramatist, Beaumarchais, the story concerns a pair of betrothed servants, Figaro and Susanna, who are eagerly awaiting their forthcoming wedding. But a problem arises over the Count's amatory interest in Susanna. The Count, who is Figaro's master, has foresworn the traditional *droit du seigneur*—the right of a lord to sexually possess a female servant on her wedding night—but he hopes to achieve secretly what he has renounced publicly. The play is filled with plots, counterplots, and subterfuge. The Count is eventually bested by his "inferiors" (with the aid of the forlorn Countess), and Figaro and Susanna get to enjoy their first night without intrusion. Democracy has won the day against outworn feudal principles.

Wolfgang Amadeus Mozart (1756–1787). Long after his death, Mozart was portrayed as an innocent genius crowned with a halo of ethereal remoteness. In truth he was extremely down-to-earth, and as an opera composer his greatest virtue lay in creating vivid human characters.

Writing during the reign of Louis XVI and Marie Antoinette, Beaumarchais poked fun at the very society which supported him. Surprisingly, his royal patrons enjoyed his well-aimed barbs, and the play became a great popular success. Yet, as fine a drama as it is, the continuing fame of Beaumarchais' *The Marriage of Figaro* today (at least outside of France) must be attributed to the opera which Mozart and his librettist, Lorenzo da Ponte, derived from it.

Some twenty-four years Beaumarchais's junior, Mozart was born in the little mountain town of Salzburg, Austria in January 1756. As a youngster he amazed everyone with his musical talent. He began music study at the age of four and was touring the continent as pianist, violinist, and composer by the age of seven. Even more remarkable than his precocity was his ability to survive the critical postyouth years without burning out his talent (as has often been the case with musical prodigies);as an adult Mozart reached the heights of consummate mastery. He was a prolific composer and left the world an enormous and varied repertoire at his premature death at age thirty-five (in 1791). Among his most successful works are his operas. Even today, after two hundred years, Mozart remains perhaps one of the three greatest composers of opera (in company with Verdi and Wagner).

Long after his death Mozart was portrayed by biographers as an innocent child genius, crowned with a halo of ethereal remoteness. But do not let the courtly wig and satin breeches in his portraits fool you; Mozart was no prig! In truth he was extremely down-to-earth and even loved to indulge in crude humor. (His personal letters reveal him a devotee of what would now be called "bathroom humor.") Thus, Mozart could easily enter into the democratic spirit of Beaumarchais's underdog protagonists. As an opera composer his greatest virtue lay in creating vivid human characters. All the roles of *The Marriage of Figaro*—shrewd Figaro and pert Susanna, the wily Count and the hassled Countess, the giddy adolescent Cherubino and the scheming voice teacher, Basilio—depict believable persons to whom we can respond just as if we had met them in real life.

On the other hand, the period and setting of *The Marriage of Figaro* stretch back some two hundred years before the present day, with costumes and scenery reminding us of the world of George Washington and Benjamin Franklin. After a scintillating overture, the first act curtain rises on an eighteenth-century room which Figaro and Susanna are to share once they are married. We find the young couple happily occupied with details of their upcoming nuptials. The orchestra plays cheerful "measuring music," as Figaro busily marks off the room's dimensions (with an eye to placing various pieces of furniture). Susanna is interested in a new hat she is trying on. Mozart skillfully provides contrasting music for the two performers. Figaro is the first to sing, and then Susanna follows with her "hat music"—a lovely, lyrical melody.

Example 65

MOZART, *The Marriage of Figaro,* Opening of Figaro–Susanna Duet (Figaro's Measuring Music) [Orchestral Score Reduced for Piano]

Marriage and Social Class

Example 66
Susanna's "Hat" Music

O - ra si, ch'io son con - ten - ta, sem - bra
Yes, I think it's most be - com - ing, just the

fat - to in ver per me, sem - - bra
sort of hat for me, just the

Figaro resumes his measuring music, joined by Susanna vying for his attention. Eventually breaking out of his absorption, Figaro pays Susanna a handsome compliment—to the tune of the hat music, which continues, as the blissful pair finishes the duet. (But the very last phrase of the orchestral coda reverts to the introductory measuring music.)

After this happy opening number, Susanna introduces a sobering thought which she presents in the declamatory style known as *recitative*. (That is, there is no identifiable melody, and the rhythm and form are dictated mainly by the requirements of the verbal text. The accompaniment is usually supplied by a single keyboard instrument—harpsichord or piano.) Susanna complains that their room-to-be is all too conveniently located between the Count's and the Countess's separate bedrooms. Figaro does not comprehend her objection; it seems a highly practical arrangement to him. She gives her reasons in the second formal number of the opera, another duet. After the orchestra introduces the first theme, Figaro sings, "Suppose that during the night the Countess should need you. All she has to do is ring ('ding, ding') and you'd be there in two steps." The key of the music changes, and we hear a variant of this melody as Figaro points

Music and Society

out that he could just as easily jump at his master's call ('don, don'). Now the music changes from major to minor as Susanna raises the possibility of the Count sending Figaro far away on a purported errand, only for the count to spring to *her* bedside ('din, din, don, don') in no time flat. Figaro is horrified by Susanna's words and begs her over and over to be silent ('pian, pian'). In the second part of the duet, Susanna agrees to tell Figaro the reasons for her anxiety. Mozart sets this scene with an uncanny combination of cheerful verve (retained from the first part of the duet) and sharp intensity, anticipating many similar moments in ensembles spread throughout the opera. Often a sense of serious import is added quite literally by a single orchestral note. Compare Example 67a with its repetition in Example 67b. The voice parts are identical (except for the last note of the phrase), but the accompaniment adds two marvelous dissonances in the second and third measures of the repetition.

Example 67

The Marriage of Figaro, End of Second Duet Between Susanna and Figaro

Marriage and Social Class

Returning to recitative style, Susanna informs Figaro that of late the Count has been showing her all too much attention. As Susanna exits, the character of the recitative changes, with the orchestra augmenting the keyboard accompaniment and the general tone turning slightly ominous. Figaro commences a monologue warning the Count that he will make a steadfast opponent to the Count's seductive improprieties. Figaro then sings a three-part aria which contrasts an ironic minuet style (part 1) with an angry presto (part 2). The third part of the aria reverts to an abbreviated reprise of the first part, and the orchestra finishes with a brief coda imitating the second part.

As the opera progresses, the Countess, Susanna, and Figaro hatch various plans to catch the Count off guard. The second act finale is possibly the finest ensemble scene in the operatic repertoire. It escalates from a duet between the Count and Countess, to a trio with the two of them and Susanna to a quartet including Figaro, to a quintet with an alcoholic gardener, and finally to a *tutti* with three other secondary characters. Susanna's and Figaro's wedding ceremony occurs during the third act finale, but the occasion is marred by note passings, suspicious looks, and snide comments. However, by the end of Act IV the Count has been caught red-handed and promises to mend his ways. Although everyone knows better than to believe him, the sanctity of the marriage vows between Figaro and Susanna has survived, at least for the moment, and a victory may be claimed for the common person and democracy. It is certainly no coincidence that both the original play and the opera were written in the same period that witnessed the French and American uprisings against royal/aristocratic tyranny.

Listen to the opening scenes of Act I, followed by a selection of excerpts of your own choice from the remaining three acts. Because an opera is a musical setting of a drama, your appreciation of the music will depend on how well you comprehend its verbal content. Be sure to keep a copy of an English translation of *Figaro* close at hand, consulting it frequently as you listen. (For further comments on following an opera text, or *libretto*, see "The Languages of Opera" following.)

BASICS: MUSIC AND THEATER

The Rise of Opera

The first experiments in opera took place in Florence, Italy, at the beginning of the seventeenth century, marking the beginning of the Baroque period. The early creators of opera intended to revive the art of dramaturgy as they believed it had been practiced in ancient Greece. The classic myth of Orpheus—the legendary poet and singer of Thrace—provided an ideal subject for their initial efforts, and in the year 1600 Jacopo Peri and Giulio Caccini jointly composed an opera, *Euridice*, based on the Orpheus legend. Subsequently the two composers individually published their own versions of the opera. In these first operas words take precedence over music, which is employed merely as a vehicle and never for its own sake. The musical style is extremely simple, even bare. Speech rhythms predominate in unornamented melodies coupled with spare accompaniments; the musical texture is essentially that of recitative. In later operatic styles words are repeated often, thereby allowing the composer "time" to work out elaborate musical ideas. But in these early operas word repetition is virtually unknown, and there are few if any set musical numbers.

A few years after the Peri/Caccini experiment, Claudio Monteverdi (1567–1643) based his first opera, *Orfeo, Favola in Musica* (Orpheus, a Musical Fable), on the same mythological subject. This opera is considerably more intricate than its predecessor, calling for a large and varied orchestra and including set pieces for soloists and chorus. Word repetition is still uncommon, and therefore the musical numbers remain brief. But superb melodies abound—some highly ornamented—and the music is no longer relegated to a subsidiary position. Unlike Peri and Caccini's opera, *Orfeo* has withstood the test of time. It offers beautiful music, and is eminently stageworthy as well.

Even though Monteverdi's compositional style is relatively ornate compared to other early opera music, it nevertheless fulfills the Florentine requirement that serious drama be presented in a simple and straightforward manner. It was not long, however, before Baroque operas began to acquire stylistic affectations; consequently, by the middle of the eighteenth century, the dramatic impact of opera had considerably diminished. The rise at this time of Classical styles coincided with a reform movement in operatic composition and performance practice. The most important composer associated with this movement was Christoph Willibald Gluck (1714–1787). Like Monteverdi, Gluck composed an opera founded on the Orpheus legend. Although it appeared a few years prior to the real beginning of the reform movement, Gluck's *Orfeo ed Euridice* exhibits a tendency toward simplicity and directness. To begin with, there are just three characters: Orpheus, sung by a mezzo-soprano, and Eurydice and Amor (Cupid), both sung by sopranos. The music ably serves the text, and there are no extraneous arias merely to show off a singer's technical prowess. Furthermore, the opera is limited to three acts, each of which is quite brief.

Christoph Willibald Gluck (1714–1787), the most important composer associated with eighteenth-century reforms in opera, specialized in serious operas.

Marriage and Social Class

Gluck specialized in serious operas (*opera seria*), which for all their musical beauty sometimes seem a bit wooden for modern tastes. At the time of Gluck's death, Mozart was just reaching maturity as an opera composer, and, although he made several notable attempts in Gluck's serious idiom, Mozart's greatest successes were all comedies. Of course, as our observations on *The Marriage of Figaro* have shown, not all comedies eschew serious content. Admittedly Mozart's *Abduction from the Seraglio* is mainly a nonsensical farce, but his other comic masterpieces—*Don Giovanni, The Magic Flute,* and *Così fan tutte* (*That's the Way Women Are*)—contain, along with *Figaro,* many moments of poignancy, philosophy, and/or deeply felt sentiment. The comic opera genre, while already popular in Italy in the early eighteenth century, was perfected only in Mozart's hands. Mozart makes you laugh, but at the same time he makes you think. No other composer has wedded so well the funny with the meaningful, the light heart with the thoughtful mind. (*Don Giovanni* is discussed in Chapter 21, and other material on *The Magic Flute* is found in Chapters 5 and 25).

The Languages of Opera

With Italy the birthplace of opera, the Italian language reigned as the principal operatic tongue for about two hundred years (1600–1800), and not just within Italy's borders. Thus, George Frederick Handel (1685–1759), one of the outstanding opera composers of the Baroque period, was German by birth and most of his life an Englishman by residence, yet he nonetheless produced numerous operas in Italian. In those days, English and German—not to mention the less prestigious European languages—were considered unsuited to the ears of the operatic elite. Outside Italy the only country where composers could consistently write in the language of their audience was France (e.g., Lully and Rameau). Otherwise, musicians who wanted to write an opera did so in Italian.

Mozart was one of the first to write an opera in German. As a youngster of twelve, he composed a brief operatic comedy, *Bastien and Bastienne.* The story concerns a pair of young lovers whose idyllic romance is disturbed by misunderstandings and jealousy but is then restored through the ministrations of their friendly local magician. Since German was Mozart's mother tongue, it should come as no surprise that, with the exception of the magician's incantations, the text is sung entirely in German. But this is not the case with other Mozart operas, such as *Le Nozze di Figaro* (*The Marriage of Figaro*) and *Don Giovanni.* These operas were not only composed in Italian, but during Mozart's lifetime were performed untranslated in Vienna, Prague, and other musical centers outside Italy. Mozart's patrons were highly cultivated, and considered it perfectly natural to hear his operas sung in Italian. (Mozart's two full-length German operas, *Abduction from the Seraglio* and *The Magic Flute*, were exceptions to the rule.) Carl Maria von Weber (1786–1826) and Richard Wagner (1813–1883) were the first important German opera composers to rebel against Italian libretti altogether.

There is an interesting dichotomy between the ways in which Mozart treated his Italian and German libretti. In the former, conversational dialogue is sung in recitative style, whereas the German operas contain spoken dialogue in addition to or instead of recitative. The consistent alternation between spoken dialogue and musical "numbers" became the format for the comic opera of the nineteenth century—the *operetta*—which in turn led to the *Broadway musical* as we know it today.

Music and Society

So starting in the seventeenth century a certain Italian "colonialism" held sway in the realm of opera for more than two centuries. By the present day, however, the practice has changed considerably, and most European opera houses present operas in the language of the audience. During the winter season in Salzburg (Mozart's birthplace), you can hear *Figaro* in German (*Figaros Hochzeit*), although it reverts to Italian during the prestigious international music festival held there each summer. Danes hear Mozart in Danish, regardless of whether the original libretto is German or Italian. The French listen to Wagner's German texts translated into French, and correspondingly the English hear the Frenchman Gounod sung in English.* In the United States, however, there is still a tendency to mount operas in the original languages. The Metropolitan Opera once experimented with alternate performances of Puccini's *La Bohème* in Italian and English, but most of their clientele preferred the Italian original (based on a French novel!). It is not difficult to see why: the numerous consonants and diphthongs of English are hard to project in a cavernous, unamplified opera house; Italian, with its many vowels and relatively few consonants, is much better suited to opera singing. Singers prefer it to English, and so do their customers.

Almost all recorded operas are performed in the original languages. This creates a special problem for English-speaking listeners, since most of the great operas were composed by non-English-speaking composers (Mozart, Verdi, Wagner, Puccini, etc.). Those wishing to develop an appreciation for opera must rely on printed translations of the libretti. And following a translated libretto can represent no small challenge, especially for those who wish to keep pace with the music. The trick is to keep an eye on the original text, listen for key words, and then switch over to the English equivalents. Single words and entire phrases may be repeated and re-repeated, making the whole procedure quite complicated. Some people prefer to start by reading a synopsis of the plot and then settle back to listen to the opera purely as music. This approach can be satisfying only to a limited extent. Since opera is a combination of music and drama, one needs to follow *both* to absorb the operatic experience fully.

The English Comic Opera Tradition: Gilbert and Sullivan

To date, few renowned operas have been written in English. Notable exceptions are *Dido and Aeneas* by Henry Purcell (1659–1695), *The Rake's Progress* (1949) by Igor Stravinsky, and several operas by Benjamin Britten (1913–1976). But if you are on the lookout for first-rate English-language music dramas, do not pass over the operettas of W. S. Gilbert (1836–1911) and Sir Arthur Sillivan (1842–1900). For all that their works are steeped in the era of Queen Victoria (late nineteenth-century), their structure and ambience derive strongly from the Mozartian comic opera tradition. And because they require no translation, "G&S" operettas offer the American listener a perfect wedding of words and music. It is not just that the singers' words are easy to understand; in addi-

---

*There is a special irony in rendering into English Italian libretti derived from original English dramas—for example, Verdi's settings of Shakespeare's *Macbeth, Othello,* and *The Merry Wives of Windsor* (*Falstaff*). Similarly, German audiences must often be amused at hearing translations of French libretti based on the original German of Goethe's *Faust* (in the operas by Berlioz and Gounod—see Chapter 22).

Light opera collaborators Sir William Gilbert, (right) librettist/lyricist (1836–1911) and Sir Arthur Sullivan, (left) composer (1842–1900).

tion, the music fits the words in a way that is inevitably sacrificed when a foreign text is translated into English.

Many people have acquired a bias against G&S as a result of having heard their works performed by children. (Mozart's operas would also suffer if performed by youngsters!) This is unfortunate, for Gilbert and Sillivan were both artistic craftsmen of high caliber. Gilbert was a brilliant wit, on a par with Oscar Wilde, and his lines require delivery by well-trained sophisticated adults. And, although Sullivan's "serious" music is no better than that of most other British composers of his time (the nineteenth century being generally a poor time for English music), his operetta music is very skillfully constructed, full of delightful melodies, and closely molded to the twists and turns of the plots.

In their humorous way, G&S shows offer a multitude of barbs aimed at the follies and foibles of Victorian England. Almost every plot displays a romantic couple separated by social rank: the son of the great Mikado loves humble Yum-Yum, a school girl (*Mikado*); Mabel, daughter of a haughty *nouveau riche* major general (who has purchased a manor replete with ancestoral ghosts), loves Frederick, a pirate apprentice (*The Pirates of Penzance*); the high-born Casilda loves Luis, a drummer-boy (*Gondoliers*). Nowhere is class distinction treated more brilliantly than in *H.M.S. Pinafore*. Here we have a three-way class confrontation: Sir Joseph Porter, first lord of the Admiralty, wishes to marry Josephine, daughter of the captain of the *Pinafore*; she, however, loves Ralph, a lowly sailor aboard her father's ship. Josephine is upper-middle class, whereas Sir Joseph—by dint of highly polished mediocrity—has achieved entrée into the aristocracy.

Josephine, well aware of the great disparity in rank between herself and Ralph, initially conceals her passionate feelings. When Ralph finally declares his love, Josephine acts the part of the shocked lady and rejects him summarily. But a moment later, in an aside, she touchingly expresses her wish to surmount the class differences which separate them. It takes a determined threat of suicide before Ralph succeeds in

A contemporary artist's engraving (1878) of *H.M.S. Pinafore*. From left to right: Poor Little Buttercup, the Captain, Josephine, Ralph, Sir Joseph Porter, and Dick Deadeye.

breaking through Josephine's veneer. Having finally acknowledged her true feelings, she agrees to elope with him. The first act ends with a rousing chorus in honor of social equality.

Josephine's second act aria is a brilliant exposition of the problems facing her as she struggles to cross social boundaries and marry "down." The whole thing is treated as a parody of a grand opera *scena* (extended aria). Josephine sings a long recitative contrasting "papa's luxurious home hung with ancestral armour and old brasses . . . and Venetian fingerglasses," with "a dark and dingy room in some back street with stuffy children crying . . . and clothes hanging out all day a-drying, with one cracked looking glass to see your face in, and dinner served up in a pudding basin!" In the aria proper, Josephine compares Ralph's poverty and poor education with "his trusty heart and honest brown right hand." (An anticipation of D. H. Lawrence's Lady Chatterley and her earthy lover?) The aria ends with the unanswered question, "Oh God of love and God of reason, which of you twain shall my poor heart obey?" In the end there is no need to answer the question, for, in the manner of Wilde's *The Importance of Being Earnest*, Ralph and the Captain reveal exchanged identities (having as babies been switched by their befuddled nurse, poor little Buttercup). On being informed of the Captain's and Josephine's sudden demotion in social status, Sir Joseph loses all interest in her, whereas Ralph is only too willing not to allow his sudden rise in fortune to interfere with the fulfillment of his matrimonial desires.

THE FAMILY

Once a couple has surmounted society's obstacles to marriage, its problems are just beginning. Raising a family is no easy task; pitfalls lie in every direction. The recent Broadway musical *Fiddler on the Roof* offers a good case in point. Tevya and Golde are an older married pair who have been raising five daughters in the anti-Semitic atmosphere of late nineteenth-century Russia. Tradition has always ruled the family; now it is starting to weaken. One of the daughters does not want to obey her father's injunction to marry an old widower, for she loves a young man of her own age. "Love," Tevya asks, "love?" He turns to Golde, his wife of twenty-five years, and asks if she loves *him*. The musical number prompted by this question is no romantic love duet, but rather a serious consideration of what holds a family together—namely, necessity! Golde sings, "I've washed your clothes, borne your children, cooked your meals—what do you mean, do I love you?"

The theme of the pioneer spirit in a hard-working family is found in many musical compositions, both classical and popular—for example, Aaron Copland's ballet, *Appalachian Spring*. Leonard Bernstein's short comic opera *Trouble in Tahiti* (1952) shows another aspect of family struggle—the conflicts of modern American suburban life. The sole protagonists are a married couple who have long ceased to love each other. They have plenty of money, high social position, a healthy son, yet happiness eludes them. Their situation is presented in a humorous vein (accompanied by a trio of commentators who sing in a 1940s radio commercial style), but—underneath and alongside the humor—tension and even bitterness continually bubble up. The man finds relief in his work and recreation, the wife sees a psychiatrist. They stick together for the sake of their son. Sometimes they spend an evening together at an escapist movie, such as *Trouble in Tahiti*, an imaginary film from which the opera takes its title. In less than an hour of musical theater, Bernstein cleverly illumines the predicament of many modern American families.

WAGNER, DAS RHEINGOLD

At the opposite pole from Bernstein's sociological gem is Richard Wagner's monumental *Ring of the Nibelung*, a cycle of four interrelated music dramas, three of which last upward of six hours apiece. Born in Germany in 1813, Wagner was destined to become one of the front-rank composers of the nineteenth century. He was largely self-taught, taking inspiration especially from Beethoven and Carl Maria von Weber, both of whom made important early contributions to the field of German opera. Wagner soon became a standard-bearer of German cultural nationalism. Many of his works are founded on German/Nordic mythology, and his music is inseparable from the extensive German libretti which he himself wrote. (Most other famous opera composers have relied on texts provided by others. For example the libretti of Mozart's *The Marriage of Figaro* and *Don Giovanni* were written by Lorenzo da Ponte.) Indeed, Wagner was so initmately involved in the Germanist movement that his music later became the rallying cry for the twentieth-century nationalistic drives which promulgated Germany into World Wars I and II. An avowed anti-Semite, it would appear that had Wagner lived in the 1920s and 1930s he would have espoused the Nazi crusade.* But we should not condemn Wagner too quickly, for he held many conflicting views and was in some respects a genuine humanist.

> The scene is the New School for Social Research. The speaker is Thomas Mann, noblest and greatest of anti-Hitler Germans. He is expounding his love and admiration not only for Wagner the musician but for Wagner the thinker. Mann is referring to Wagner's prose: "essays of astonishing intelligence." Flashback to Germany: Hitler's "favorite reading is the "political compositions of Richard Wagner."[1]

At one point early in his career, Wagner—the future proto-Nazi—even engaged in leftist agitation alongside the Russian anarchist, Mikhail Bakunin, and was subsequently exiled from Germany for helping foment the uprisings of 1848–1849.

Whatever the nature of Wagner's political and social views, he was one of the great musical geniuses of his time. He conceived operas of enormous magnitude, with music of previously unheard of difficulty, requiring great stamina and endurance from singers and instrumentalists alike.† Wagner also set new standards for staging, scenery, and lighting—in fact he lobbied successfully to have a new opera house constructed (in Bayreuth) to satisfy his theatrical requirements. (The Festspielhaus in Bayreuth is now a Wagner shrine. A festival of his music dramas is held there every summer.) Even Wagner's love life was impressive. After going through one wife and several mistresses, he made off with Liszt's daughter, Cosima, who was the wife of his colleague, the conductor Hans von Bülow. Late in life he fathered several children, naming two of them after his heroic operatic "offspring," Isolde and Siegfried.

If you enjoy tales from Greek mythology and/or Tolkien's *The Fellowship of the Ring*, you may well take pleasure in Wagner's interpretation of the Nordic epic, *The Ring of the Nibelung*. Wotan, king of the gods, is the northern equivalent of the Greek Zeus. He is married to the unamiable Fricka, but has often consorted with other females, both mortal and godly. The story of the *Ring* is extremely complex, but it hinges (in Wagner's version) on the structure of society and the sanctity of the family. George Bernard Shaw, a distinguished music critic before achieving stature as a playwright, wrote a monograph, *The Perfect Wagnerite*, interpreting the *Ring* cycle as a social manifesto.[2] An alternative interpretation of the *Ring's* social message has been proposed by the American essayist, Elmer Davis. He regards the story of Wotan as

---

*Adolf Hitler, a fervent admirer of Wagner's music, was introduced to his widow in 1923. For more on this subject, see Peter Viereck's *Metapolitics, The Roots of the Nazi Mind*, esp. Chapter VI, "Hitler and Wagner," New York, 1941, pp. 126–143.

†Not everyone could withstand the pressures of Wagnerian productions. The first heroic tenor lead in *Tristan und Isolde* caught cold at the premier and died shortly thereafter! And his wife, the first Isolde, suffered a nervous collapse and was for a time given to delusions. See Elliott Zuckerman, *The First Hundred Years of Tristan*, New York, 1964, pp. 57–60.

The Family

the greatest apologue ever written of the life of the Average Man . . . the man whose ambitions, by no means wholly unselfish, still aim at socially useful ends; who catches a vision of good things that he hopes to accomplish, and then finds himself in middle age impotent to accomplish them, paralysed by his innate shortcomings and by the ineluctable consequences of his own mistakes.[3]

Here is Davis's version of what happens in the first of the four music dramas, *Das Rheingold* (The Rhine Gold):

Wotan's troubles, like those of most young married men, began when he became a home owner. Up to that time he had apparently done pretty well; when we first see him he is the executive of a considerable organization, he has made some advantageous contracts, and he is successful enough to enlist the services of a smart lawyer, Loge, who can be depended on to find a loophole in any contract that may prove inconvenient. Wotan also has a wife, Fricka, whom he had wanted badly enough before he got her (or so he says) to have given his only remaining eye for her. (He had spent the other one for his education.)

Nevertheless, there are already signs of tension between husband and wife. "I like women too well to suit you," he confesses; but as yet other women are no problem in themselves; they are only the symptom of a restlessness in Wotan, an itch for variety, that Fricka cannot share. So, agreeing with Herbert Hoover that nobody ever sang "Home, Sweet Home" to a bundle of rent receipts, she has fallen in with Wotan's project of acquiring a suburban home, in the hope that her husband will be so proud of his establishment that he will stay at home in the evening. (Plenty of apartment wives will recognize her feelings.) So badly does she want the house that she is not much worried about the price; her husband is doing well in the world, he has assured her that they can afford it; with the self-confidence of a rising young executive he has left her out of the negotiations with the contractors—and now she and her husband suddenly discover that the new home will cost more than they can pay.

Wotan gets out of this difficulty more luckily than the average young man—thanks to his lawyer. Usually such talent as Loge's serves the title company; with his

In a scene from *Das Rheingold,* Loge and Wotan visit Alberich, who, boasting of his power, turns himself into a huge serpent. When Loge questions whether Alberich can also make himself small, Alberich becomes a toad and is captured.

Music and Society

professional skill backing up Fafner's brutal violence, the home owner goes into peonage for the rest of his life. But Wotan pays for his house only by letting himself in for something even more inconvenient than mortgages; he raises the money by the first unmistakably crooked deal of his life, behaving so badly that even his lawyer is ashamed of him. Wotan has overcome his moral scruples, Shaw points out, by working up a moral fervor over the misuse Alberich would have made of the money which Wotan intends to employ for worthy purposes; but presently he meets a woman (a widow with three children, older, more experienced, and wiser than his wife) who recalls him to reality. He has behaved badly because it seemed at the moment that it was the only way out; and thereby he has started a chain of consequences whose end is far beyond his seeing. Always after that he must worry, and be a little afraid.

For the moment Wotan has triumphed and triumphed very splendidly as the rainbow bridge leaps across the chasm, and the gods cross over it to Walhall on the distant heights. . . . What was once the music of the future is already, to a good many people, the music of the past; and it may be that no one can be deeply moved by it who did not get his emotional set before the nineteenth century went out. But there is an emotion that most men are lucky enough to experience at least once or twice in their lives, an emotion without which no man's life is complete: the feeling of now-at-last-I'm- beginning-to-get-somewhere. The sudden startling glimpse of a rainbow brilliance as some long-sought objective that has cost work and worry, anxiety and apprehension and self-denial and pain, is at last attained—the triumphal culmination of a long struggle, opening the way (so it seems in that exalted moment) to even greater triumphs beyond. These words are pitiably inadequate; no words that I have ever seen in print are adequate to describe this particular feeling. Once and only once, to my perhaps archaic taste, it has been expressed adequately—by the rainbow music at the end of *The Rhine Gold*. . . . Yet presently, interwoven with that music, you begin to hear other themes—reminders of what the triumph has cost, of the hidden forces, irrational and incalculable, that have been aroused. Wotan has done something wrong and he knows it; he keeps up his front, but precisely because he is a fairly decent god, as gods go, he never quite gets over it.

As *Das Rheingold* ends, the gods ignore the Rhinemaidens' cries for their lost gold and walk across the rainbow-bridge to Valhalla.

The Family

Nor is the stirring up of hatred, the unleashing of a curse, the only cost of Walhall; something irreparable has happened to Wotan's relation to his wife. Before this real-estate transaction she may have worried about his restlessness, but she respected him; he might be just a big grown-up boy in some ways, but nobody could deny his business ability. Now Fricka has to recognize that her husband made a fool of himself, that only Loge, whom she despises, saved the family from disaster. Moreover, a marital harmony that had survived ordinary stresses cracked wide open in a money crisis; husband and wife under pressure displayed unsuspected motivations, utterly irreconcilable standards of value; everything each of them did got on the other's nerves, they lost their tempers and blurted out unpleasant truths that can never be forgotten. The quarrel is over, they move into Walhall; but an indispensable illusion has been shattered, Fricka can no longer respect or trust her husband. . . . While Wotan, recalling how maddeningly his wife nagged him when he was worrying his head off about money, finds his thoughts going back to that widow he lately met, and her refreshingly realistic point of view. It could do no harm to look her up again—with no sentimental intentions, of course; his interest in Erda is purely intellectual. . . .

You can read in *The Rhine Gold*, says Shaw, the whole tragedy of human history; and you can also read in it such a tragi-comedy as is played out a dozen times a year in every commuting suburb. There stands the House, acquired at such a cost, and not in money alone; still it is a good house, and the young people have taken title and moved in, even though the mortgage hangs heavy over their heads; the quarrel that broke out during the negotiations with the title company has been made up, and now they are going to live happily ever after.

But nothing will ever be quite the same again.[4]

Davis goes on to interpret the remainder of the *Ring* cycle in terms of the compromises people make in their struggle to forge a society in which they can survive. We shall stop here, for, while *Das Rheingold* is the least familiar *Ring* opera, it is also the only relatively short one. (It consists of one long act comprised of four scenes. The first act of the second opera, *Die Walküre*, is discussed in Chapter 29.) Reading a synopsis of *Das Rheingold*, untempered by Davis's interpretation, you might well be induced to throw up your hands in despair at the crazy intermix of dwarves, mermaids, giants, and gods (including the familiar Donner, god of thunder). But assisted by Davis you can begin to comprehend the magnificent ramifications of Wagner's version of the *Ring* epic. It involves the nature of government, the quest for power among various segments of society—indeed the structure of the entire human universe.

Das Rheingold offers several musical highlights worthy of your attention. To begin with there is the long drawn-out prelude setting the mood for the first scene, which takes place at the Rhine River. This prelude is famous for prolonging a single E♭ major triad for 136 measures—a record for harmonic endurance!—as Wagner masterfully renders the flowing waters. In this scene three swimming mermaids are guarding a magical ring and an enormous treasure of gold. The second scene depicts the majesty of the gods in resplendent musical colors (Example 68). Here you may experience Wagner's superb writing for brass instruments, an aspect of instrumentation in which he pioneered. Scene 2 also introduces the brothers Fafner and Fasolt, giants who have constructed the new castle for the gods. Wagner portrays them with delightful humor. Later we encounter Loge, the crafty god of fire (Example 69).

Music and Society

Example 68
WAGNER, *The Ring of the Nibelung,* Castle *Leitmotif*

Example 69
Loge's *Leitmotif*

Feeling that traditional opera techniques did not do sufficient justice to the dramatic element, Wagner developed a novel treatment of opera structure; he even coined the term *music drama* to replace the older term *opera.* Wagner's new method involved the principle of the *Leitmotif:* each important character, concept, and object is assigned a specific musical motive which recurs whenever relevant. Thus, the *Leitmotif* signifying the castle of the gods (Example 68) appears often in *Das Rheingold,* as well as whenever reference is made to the castle in the other three *Ring* music dramas. It is especially prominent in the first act of *Die Walküre* and in the concluding scene of *Götterdämmerung (Twilight of the Gods).* Loge's motive (Example 69) is heard in the Magic Fire Music at the end of *Die Walküre* and again at the end of *Siegfried*—both times associated with a fire-encircled mountain. In *Siegfried,* one of the *Rheingold* giants kills his brother and then turns himself into a dragon in order better to defend the horde of gold which is now exclusively his. When the young hero Siegfried arrives at the dragon's lair, the orchestra plays the giants' earlier motive in mildly distorted form as counterpoint to Siegfried's high-spirited hunting-horn motive.*

*An illuminating and exhaustive guide to the Leitmotifs of the *Ring* cycle is provided in a three-record set, "An Introduction to *Der Ring des Nibelungen,*" performed by Georg Solti and the Vienna Philharmonic Orchestra, with spoken commentary by the English musicologist, Deryck Cooke. London Records RDN S-1.

The Family

Siegfried confronts Fafner, one
of the *Rheingold* giants, who has
turned himself into a dragon.

A graphic scene of stunning proportions is found in the Anvil Music of Scene 3. One recording of this passage utilizes no less than eighteen separate anvils (London Records, Georg Solti conducting). And, finally, in Scene 4, we hear the splendiforous Rainbow Music, as Donner gathers the mists about him and creates a rainbow bridge on which the happy gods cross the skies to enter the portal of their new castle. (Reread Davis's vivid account of this passage.) The Rainbow Music leads to a reprise of the castle motive (Example 68), while from the depths we hear once again the music of the now gold-deprived Rhinemaidens.

It is perhaps ironic that Wagner composed almost no purely instrumental music, for his music dramas can compete with any orchestral music ever written. Indeed, he was second to none in creating descriptive sketches for orchestra (e.g., the Magic Fire Music and Siegfried's Rhine Journey).* While other opera masters (Mozart, Verdi, Puccini) artfully used the orchestra to support the voice, Wagner often put the orchestra in the forefront, making the singers function mainly as a complement to the principal orchestral "action." This technique relates to the *Leitmotif* principle already discussed; the orchestra "tells" the story by introducing and reintroducing *Leitmotifs*. Wagnerian orchestral excerpts serve beautifully as a bridge into the strange and wonderful world of his music dramas. Any of the numerous available recordings are recommended as preparation for listening to the full-scale music dramas.

*Willa Cather based one of her finest short stories, *A Wagner Matinee*, on the experience of attending a concert of Wagner orchestral excerpts.

Music and Society

A Mozart opera alternates concerted musical numbers and declamatory passages of recitative or spoken mono/dialogue. Its musical numbers encompass solo arias, ensembles for two or more characters, and choruses. Each of these numbers is tantamount to a short movement of a sonata or symphony; that is, the musical content of a given number—its melody, rhythmic figures, orchestration, and so on—is essentially independent of the musical content of other numbers within the same opera. These numbers sometimes have the effect of halting the dramatic continuity, as one or more of the protagonists express their thoughts and feelings, with the action resuming only as the musical number concludes. On the other hand, some of the most beautiful music occurs in precisely those passages where there is the least dramatic content. This tension between musical and dramatic priorities underlies the controversy that was to arise in operatic circles after Mozart's death in 1791.

The Mozartian tradition was carried on most directly by Gioacchino Rossini (1792–1868), an Italian composer of primarily comic operas. (His *Barber of Seville* is based on the first play of Beaumarchais's *Figaro* trilogy—see Chapter 13.) Rossini undoubtedly possessed a remarkable flair for musical comedy, but his music lacks Mozart's substance and subtlety. Other early nineteenth-century opera composers, both in Italy and France, continued the Mozartian dichotomy between concerted numbers and spoken or sung declamatory passages. German opera, however, mainly in the hands of Wagner, moved in the direction of a continuous, less stylized flow. A Wagner music drama consists of an unending web of singing, much like a sung play. Wagner dropped recitatives accompanied merely by keyboard; the orchestra now performs throughout and is almost always of central importance. Most important, there are few separate arias or ensembles, so the music rarely interrupts the dramatic continuity. Lest the Wagnerian model appear superior to the Mozartian legacy, the matter is not

Italian composer Gioacchino Rossini (1792–1868). Photograph by Felix Nadar.

that simple. Both composers could create extraordinary musical/dramatic excitement on stage, yet each was capable of devising slow and dull dramatic passages as well. Mozart's arias sometimes intrude on the dramatic action, and Wagner's penchant for morose intellectual exchanges often results in static stretches of torturous dimensions.

The principal Italian opera composer of the Romantic period was Giuseppe Verdi. Verdi modified the Mozartian model by using fewer recitatives and accompanying these with orchestra. (The keyboard no longer figured in the nineteenth-century opera

Giuseppe Verdi (1813–1901). Photograph by Felix Nadar. Verdi and Wagner were born in the same year, but as opera composers they had exceedingly different methods for achieving dramatic intensity— Verdi relying on exquisite, lyrical melodies, Wagner on shifting harmonies and textures.

pit.) With one exception Verdi's operas are tragic melodramas. Although they contain concerted numbers, they also include extended scenes more in keeping with the Wagnerian principle of continuous music drama. Verdi and Wagner were born in the same year, 1813, but as composers they were exceedingly different. For one thing, Verdi preferred to base his operas on plays by Shakespeare (*Macbeth, Othello*), Victor Hugo (*Rigoletto*), and Dumas (*La Traviata*), whereas Wagner leaned toward primordial stories grounded in mythology (*The Ring of the Nibelung*) and medieval romance (*Tristan and Isolde, Lohengrin, The Mastersingers of Nürnberg*). Verdi, like Mozart, relied on the collaboration of librettists, whereas Wagner wrote his own texts, occasionally even publishing them apart from the music. Wagner developed the expressive technique and size of the orchestra, often allowing it overpowering volume; indeed, a special breed of "heroic" singer has arisen to cope with the enormous demands of the Wagnerian orchestra. Verdi always restrained the orchestra—it accompanied but never competed with the singers. And Verdi generally resisted the new *Leitmotif* technique introduced so effectively by Wagner (see the discussion of *Das Rheingold*), although it occasionally crept into his operas (as when the love themes from Acts I of *La Traviata* and *Otello* recur in the death scenes of those operas). Finally, the two composers differed greatly

Music and Society

in their approaches to vocal writing. Verdi maintained the old Italian tradition of *bel canto*, weaving long and beautiful melodic lines which fit the natural capabilities of the voice to perfection. Wagner broke with the bel canto tradition, composing vocal lines so demanding that only the bravest singers dare essay them.*

If Verdi differed so significantly from Wagner, he is also easily differentiated from Mozart. For instance, Verdi's concerted numbers ordinarily are longer and more complex than Mozart's (the latter's extended finales most distinctly excepted). Choral singing figures much more prominently in Verdi, and the whole singing style is changed, with Verdi calling for larger voices, accompanied by a larger orchestra than Mozart's. (Verdi represents something of a bridge between the styles of Mozart and Wagner.) Also, Verdi often gave his singers more sustained melodic lines than Mozart, although both were supreme with regard to melodic invention. On the other hand, Mozart's vocal style requires of singers a certain nimble finesse, unlike the vocal lines of Verdi and Wagner. Perhaps the most important characteristic of Mozart's operatic music is his delightful sense of musical humor. Little humor is to be found either in Verdi's or Wagner's theatrical works. Verdi's only Mozartian opera is his swan song, *Falstaff* (1893), the aging Italian's sole comedy. Like Verdi, Wagner also wrote only a single comic opera, *The Mastersingers of Nürnberg*, but this work is less Mozartian than *Falstaff*, due to Wagner's enormous orchestra, large chorus, three acts lasting more than an hour each, and a rather heavy-handed sense of humor. The work is lightweight only by comparison with Wagner's other music dramas.

The styles of Verdi and Wagner merge in the operas of Giacomo Puccini (1858–1924). An Italian, Puccini imitated Verdi's mellifluous vocal style but also wove the *Letimotif* into his orchestral fabric—most notably in *La Bohème* and *Tosca*. Wagner's most direct operatic descendant was the German composer Richard Strauss (1864–1949), especially in the stark music dramas *Elektra* and *Salome*. As much as he was a devotee of Wagner, Strauss also greatly loved Mozart, and composed a comedy in Mozartian vein, somewhat akin to *The Marriage of Figaro*, albeit with *Leitmotifs*. This opera, *Der Rosenkavalier* (*The Rose Bearer*), concerns the bumptious but highly pedigreed Baron Ochs, who wishes to marry "down" into a middle class but ever so *nouveau riche* businessman's family, and the resistance of the pert Sophie to allying herself with a male chauvinist oaf. Her father is determined to see the marriage materialize, since he lacks standing among the nobility (his ownership of twelve stately Viennese houses notwithstanding). In the end, true love bests veniality, and Ochs is sent packing without his bride.

During the middle of the nineteenth century a new form took root known as *operetta*, or light opera. Its ambience derived from the style of Mozart's German comic operas, *The Abduction from the Seraglio* and *The Magic Flute*. The spoken dialogue in these new works was full of jokes, and their plots were often nonsensical. Two famous examples are *Die Fledermaus* (*The Bat*), by the waltz king, Johann Strauss, Jr. (1825–

*When Wagner's *Lohengrin* was first performed in Italy (in the midnineteenth century), there was much anti-Wagner sentiment in that country. The elder statesman of Italian opera, Rossini, attended the performance, and afterward was mobbed by his younger fellow musicians wanting his opinion of the controversial new work. "I have learned," he stated sagely, "that it is unwise to judge a new and complex work after a single hearing." And then he added slyly, "And since I never intend to hear this work again, you will never learn what I think of it!"

The Family

1899, no relative of Richard Strauss), and *Orpheus in the Underworld,* by Jacques Offenbach (1819–1880). The latter is of special interest because it is based on a story used in the earliest operatic efforts, as well as in later reforms of opera (Chapter 13). In Offenbach's hands, the legend of Orpheus and Eurydice was transformed into a ridiculous spoof. Gluck's earnest chorus is now replaced by a petulant individual singer, Public Opinion, and Orpheus is a violinist, Director of the Conservatory of Music at Thebes (Greece). He and his wife Eurydice quarrel incessantly. She is sick unto death (*sic!*) of listening to him practice his new concerto, and anyway she is in love with Pluto, the God of the Underworld. (He visits Earth disguised as a shepherd.) Husband and wife unsuccessfully implore the gods to liberate them from each other, and Pluto finally decides that death is the only possible escape open to Eurydice (an appealing idea since Pluto resides in Hades himself.) The two illicit lovers yearn for (her) death, to which Orpheus is perfectly amenable, but Public Opinion steps in demanding that Orpheus rescue his wife from death's clutches. After all kinds of machinations, intrigue, and generalized hanky-panky involving Jupiter, Pluto, Cupid, Venus, and other gods, Orpheus reluctantly obeys Public Opinion and goes down to reclaim his wife. Pluto releases her, but only under the condition that Orpheus not look back at her until safely back home on Earth (one of the few parts of the spoof consistent with the legitimate version). Jupiter, who himself is attracted to Eurydice and prefers her to remain in Hades, tricks Orpheus into gazing at Eurydice; so in the end the two spouses live (die) happily torn asunder, with only Public Opinion disgruntled. The light-hearted spirit of the operetta is expressed in the rambunctious "Can-Can" for which the work is best known.

Example 70
OFFENBACH, *Orpheus in the Underworld,* "Can-Can"

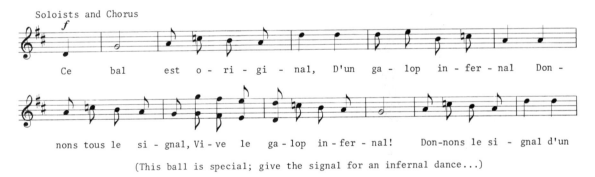

(This ball is special; give the signal for an infernal dance...)

Jacques Offenbach (1819–1880).
Photograph by Felix Nadar.

The new operetta composers quickly achieved popularity all over Europe: Strauss in Vienna, Offenbach in Paris, and (Gilbert and) Sullivan in England. By the end of the century the operetta genre had taken root in America as well, as represented by Victor Herbert (*Naughty Marietta, Babes in Toyland*), Rudolf Friml (*The Vagabond King*), and Sigmund Romberg (*The Student Prince*). Soon a new kind of operetta was born— the *Broadway musical*, with music veering ever further from the classical orientation of European nineteenth-century operettas. A new brand of singing actor developed, such as Al Jolson, Gertrude Lawrence, and Alfred Drake. With the rise of the great new moving picture industry, the Broadway musical became a vehicle for the Hollywood spectacular, with "casts of thousands."

163

The Family

America boasts a long and impressive line of light opera composers: Irving Berlin, George Gershwin, Cole Porter, Jerome Kern, Richard Rodgers, Kurt Weill, and Leonard Bernstein, to name only some of the most illustrious. Their best works—*Show Boat, Kiss Me Kate, Lady in the Dark, Porgy and Bess, Oklahoma!, Carousel, South Pacific,* and *West Side Story,* among others—are classics of the American stage. Still later newcomers to the Broadway musical theater are rock shows, such as *Hair, Tommy,* and *Jesus Christ Superstar.* Although their musical styles and song delivery are entirely pop oriented, they still retain the essential operatic format used by Mozart. *The Marriage of Figaro, Orpheus in the Underworld, H.M.S. Pinafore, South Pacific, Hair*—all share a common lineage, no matter how much they differ on the surface. Together they represent the best of the heritage of light opera.

The successful Broadway musical team of Richard Rodgers, composer (b. 1902), and Lorenz Hart, lyricist (1895–1943). Photograph by Nickolas Muray.

Music and Society

SOCIETY: REAL AND IDEAL

We have found light-hearted musical treatments of class conflict in Mozart's *The Marriage of Figaro* and Gilbert and Sullivan's *H.M.S. Pinafore* and an imaginative social allegory in Wagner's *Das Rheingold*—works originating in the eighteenth and nineteenth centuries. For a starker, more realistic interpretation of society's ills, we shall move now to the twentieth century. In this chapter we will encounter two of the most challenging achievements of the modern musical theater. The two works bear much in common: they were produced in the 1920s by composers steeped in the heritage of Classical/Romantic German music, and they each direct harsh attacks on society which are powerful both in dramatic thrust and musical expression. But there are also important differences. Kurt Weill's *The Threepenny Opera* exemplifies "people's music," as a kind of proletariat opera that blends the earnestness of grand opera, the realism of modern drama, and the compositional styles of popular music. Alban Berg's *Wozzeck* adheres more closely to the traditions of grand opera, but in a dissonant, atonal style. Taken together, these two works stand for the best the modern musical theater has to offer in depicting the evils of society.

The early nineteenth century was a period of great optimism. All over Europe, and in America too, people began to think they could control their destinies, improve their economic lot, and win political freedom. Unfortunately, there was a tendency, particularly in Europe, to entrust these hopes to a single, charismatic leader—Napoleon, Bismarck, Hitler. Beethoven was originally much taken by Napoleon, believing him capable of breaking down the old barriers to national independence and personal liberty. Later Beethoven lost faith in the French militarist, seeing in him simply another enslaver of the European peoples. Beethoven's social aspirations, and their expression in his music, are discussed in the concluding section of this chapter.

WEILL, THE THREEPENNY OPERA

The London season of 1728 witnessed the first performances of John Gay's new production, *The Beggar's Opera*. Combining spoken dialogue and sung ballads (some already known, others newly composed), the work displays the grimness of life among the indigent and the crime spawned in their midst. London audiences were shocked (and delighted) by the down-to-earth nature of *The Beggar's Opera*, a far cry from the overstylized historical romances of contemporary grand opera. In 1928 a variant of this work was produced by the German team of composer Kurt Weill and playwright Bertolt Brecht. *Die Dreigroschenoper* was a tremendous hit when it first came out and was equally successful in its American adaptation twenty-five years later. The lapse between the dates of the German and American premieres can be attributed to the Nazi takeover of Germany in the 1930s. Hitler suppressed *Die Dreigroschenoper*, due in

Contemporary engraving (1728) of *The Beggar's Opera*. Macheath with Lucy and Polly.

equal measure to Weill's Jewish background and Brecht's Communist sympathies. What with the exigencies of World War II on both sides of the Atlantic, the work was temporarily forgotten. Meanwhile, Weill made a name for himself on Broadway (see Chapter 10), so it was just a matter of time until the show would be revived in an American version. Weill died in 1950, missing by a couple of years the triumphant rebirth of *Die Dreigroschenoper* as *The Threepenny Opera*. (The transformation was accomplished by Marc Blitzstein, himself the composer of the socialist-oriented *The Cradle Will Rock*.) *Threepenny* opened at the Theatre de Lys in New York's Greenwich Village in 1954. Despite its foreign origin the show became an instant American classic, with the New York production alone running for several years. Recordings of the work both in German and English (some featuring the composer's widow, Lotte Lenya) remain continuously available in record stores.

Music and Society

When Weill and Brecht first met in Berlin during the mid-1920s, they were already established as "serious" contributors to their respective fields. But each of them also had an itch to communicate more directly to a larger audience.

> Both men had achieved a certain fame in intellectual circles but were anxious to escape from the limited, ivory tower atmosphere in which they felt trapped. . . . What they hoped . . . to achieve was a new form of popular musical theatre, a *Zeitoper,* that would reveal the true spirit of the times in which they lived.[1]

How should the times in which Weill and Brecht lived be described? For one thing, there was a wonderful sense of hopefulness, as post–World War I Germany struggled to establish a democratic society. On the other hand, the German ego had been seriously wounded as a result of losing the war. Incredible poverty and inflation (like nothing we know today) and the fear of communism following the Russian Revolution of 1917 ultimately overcame the spirit of hope, and engendered the rise of the Nazi party, with its racist philosophy of Aryan supremacy and anti-Semitism, and its destruction of democratic ideals. The Broadway show and film, *Cabaret* (based on Christopher Isherwood's *Berlin Stories*), gives a good sense of the desperation in Germany at the time *Die Dreigroschenoper* was conceived.

The Threepenny Opera is outstanding both as drama and as music, a cut above the average Broadway musical, but not quite an opera either. Weill's music—all freshly composed with the exception of Mr. Peachum's "Morning Hymn"—reaches the artistic level of the best theater music of Gershwin and Bernstein, but its style is unique. Weill and Brecht succeeded in revealing the social horrors of urban London (updated to the nineteenth century)—something like the scenes Dickens brought to light in the novel *Oliver Twist.* Weill's catchy tunes are meant to be sung by actors, not trained singers, and the orchestral backup is supplied by a small jazz combo. In this way Weill hoped to rid the work of the elitist tinge of grand opera.

The show opens as the narrator sings "Mac the Knife." This hit song tells of murder and mayhem. For Mac, stealing and violence are the only way to survive.

Example 71
WEILL, *The Threepenny Opera,* "Mac The Knife"

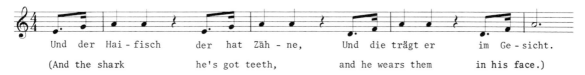

Und der Hai - fisch   der hat Zäh - ne,   Und die trägt er   im Ge - sicht.
(And the shark   he's got teeth,   and he wears them   in his face.)

The show is saturated in cynicism. When beautiful young Polly tells her parents, Mr. and Mrs. Peachum, that she loves Macheath, they vent their annoyance by disparaging young people and their notions of love. (The Peachums, like Dickens's Fagin, run an establishment for fake beggars and thieves.) When a bunch of thugs needs entertainment, they sing, "Let's go barmy and join the army" and envision seeing the world and cutting down the civilian population at will. Mac's close friend is Tiger Brown,

Society: Real and Ideal

Georg Grosz's drawing illustrates the brutality and bitterness of poverty underlying Weill's *Threepenny Opera*. The drawing is ironically captioned with a line from Rilke: "Poverty is a great glow from within."

chief of police, who always tips Mac off before staging a raid. This means that, while Mac is on the "most wanted" list, he never fears being caught. One of Mac's former girl friends is Jenny, a down-and-out whore who fantasizes gaining absolute power and wiping out all her enemies ("Pirate Jenny"). The Peachums, who do not appreciate their son-in-law, eventually "corrupt" Tiger Brown into turning on his friend, and Mac is subsequently jailed and sentenced to be hanged. All ends well, however, for at the last minute Queen Victoria grants Mac a reprieve, assigns him an annuity of ten thousand pounds a year, and raises him to the peerage. Who says crime doesn't pay?

Music and Society

The *Threepenny Opera* is a forum for lower-class realism. To appreciate fully its musical/dramatic impact, you should see the work, or at least read the spoken script in addition to hearing the music. The music alone will give you a good sense of the work's ambience, but it behooves you to read the play as well. Listen to the first few songs several times—until you get a feeling for the unique flavor of Weill's musical style—and then proceed through the rest of the show. You should expect to find the music challenging and enjoyable in equal measure.

BERG, WOZZECK

Kurt Weill was raised under the star of the "classical" school of Mahler, Strauss, and early Schoenberg, but he achieved his greatest successes in the field of popular music. By contrast, Alban Berg (1885–1935) functioned exclusively in the realm of serious music. As a youth Berg's interest in music was intense, but he began formal music study only at the age of nineteen. His sole teacher was the controversial Arnold Schoenberg, who was soon to achieve notoriety for his pioneering experiments in atonal composition.* (Berg wept when his mother suggested he leave Schoenberg's tutelage for a traditional conservatory education.) Schoenberg was a thorough and inspiring pedagogue, but life for the master and his handful of devoted pupils was not easy in musically conservative Vienna.

> To belong to this circle was tantamount to belonging to a small army of revolutionaries who, under their leader, were besieged on all sides and against whom the most violent attacks were constantly launched by the Establishment.[2]

Nevertheless, despite the modernity of his own compositional style, Berg was destined to attain fame and even some degree of fortune. Indeed, his opera *Wozzeck* (1925) initially won a greater following than any of his teacher's music.

Berg based *Wozzeck* on an extraordinary drama written roughly one hundred years earlier by the German intellectual and revolutionary, Georg Büchner (1813–1837). The plot concerns a poor, half-demented soldier, Wozzeck, who is controlled by a sadistic captain, himself of dubious sanity. Berg rearranged the drama into three acts and fifteen scenes, with musical interludes covering many of the scene changes. A fascinating insight into the genesis of the opera is provided by Hans W. Heinsheimer in his memoirs of life in Vienna during World War I.

> *Wozzeck* had been almost ten years in the making. The spark that ignited the fire was struck in May 1914 when Berg attended several performances of Georg Büchner's fragmentary drama *Woyzek* at a Viennese theater and decided to use the play for an opera. A few months later, war broke out. Berg was drafted. Work had to stop, but *Wozzeck* was now forever with him. When one of his pupils visited him in the barracks, he spoke long before the chorus of the sleeping soldiers in *Wozzeck* was written, about his sleepless, tormented nights. "Did you ever hear many people

---

Atonality refers to music which is not centered in a key. (The concept of *key* is explained in Chapter 9.) Schoenberg eventually founded the method of composition known as the *twelve-tone system*—see Chapter 22.)

Society: Real and Ideal

snore at the same time?" he asked. "This polyphonic breathing, rattle, and moaning is the most original chorus I've ever heard. It is like music of primeval sounds emerging from the abyss of the souls."

The whole aspect of the army and the people he encountered—doctors, drum majors, captains, and many poor downtrodden Wozzecks—drove him closer and closer to identifying himself with the soldier in Büchner's play and his futile struggle against the powers of eternal, universal brass. His delicate health kept him from service at the front, but life in the barracks, the monotony of, to him, senseless training and watch duties, the treatment he received from the noncoms who ordered him around, made army existence a physical and mental torture. What a strange, mysteriously fitting atmosphere for a sensitive artist who had chosen his subject before he had experienced wozzeckian army torments himself.[3]

In dramatic content, *Wozzeck* matches the stark realism of *The Threepenny Opera*, but, in contrast to Weill, Berg's atonal compositional style can hardly be described as "popular." Indeed, when you first listen to this music you may find yourself unwilling to tolerate its dissonance. Of course, there is much dissonance in the music of earlier tonal composers, but most of it is promptly resolved; the dissonance is controlled within a consonant framework. In Berg's music, however, the dissonance tends to be left unresolved: one clashing chord follows another, unsoftened by intervening consonances. Against this strikingly dissonant style the German text sounds especially harsh and guttural. But Berg's music is not as difficult as it may at first seem. Once you have crossed the barrier of unfamiliarity you should find it as accessible as the music of Berg's contemporaries, Richard Strauss and Claude Debussy. The effort is worth the making, for *Wozzeck* is one of the finest music dramas of the twentieth century.

The opening of Scene 1 is dominated by the Captain's idiotic ravings, sung in a high, effeminate-sounding tenor voice. He ridicules Wozzeck's ignorance and immorality, playing hard on the fact that Wozzeck lives with his woman Marie "without the blessing of the church." Wozzeck at first says little, restricting himself to wooden monosyllabic replies. Gradually, however, he becomes more outspoken, eventually achieving a righteous vocal eloquence as he quotes Jesus in support of the downtrodden: "Suffer the little children to come unto me." The music may seem to lack melody, but with repeated listening you will be able to detect distinct musical themes that function like the *Leitmotifs* of Wagner's operas. (See the discussion of *Das Rheingold* in Chapter 14.) One of the principal motives is heard as Wozzeck agonizingly cries out: "Wir arme Leute!" ("We poor people!")

Example 72
BERG, *Wozzeck*, Act 1, Scene 1

Wozzeck *f*

Wir ar - me Leut!   Sehn Sie,   Herr Hauptmann, Geld, Geld!   Wer kein   Geld hat!
(We poor people!   You see, Captain,   it's money, money! Those who have no money..)

Strings
molto f

Alban Berg (1885–1935) at the age of 24. In dramatic content, *Wozzeck* matches the stark realism of *The Threepenny Opera*, but Berg's compositional style is atonal and can hardly be described as "popular."

171

Society: Real and Ideal

Wozzeck continues:

You see, Herr Captain, it's money, money! Oh, the one who has no money! Just let one of us try to bring one of his own kind into the world in a moral way! One's made of flesh and blood! Oh, if I were a fine gentleman, and had a proper hat and watch and a monocle and could talk gentleman-like, then I'd be virtuous allright!

The music now becomes extraordinarily gentle, as a solo violin plays Example 72 in a high register, and Wozzeck says, "It must be wonderful to be virtuous, Herr Captain." Quickly the musical mood reverts to the earlier severity, and Wozzeck grimly sings, "But I am just a poor fellow. For people like us nothing is blessed either in this world or the next." The orchestral sound throbs threateningly and Wozzeck goes on, "I bet that if *we* got into heaven we would make some thunder!" The Captain does not quite know what to make of this outburst and tries to pacify Wozzeck: "I know, you are a good fellow, a worthy person. But you think too much. . . ."

The "arme Leute" motive is heard again during the orchestral interlude which follows this first scene. (It is also one of the motives heard in the final orchestral interlude of Act III, just preceding Scene 15—following Wozzeck's suicide by drowning. Here Berg recapitulates several of the opera's main themes, expressing in all their painful dissonance the miserable condition of downtrod humankind. The music is more tonal than atonal—heavy, lyrical, minor—and bears some resemblance to Part I of Ives' *Washington's Birthday* —see Chapter 8.)

Melodies of a more traditional kind are heard in the next two scenes of Act I. In Scene 2 Wozzeck is out on patrol with another soldier, Andres. Wozzeck becomes agitated by the blood red of the setting sun, and Andres tries to calm him by singing a folk song. In Scene 3 we meet Wozzeck's common-law wife, Marie. To the accompaniment of a conventional marching tune, Marie and her young son marvel at the handsome Drum Major, parading beneath their window. Marie expresses herself in a blending of singing and speech known as *Sprechstimme*. Then she gently sings the child asleep with a traditional German lullaby. But the peaceful scene is disturbed as Wozzeck enters, still bewitched by the blood-red sky. The scene ends as he leaves to return to duty, and Marie comments: "That man! So distracted! He didn't even notice his child."

In *Wozzeck* Berg attempted to depict the pain and realism of life among the impoverished. There is nothing "pretty" either in the life of its protagonists or in the music itself. But "pretty" and "beautiful" are not synonymous, and the harsh realities of *Wozzeck* offer a welcome contrast to the easier and prettier styles of earlier periods. Allow yourself to develop a sensitivity to Berg's music—it will add another dimension to your overall musical experience.

BEETHOVEN, EROICA SYMPHONY

Perhaps the greatest novel ever written relates one of the grandest social and military adventures of modern times, Napoleon's unsuccessful attempt to conquer the European continent. The novel is *War and Peace* by the Russian social philosopher, Leo Tolstoy (1828–1910). Prokofiev composed a huge opera based on this book, but the musical work which perhaps most closely matches its spirit and scope is a non-stage work composed some fifty years before Tolstoy's masterpiece appeared in print: Beethoven's *Symphony No. 3 in Eb Major*, Op. 55.

172

Beethoven held great hopes for improvement of the social condition of the European peoples and at first believed that Napoleon would elevate the common people by establishing truly democratic governments to replace the old aristocratic systems prevailing throughout Europe. The title page of the *Eroica Symphony* was initially inscribed by Beethoven, "Sinfonia grande: Buonaparte." But, when Napoleon proclaimed himself emperor, Beethoven angrily crossed out the inscription and wrote instead, "Sinfonia eroica composta per festeggiar il sovvenire s'un gran huomo" ("Heroic symphony composed to celebrate the memory of a great man"). Since that time, the *Eroica*—itself a revolutionary work in a purely musical sense—has become associated with the pursuit of freedom through the overturning of old orders. For many the *Eroica* represents one of the pinnacles of music history. H. L. Mencken, the social critic and author of the authoritative *The American Language,* was also (like George Bernard Shaw) a talented music critic. Here are some of his comments on the *Eroica*:

> Surely the nineteenth century was not deficient in master musicians. It produced Schubert, Schumann, Chopin, Wagner, and Brahms, to say nothing of a whole horde of Dvořáks, Tchaikovskys, Debussys, Verdis, and Puccinis. Yet it gave us nothing better than the first movement of the *Eroica*. That movement, the first challenge of the new music, remains its last word. It is the noblest piece of absolute music ever written in the sonata form, and it is the noblest piece of program music. In Beethoven, indeed, the distinction between the two became purely imaginary. Everything he wrote was, in a way, program music, including even the first two symphonies, and everything was absolute music. . . .

H. L. Mencken. Like Shaw, Mencken was not only an important social critic and literateur, but also started out as a music critic.

> The older I grow, the more I am convinced that the most portentous phenomenon in the whole history of music was the first public performance of the *Eroica* on April 7, 1805. The manufacturers of program notes have swathed that gigantic work in so many layers of banal legend and speculation that its intrinsic merits have been almost forgotten. Was it dedicated to Napoleon I? If so, was the dedication sincere or ironical? Who cares—that is, who with ears? It might have been dedicated, just as

Society: Real and Ideal

well, to Louis XIV, Paracelsus, or Pontius Pilate. What makes it worth discussing, to-day and forever, is the fact that on its very first page Beethoven threw his hat into the ring and laid claim to immortality. Bang!—and he is off. No compromise! No easy bridge from the past! The *Second Symphony* is already miles behind. A new order of music has been born. The very manner of it is full of challenge. There is no sneaking into the foul business by way of a melifluous and disarming introduction; no preparatory hemming and hawing to cajole the audience and enable the conductor to find his place in the score. Nay! Out of silence comes the angry crash of the tonic triad, and then at once, with no pause, the first statement of the first subject—grim, domineering, harsh, raucous, and yet curiously lovely—with its astounding collision with that electrical C sharp. The carnage has begun early; we are only in the seventh measure. In the thirteenth and fourteenth comes the incomparable roll down the simple scale of E flat—and what follows is all that has ever been said, perhaps all that *will* be said, about music-making in the grand manner. What was afterwards done, even by Beethoven, was done in the light of that perfect example. Every line of modern music that is honestly music bears some sort of relation to that epoch-making first movement. . . .

It must have been a great night in Vienna. . . . They went to hear "a new grand symphony." . . . What they found in the Theater-an-der-Wien was a revolution.[4]

One must listen to the entire first movement to gain an appreciation of the special place the *Eroica* holds in the hearts of music lovers. The movement breaks down into the customary four parts—*exposition* (repeated), *development, recapitulation,* and *coda.* (For a review of these terms, see the discussion of sonata form in Chapter 12.) Beethoven widened the scope of the exposition by including an astonishing variety of melodic ideas—no less than six independent themes. The development section is extremely long by the standards of the Classical period. After in-depth exploration of three of the exposition themes, a thrillingly dissonant chord progression leads into one of the more revolutionary musical aspects of the *Eroica*, a brand-new theme introduced *after* the completion of the exposition section. Another remarkable passage occurs just at the end of the development section: After reaching a fortissimo highpoint, the music turns mysteriously quiet, with the violins alternating between trembling bows (*tremolo*) and plucked strings (*pizzicato*). When the music has reached its softest point, the French horn starts to play the long-awaited return of the first theme, as if to commence the recapitulation. But strangely the violins lag behind, playing the "wrong" chord. Suddenly the full orchestra enters on the same chord as the violins, covering up what in retrospect seems to have been a "blooper" by the horn. Only now does the recapitulation begin in earnest. This passage represents one of the most exciting moments in the orchestral literature.

Music and Society

Example 73

BEETHOVEN, *Eroica Symphony*, 1st Mvt., End of Development Section

Society: Real and Ideal

According to the traditional formulation of sonata form the recapitulation supposedly restates the themes of the exposition, one after the other. But almost from the outset the *Eroica's* recapitulation deviates from the exposition. For no sooner does the main theme encounter what Mencken described as "its astounding collision with that electrical C sharp" than the C sharp functions surprisingly as a D flat, and the music courses off into another key.*

Example 74
Comparison of Beethoven's Treatment of the "Electrical" C♯s in the First Movement of the *Eroica Symphony:*

(In the exposition, the bass C♯ moves to D; in the recapitulation, it moves to C♮.)

All in all, the differences between the first parts of the exposition and recapitulation exceed those of virtually every other corresponding pair of sonata-form sections in the Classical repertoire. After this, however, things settle down to normal, and the next surprises do not occur until the coda. This final section attains more than half the length of the already lengthy development section and really counts as a second development—that is, as another review of the great variety of musical material presented in the exposition and recapitulation. It includes the theme first introduced in the development, as well as one of the exposition themes not treated in the development proper.

We are now in a position to differentiate two works in the same genre by the

*C♯ and D♭ are equivalent names for the same note—as explained in Chapter 9. A composer ordinarily selects a note name according to the general direction of the musical motion and in particular the key currently in use. The C♯ of measure 7 of the exposition simply ornaments the note D, itself a member of the E♭ major scale; at the corresponding point in the recapitulation—measure 402—Beethoven moves away from C♯ as if it were D♭ leading to C♮ and on to the key of F major (See Example 74).

Music and Society

same composer: Beethoven's *Eroica* and *Pastoral* symphonies (see Chapter 1 for the *Pastoral*). Both are true representatives of the Classical period, yet are also vastly different in character. The *Pastoral* seems almost casual compared to the intensive energy of the *Eroica*. Moreover, the individual *Eroica* movements last longer than the corresponding *Pastoral* movements. The second movement of the Eroica is a huge, square-cut funeral march, whereas the second movement of the *Pastoral* is the easy-going and conversational "Scene at the Brook." The *Eroica*'s Scherzo packs a much harder punch than the Pastoral's Peasant Dance, and the enormous creative vitality of the *Eroica* finale—a mixture of several different forms—makes the *Pastoral* finale seem tame by comparison. (This is not to suggest in any sense that the *Eroica* is better than *Pastoral*, but merely to emphasize the distinct individuality of the two works.)

Given its title, is the *Eroica* a genuine program symphony? Certainly not, if compared with later works like the *Pastoral*, Berlioz's *Harold in Italy* (Chapter 11) and *Symphonie fantastique* (Chapter 28), and Liszt's *Faust Symphony*. In any case, only the first two *Eroica* movements are thought to pertain to Napoleon. If only half of the *Eroica* is a "Napoleon Symphony," then what of the last two movements, the scherzo and the finale? The main theme of the finale is one that Beethoven had previously used in a set of piano variations and in his ballet, *The Creatures of Prometheus*. Was there in Beethoven's mind a connection between Napoleon, the great military leader, and Prometheus, the mythological Greek god who stole fire from Mount Olympus to give to humankind? For the answer to this question let us turn to Anthony Burgess, erstwhile composer as well as author of several successful novels (including the source of Stanley Kubrick's controversial film, *A Clockwork Orange*). Burgess has written a book entitled *Napoleon Symphony, A Novel in Four Movements*.[5] The dust jacket bills the book as "An hEROICAl novel, a grand and loving tragi-comic symphony to Napoleon Bonaparte, by Burgess out of Ludwig van, that unteases and reweaves Napoleon's life into a pattern borrowed—in liberty, equality, fraternity—from Beethoven." Beethoven himself does not figure in the novel, but at the end of the book the author offers an *Epistle to the Reader*, composed somewhat in the style of the late verse humorist, Ogden Nash. Here Burgess suggests (among other things) a solution to the riddle of the *Eroica Symphony* and its purported programmatic content. Let these be the last words on the subject:

> The first two movements of the Eroica,
> Although (but need I tell you this?) they are
> Organized sound, no more, to awe the ear,
> Yet do suggest some hero's brief career.
> The Allegro: see him live and vigorous,
> Striding the earth, stern but magnanimous,
> In love with order, his regretful strife
> Devoted to the ennobling of our life.
> The *Marcia Funebre*: already dead,
> The ironic laurels wilting round his head,
> He's borne to burial; we weep, we hear
> The purple orators about his bier—
> That character, how noble; and how great
> Those exploits in the service of the State.

Society: Real and Ideal

He rests in peace beneath this hallowed shroud,
Quite dead, and resurrection's not allowed.
But stay—there are two movements still to run:
The subject's buried; what's then to be done?
The *Scherzo*—how? The brisk *Finale*—who?
Beethoven smiles: "What I propose to do
Is to invoke another noble creature,
No child of Nature, but of Supernature.
The vague historical—that's finished with;
Now the particularity of myth."
What myth? What hero? Aaaaah—Prometheus.
Beethoven makes it fiery-clear to us
In his *Finale* who the hero is.
He takes a bass and then a theme from his
Own ballet music on Prometheus, then
Builds variations till the count of ten.
The *Scherzo*—is it fancy that hears roar
The flames which from the gods the hero tore
To bring to man? Those horns—what are they doing?
The hunt is up, it is the gods pursuing.
In Plutarch's *Lives* the heroes go in pairs—
One fabulous and one historic. There's
The origin, one thinks, of this device:
The heroic is displayed not once but twice.[6]

MUSIC AND CHILDREN

The world of literature abounds in classics written for and about children: A. A. Milne's *Winnie the Pooh,* Lewis Carroll's *Alice's Adventures in Wonderland*, Antoine de St. Exupery's *The Little Prince*, James Barrie's *Peter Pan*, and so on. Books of this sort appeal also to adults; the simplicity and directness of the stories are a joy to all. Correspondingly, a considerable musical repertoire exists for the purpose of entertaining and enlightening young audiences. This repertoire provides an excellent escape from the concerns of the adult world; children's music is always easy to listen to and usually charming and engaging as well. So, despite your having long since outgrown childhood, you are invited to sit back and relax among the pleasantries of this special musical world. You will encounter works by Saint-Saëns, Britten, Debussy, and Orff. One of the featured works, Britten's *The Young Person's Guide to the Orchestra*, culminates in a *fugue,* a musical form which has been popular since the beginning of the Baroque period. Chapter 16 concludes with an essay surveying the essential features of fugal composition.

SAINT-SAËNS, CARNIVAL OF THE ANIMALS

Camille Sainte-Saëns (1835–1921) was a potent force in French musical life during the second half of the nineteenth century. During the Impressionist period starting at the turn of the century, however, Saint-Saëns represented a conservative influence, finding himself unable to participate in the "radical" new trends initiated by Debussy and Ravel. Today few of Saint-Saëns's compositions are played widely outside of France, but a notable exception is the perennial children's favorite, *Carnival of the Animals.* Like *Alice in Wonderland*, this work is aimed at children, yet beguiles adults. It is a collection of fourteen separate pieces picturing a wide spectrum of animal life—mostly your ordinary zoo animals, such as elephants, turtles, birds, and lions. However, one of the pieces depicts an animal found only in a musical zoo—the pianist! And indeed, two pianos are included in the rather limited orchestra for which Saint-Saëns scored the work; strings, flute, clarinet, and glockenspiel are the other instruments. *Carnival of the Animals* is primarily a spoof, unlike musical bestiaries by Ravel, Poulenc, Stravinsky and others, which are humorous in many cases, but not spoofs (see Chapters 4 and 5). As you listen to it, you will hear a number of borrowed tunes, such as "Twinkle, Twinkle, Little Star" and the "Can-Can" from Offenbach's *Orpheus in the Underworld* (itself a spoof—see Chapter 14, Example 70). The *Carnival* is a kind of *suite,* a collection of independent and for the most part unconnected short pieces. Its best known section is "The Swan," a cello solo accompanied by two pianos which has become a vehicle for ballerinas. The immaculate music is quite in keeping with the graceful character of

French composer and organist, Camille Saint-Saëns (1835–1921). Photograph by Felix Nadar.

a swan. (You may want to compare Saint-Saëns' "Swan" with Ravel's lovely song about a swan in *Histoires naturelles* — see Chapter 4.)

The graceful lines of "The Swan" are not typical of the musical portraiture one encounters in the *Carnival*. Instead, raucous good humor is the prevailing characteristic. For example, "Turtles" includes the brilliant "Can-Can" mentioned above, but now with the rushed tempo of the original replaced by slow lugubrious notes representing the dignified gait of the turtle. At one point the hee-hawing of donkeys is suggested by string *glissandi* and *harmonics* — the former a sliding of the finger up and down the fingerboard, the latter thin high notes produced by just barely touching certain "nodes" which divide a string in halves, thirds, fourths, and so on. You will recognize the familiar cuckoo, as the clarinet imitates the ending of the second movement of Beethoven's *Pastoral Symphony* (see Chapter 5). The jumpiness of the kangaroo is suggested by *grace notes* — extremely short notes which immediately precede "regular" notes. (For an illustration of grace notes, see Example 6 in Chapter 4, above.) The section entitled "Fossils" is especially amusing in that it contains a potpourri of familiar tunes (fossils themselves): several French folk songs, a brief excerpt from Rossini's comic opera, *The Barber of Seville,* and even the main theme from Saint-Saëns's own *Danse macabre,* now played on the glockenspiel and recurring as a refrain throughout this section.

Some years ago, Ogden Nash, the late American poet-humorist, wrote a set of verses to be recited as an introduction to each section of *Carnival of the Animals.*

Nash's poems can be heard on some, but not all, recordings of the work. In one of the poems he alleges that Saint-Saëns chose to portray animals as opposed to people because of his annoyance with the human race for mispronouncing his name. According to Nash, the composer suffered *pains* when people pronounced his name "Saint-*Sains*."*

The final section of the work brings back some of the themes heard earlier, thereby suggesting a menagerie of all the animals. Nash introduces this part by rhyming "Animale carnivale" with "Grand finale" (sound the final e!).

BRITTEN, THE YOUNG PERSON'S GUIDE TO THE ORCHESTRA

In contrast to the spoofing nature of Saint-Saëns's *Carnival,* Benjamin Britten's *Young Person's Guide* is a serious pedagogical tool for introducing the various instruments of the modern orchestra. At his death in 1976 Britten was the ranking British composer, having achieved success in many genres, including opera (*Peter Grimes, Death in Venice*), solo vocal music, liturgical music, and various works for large and small orchestral ensembles. Britten based his *Young Person's Guide* on a well-known theme of his musical ancestor, Henry Purcell, the leading English composer of the late seventeenth century.

Example 75

BRITTEN, *A Young Person's Guide to the Orchestra*, Theme (by Henry Purcell)

Britten first uses this theme to introduce each of the four families of the orchestra (strings, winds, brass, and percussion) and then proceeds with a variation for each instrument, starting with the flute. A narrator provides information about each instrument just prior to its variation. Purcell's theme opens with an *arpeggio* (four notes, a linear statement of the tonic triad) which is easily recognized in a few of the variations, for example, the one for oboe:

*Certainly the student first encountering classical music may find pronouncing composers' and performers' names painfully difficult. In French final consonants are silent, but there are important exceptions, such as the final *z* of Berlioz and the final *s* of Saint-Saëns. On the other hand, you should say something like "Sahwnz," as opposed to "Saynes." The intricacies of composers' names can be considerable, especially when more than one pronunciation is acceptable. Americans stress the first syllable of Berlioz, but the French accent the last syllable, dividing the full name into two, rather than three, syllables (Ber-lyoz). Americans and French both emphasize the first syllable of "Debussy," but the resemblance ends there, especially in regard to the *u*. German is no less problematical: In "Mozart" the *z* sounds like our *ts,* and in "Wagner" the *w* is equivalent to our *v.* Sometimes we have no problem pronouncing a name we have often heard, but then we misspell it. Among the most frequent mistakes are adding an *e* in "Haydn" and leaving out the *h* in "Beethoven."

Music and Children

Example 76
A Young Person's Guide, Oboe Variation

But for the most part the Purcell theme is hard to detect, and the effect is more that of a suite than a typical set of variations. (For an explanation of traditional variation form, see Chapter 18.)

The *Young Person's Guide* ends with a fugue in which the various instruments play the subject in the same order wherein they previously appeared. (An essay on fugue is found later in this chapter.) The fugue subject is very fast, with Purcell's original theme all but obliterated.

Example 77
A Young Persons's Guide, Fugue Subject

Just before the fugue begins, the narrator announces that at its conclusion the entire orchestra will join together to play Purcell's majestic theme. But, if you listen closely, you will hear it played in a quick "sneak" entrance by the winds (combined with the fugue subject in the strings) just before the brass commence the full-blown Purcell theme in its original slow tempo. Much of this finale recalls the music of the Russian, Sergei Prokofiev (1891–1953). Britten may have intended this resemblance as homage to the creator of the ever-popular children's piece, *Peter and the Wolf*. Britten's fugue also suggests the first movement of Prokofiev's charming *Classical Symphony*.

Claude Debussy (1862–1918).
Photograph by Felix Nadar.

DEBUSSY, CHILDREN'S CORNER

In one of the funniest parts of *Carnival of the Animals*, entitled "Pianists," we hear some of the familiar five-finger exercises that budding piano majors seem to practice so much of the time. Claude Debussy designed a similar spoof in "Dr. Gradus ad Parnassum," the first section of his piano suite, *Children's Corner*. Debussy drew the title from a time-worn collection of keyboard exercises ("Dr." was his own idea); it means something like "graded ascent to perfection." Debussy's "Gradus" is a lovely piece, quite aside from its effectiveness as a pianist's practice piece, for despite the fast finger work it embodies a lyrical warmth quite uncharacteristic of exercises of this sort. The entire suite, which Debussy composed for the entertainment of his young daughter Emma, contains five other charming pieces: "Jimbo's Lullaby," "Serenade for the Doll," "Snow Is Dancing," "The Little Shepherd," and "Golliwogg's Cake-Walk."

The last adroitly spoofs the famous opening passage of Wagner's music drama, *Tristan und Isolde*. Debussy grew up during a period of fanatical worship of Wagner, whom his adherents regarded as a revolutionary musical messiah. Debussy's earliest compositions, especially his songs, give ample evidence of Wagner's influence, but Debussy soon moved out in his own direction, independent of the post-Wagnerian impulses of his contemporaries Mahler, Schoenberg, and Richard Strauss. Ironically it is Debussy whom music historians and critics now perceive as the first genuinely modern composer; it is on his shoulders (rather than on Wagner's) that the mantle of musical revolutionary properly belongs. Nearly a century after his death Wagner's music no longer seems radical, any more than the music of his putative archrival, Brahms (see Chapter 19, "A Musical Controversy"). Both composers represent the culmination of the traditional tonal styles and procedures of Romanticism. Debussy retained elements of tonality but also created new tone combinations very much unlike any music of the past.

"Golliwogg's Cake-Walk" demonstrates that Debussy was not above twitting the fervent Wagnerians in his midst. Compare the sensuous opening of the Prelude to *Tristan und Isolde* with Debussy's jocular treatment thereof in "Golliwogg":

Example 78a
WAGNER, *Tristan und Isolde*, Prelude (Opening)

Example 78b
DEBUSSY, "Golliwogg's Cake-Walk," *Tristan* Spoof

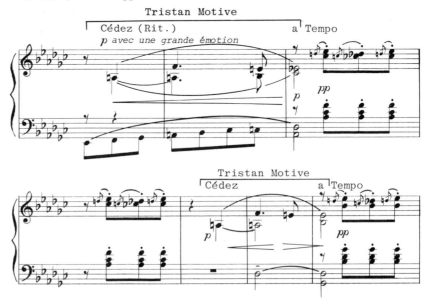

Music and Society

Carl Orff, a contemporary German composer (b. 1895), is a name associated with a method of teaching musical rudiments to children. His approach lays heavy emphasis on rhythmic development, using specially constructed "Orff" instruments. There is nothing unsophisticated about the music of Orff's opera, *Die Kluge* (The Clever Woman), yet in some respects, like children's music, it is extremely simple. This simplicity is mainly effected by the static harmony. Orff unhesitatingly stays on a single chord— usually a simple major or minor triad—for great stretches of musical time, often repeating the same melodic motives over and over as well. In the opening scene an old man sits in prison, bewailing his fate. Again and again he sings the same words to almost identical music, all within a single harmony: "Oh, if only I had believed my daughter, only believed my daughter, oh if only I had believed. . . ." The music is highly energized through rhythmic accents but is otherwise uneventful. Orff appears to have adopted Stravinsky's beloved *ostinato* (repeated motive) concept (see *The Rite of Spring* discussion in Chapter 30), making it the central element of his musical constructions.

When Orff finally does change harmony (for no one can write an entire opera on just one chord!) he still remains faithfully within the given tonic key. The music is almost totally nonchromatic in inflection and also generally avoids modulations from the tonic to other keys. The effect is surprisingly modernistic, inasmuch as even the simplest Classical pieces hint (even if only temporarily) at other keys. The modernistic quality of Orff's music is actually quite anachronistic, for it has been many centuries since tonal music was conceived of in such simplistic *diatonic* (i.e., nonchromatic) terms. As early as the Renaissance period chromaticism was introduced as a constituent element of tonal composition. By the beginning of the Baroque period (circa 1600) chromatic modulation from one key to another had become a commonplace "event." We now take it for granted that when we hear a piece in, let us say, C major we can expect incursions into closely related secondary keys such as A minor, F major, and G major (using, respectively, the chromatic notes G♯, B♭, and F♯), as well as motions to more distant secondary keys. Orff's innovation was to substitute pure diatonicism for the tonal chromaticism with which we are so familiar. Many modern composers (including rock composers) have experimented with integrating older compositional procedures with newer ones, but probably none has achieved a degree of "originality" to match Orff's insistent avoidance of chromaticism. (A review of the fundamentals of the tonal system, as explained in Chapter 9, may assist the student in appreciating Orff's uniqueness.)

Ingenious as Orff is, his static harmonic textures can be wearying with too much exposure. But the special virtue of Orff's music is that his is one of the very few modern styles which anyone can appreciate on first hearing. The story of *Die Kluge* is strange and intricate. An old man has come upon a gold mortar, but with no sign of its pestle. He decides to present the mortar to the king, hoping thereby to receive a big reward. The old man's daughter shrewdly warns him that the king will ask for the pestle and then accuse the man of hiding it. The daughter's prophecy comes true, and the old man is thrown into jail. In his distress the man repeatedly wails, "Oh, if only I had believed my daughter." Curious, the king sends for this clever daughter and sets her three riddles. She solves them handily, and he marries her on the spot! However, . . . and the story goes on and on, a complex fairy tale for adults. Orff's music is enjoyable for children, yet intricate enough to entertain older folks. Orff is one of the more successful composers of the midtwentieth century.

BASICS: FUGUE

A fugue is an instrumental or vocal work in which a given theme is subjected to various kinds of treatment—transposition, curtailment, inversion, extension, and so on. A fugue is differentiated from other structures in which thematic transformations occur by its "singlemindedness," for there is virtually nothing in a fugue not connected with the treatment of its theme. This very intensity of thematic treatment dictates a special term for a fugue's theme—to wit, *subject*. In this essay we shall consider various aspects of the fugal treatment of fugue subjects.

Consider a typical classical melody in a song or sonata. The melody is usually presented in the top, or soprano, "voice," accompanied by chords built up from a bass line. This is known as *homophonic texture*. In a fugue, the texture is *polyphonic*, in that no one voice supersedes any other voice in melodic precedence. Thus, fugal texture is a web of interwoven contrapuntal lines. The subject (or motives selected therefrom) is almost always present in at least one voice, sometimes in two or more voices simultaneously. The number of voices may vary from two up to many, but three to five is normal. During the presentation of the subject secondary contrapuntal material may also be heard in other voices, but no one voice dominates the others; the full subject is heard with more or less equal frequency in all voices. (The term *voice* is used in discussions of instrumental, as well as vocal, fugues.)

Most fugues begin with the presentation of the fugue subject in one voice while the others remain silent. As the first voice completes the initial statement of the subject, a second voice introduces it higher or lower than the first voice. This is known as the *answer*. Meanwhile the first voice continues with counterpoint to the second voice. This is known as the *countersubject*.

Example 79

BACH, *The Well-Tempered Clavier*, Vol. I, *Fugue in C Minor*, Opening

(continues in Example 80)

Music and Society

Examining Example 79 you will notice that the answer lies higher than the subject: voice 1 starts on C, an octave higher than middle C, while voice 2 starts on G, a perfect fifth higher than that. This is the normal relationship between subject and answer, the answer lying a perfect fifth higher, or a perfect fourth lower, than the subject.*

The third voice normally enters an octave higher or lower than the first voice. This entrance may take place immediately upon the conclusion of the answer in voice 2, or may occur after a short episodic delay. Brief *episodes* of this sort occur frequently throughout a fugue, and this is the first juncture at which one may appear. Most episodes are based on short motives abstracted from the fugue subject. In his *C Minor Fugue*, Bach introduced a two-measure episode before bringing in the third voice.

Example 80
C Minor Fugue, First Episode and Entrance of Voice 3

This first episode consists of three statements of the basic five-note motive which characterizes the subject, the third one being extended by two beats so that voice 3 enters just after the next bar line. Looking back at Example 79, you will note that the complete subject consists of three two-beat statements of the basic motive followed by an extension to the end of measure 2. How is one to detect the difference between the *subject*, with its three statements of the basic motive, and an *episode* also comprising three successive statements of the basic motive? *Answer*: In the subject each basic

*The pitch located a perfect fourth lower than the first pitch of the subject is the *octave equivalent* of the pitch located a perfect fifth higher than that first pitch. Although the pitch contours and rhythmic figures of the answer and other statements of the subject remain essentially unchanged with respect to the initial subject, the precise interval sizes may vary. Thus, in Example 79 the perfect fourth between the third and fourth notes of the subject (C down to G) is converted into a perfect fifth (G down to C) in the answer.

motive starts with the first pitch of the subject, whereas in the episodes the basic motives begin on different pitches. Thus in Episode 1 the basic motive starts successively on E♭, F, and G; in the first statement of the fugue subject, the three basic motives all start on C. (In general, episodes involve moving sequentially up or down, or zigzagging in both directions.)

In Episode 2 the initial pitches of the basic motive are G, C, F, and B♭ (see Example 81). In the following measure the basic motive commences on E♭. This turns out to be the beginning of the full subject, as confirmed by the fact that E♭ also commences the next two statements of the basic motive.

Example 81
C Minor Fugue, Episode 2 and New Entrance of Subject

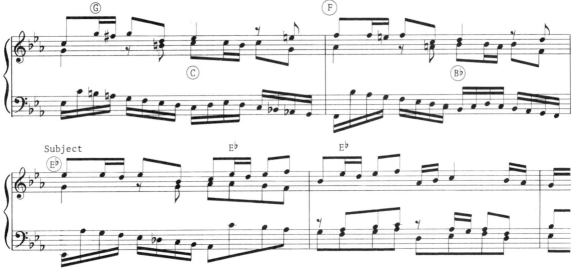

Writing a good fugue requires a combination of musical inspiration and a flair for intellectual games. The composer of a fugue faces the challenge of ingeniously applying fugal techniques while infusing the piece with the same high-level aesthetic qualities one expects in any good music. In his *C Minor Fugue* Bach combines crafty acumen with musical humor by momentarily implying a new entrance of the subject in voice 1 (see Example 80, end of second measure). This carries the implication of a two-voice fugue (since a fugue subject is always presented once in each voice before being repeated in any other voice), but a moment later voice 3 enters on middle C (an octave lower), and the "proper" third statement of the subject is heard. This being a three-voice fugue, the completion of the subject in voice 3 marks the end of what is known as the fugal *exposition.* The remainder of the fugue alternates between episodes and complete statements of the subject. Incidentally, in a four-voice fugue, the fourth voice starts an octave above or below the second voice; in a five-voice fugue, the fifth voice begins on an octave equivalent of the first and third voices; and so on.

Music and Society

It is quite common for a countersubject to be repeated frequently throughout a fugue. Thus, after Bach's initial presentation of the countersubject in measure 3, it is heard in the soprano voice in measure 5 (see Example 80), and it is then heard again in the bass voice of measure 11 (see the third measure of Example 81). There is even a sense of a secondary countersubject. Compare the middle voice of measures 3–4 with the middle voice of the last measures of Example 81. Here the repetition of the pitch contours is only approximate, but the rhythmic imitation is virtually exact.

Example 82
Middle Voice Secondary Countersubject of Examples 80 and 81

With the entrance of the third voice (in measure 7), the texture offers numerous vertical chords. Nevertheless, the emphasis continues to be linear, the chordal harmonies seeming almost incidental to the contrapuntal activity. This is in marked contrast to the conventional melody-*cum*-accompaniment associated with homophonic styles. In a fugue all voices are structurally equal—each is melodic, yet each also accompanies the others. In other words, a fugue represents a special instance of "structural democracy" in music. (Another instance is the *round*, such as "Frère Jacques.")

On the completion of the exposition, a fugue begins moving through a succession of secondary keys. We have been surveying a fugue in the key of C minor, so the first three statements of the subject are in that key. But, starting in measure 11 (middle of Example 81), the subject is presented in two different keys, the first being the relative major key, E♭ major. Like most fugue subjects, the one Bach devised here lends itself well to modal alteration; that is, it sounds good either in major or minor. This is a relatively short fugue, and Bach takes us through only one other secondary key (G minor) before returning to the original tonic, C minor. In longer fugues the subject is ordinarily presented in numerous secondary keys. The various intervening episodes, based on motives derived from the subject and/or countersubjects, usually function as modulatory transitions from one key to another.

At the very end of a fugue the composer may elect to introduce extra voices to make the conclusion more impressive. Bach completed the C *Minor Fugue* with a statement of the subject in the top voice over a sustained octave C in the bass part. (This is called a *pedal point*.) The final chord is a C major triad in five (rather than three) voices. In these final measures the texture is exceptionally homophonic, with the subject being treated in the traditional manner of a melody predominating in the soprano voice.

Music and Children

Example 83
C Minor Fugue, Homophonic Conclusion. Pedal Point in Bass

      Fugues vary according to (1) size and tempo of subject, (2) number of secondary keys, (3) instrumentation and/or vocal forces, and (4) sophistication of transformational techniques. Here we shall briefly consider factors (1) and (4).

Size and Tempo of Subject

      Despite the brevity of Bach's *C Minor Fugue*, its subject is relatively long. Many fugue subjects are briefer (and of course some are even longer). The *C♯ Minor Fugue* from the first volume of Bach's *Well-Tempered Clavier* has one of the shortest on record: it consists of just four tones! In this fugue the initial entrance of the subject is in the lowest voice, with subsequent statements entering successively higher. The tempo is slow. The *B Minor Fugue* with which Bach closes Volume 1 of the *Well-Tempered Clavier* is also slow, but differs from the *C♯ Minor Fugue* in bearing one of his longer subjects:

Example 84
BACH, *The Well-Tempered Clavier*, Vol. I, *Fugue in C♯ Minor*—4-Note Subject

Example 85
The Well-Tempered Clavier, Vol. I, *Fugue in B Minor*

Beethoven composed relatively few fugues, but some of them are based on extremely long subjects. See his *Hammerklavier Sonata*, Op. 106, last movement, for piano, and his *Grosse Fuge*, Op. 133, for string quartet.

Sophistication of Transformational Techniques

A composer may introduce a new subject somewhere in the middle of an extended fugue. In this case the second subject will eventually be combined with the first subject, the two interacting with each other as countersubjects. Complex fugues also tend to exhibit sophisticated transformational techniques, such as *stretto, inversion, diminution,* and *augmentation*.

Stretto. This term signifies decreasing the time lapse between the beginning of the subject and its answer. That is, an answer normally commences only as the subject is completed, but a composer may elect to start the answer "prematurely," producing an overlapping effect. Compare Examples 84 and 86, representing different parts of Bach's *C♯ Minor Fugue*. In Example 84 the answer commences *after* the fourth note of the subject; in Example 86 the alto answer coincides with the third note of the subject. The stretto technique in Example 86 actually involves two subjects, as illustrated in Example 87.

Example 86

The Well-Tempered Clavier, Vol. I, *Fugue in C♯ Minor*, Stretto of Two Subjects (see Example 87)

Example 87
Clarification of Strettos in Example 86

Principal subject/answer overlaps (stretto)

Secondary subject overlaps

Mirror image: the standing heron is, musically speaking, "inverted at the unison," while soaring birds etch a pattern in the sky that is reflected in the water below. The scene provides a graphic representation of a melody heard in its original form as well as in inversion (see page 194).

Inversion. This term signifies the mirroring of a subject. In its inversion each interval of the original theme is copied in the *opposite direction*. Examine the principal fugue subject of Bach's *Art of the Fugue*,* Example 88, and then observe its inversion in Example 89. As you can see, the rhythmic configurations remain unaltered, and each successive intervalic distance is essentially the same (fifth-third-third-second-second-second, etc.). The directional change is responsible for the mirroring effect.

Example 88
BACH, *Art of the Fugue*, Fugue 1

Example 89
Fugue 4 (Inverted Subject)

Diminution and Augmentation. These terms signify decreasing or increasing the duration of a subject. Fugue No. 7 of *Art of the Fugue* exhibits stretto, inversion, diminution, and augmentation, all at once. To begin, the original subject has been elaborated with ornamental passing notes and dotted rhythmic figures:

Example 90
Art of the Fugue, Ornamented Version of Principal Subject

*Art of the Fugue, Bach's last major composition, is a compendium of fugal techniques.

194

Music and Society

Example 91 illustrates the first eight entrances of the subject and answer. Comparing the first entrance with Example 90, you can see that the time values are halved, and the subject is completed in two measures, instead of four. This is known as diminution. Again using Example 90 as a reference, you can see that the second entrance is its mirror, but now with unchanged time values. Next comes a diminution of the inverted answer (in which the intervals are similar but not identical to the subject). The fourth entrance is a bass augmentation of this inverted answer; that is, it lasts *eight* measures rather than the normal four (or the two measures of the diminution—the fourth entrance actually lasts four times the duration of the third entrance!). The next four entrances are all diminutions, as indicated in Example 91. Three of these begin and end before the bass augmentation itself is completed.

Example 91

Art of the Fugue, Breakdown of Transformations of Ornamental Subject, Fugue 7

Now examine the interaction of these entrances and transformations as they occur in the score.

Example 92
Art of the Fugue, Fugue 7, Combining Inversion,
Stretto Overlaps, Diminution, and Augmentation.

Fugal techniques may be found in works which are not exclusively fugal. For example, it is not uncommon to find fugal passages (*fugatos*) in developments and other sections of sonata forms. One of the best known examples is the stirring fugato which closes Mozart's *Symphony No. 41 in C Major*, the *Jupiter*. A special imitational technique related to fugue is *canon*. The simplest canons are rounds, such as "Three Blind Mice" and "Row, Row, Row Your Boat," in which different parts of the tune make suitable counterpoint to all the other parts. A more sophisticated approach is found in concert works, such as Bach's *Goldberg Variations* for harpsichord.* The idea here is that the tune is faithfully imitated, as in a round, but not necessarily starting on the same pitch. Other voices provide free counterpoint, without imitating the canonic melody.

*Bach composed an extensive set of thirty variations for a brilliant young harpsichord virtuoso, Johann Gottlieb Goldberg (1727–1756).

Example 93
BACH, *Goldberg Variations*, No. 21, Canon at the Seventh

Transformational techniques, such as inversion, diminution, and augmentation, may be found in polyphonic textures that are not specifically fugal. Brahms introduced augmentation at several points in his *German Requiem* (see Chapter 32, Examples 230 and 231). Rachmaninoff's *Rhapsody on a Theme of Paganini* illustrates an unusual application of inversion. In most cases an inverted melody sounds much like its model, as in Bach's *Art of the Fugue* (see Examples 88 and 89). However, Rachmaninoff conceived of an inversion of the Paganini theme which sounds deceptively like a lush, superromantic Rachmaninoff original. The striking difference between the model and its inversion is achieved through a change in tempo, substitution of triple for duple meter, distortion of some of the durational values, and the addition of arpeggiated chords in triplet rhythmic groupings. Compare Examples 94a and b.

Example 94a
PAGANINI, Theme from *24th Caprice*

Music and Society

RACHMANINOFF, *Rhapsody on a Theme of Paganini,*
Variation 18 (Inverted Theme in Db Major)

Example 95 illustrates the inversional relationship of these apparently unrelated themes, with the inversion transposed to the key of A major (matching the A minor tonic of the Paganini original). Another element of contrast stems from the fact that Paganini's theme is in minor, Rachmaninoff's transformation in major.

Example 95
Inversional Relationship Between Paganini & Rachmaninoff Themes (The Latter Transposed to A Major). See Examples 94a and b.

The twelve-tone method of composition makes extensive use of the inversional techniques of Bach and his Baroque contemporaries, but in a *serial* manner which tends to disguise the melodic correspondences between a model and its transformations. (See the discussion of Schoenberg's *Phantasy for Violin with Piano Accompaniment,* Chapter 22, and notably Example 120).

MUSICAL DEMOCRACY: CHAMBER MUSIC

Music is a social lubricant; hardly any type of group interaction exists without it. Music accents social events such as parties, dances, baseball games, political rallies, and even supermarket shopping. People sing as they work, children sing at camp and school. Music accompanies ballet, theater, radio, and television. It serves the church. A survey of music in all its functions could easily fill an entire volume. Here we shall limit our observations to a single facet of the social side of music, namely, music for friends to get together and play. Not to study, or to rehearse for future performance, but simply to play in the here and now for the sheer aesthetic and recreational fun of it. This is the world of music for small ensembles (*chamber music*). Vocal chamber music ranges from medieval motets and Renaissance madrigals to modern unaccompanied (*a cappella*) anthems and barbershop quartets. But we shall concentrate here exclusively on chamber music geared to small groups of instrumentalists.

There was a time when making "homemade" chamber music was a commonplace activity; chamber music lovers who wanted to indulge their desires were forced to seek out others of like interests and abilities. Nowadays, radio, television, and the phonograph have restructured our recreational home life, and to recreate chamber music one need only turn on the radio or put on a record. Of course, genuine chamber music enthusiasts still prefer the "do-it-yourself" approach, rather than listening to others perform. A veritable army of chamber musicians is to be found in city and country—blowing, sawing, and thumping away to their hearts' content.

Human animals being gregarious creatures, the popularity of ensemble playing (in popular jargon, *jamming*) is hardly surprising. Of course, orchestras offer group-playing experience too, yet many musicians eschew large ensembles, and, indeed, the difference between small ensembles and large orchestras is a critical one. The particular gratification of playing chamber music stems from the absence of a conductor. An orchestra requires strict obedience from its members. All of them (especially the string players) are expected to surrender their individuality in favor of a mass melding which reflects (ideally) just one performer's interpretation—the conductor's. By contrast, the small ensemble allows the player a great deal of solo responsibility and freedom, leading to a corresponding increase in attention from the other players (as well as listeners). The small ensemble effects a perfect compromise between the extremes of solo and orchestral playing.

Small ensembles come in many forms and sizes: trios, quartets, quintets, sextets, and even larger groups (but not much larger if they are to manage without the help of a conductor). For most music lovers, and certainly for all string players, the ensemble of choice is the string quartet. Several factors underly this preference. For one thing, smaller combinations (duos and trios) usually include a keyboard instrument—the

The Lasalle String Quartet in concert. The experience of a live performance is more gripping than hearing it on a recording.

most common one being the piano—which string players generally prefer to shun due to its dominating size and range. Furthermore, good string players will alter or inflect a given tone, pushing its pitch up or down ever so slightly (depending on the other pitches being played), resulting potentially in a remarkably fine blending of sounds, whereas pianists miss out on this kind of subtle interaction and must be content to strike each key with no further control over the resulting pitch. Of course, the very flexibility of string playing can easily lead to out-of-tune playing (faulty *intonation*), and for that reason one is always relieved to hear accurate string intonation. On the other hand, pianos are often out of tune to start with, requiring elaborate and time-consuming effort to restore them to tolerable pitch levels.

Another aspect of the superiority of the string quartet is the fact that the availability of many fine compositions for smaller and larger ensembles notwithstanding, nothing can match the literature for string quartet. This state of affairs can be attributed partially to the fact that Western composers have long conceived of music in four "parts"—much like choral music for four voices: soprano, alto, tenor, and bass. Quartets of instruments that play mainly one note at a time are particularly well suited to this tradition. Add the fact that string instruments are generally thought to exhibit greater tonal variety and expressiveness than wind and brass instruments, and you begin to understand the string quartet's popularity—it happily combines ideal size, perfect balance, and maximum expressiveness. The string quartet is the chamber music ensemble *par excellence*.

WHIT BURNETT: "THE EVERLASTING QUARTET"

The spirit of the wonderful pastime of quartet playing is indelibly captured in Whit Burnett's charming story, *The Everlasting Quartet*,[1] which is reproduced here in full. Burnett, himself an enthusiastic quartet member, addressed himself to the musical connoisseur, making no attempt to clarify the "in" aspects of his story. Therefore, explanatory annotations have been added to help the reader enjoy its delightful and humorous details. Read the story once straight through for continuity; then go through it a second time with the help of the supplementary information.

1

This is a story told me by a Welshman, an amateur musician, who had the wit to recognize the architecture of sublimity when he saw it. He was a man past middle age, with a huge, dark scimitar of a nose, and shaggy brows, and a wave of black hair—quite handsome in his way, but unmarried, and capable, one suspected, of a kind of dark humor, or irony. His name was Evan Evans, and he was a lawyer and a singer.

It is such a simple story, really. There is not even a woman in it, for a viola player's wife, who was not even present, can hardly be considered a participant. It could be retold in a flash—and yet that would not do justice to the theme, the passion of devotion of the four men involved.

One, I believe, I met once. I have a vague remembrance, in some little orchestra, of slight, sandy-haired Stevens. . . . He had a remarkably cheap, unusual violin. The Welshman later showed it to me. And I thought then, when he held the instrument in his hand, there was something wild and unearthly in his eye, as if he were remembering a glimpse of some other world.

The Welshman was also a fiddler, if not a very good one, and the love of his life was to sit down of an evening with a few pickup string men and play a humble second through the classics.

"String men" simply means string players. You will have to forgive the implied male chauvinism; this story was written nearly thirty years ago. Women, like men, play in string quartets, although somewhat rarely in professional quartets. One of these days, if it has not already happened, an all-female quartet will reach the concert stage. One of the members of the venerable Quartetto Italiano is a woman, but even here there is a hint of chauvinism, for she is the second violinist—which is to say that her role is much less noticeable and brilliant (though no less essential) than the first violinist's. In other words, she plays "second fiddle" to his more prominent leadership role. (Notice that in the same sentence the author refers to "a humble second.")

So it is not such a strange thing that at one time or another Evan Evans knew them all, their manners and their morals and even the make of their instruments.

It happened in Brooklyn, where there is frequently to be found the string player, usually a moody, melancholy fellow, not quite good enough to be a soloist, not steady enough to be a professional, who is not geared by nature for orchestras. If he is, for example, a viola player, he is always seated in front of the trombones and cornets, and, on a full attack, the tin pans of hell seem suddenly to crash in his skull, and the delicate thing in his soul which makes him a player on a mellow string is shattered and, at the next tuning up of the Brooklyn Home Symphony, while the horns are out in number, the viola has disappeared. Lost, dead, perhaps, but usually just forlornly absent, wishing somehow he could find a friendly string quartet.

Fiddle players are plentiful, but viola players are rare. Even their instruments are not easy to find, and like the performers themselves they come in odd sizes, no two quite alike, with odd-sized necks and different-sized bellies, and lengths which vary in inches.

Such a man was Arthur Nilson, a viola player.

Music and Society

The viola is an oversize violin. The lowest note of the violin is G below middle C, whereas owing to its larger size the viola can reach down a whole octave below middle C. Tradition has it that viola players are frustrated violinists or, at any rate, violinists who prefer to be big frogs in a little pond rather than vice versa. (There are always fewer violists around than violinists.) The viola, awkward to hold and to play, compares to the trim violin like the string bass to the cello. (The bass itself is so ungainly that it almost never figures in chamber music and is mainly an orchestral instrument.)

Mr. Nilson was a tall, lean, Danish kind of chap, silent and thoughtful, and not quite successful at anything, a fiddle player who never had the fire for virtuosity and so "took up" the viola. That is, in his case, he clasped to his bosom the sad sweet alto of the viol family and, as his interest quickened to the almost hopeless task of conquering his new love, he saw, I was told, his wife depart his bed and board—that very day she had gone to live with her mother. It didn't much matter, for his passion was elsewhere. The viola is a challenge even to experts; to Arthur it was the test and fulfillment of his higher self. Anyway, he privately thought, his wife had the voice of a guinea hen, a high aggressive petulance of squawk, like a squeaking door with will power. Still, she always saw that he was well fed, and he didn't quite know what he would do without her.

The day it all began was a fair one. Brooklyn crashed to left and right, cars and trolleys and buses clattered and whirred on by, and there stood Arthur Nilson on a corner at Fulton, his viola case under his arm, big end to—he'd been for a soundpost adjustment—when this little man came up behind him, touched his arm, introduced himself politely, and the first of the dreadful consequences began to fall in line.

The man who accosted him, the Welshman said, was Old Herr Stoeffel.

"Excuse me," Stoeffel said, "I hope you don't mind. But that instrument—isn't it a viola?"

"Why yes," admitted Nilson. "It is."

And his eyes, of course, immediately took on life. Viola players not only sense that they are an isolated group, not much wanted in the society of really showy players, but they feel, as individuals, alone in the world. That anyone should recognize even the case as that containing a viola and not just a violin meant that here was someone indeed—it could only be a quartet player, and quartet players are in the seventh rank of angels.

"I thought so," said Old Stoeffel. He was a stocky, squat little German-American with a sense of persistence. "It wouldn't be, also, that you play occasionally in a string quartet?"

"Yes, it would be," said Arthur eagerly. "I was in a quartet four years, until our second violin walked into an open elevator shaft. By accident, of course. All the other second fiddles we tried were difficult. Married. Or busy. Or they moved away. . . . It broke up the quartet."

"I see," said Stoeffel, rocking back and forth on his heels and nodding sagely. "So you fell back on the Beethoven trios, for a while, and even the Dvořák terzetto . . ."

"As a matter of fact, we did."

"It didn't work. Even Beethoven knew it wouldn't work for very long. There is no balance in three. And it was all good enough to get sore at the second fiddle and write him out, as Beethoven did, but three is not good, in anything—somebody is al-

Musical Democracy: Chamber Music

ways the mother-in-law. Second fiddlers are no *verdammt* good. Still, you cannot have a quartet without a second fiddle."

There exists only a very small repertoire for string trio (consisting of one violin, one viola, and one cello). Presumably, as Herr Stoeffel says, "there is no balance in three," meaning that the lower-voiced viola and cello outweigh a solitary high-register violin.

No bus came. The conversation continued. Herr Stoeffel suggested, finally, that since it was a bright sunny day, and a good dry one too, the instruments would be in fine voice and wouldn't the viola player like to see, if he wasn't too busy, if they couldn't rake up a couple of fiddle players; he would get out his "old dog box," and they might play a few quartets.

Old Stoeffel's instrument was the cello.

2

At the time, happily, Mr. Nilson was unemployed. The amount of time he spent practicing on his instrument had rather depleted his energy, and going up and down stairs in the department store basement where he had presided at a kitchen hardware counter had proved rather wearing. One day he quit, and although he had only a few dollars left, he had not really begun yet seriously to look for re-employment. He wanted first to get through the *Kreutzer*, arranged for viola, and then he was going out and battle the world.

Rudolphe Kreutzer, a French diplomat of German extraction, composed a set of *Forty-two Etudes and Caprices* for violin, also known as the "Violinist's Bible." The Kreutzer etudes are studied by all violinists and (in transcription) violists and are just what a fairly advanced but out-of-practice amateur violist would be likely to turn to for a little technical brushing up. Today Kreutzer is remembered for having received Beethoven's dedication of his great *Sonata in A Major*, Op. 47 (1803). (Known as the *Kreutzer Sonata*, the fame of this work is such that the great Russian writer, Leo Tolstoy, wrote a short novel bearing the same title. In it a man and woman play Beethoven's sonata together and then purportedly become illicit lovers. See the end of Chapter 27 for further discussion of this novella.)

Unfortunately the meeting with Stoeffel was the event which was to preclude this forever.

He hesitated only an instant. He knew his wife would be expecting him to come for her, which he knew he would probably do. . . .

"I would be only too glad," said Arthur. "When it comes to playing quartets, I would rather play than eat."

He could have said nothing to bring more joy to Old Stoeffel. His square and rugged face abeam, he took Mr. Nilson by the arm and off they went up Fulton, only stopping for a necessary moment at a rooming house en route where they picked up Mr. Stevens.

"In Mr. Stevens," the cellist said, "you will find a second violin player *vom Herz aus.*"

Mr. Nilson shook hands, and the three were on their way.

"I would rather play," said Mr. Stevens, from behind his unrimmed glasses, "than eat."

And while it was not a new phrase, it was the password of the devotees.

"Ja," agreed Old Stoeffel, striding alone, "even he often does."

And, if it is the Stevens I think I met once, playing in the Catholic amateur orchestra, it is possible that in those lean days he often went without a meal or two. He seemed to me a rather weak character, however dependable and solid in sustaining his part. His hair was thin and had been red, his eyes a pallid blue, soft and gentle behind his spectacles; and among the great violins of the world, he had no fine old Italian master, nor even one of the lesser Italians, old or new, nor even a German made by the numerous brothers Klotz, nor yet a common Czech made by the unskilled hands of peasant girls. It was Japanese. But even on a Japanese fiddle, Evan Evans said, Stevens made music.

On the way up Fulton, Old Stoeffel talked continuously. Perhaps he had never been so wound up with unspent bow strokes in his life. Perhaps he had not played quartets for as much as a month. And here, at last, he was assembling a group, and the day was shaping fine.

Only once on the way did Mr. Nilson suggest, a little worriedly, that perhaps he ought to make a phone call.

Stoeffel's quarters were an old brownstone basement where he kept his cello and his cameras, for in the good days he was a photographer, and oddly, for a confirmed bachelor, he specialized in children's portraits. But hardly anybody in those days had much extra money to have portraits of their children—the kids cost enough as it was, there was no need of reminding their parents for all posterity. Der little mutts, anyway, said Stoeffel. For he did not like photography, it was a business. He had rather been a professional cellist, but while his application was excellent, his technique was not—he was never quite sure of the highest positions. Indeed he had once disgraced himself, but with an orchestra, so that, of course, didn't count—he had a solo and it was to end on one of those slide-home-to-base notes up near the bridge in the highest treble register, and being a little nervous, for everyone was to hear this note, he chalked the point on the finger board and at the concert he slid up the neck in unholy abandon, sure of himself and the note, until he smashed out the wrong note—sour—which everyone heard, for some devil just before the concert had moved the chalk mark.

As we have said, a pianist produces a tone by depressing a key. By contrast, string players have nothing but an undifferentiated fingerboard, somewhere along which they must locate each pitch. (The pianist experiences a similar challenge when required to make fast hand leaps with next to no time to "aim.") The guitar is equipped with *frets*—metal strips placed at intervals across the fingerboard—saving the guitarist much guesswork. But frets attached to violins and other orchestral string instruments would impede a performer's flexibility and virtuosity. Beginning string players learn to locate pitches according to "positions," starting with the first position and slowly working up to the higher ones. The thumb of the left hand cradles the fingerboard, and each finger is used for one pair of pitches. For example, a violinist starting on the open top string (E) in the first position would play F and F♯ with the first (index) finger, G and G♯ with the second, A and B♭ with the third and B♮ with the pinky. So, confronted with a printed note, the player must instantly select the string on which to play it and decide which position to head for. (This challenge is compounded by the fact that many pitches are located on more than just one string.) Once the correct position is determined, there remains the choice of which finger to press onto the string, although ordinarily the whole process occurs so quickly that it becomes a matter of a single question:

205

which string—which position—which finger? In the story old Stoeffel had decided to cheat by drawing a chalk mark across the fingerboard, thereby predetermining the location of the fearful high note in his solo (the chalk mark functioning like a fret on a guitar). But when the time came he apparently missed the mark, or else had put it in the wrong place to begin with. Professional string players never indulge in chalk marks, although undoubtedly there are times when they might like to.

In addition to the virtuosity required of a string player's left hand, the right hand must accomplish numerous effects, such as playing two or more notes per bow stroke, *pizzicato* (plucking the string rather than bowing it), and so on. If you perceive a resemblance between the dexterity of a trained string player and the deftness of a skilled athlete, you're right. (The comparison applies to other instrument families as well.) Music and athletics both require years of strenuous training if excellence is to be achieved.

> Stoeffel found the cello, the only properly dusted object in his room.
> *"Ein Moment!!"* He leaned it on his chair. "I go up in the hall and telephone Rennie."
> "He is a First?" asked Nilson.
> "What a First!" said Stevens. "And he will drop absolutely anything if you just say one word, Quartet."

As already observed, there is a considerable difference in the kind of playing expected of the first and second violinists of a quartet. The first is the leader or quasi-conductor, nodding or giving a bow stroke in place of the conductor's baton beat. The other three players ordinarily look to the first violinist for guidance in setting a tempo, ritard, acceleration, or other nuance. Moreover, the first violin part usually carries the lion's share of melodic lines, scale passages, and roulades, whereas the second violin part is comparatively subdued, functioning primarily as an inner-voice filler.

> A familiar in Stoeffel's basement, Mr. Stevens dug out the half-rusted iron stands and arranged the four straight chairs in the proper semicircle under a stand lamp with a good bright bulb, for, bright as it was outside, Stoeffel's quarters were a bit gloomy.
> The cellist had hardly more than returned and tuned up when the front door flew open and there stood the First.
> He was a wild-eyed Italian, with double-lensed glasses, behind which popped the eyes of the true fanatic, sharp, bulbous, darting everywhere at once.
> "Gentlemen!" shouted Rinaldo del Jolio. And he saluted with his outthrust fiddle case. And in less time than it takes to tell it he was seated, tuned and ready for the opener.
> Herr Stoeffel thrust forward, with one foot, a tall stack of the Edition Peters.
> "So! What shall it be?"

The Edition Peters, or Peters Edition, is one of the largest music publishing houses on either side of the Atlantic. Their catalog includes the major part of the standard chamber music repertoire.

3

> It is not necessary to tell any player in a string quartet, anywhere in the world, that of course they started with a little Haydn. All quartets, everywhere, start with a little

Haydn, and it comes from the *30 Berühmte,* and if it doesn't at first sound so *berühmte* it sounds better as time goes on.

In German "30 Berühmte" means "30 Famous [Quartets]." Haydn composed so many works in this genre that thirty of them have been assembled in a multivolume collection that satisfies all but the most intrepid quartet players. (As you will see, Herr Stoeffel and his friends were among those interested in digging out the more obscure Haydn quartets.)

Old Stoeffel leaned into his cello, grasped between his knees like some beloved mount, and on his face was that lost rapture of the *Kammerspieler* of old.

Kammerspieler means "chamber player."

Mr. Stevens, as second, soberly beat time with his left foot, the anchor of the seconds; Arthur Nilson, when he found that he was just about as good as his companions, achieved a kind of otherworld serenity, which in the *adagio* became sheer love itself, and it was with reluctance he let go of the rich gold tones when, at times, he produced them.

Adagio means very slow. (See Chapter 3 for other Italian tempo terms.) The viola is awkward in fast passages; it lends itself more to drawn out mellow tones at slow tempi.

The first violin, Rinaldo del Jolio, was fire and steam and energy itself, and grace, too, and delicacy when the mood required. He was the lark, in The Lark, and Old Stoeffel was the root and the trunk of the oak; and when it came to Mozart, Del Jolio was the hunter and the hound and the fox, and behind him, with him, beyond him, with him again, were the others, Mozartian riders, the horns of the Hunt echoing and re-echoing from cello to viola, all coattails flying through the measures.

Many musical works bear descriptive titles, in most cases not selected by the composers (as in Beethoven's so-called *Moonlight Sonata* for piano). The *Lark* refers to Haydn's *Quartet in D Major,* Op. 64, No. 5; the *Hunt* is Mozart's *Quartet in B♭ Major,* K. 458. The score of the *Lark* exhibits nothing obviously birdlike other than possibly the opening high violin theme of the first movement. The opening theme of the *Hunt* suggests a hunting song.

Example 96
a) MOZART, *"Hunt"* Quartet, K. 458, 1st Mvt.

Example 96

b) HAYDN, "Lark" *Quartet* (No. 67), 1st Mvt.

And so the day passed, celestially.

"Anybody tired?" asked Stoeffel, who looked hardy as a bull fiddler. It was long past dark.

"Tired!" sneered Rinaldo del Jolio. "How can anybody be tired when we have done only five Haydns and six Mozarts? And those only the chestnuts!"

The number of quartets played already far exceeds what an amateur group would ordinarily tackle in one sitting. A "chestnut" is an extremely popular work, like Beethoven's "Fifth" in the symphonic literature.

"I am as fresh as a daisy," said Mr. Stevens, although the fiddler's neck was beginning to show a bit red beneath his jaw.

"I could die playing such music," said Arthur Nilson, with warmth. For here, indeed, were players, four who spoke as one, four whose voices blended from their instruments to weave ineffable patterns in the air. . . . There was nothing in life like this.

"I hope nobody is married," said Old Stoeffel, at the next brief pause. He looked accusingly at Nilson. "Wives are always expecting a person home."

"I am not married," said Stevens, needlessly, with pride.

Mr. Nilson awoke from his brief reverie of bliss—the bliss of music, not marriage.

"Oh," he said, "I forgot . . ."

They looked at him with alarm.

Music and Society

"It's all right," Mr. Nilson set them all at ease, although he himself still looked a bit anxious. "After all, my wife was a guinea hen."

"You know," said Del Jolio as the breather continued, for good quartet players do take breathers, although they can well play, if they are good players, without a stop till morning, "a funny thing. My girl used to tell me she was interested in me because she loved my music. The closer we got to getting married, the more often she told me I spent too much time on the very thing she liked about me most—music. Believe me, I saw what was coming out of that. I dropped her like a brick."

"Lucky for you," said Mr. Stevens. "Remember little Hermanson, the oboe?"

"Oboes are crazy," said Del Jolio dogmatically.

"Yes," Mr. Stevens concurred. "But he had a wife who was very irritating. She objected to his practicing. It did something to her head."

"It does something to the oboe player, too," said the First.

"They had row after row, but Hermanson had to practice to keep his lip up. One day when she broke in on him he killed her. He is leading the orchestra Up the River now. He was a neat fellow, very orderly, too. He cut off her ears so he could stuff her down a drain pipe."

"Schluss mit den vimmin!" said Stoeffel, handing out parts. "Bitte, mein' Herren—Schubert!"

"Schubert!" agreed Mr. Nilson.

And so there was Schubert, the one in A minor, with the lovely andante theme from Rosamunde, which of course led to the harrowing and exciting Death and the Maiden, more exhilarating than the chase of any earthly female.

Like other composers before and since, Schubert was wont to reuse favored melodies, as in the Quartet in A minor, which shares a theme with his incidental music to the drama Rosamunde. (The same theme also shows up in his piano Impromptu in Bb, Op. 142, No. 3.) The second movement of Schubert's Quartet in D Minor is based on his song, "Death and the Maiden" (analyzed in Chapter 31). It may seem strange that after the early Classicists Haydn and Mozart, Herr Stoeffel bypasses Beethoven and proceeds directly to the late Classicist Schubert. Beethoven was born in 1770, fully a generation before Schubert's birth in 1797. However, Schubert matured as a composer much faster than Beethoven, and, since nearly all their output originated during the first quarter of the nineteenth century, the two can be regarded as virtual contemporaries. (Schubert's death in 1828 followed Beethoven's by only one year.) Still, why Schubert before Beethoven? The answer may lie in the fact that many music lovers view the Beethoven string quartets as the summit of the quartet literature; indeed, there are those who consider his late quartets (dating from 1823) the finest music ever composed, irrespective of medium and genre. (For more on this subject, see Chapter 27.)

"When we get through all the music I have," said Stoeffel some hours later, "I have a big surprise. I saved it."

The night had gone. It was early in the morning.

"This is a very practical apartment," said Mr. Nilson, sweating now, a trifle. "Nobody seems to object after eleven."

"The people on the next floor are away for the summer," said Stoeffel, "and nobody higher up hears anything. We can play right on."

They finished all the early works of Beethoven and were in the Rasoumovsky period when the sun came up. By this time the tones of all were really golden.

Musical Democracy: Chamber Music

The three *Rasoumovsky Quartets*, Op. 59, represent middle Beethoven, in contra-distinction to the six early quartets, Op. 18, and the late quartets, commencing with Op. 127. Rasoumovsky, a Russian nobleman living in Vienna, was a friend and support-er of Beethoven.

Mr. Stevens's left arm required a little shifting.

"You're not getting *tired!*" frowned the Italian First.

But he did condone a moment's rest.

"I like your viola," he said to Mr. Nilson. He reached for the big dark somber in-strument and turned it about with a knowing eye.

"Yes," said Nilson, "it has a nice tender tone."

"Ah, the tender tone!" said Del Jolio. "Once I had a job with Rosenthal next to Carnegie Hall. Would you believe it? I used to repair fiddles. The cheap ones. I was quite good, too, But it was a terrible bore. The customers were fantastic. I got most-ly amateurs. They were always griping at their instruments. I was glad to quit.

"There was one fellow came in the shop with a fiddle and asked me if I could give it a tender tone. That's what he wanted, a tender tone.

"I told him I could shift the bridge, change the strings, maybe alter the position of the sound post. I told him what I could do. But he looked at me so skeptically I couldn't figure him out. Finally, the cheap skate, he put the fiddle under his arm and walked out. 'I think,' he said, 'I see what I can do myself. I want a really tender tone.'

"About a week later he came back to the shop with the fiddle in a bag. It was all to pieces. The tailpiece was off, the ribs apart, the neck was in a pocket of his jacket, and the back and belly were lying on the counter like platters.

"'My heavens, my good man!' I said. 'Is this the same fiddle? Is this the instru-ment from which you wanted a tender tone?'

"I must say the fellow hung his head.

"'Well, speak up, man,' I said. 'What in heaven's name did you do with the fid-dle?'

"'Well,' he said, 'finally, I boiled it!'"

"Very funny. Ha-ha. Now," said Stoeffel, "back to work!"

And the quartet buckled down again to business.

It must have been quite late the next day when Herr Stoeffel felt the time had come to spring his big surprise.

It seemed there was a lawyer, an amateur musician, who lived half a mile out toward Flatbush, who was a friend of Stoeffel's, and the lawyer had recently come into possession, as a collector, of the entire musical library of the famous Gneisel Quartet. He had simply bought it, having money, and he had asked Stoeffel to cata-logue it for him.

"What is so supremely obliging of my friend"—Stoeffel radiated his appreci-ation—"is that at this moment he is in Wales attending some Folk Song Sing or other, although he cannot sing a true note and is only Welsh through his great-grand-mother.

"And being in Wales," he added, "he has left his house empty. And the music fills a whole room! And all we have to do is pick up our stands and take the bus to his door, and then we can really sit down, without disturbance, and play some quar-tets—quartets I bet you never heard of."

"I have always wanted to play a little Reger," said Mr. Nilson. "We never got around to Reger when I had my quartet."

Music and Society

Max Reger was a German composer who died during World War I. His music is rarely played today, yet is not entirely forgotten either.

"If he has a real library," put in Mr. Stevens, "there are dozens of Haydns you don't find in the *Berühmte*."

"What are we waiting for?" Del Jolio arose with his fiddle and jammed on his hat. Impatiently, like the leader he was, he waited, foot in the stirrup, ready to charge the unknown.

4

It was this move, according to my informant, which was fatal. It was the one step too much. It opened to the players a world of treasures, and it was simply more than mortal could stand.

On the way to the Welshman's house everyone was busy with speculations as to just what they might find.

"Everything standard, of course," Del Jolio was muttering to himself. "The Gneisels played the whole classical repertoire."

"The Russians—all the Russians," Herr Stoeffel added.

"A little Boccherini might be nice," said Nilson.

And in the eagerness of expectation no one—absolutely no one—thought of lunch, although it was now again near sundown.

But Old Herr Stoeffel did think to buy several dozen large white candles, explaining that, at the Welshman's house, with him away, there were neither lights, nor bells, nor telephones.

Thus they arrived at the big old brownstone, buoyed up only by the spirit. Nothing more substantial.

And after the key was turned and the music unfolded, only then did Herr Stoeffel think to mention food.

"I hope nobody is getting hungry," he said, in a low voice. He half hoped nobody would hear. "We have all this music before us."

"Hah!" snorted Rinaldo. He looked around, almost fiercely.

"No," said Mr. Stevens. "I have said it. I would rather play than eat."

"*Also!*" said Old Stoeffel, pulling up his A. "Let us hear no more about it. Fried fish! Phaw!"

"Also" in German means something like "all right, then." "Pulling up his A" means tuning the A string (the highest on the cello), which presumably had gone flat. It is next to impossible to play with good intonation in the absence of properly tuned open strings, which is accomplished with the aid of tuning pins set into the neck of the instrument. In extremely humid or dry atmospheres the pins can easily stick or slip, which explains why string players often take a long time to tune. Even then a string may go out in performance, requiring retuning at the end of a movement.

"I am not hungry," said Mr. Nilson, who, for the last time, was thinking of his wife. She did love to see him eat. . . .

And thus began a session of quartet playing which, in all history, has never been surpassed. In a deserted house, near Flatbush, on a side street, in a room the proper size to give back a moderate *fortissimo*,

211

The author's point is that the acoustics of the room allowed the players a good resonant tone.

> four lovers of the art of chamber music sat down, in full possession of their faculties —indeed with faculties attuned to concert pitch—in the total absence of an audience, for audiences have never been sought by your true chamber music players— and from Palestrina to Bartók, the four fellows fiddled . . . and fiddled . . . and fiddled. . . .

Palestrina was a sixteenth-century master of vocal composition. What piece Herr Stoeffel and his colleagues could have played by him is a mystery, unless it was an arrangement. Bartók was an outstanding twentieth-century Hungarian composer (see Chapter 6) who produced six first-rate string quartets.

> They fiddled low and they fiddled loud, they fiddled *adagio* and they fiddled *prestissimo*, they fiddled through the wildness and the pathos of Smetana, and they glowed in the sentimental honey of Borodin, faced each other through the thick harmonic woods of Brahms, waxing soft and beatific in the serenities of Franck. They fiddled the classics of the masters, and wandered into the half-forgotten mannerisms of the Dittersdorfs and others of their kind; they played the archaic and the modern. They found hand-copied reproductions of the *In Nomines* of Byrd and Brewster, and *Sonatas a quattro* by Scarlatti and a lone rare *Ricercari a 4 voci*; and then, in contrast, they ventured out into Debussy's glazed lakes of tone and were swept along by the rhythmic rushes of Prokofiev.

Smetana, a Czech composer of the midnineteenth century, and Borodin, a Russian of the same period, both emphasized nationalistic elements in their music (see Chapters 6 and 7). Their German contemporary, Johannes Brahms (1833–1897) ranks with Beethoven as one of the greatest of the greats; he composed three string quartets, as well as other string works for five and six players. César Franck (1822–1890) was a leading French Romantic composer. Carl Dittersdorf, a minor Classical contemporary of Beethoven, is noteworthy for having published an autobiography. "In Nomine" is a plainchant melody drawn from medieval Catholic liturgy (see Chapter 23). William Byrd (1543–1623?) was a pillar of English music during the reign of Queen Elizabeth I. Brewster's name is unfamiliar but may be a variant of (Thomas) Brewer, born in London in 1611. (Brewer is remembered mainly for the size and redness of his nasal appendage when demonstrating his capacity for imbibing the nectar of the grape!) Scarlatti, presumably Alessandro and not his son Domenico (an important composer of harpsichord music), lived at the turn of the eighteenth century, whereas Debussy and Prokofiev created their principal *oeuvres* just prior to or during the first part of the twentieth century.

> If, in Stoeffel's casual library, music had seemed to have been created at times past for the sake of the players, here in the collector's home, amid these treasures of the spirit, the players seemed to have been created for the sake of the music, and in this sphere, a realm of sounds, four lone men, with no allegiance other than to this, were lost to the world, and they who had rather play than eat just played . . . and played . . . and played . . . and played. . . .

The Welshman came home late in the fall. His stay in Wales had been a pro-
longed one. He had had a lovely time, and music was in his veins, singing *Fal la la*
with the Welsh. Evan Evans was rather looking forward to finding Old Stoeffel and
sorting out the music.

The lawyer had not expected to find Old Stoeffel where he found him—nor any
of the others, including Mr. Nilson. But there they were. No one had ever missed
them. No one had even looked.

They were all still seated, slumped a little, their instruments glued to the chins of
the three fiddlers—and all was quiet, as if at the end of a peaceful *cantabile* the
choir of musical sounds had thinned away, *diminuendo*, into final silence—and Old
Herr Stoeffel, motionless, still gripped his cello between his well-starved knees.

The candle wax lay white on the Welshman's carpet.

It was, of course, the perfect quartet. It is a rare thing to find a quartet which can
meet at a time to suit everyone. Four individuals have four separate lives. It is rare,
when you find four good players, that one doesn't have to leave before the others
are satisfied. Here was a meeting not only of minds and talents, but a meeting of
spirits. It could happen only once in a lifetime. And they all simply played themselves to death.

I have never had any reason to doubt the Welshman's story. As I say, he was himself a fiddler. Nilson and Stoeffel and Del Jolio I never knew. But the cheap little
Japanese fiddle that Stevens used to play on is still in Evans Evans's collection.

"A memento," he explained, "of a great artist—four great artists!"

It was a Nipponese imitation of a Stradivari.

Antonio Stradivari (1644–1737) was the most renowned of the great seventeenth-
century violin makers. In our day owning a "Strad" is the secret fantasy of every serious violinist.

"In a good quartet," he said, "even the second fiddle is beautiful!"

He was right. He would know. And I haven't any doubt that ringed around in
their proper chairs in heaven are now the four greatest amateur quartet players of
all time—Old Herr Stoeffel, the organizer, the pack horse of the dog box, unde-
feated; Del Jolio, the egoist, making commanding eyes at the thirty-second note
runs; Mr. Stevens, in his unrimmed glasses, nothing, it is true, by himself, but strong
among his kind;

Here again is a reference to the difference between first and second violinists.
Thirty-second notes are normally very fast (eight of them occurring in a single quarter-
note beat) and are characteristic of the spectacular passages that a first violinist is expected to play, often at sight (i.e., with no previous exposure to the music). By comparison, Mr. Stevens, the second violinist, is "nothing . . . by himself."

with Arthur Nilson, free from his conscience forever, sweetly blending in on his ten-
der-toned viola—and in the *pizzicato* passages the whole quartet airily outplucking
all the angels of heaven and their harps.

This is a reference to Beethoven's *Quartet in E♭ Major*, the *Harp*, Op. 74, which includes a good deal of pizzicato playing in the first movement.

Entertaining as Burnett's story is, it also represents a fairly thorough survey of the string quartet literature. Having read about it, it is now time for you to do some listening. There are three possible ways for going about this. Locate an amateur string quartet and ask permission to sit in on their readings. Go to a concert presented by a professional quartet. Or listen to recordings. For most readers the last option is going to be the most practical, but the others are definitely worth trying. In this case, seeing enhances hearing: the total experience of a live performance far outweighs the mere hearing of it on a recording.

Where should you start? You may follow the order of the quartets mentioned in the story, or your teacher may offer other suggestions. One idea would be to begin with Schubert's beautiful *Quartetsatz in C Minor*, since it is just a single movement (of an unfinished quartet—most quartets consist of four movements). Beethoven's *Quartets,* Op. 59, Nos. 2 and 3, include Russian folk themes, in deference to the nationality of Count Rasoumovsky, in whose house they were first played. (The Russian melody of Op. 59, No. 2 is heard also in the "Coronation Scene" from Mussorgsky's opera, *Boris Godunov.* See Example 26, Chapter 7.) Or perhaps you would prefer starting with a twentieth-century master, such as Bartók or Schoenberg. For the latest innovations in the quartet repertoire, consult the Vox album, "The Avant Garde String Quartet in the U.S.A.," which includes works such as George Crumb's *Images I: Black Angels* for electrified string quartet. Wherever you start, listen to at least one work from each of the three fertile quartet periods: Classical, Romantic, and Modern.

You may also want to sample the literature for string quartet and one extra instrument. There are several outstanding piano quintets (string quartet plus piano), most notably by Schumann, Brahms, Dvořák, and Franck (one each) plus Schubert's unusually scored *Trout Quintet* (based again on an original Schubert song tune) for piano, violin, viola, cello, and double bass. Mozart and Brahms each composed a clarinet quintet, Schubert a superb cello quintet, and Mozart several stunning viola quintets—all calling for a combination of string quartet and one other instrument (specified by the

Trio with piano, violin, and cello. Victorian chamber music illustrated in *Harper's Weekly,* 1876.

title). Schoenberg's *String Quartet No. 2 in F♯ Minor* turns into an unusually scored quintet with the inclusion in the last two movements of a soprano solo in settings of poems by Stefan Georg.

If you like chamber music with piano, you will want to examine the literature for one or two instruments and piano: violin sonatas by Mozart, Beethoven, Brahms, Franck, and Debussy; cello sonatas by Beethoven, Brahms, and Debussy; clarinet sonatas by Brahms (optionally for viola); trios by Beethoven, Schubert, Mendelssohn, Brahms, Dvořák, and Ravel. Mozart, Schumann, Brahms, and Fauré composed fine piano quartets (piano plus string trio). There is also music for piano combined with wind and/or brass instruments. For example, the scintillating *Sextet* by the Frenchman Francis Poulenc (1899–1963) calls for piano, flute, oboe, clarinet, bassoon, and French horn. The German composer Paul Hindemith (1895–1963) devised sonatas for virtually every orchestral instrument, no matter how neglected as a solo instrument—tuba, bassoon, and English horn—each accompanied by piano. Going back a few hundred years, virtually all chamber music originating in the Baroque period includes harpsichord, sometimes only as *continuo* background, but often as a solo instrument as well.*

There is also an impressive repertoire of brass chamber music from the pens of Giovanni Gabrieli, Claudio Monteverdi, and Heinrich Schütz, the Italian school of the sixteenth and seventeenth centuries. (Schütz was German, but lived for several years in Italy.) For those interested in early instruments, the fourteenth and fifteenth centuries offer a wealth of chamber music for recorders, sackbuts, shaums, viols, and the like. Many Baroque works combine instruments with one or more solo voices; try Schütz (1585–1672) and Dietrich Buxtehude (1637–1707) in addition to the eighteenth-century giants, Bach and Handel.

All in all, the chamber music repertoire is immense. Since you are likely to want only a sampling at first, the string quartet is a good place to start. And then, should you turn into a chamber music buff, there are all these other specialties awaiting your aural investigation.

---

*In our own time, the American Elliott Carter (b. 1908), imitating a familiar Baroque combination, has composed a *Sonata for Flute, Oboe, Cello, and Harpsichord.*

Terms preceded by (•) are included in lists for Units 1 and/or 2.

General and Historical

ensemble scene (146)
- finale (146)
  libretto (148)
  Orpheus (146, 162)
- program music (173)
  Ring of the Nibelung (152)
- tutti (146)

Instrumental Music

chamber music (200)
- development (174)
- exposition (174)
  families of the orchestra (181)
- overture (142)
- pizzicato (174)
- recapitulation (174)
- scherzo (177)
- sonata form (173)
- suite (179)
- tremolo (174)

Vocal Music

- aria (146)
  bel canto (161)
  duet (143)
  music drama (157)
  opera (146 ff)
  operetta (148, 161)
- recitative (144)
  round (197)
  Sprechstimme (172)

Theory (General)

adagio (207)
arpeggio (181)
atonality (169n)
- canon (197)
- coda (146, 174)
- dissonance (170)
  homophonic (186)
  Leitmotif (157)
  octave equivalent (187n)
- ostinato (185)
  pedal point (189)
  polyphonic (186)
  tonic triad (174)

Theory (Fugue) (186 ff)

answer (186)
augmentation (194)
countersubject (186)
diminution (194)
episode (187)
exposition (188)
inversion (194)
stretto (191)
subject (186)
voice (186)

MUSIC AND IDEAS

"Has it been noticed that music liberates the spirit? gives wings to thought? that one becomes more of a philosopher the more one becomes a musician?" So wrote Friedrich Nietzsche, one of the most important philosophers of modern times (and an amateur composer himself).[1] But, if music inherently expresses ideas, it is nevertheless only since Beethoven that one discerns explicit verbal messages in musical compositions. Of course, earlier composers had written music embodying both religious and secular ideas. But when Palestrina composed a mass or Bach a passion, the ideas expressed were not their own—neither composer was speaking his own mind outright. In the nineteenth century the situation changed, starting with Beethoven's inclusion of Friedrich Schiller's rapturous invocation of universal brotherhood, "Ode to Joy," as the text of his *Symphony No. 9.* Even though Beethoven penned only a brief preface to Schiller's poem, the music somehow comes across as if he had conceived the entire text himself. Furthermore, his combination of words and music was not intended for performance within the confines of church ritual (albeit a Protestant hymn was later to be derived from it) or in an opera house; instead the concert hall itself was being transformed into a philosophical forum. And, since Schiller's paean to brotherhood now enjoys worldwide familiarity largely due to Beethoven's setting, we can truthfully affirm that, in Nietzsche's words, music has given wings to thought.

Unit 4, *Music and Ideas,* presents various musical works in which composers have set forth philosophical messages. Chapter 18 deals explicitly with the finale of Beethoven's *Symphony No. 9.* Since the structure of this movement is a modified set of variations, the chapter also includes a discussion of the basic form known as *theme and variations.* Mozart's *Piano Sonata in A Major,* first movement, is analyzed as an illustration of this much employed form.

Chapter 19 proceeds to philosophical expressions by composers of the Romantic period, featuring brief considerations of works by Richard Strauss and Gustav Mahler. It was during the Romantic period that program music gradually assumed importance in the orchestral repertoire. A background essay takes up the controversy created by this new form of music, particularly as represented in the "warfare" which long ensued between the programmatic adherents of Wagner versus the purists who admired Brahms.

Chapter 20 moves into the present century, dealing with a variety of compositional approaches involving philosophical messages of one kind or another. Charles Ives, John Cage, and George Crumb are profiled. A background essay considers the innovations and inventions of a host of modern composers who have expanded the boundaries of instrumental sound. Since the most important new sounds appear to be those produced or modified electronically, a brief history of electronic music is included.

The last two chapters of Unit 4 raise a different aspect of the interrelationship of ideas and music, namely, the position of music as a subject of literature. In Chapter 21 we look at Mozart's *Don Giovanni* as it figures in several important literary works by such authors as E.T.A. Hoffmann, Søren Kierkegaard, Hermann Hesse, and George Bernard Shaw. In Chapter 22 we examine the Faust legend in music, especially with regard to Thomas Mann's novel about a composer, *Doctor Faustus*. This chapter also provides us with an opportunity to consider the modern compositional method known as the *twelve-tone system*. Schoenberg's *Phantasy for Violin*, Op. 47, is the featured piece.

Music and Ideas

THE COMPOSER AS PHILOSOPHER

18

BEETHOVEN, SYMPHONY NO. 9 IN D MINOR, FINALE

Beethoven's *Symphony No. 9* is a monumental work, by far the composer's longest symphony. The first three movements are scored for orchestra alone, but the fourth movement calls for four vocal soloists (soprano, alto, tenor, and bass) and a large chorus. Although the three purely orchestral movements rank among Beethoven's finest, it is the finale which accounts for the symphony's great popularity. The presence of solo and choral voices adds an exciting new dimension hitherto unknown in symphonic music, and the inspired main theme is a perfect vehicle for expressing the noble sentiments of Schiller's text.

Example 97
BEETHOVEN, *Symphony No. 9*, Finale, Main Theme

A model of purity and simplicity, this theme is the basis for a complex series of variations of considerable grandeur and virtuosity. As you listen to the music you will be able to recognize the theme in its various guises, but you may be confused by the multitude of switches from orchestra alone to various combinations of soloists, chorus, and orchestra. The following listening guide is intended as a musical scorecard to help you find your way in the music. It will be convenient to divide the movement into three large-scale sections which break down further into a total of fourteen smaller units. Section I, the introduction, is scored exclusively for orchestra. Section II, representing the principal portion of the movement, brings in the vocal soloists and the chorus. Section III is an extensive coda for all the participants.

Ludwig van Beethoven (1770–1827) was a link between the Classic and Romantic periods in music.

Section I: Introduction

The movement opens with a brass-winds-percussion chord of piercing dissonance, erupting into a phrase of ferocious vigor. The cellos and basses follow with an imitation of vocal recitative, anticipating the actual vocal recitatives which occur later in the movement. After a second brass-winds-timpani outburst and still more cello-bass recitative, the music changes abruptly to a brief quotation from the first movement of the symphony (soft sustained winds, tremolo strings). Further recitative passages lead to other short quotes from the second and third movements: first the quick-footed scherzo (staccato winds and pizzicato strings) and then the gentle slow movement (winds and French horns). (With these excerpts from earlier movements Beethoven seems to be telling us that the music to come is to be the most important of all.) Only after still another recitative phrase do the winds hint at the principal theme of this, the fourth and final movement (see Example 97). One last passionate cello-bass recitative, heavily punctuated by brass and woodwind chords, leads to the next part of the introduction.

We now hear the main theme, played by cellos and basses without adornment or accompaniment. A brief series of orchestral variations follows:

1. The violas take the theme, accompanied by independent melodic lines (*counterpoint*) in the lower strings and bassoon.

2. The first violins take the theme, with more counterpoint in the lower strings and second violins, and some doubling of the theme in the bassoon.

3. The whole orchestra comes in loud, with the theme in the winds and brass. A considerable extension of the theme completes the orchestral introduction.

Music and Ideas

Section II: "Ode to Joy"

The full orchestra repeats the dissonant chord heard at the outset of the introduction, commencing what appears to be a full-fledged restatement of that section. But now the cellos and basses are replaced in the recitative passages by the bass soloist himself. His first words explain the dissonance of the opening chord. "Oh friends, not these tones!" he sings, "but rather let us raise our voices in more pleasant and joyous sounds." (These opening words are Beethoven's, not Schiller's, whose ode is now unthinkable without Beethoven's penned introduction; their philosophical significance was underscored when in 1914 the novelist Hermann Hesse entitled an essay opposing World War I with Beethoven's opening phrase, "O Freunde, nicht diese Töne!") As if in response to the bass's admonishment the radiant principal theme now returns in full glory.

Example 98
Symphony No. 9, Finale, Bass Solo Recitative

Schiller's poem consists of eight twelve-line stanzas, each subdivided into an eight-line verse followed by a four-line refrain. The rhyme scheme is a-b-a-b in the verses, but changes to a-b-b-a in the refrains, and the subdivisions are further emphasized by Schiller's having indented the refrains closer to the middle of the page. (Unlike the traditional repetition of a single refrain text after each verse, here each stanza presents a new refrain.) In his musical structure Beethoven has carefully differentiated between the verses and refrains, as will be illustrated below.

The bass soloist now sings the *verse* (lines 1–8) of stanza 1, the chorus backing him up with a repetition of lines 5–8.

> Joy, of flame celestial fashioned,
> > Daughter of Elysium,
> By that holy fire impassioned
> > To thy sanctuary we come.
> Thine the spells that reunited
> > Those estranged by Custom dread,
> Every man a brother plighted
> > Where thy gentle wings are spread.[1]

The Composer as Philosopher

Following a short orchestral interlude, the four soloists sing the main theme for the verse of stanza 2 ("Wem der grosser Wurf gelungen . . ."). (Note that the refrain of stanza 1 has been omitted for now.) As before, the chorus repeats the last four lines of the verse, while the refrain is again omitted (as in the previous stanza).

> Who that height of bliss has proved
> > Once a friend of friends to be,
> Who has won a maid belovèd
> > Join us in our jubilee.
> Whoso holds a heart in keeping,
> > One—in all the world—his own—
> Who has failed, let him with weeping
> > From our fellowship be gone!

The two male soloists start the third stanza ("Freude trinken alle Wesen . . ."), with their female counterparts joining in somewhat later. The main theme seems to vanish, but it is merely disguised by embellishments, first in the bass part, then in the alto and finally the soprano parts. The main notes of the theme are indicated in the circled notes in Example 99.

Example 99
Symphony No. 9, Finale, Embellished Treatment of the Main Theme
(See Circled Notes)

Music and Ideas

All drink joy from Mother Nature,
  All she suckled at her breast,
Good or evil, every creature,
  Follows where her foot has pressed.
Love she gave us, passing measure,
  One Who true in death abode,
E'en the worm was granted pleasure,
  Angels see the face of God.

Once again the chorus repeats the second half of the verse, and the refrain is omitted. A brief choral-orchestral passage serves as transition to the next section, which is for instruments alone.

The music is now very soft, as we hear gentle "bleeps" from the bassoons, contrabassoon, and bass drum. The meter changes from a simple $\frac{4}{4}$ to two triplet groupings per measure ($\frac{6}{8}$). Beethoven marked the new section "alla marcia," and sure enough the music turns into an elegant march, with the bass drum, triangle, and cymbals providing the "tsing-booms." As the principal theme begins in the piccolo and other wind and brass instruments, we notice the absence of strings; we are listening to a genuine military band! The theme is now converted into a regular alternation of long and short notes, replacing the even durations of its original form (as shown in Example 97).

Example 100
Symphony No. 9, Finale, "Band" Version of Main Theme

After the "band" plays the theme all the way through once, the tenor soloist enters with the refrain of stanza 4 ("Froh, froh wie seine Sonnen"). The theme remains in the orchestra while the tenor sings a countermelody against it. The choir joins in, and the soloist sings an ever more florid line, culminating at the top of his range in a high B♭.

Gladsome as her suns and glorious
  Through the spacious heavens career,
  Brothers, so your courses steer
Heroes joyful and victorious.

Simultaneous with the tenor's B♭, the orchestra commences an extended *fugato* based on a variant of the main theme. It starts in the bassoons, cellos, and basses, then moves to the first violins, and later comes back to the cellos (at first with violas but without basses). At the same time, other instruments play a spirited countermotive.

223

The Composer as Philosopher

The fugal passage continues for an extended period, eventually climaxing as all the instruments play a series of accented octaves. Suddenly all the instruments drop out except for two French horns playing an octave F♯. The oboes and bassoons then quietly commence the main theme but do not get past the third note. There is a reason for this: they are playing in the key of B major, whereas the main key of the movement is D major, and Beethoven is ready to return to this key. The oboes and bassoons try the theme again, this time in B minor. This still is not the right key, of course, but at least it is closely related to D major—in fact B minor and D major share the same key signature of two sharps. Meanwhile the two horns patiently continue their F♯s (which fit into all three keys), as if aware that eventually the right key will come into focus. Finally, even softer than before, the oboes (accompanied by horns) get it right, playing the first three notes of the main theme in D major.

At this point the chorus and orchestra resume in full force, presenting the complete main theme, once again with the verse of stanza 1 ("Freude, schöner Götterfunken"). The choir restores the theme to its original ⁴₄ meter, but the strings continue the ⁶₈ triplet figures in their accompaniment.

We have now arrived at a crucial moment in the musical structure: a majestic new theme is introduced as the choir at long last renders the refrain of stanza 1 ("Seid umschlungen, Millionen!"). The music is loud and forceful, with the men singing out in stentorian fashion.

Example 101
Symphony No. 9, Finale, Theme 2 (Stanza 1, Refrain)

Millions in our arms we gather,
To the world our kiss be sent!
Past the starry firmament,
Brothers, dwells a loving Father.

Why, at this late point in the movement, does Beethoven turn back to the refrain of the first stanza? Read on—it is all explained below.

The refrain of stanza 3 ("Ihr stürzt nieder, Millionen?") is presented in a contrasting passage of slow and solemn dignity.

Fall ye millions, fall before Him,
Is thy Maker, World, unknown?
Far above the stars His throne
Yonder seek Him and adore Him.

Music and Ideas

We have now reached the climax of the movement, and it is in this section that we discover the *musical* solution to the riddle posed by Beethoven's separation of the verse and refrain of stanza 1 earlier in the movement. It turns out that Theme 2 (Example 101) can be set as counterpoint against a modified version of Theme 1 (Example 97). A new triplet (long-short) version of Theme 1, sung by the sopranos, combines with Theme 2 (altos), and thereby the words of both the verse *and* refrain of stanza 1 are heard *simultaneously*. The tempo marking is "allegro energico, sempre ben marcato," meaning "fast and energetic, with lots of accents throughout." Each of the two themes is taken up successively by the various sections of the chorus. By the end of this rather lengthy passage the entire orchestra is playing in fullthroated support of the chorus.

Example 102

Symphony No. 9, Finale, Themes 1 and 2 Combined

Finally, we hear a quiet and *misterioso* treatment of the refrain of stanza 3.

Section III: Coda

The concluding portion of the movement consists of several short settings of the verse and refrain of stanza 1. With the exception of a couple slow interruptions, the general effect is of continuous acceleration, eventually reaching *prestissimo* (Theme 2). After a final brief but intense slow passage, the symphony concludes with a rousing multi-repetition (*ostinato*) of the first two measures of the main theme tagged by tonic scales and triads—a veritable musical explosion of universal humanistic love!

BASICS: THEME AND VARIATIONS FORM

Although the finale of Beethoven's *Symphony No. 9* includes several variations on its famous theme, as a whole the movement extends beyond the scope of an ordinary set of variations. In this essay we shall examine the essentials of simple theme and variations form.

To begin, in planning a set of variations a composer may select an original theme (possibly derived from an earlier work) or else opt for a theme by a different composer.

225

Of the latter sort, Brahms composed piano variations on themes by Handel and Paganini and an orchestral set on a theme attributed to Haydn. Sometimes a composer chooses a traditional folk or patriotic theme, as in Beethoven's and Charles Ives's variations on "God Save the King," also known as "America," and Mozart's variations on the tune we know as "Twinkle, Twinkle, Little Star." Once having selected a suitable theme, the composer then creates a series of variations, three or more in number. There is no upper limit to the number of variations in a given set; however, few sets exceed in length Beethoven's monumental set of *Thirty-three Variations on a Waltz by Diabelli.** A smaller set often constitutes a single movement within a larger work (sonata, concerto, symphony), as in the case of the theme and three variations which comprise the slow movement of Beethoven's *Piano Sonata in G Major*, Op. 14, No. 2. Larger variation sets ordinarily stand alone as separate and complete entities.

Each variation within a given set normally retains the internal structure of the theme upon which it is based. For example, where the structure of a theme is characterized as *A–B–A–B–A* (as in the finale of Beethoven's *Symphony No. 9*), each of the variations can be expected to exhibit a similar internal organization. In each subsequent variation the given melody is subjected to rhythmic disguises and other kinds of distortions, yet remains fundamentally unchanged throughout. Similarly, the harmonic structure of the theme is at least partially retained, most noticeably at the beginnings and endings of phrases.

By way of illustrating the variety of compositional techniques employed in traditional variations form, we now proceed to a detailed examination of the six variations on an original theme which comprise the first movement of Mozart's *Piano Sonata in A Major*, K. 331. The theme is divided into two separate sections, each of which is repeated. Section 1 consists of two four-measure phrases which begin alike but conclude with different *cadences*. Section 2 breaks down into three subsections: (1) a new contrasting phrase, (2) a return of the original phrase, and (3) a brief coda. (See Example 103.)

Although relatively simple as compared with the complexities of the ensuing variations, Mozart's theme itself represents a variation, or fleshing-out, of a simpler melodic/harmonic framework, as partially illustrated in Example 104. This framework will serve as a point of reference for our consideration of the six successive variations.

---

*Diabelli was a music publisher who conceived the curious notion of asking a number of different composers each to compose a single variation on his waltz theme. Among those who complied were the eleven-year-old Liszt and the twenty-five-year-old Schubert. Beethoven, becoming intrigued with Diabelli's rather uninspired theme, ignored the conditions of the request and created his largest set of variations. It is uncertain whether anyone ever actually performed Diabelli's composite set, but the Beethoven work has become a mainstay of the pianist's repertoire.

Music and Ideas

Example 103

MOZART, *Piano Sonata in A Major*, K. 331, 1st Mvt., Theme

Example 104

Structural Framework of Measures 1–4 (See Example 103)

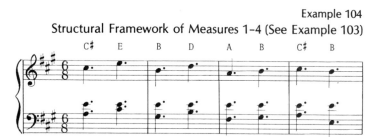

The Composer as Philosopher

Variation 1   The right-hand part adds ornamental notes which hover around the soprano (i.e., top line) notes of the framework. For example, in measure 1 the framework notes C♯ and E are embellished by B♯, D♯, and F♯ (see Examples 104 and 105). Meanwhile the left-hand framework chords are deflected from the metrically accented first and fourth beats of each measure to the weaker second and fifth beats.

Example 105
A Major Variations, Opening of Variation 1

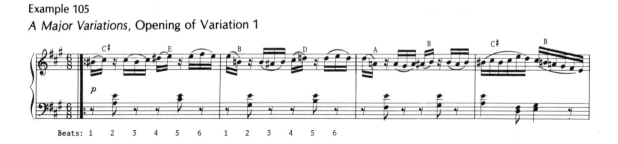

As indicated above, after measure 4 of the theme Mozart simply started out again as before but with a different cadence in measures 7–8 (see Example 103). By musical analogy, in Variation 1 we might expect measures 5–8 to adhere closely to measures 1–4, but, instead, Mozart introduced *new* variational material in this second phrase. Whereas the first four measures are soft and relaxed, the second four measures are loud and dynamic, with an insistent repeated-note figure in the left hand. In measures 5–6 the melody consists of the framework soprano notes filled in by ornamental passing notes, while in measures 7–8 the melody is virtually identical to the corresponding measures of the theme.

Example 106
Variation 1, Measures 5–8

The second half of Variation 1 restores the lighter style of the opening phrase, but the heavier style recurs once again in the two-measure coda. Mozart retained this duality between light and heavy variational styles in all but one of the remaining five variations.

Variation 2   Here the soprano line ornamentation is reminiscent of measures 5–8 of Variation 1—compare Examples 106 and 107. The left hand accompanies with a "drone" figure in triplet sixteenth notes—the first note of each triplet grouping representing the true bass line, closely derived from the framework bass part, and with the

Music and Ideas

continuously repeated second and third triplets, D♯ and E, representing the droning inner voice (compare Example 107 with Example 104). In measures 5–8 the triplets appear in the right-hand part, but with the melody of measures 1–4 left almost unaltered. And once again, as in Variation 1, the second phrase is loud in contrast to the soft initial phrase.

Example 107
Opening of Variation 2

Example 108
Variation 2, Mm. 5–6

Variation 3 Up to now the key of the variations has been A major, as indicated by the three sharps of the key signature. Can you imagine the sound of the original theme transformed into A minor? With no sharps in the key signature the heavily emphasized framework C♯s would be replaced by C♮s. The gentle flowing variation you are about to hear is in the minor mode, with the soprano framework notes moving from the right hand in measures 1–2 to the left hand in measures 3–4. For the second four-measure phrase Mozart doubled the theme in octaves, *forte*.

Example 109
Variation 3, Mm. 1-6 (Minor Mode)

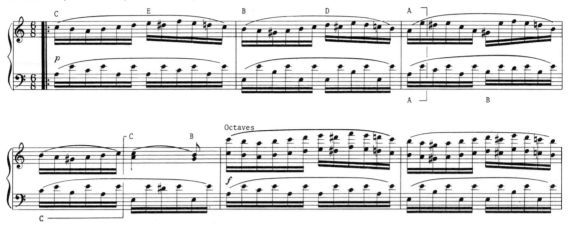

Variation 4 With A major reinstated this variation represents a three-tiered texture. The bass consists of simple percussive notes, mainly on the strong first and fourth beats of each measure; the right hand plays a middle-voice sixteenth-note figure based on the framework melodic line; and still an octave higher the left hand reaches over the right hand to play a flutelike doubling of the right-hand melody notes. This is one of Mozart's finest variational inspirations. He apparently liked it so much himself that in this one case he chose *not* to vary measures 5–8 with respect to measures 1–4; the first two phrases are nearly identical, just as in the theme (Example 103).

Example 110
Variation 4, Mm. 1-4, Three Timbres (Low, Medium, High)

Variation 5 At this point Mozart changed his tempo to *adagio*, roughly three times slower than the tempo of the theme. The long durations between eighth-note beats allow time for quick ornamental elaborations in thirty-second notes. (Paradoxically, slow variations often contain numerous fast notes.) The opening melody recalls the beginning of Variation 2, whereas the varied repetition in measures 5–8 is more like the second phrase of Variation 1.

Variation 6 The music now resumes a quick tempo, somewhat faster than the theme itself. The meter changes from two triplet eighth-note groupings per measure ($^6_8$) to a jaunty $^2_4$ march. The soft first phrase is succeeded by an exciting loud second phrase.

A brief coda of nine measures brings the variations to a close.

Music and Ideas

Several features of Mozart's *A Major Variations* are common to most sets of variations. To begin with, continuous figuration embellishes the basic notes of the melody. Rhythmically the theme consists of simple configurations, while the variations tend to successively greater complexity. With the theme in major, usually at least one variation is in minor, or vice versa. At least one variation is typically much slower than the theme, and correspondingly another variation may be much faster. Furthermore, one or more variations may exhibit a different meter from that of the theme. Any single variation may exhibit more than one kind of variational technique. In the nineteenth century, Romantic composers introduced still another variational element—*character*. This means that, along with all the technical aspects of composition, composers also juggled changes of mood. This is consistent with the Romantic interest in the expression of explicit emotions. A set of variations by Schumann or Brahms generally exhibits a greater expressive range than a set by Mozart or Haydn.

Every set of variations concludes with at least a minimal coda. Mozart's coda for the *A Major Variations* is relatively brief as compared with most codas, which often include partial or even complete extra variations (left unnumbered by the composer). In some instances the original theme is repeated with little or no change after or instead of the coda—as, for example, in the finale of Beethoven's *Piano Sonata in E Major,* Op. 109.

19

THE ROMANTIC
COMPOSER / PHILOSOPHER

Once Beethoven had established the precedent of using a text in a symphony (in the *Ninth*), other composers followed suit. Hector Berlioz (1803–1869), the iconoclastic French musician, was very much a "message" composer; nearly all his works entail a text. His dramatic symphony, *Romeo and Juliet,* projects a Shakespearean moral ultimately similar to Schiller's "Ode to Joy"—to wit, all humanity should live together in peace and harmony. Moreover, Berlioz was himself a prose writer of considerable talent. Like many composers up to the present day, he earned part of his livelihood reviewing concerts for newspapers. He also wrote portions of the libretto of his opera, *The Damnation of Faust,* and composed the words as well as the music for *Lelio,* a monodrama involving a mixture of speech (delivered by an actor) and song accompanied alternately by piano and orchestra. He published a collection of critical essays on a wide assortment of musical topics, *Evenings in the Orchestra,* and left a substantial volume of memoirs.

Robert Schumann (1810–1856), an early German Romantic composer, was fascinated by literature and founded an important music journal.

Berlioz was a great lover of literature and he particularly admired Shakespeare and Goethe. Another early Romantic captivated by literature was the German composer, Robert Schumann (1810–1856). Schumann's father was a novelist and book publisher, and at one time Schumann considered devoting his life to literary pursuits. Later, after his musical career was well established, Schumann founded a music journal dedicated to upgrading the level of music criticism in Germany. As editor he championed the music of neglected masters such as Bach and Schubert, and he played an equally important role in discovering new musical talents such as Chopin and Brahms. Literary and musical inspirations are interwoven in certain of Schumann's piano works reflecting the views of two creatures of his own imagination: the brash and impetuous Florestan and the quiet and dreamy Eusebius. These figures belong to a "secret society," the *Davidsbund*, or Society of David, a group of young idealists united in their opposition to the philistines in their midst.*

Schumann's *Davidsbündlertänze* (*Band-of-David Dances*) is a collection of short character pieces for piano, about half of them in the spirit of the dynamic Florestan, the others reflecting the gentle Eusebius. An "F" or "E" at the end of each piece indicates which character the composer was thinking of, while two of the pieces, being brash *and* reflective, receive both initials. Another piano collection by Schumann, *Carnaval*, includes three pieces relating to the Band of David: "Eusebius," "Florestan," and "The March of the Band of David against the Philistines." Much of Schumann's music criticism is enlivened by conversations ostensibly carried on by Florestan and Eusebius. Sharp differences of opinion are tempered by the wise counsels of their mentor, Master Raro. The vast collections of Schumann's aphorisms, essays, reviews, and letters have been translated into English, and are available both in complete and abridged editions.

Coming directly after Schumann was the most verbal of the great composers, Richard Wagner (1813–1883). Wagner was a central figure in nineteenth-century European intellectual circles; he loomed large in the worlds of politics and philosophy, as well as of music. At one point Wagner came under the influence of the Russian social agitator, Mikhail Bakunin, in consequence of which his blatant espousal of radical ideals led to several years of forced exile in Switzerland and France. Later he conceived a pessimistic *Weltanschauung* (world-view) similar to that of the noted German philosopher, Arthur Schopenhauer (*The World as Will and Idea*, 1819). Perhaps most important, in 1865 Wagner befriended the young Friedrich Nietzsche, whose theory of the superrace was eventually to provide the philosophical underpinning for Adolf Hitler's quest for worldwide domination.† Wagner appears not to have fully understood Nietzsche's complex ideas, and later their friendship eventually suffered an irreparable rupture. In any case it is clear that Wagner was an enthusiastic racist, and his essay, *Judaism in Music*, may have endeared him to the Nazis as much as any of his musical creations. Wagner's ideas represent a confusing and even paradoxical mixture of negativism and humanitarianism—the latter signified by his hatred of modern European society's dependency on an impoverished proletariat (harkening back to his association with Bakunin in the late 1840s).

Wagner published many volumes of prose writings, including essays, memoirs, and a volume of aesthetic theory entitled *Opera and Drama*. (For a long period after Wagner's death there was an authentic Wagner cult in Europe—and even in the culturally naive United States—resulting in an outpouring by both his followers and enemies of voluminous writings on music and musical aesthetics.) But perhaps Wagner's most

---

*The *American Heritage Dictionary* defines *philistine* as a "smug, ignorant, especially middle-class person who is held to be indifferent or antagonistic to artistic and cultural values."

†In defense of Nietzsche, some believe that his theory of the superrace, as adopted by the Nazis, was a total misrepresentation of his views, and that the "superman" represented not man over his fellow man, but man over himself, man evolving into superman by acts of will and intelligence.

impressive literary achievements are the libretti which he devised for his own music dramas. Mozart had his Da Ponte (*Don Giovanni, The Marriage of Figaro*) and Verdi his Boito (*Otello, Falstaff*), but Wagner wrote every word of his opera texts himself—in some cases even publishing them as dramatic poems independent of the musical scores. As George Bernard Shaw put it,

> A Beethoven symphony (except the articulate part of the *Ninth*) expresses noble feeling, but not thought: it has moods, but no ideas. Wagner added thought and produced the music drama. . . . Here, then, we have the simple secret of Wagner's preeminence as a dramatic musician. He wrote the poems as well as composed the music of his "stage festival plays," as he called them.[1]

Wagner founded a theory of dramatic and musical synthesis based on the use of the musical *Leitmotif*, which lends dramatic coherence to the musical fabric. Examples of the *Leitmotif* technique appear in the discussions of *Das Rheingold* and *Die Walküre* (see Chapters 14 and 29, respectively).

Having read all of this, the student first approaching Wagner's music dramas may be disappointed to find that his plots seem vastly removed from the contemporary scene. Progressive though he was, Wagner evinced no interest in depicting the wretched conditions shown in operas such as Berg's *Wozzeck* and Weill's *Threepenny Opera* (Chapter 15). Ironically, it was left to Giuseppe Verdi, Wagner's musically conservative Italian rival (Chapter 14), to project the immediacy and realism of life in the midnineteenth century. Verdi's *La Traviata* (*The Wayward Woman*) is full of arias, recitatives, choruses, and even a ballet—traditional trappings of grand opera deplored by Wagner, who preferred a less stilted, more realistic continuity akin to spoken drama. Yet Verdi based his opera on *Camille*, a true-to-life up-to-the-minute novel and play by Alexander Dumas the younger, whereas Wagner's works mostly portray other-than-human figures drawn from antiquity, mythology, medieval romances, and so on. Verdi was a dramatist interested in people, whereas Wagner was more a philosopher interested in ideas. Most of his characters are gods and/or godlike mortals. The deaths of Verdi's heroines —Violetta, Aïda, Gilda—are sad; the deaths of Wagner's Isolde and Brünnhilde are overwhelmingly tragic. As for the death of Siegfried, the great hero of the *Ring* cycle, Ernest Newman has described his funeral procession as "too vast, too universal for association with mere human death, [seeming] rather to be such music as the spirit of the universe might hear when world crashes into world at the end of time."[2]

Although Wagner applied the *Leitmotif* principle exclusively in his music dramas, other composers quickly recognized its usefulness in purely orchestral works. Franz Liszt (1811–1886), Wagner's father-in-law, conceived of a new genre, the tone poem, an orchestral work based on a "program" and similar in style to the purely orchestral passages of Wagner's music dramas. If a musical theme could represent an idea, person, or object in an opera, it could function in the same way in a composition without voices.

STRAUSS

In the late Romantic period the master of the tone poem was Richard Strauss (1864–1949), a direct musical descendant of Liszt and Wagner. Before the end of the nineteenth century he composed a series of stunning tone poems, including *Till Eul-*

Music and Ideas

enspiegel's *Merry Pranks, Don Quixote, Don Juan,* and *Death and Transfiguration.* (A detailed analysis of the last-mentioned work is found in Chapter 33.) Like Wagner before him, Strauss was an outstanding orchestral conductor, thereby developing a superb compositional sense for exploiting and combining the various instruments of the modern orchestra. (Strauss's father was a professional French horn player, and thus the young musician found easy access to orchestral and operatic music from the very outset.)

One of Strauss's tone poems is based on Nietzsche's *Thus Spake Zarathustra.*

> [Strauss's work] takes its title from Nietzsche's book of aphorisms in which the poet-philosopher suggests a superhuman way of life and outlines ethical concepts for a post-Christian society living in splendid self-confidence beyond all fettering concepts of good and evil.[3]

Nietzsche's ideas are to some extent embodied in George Bernard Shaw's play, *Man and Superman,* which is discussed in Chapter 21. The question arises here as to the degree to which a composer, as opposed to a writer, can interpret complex and weighty philosophical ideas. Here is Strauss's answer:

> I did not intend to write philosophical music or to portray Nietzsche's great work musically. I meant to convey by means of music an idea of the development of the human race from its origin, through the various phases of its development, religious as well as scientific, up to Nietzsche's idea of the Superman. The whole symphonic poem is intended as my homage to the genius of Nietzsche, which found its greatest exemplification in his book, *Thus Spake Zarathustra.*[4]

For the listener acquainted with Stanley Kubrick's film *2001—A Space Odyssey,* Strauss's opening theme will sound very familiar. (This music has also been used in television commercials to sell everything from gasoline to butter!) This is known as the

Example 111
STRAUSS, *Thus Spake Zarathustra,* World-Riddle Theme

235

The Romantic Composer/Philosopher

world-riddle theme, and is ideally suited to Kubrick's movie, which deals with such fundamental issues as the origin of humanity, its scientific development, and its religious values. The following commentary on the music reads like an interpretive summary of the film's symbolism.

> We are to suppose that . . . Zarathustra moves, during the course of the music, among mankind, weaning them from metaphysical superstitions, their dependence upon emotional impulses and passions, their narrow scientific pursuits. We further suppose that he revitalizes all of these with the light of his own nature-inspired knowledge, teaches mankind the ecstasy of nature's dance, and in due course returns to the mountains again.[5]

Kubrick exhibited keen acumen in selecting this tone poem as background music for the first part of his film.*

Strauss expressed himself in a personal vein in the tone poem *Ein Heldenleben* (The Life of a Hero). This work is said to "underscore the figure of an average man whose heroism lies in his triumph over the inward battles of life." Strauss himself wrote of the work, "There is no need of a program. It is enough to know that there is a hero fighting his enemies." But the music reveals the startling fact that the hero is none other than Strauss himself!—a fact verified by the inclusion of excerpts from his earlier tone poems. And who are the composer's enemies? Why, none other than the music critics, of course! Strauss was the rare composer who wrote his autobiography in music. In another work, the *Domestic Symphony*, he devoted a movement each to depicting himself, his wife, and his young child. An incident in the Strauss's marital life served as the plot of yet another work, the opera *Intermezzo*.

MAHLER

Just as Strauss mixed composing with a successful career as orchestra and opera conductor, so did his contemporary, Gustav Mahler (1860–1911). As composers both were masters of orchestration for mammoth-sized ensembles, yet their music exhibits distinct stylistic differences. Strauss seems more directly heir to Wagner, whereas Mahler often recalls the Classical masters, Mozart in particular. There were significant differences in their personalities, as well. Strauss was of solidly established Aryan stock, whereas Mahler, as a Jew, inhabited a hostile anti-Semitic climate. (He converted to Catholicism, largely for political reasons, as this made it easier for him to "get ahead.") Thus, where Strauss could confidently expect easy acceptance, Mahler must always face struggle—which assuredly contributed to the greater range of philosophical expression in his music. Described as a God-seeker, Mahler seems to have felt a greater affinity for Christianity and some eastern religions than for Judaism itself.

The most important musical difference between Strauss and Mahler lies in the genres in which they specialized. They shared an interest in composing lieder, but otherwise Mahler concentrated on large-scale symphonic form, Strauss on the tone poem and opera. Mahler was particularly adept as a composer of "song symphonies." Fully half of his ten symphonies contain either orchestral transcriptions of his earlier

---

*Other selections include Johann Strauss's familiar *Blue Danube Waltz* and an atonal choral work by the contemporary Hungarian composer, György Ligeti.

Gustav Mahler (1860–1911). Mahler specialized in "song symphonies." Fully half of his ten symphonies contain orchestral transcriptions of earlier songs or feature vocal solos and/or choral parts.

songs or movements actually featuring vocal solos and/or choral parts. Mahler's *Symphony No. 1* includes two transcriptions from his *Songs of a Wayfarer*, as well as a mock-humorous funeral march based on "Frère Jacques" in the *minor mode*. *Symphony No. 2* is a much grander conception, featuring soprano and alto solos and a choral setting of Klopstock's poem, *The Resurrection*, with additional lines of text by Mahler himself. The words and music express a longing for the infinite (not unlike Goethe's drama *Faust*—see Chapter 22):

> Believe, my heart, you have lost nothing.
> Everything you longed for is yours.
>
> . . .
>
> With wings I have won for myself
> I shall soar in fervent love
> To the light unseen . . .

In his *Symphony No. 3* Mahler inserted an alto solo with words drawn from Nietzsche's *Thus Spake Zarathustra*: "Oh man! Take heed . . . The world is deep, and deeper than the day remembers . . . But all joys want eternity, deep eternity." For all his seriousness, Mahler also possessed a strong humorous instinct, as attested by the lusty scherzos of his symphonies. In *Symphony No. 2* he balanced the heavy God-questing message of the final movement with an orchestral scherzo based on his earlier song, "Saint An-

The Romantic Composer/Philosopher

thony Preaches to the Fishes." In this song Saint Anthony tries to reform the various species of fish from their sinful ways:

> Despite sermons fluent,
> His flock has played truant;
> So out on the beaches
> St. Anthony preaches.
> > The fish come to listen;
> > In sunshine they glisten!
>
> The carp all were sleeping
> But now come a-leaping!
> They listen in wonder
> Their mouths wide asunder.
> > He gives them his blessing.
> > His words are impressing!
>
> The pike so ferocious
> Becomes quite precocious.
> In schools they are speeding
> To hark to his reading

However, as much as the fish enjoy his sermon, they soon backslide into their old familiar habits:

> The pike turn to fighting;
> The cod are back-biting;
> The crabs still are vermin
> In spite of his sermon.
> > His words were impressing,
> > But still they're transgressing!
> > > (translated by Yale Marshall)[6]

Mahler's adaptation of this humorous song in his otherwise portentous *Resurrection Symphony* may signify an ironic admission that all sermons, musical or otherwise, hold but slight hope of success.*

After composing the soprano solo which concludes his *Fourth Symphony*, Mahler reverted to traditional symphonic forms, scoring for voices again only in his *Symphony of a Thousand* (No. 8), based on Vergil and Goethe, which is more a massive cantata than a traditional symphony. Then, near the end of his life, Mahler created what many regard as his masterpiece, *Das Lied von der Erde* (The Song of the Earth), subtitled "A Symphony for Tenor and Alto Soloists and Orchestra," and consisting of settings of six Chinese poems drawn from a volume of German translations, *The Chinese Flute*, by Hans Bethge: "A splendid delicate, yet earth-born perfume of melancholy rises from these pages. It is as though one had entered into a kingdom of hopelessness, whose benumbing atmosphere one cannot escape."[7]

---

*The "Saint Anthony" movement of *Symphony No. 2* serves as the musical subject matter of the third movement of Luciano Berio's *Sinfonia,* a musical collage composed in 1967. See Chapter 20.

Music and Ideas

The *Song of the Earth*, even more than the music of Wagner or Strauss, epitomizes the Romantic composer as philosopher. The music transforms the poems, which are highly philosophical to start with, into extraordinarily expressive vehicles, from the tenor's first ecstatic "The Drinking Song of Earth's Sorrows" to the alto's drawn-out meditative "Farewell," which concludes the work.

A special poignancy characterizes "Farewell." It is an extremely long song, lasting nearly thirty minutes, and breaking down into three long parts, the second of which is an extensive orchestral interlude as beautiful as any music Mahler ever composed. The first pages of "Farewell" recall the opening and closing choruses of Bach's *Saint Matthew Passion*. Later the somber C minor beginning gives way to the brighter key of F major, and we hear Mahler's eternal "ticking" (as in the Adagietto of *Symphony No. 5* and the opening of *Symphony No. 9*). It is as if a universal clock were counting out the passage of time, from its inception onward to infinity.

Example 112

MAHLER, *The Song of the Earth*, "Farewell"

Still later Mahler introduced a different repetition pattern (*ostinato*), leading to one of his finest melodies, heard just before the onset of the orchestral interlude. The interlude itself is like a fantasy on the opening material of the song, the resemblance to Bach becoming even stronger.

Example 113

"Farewell," Orchestral Interlude

As the song nears completion we are reminded of Zarathustra returning to the mountains.

> Where am I going? To wander in the hills.
> I seek peace for my solitary heart.

A key image here is resignation. The ticking resumes, and the singer intones:

> I walk toward my home. I shall no longer roam
> in the distance. My heart is quiet and awaits its hour.

(It should be noted that Mahler made extensive alterations and additions to the poetry as he composed. He may have sensed his own forthcoming deliverance, for he died just after completing the work.)

Now another image emerges as the vital force of the earth reasserts itself:

> The lovely earth blooms in spring and becomes green again.

At first the music is rapturous. Then, as it gradually winds down, the alto chants again and again the final, "Ewig, ewig . . . forever and ever, throughout eternity." In Chapter 4 we observed that in *The Creation* Haydn used the most basic of chords, a resounding C major triad, to depict God's gift of light. Here Mahler used the simplest of melodic lines for the longing, peaceful setting of the word *ewig*, also in C major. There are just three pitches, the bottom notes of the major scale, E–D–C, with the D repeated: _{E-wig} _{E-D} _{e-wig} _{D-C}. In her low range the alto sings the E–D, D–C motive twice in its entirety. Then she thrice offers the first two pitches alone, with the orchestra haltingly completing each phrase. The "eternal ticking" continues throughout. Ultimately the music dissolves melodically into just the first pitch (E), while to the C–E–G of the C major triad the note A is added—producing a strange mixture of peace and yet irresolution. We have reached an ending that is no ending—a paradox in keeping with the spirit of much Oriental poetry.

In creating *The Song of the Earth* Mahler functioned as more than composer; he had become a veritable seer. A strong affinity seems to exist between Mahler's music and the novels of Hermann Hesse (1877–1962). Each of these artists has been discovered and rediscovered by increasingly larger audiences during the past generation. Both shared a tendency to explore and delineate the inner mysteries of human experience. Just as philosophy and poetry form an integral element in Mahler's music, so conversely music is an ever recurring theme in Hesse's output. His early novel, *Gertrude*, concerns a triangular relationship among a young male composer, a baritone opera star, and the soprano whom they both love. In *Steppenwolf* one of the figures encountered by Harry Haller during his wandering through the never-never land of the magic theater is no less than Wolfgang Amadeus Mozart. Music is also of central importance in Hesse's final achievement, *Magister Ludi* (The Glass Bead Game), a novel about a cultural utopia. Mahler and Hesse were both attracted to the wisdom of the East—witness *The Song of the Earth* on the one hand and *Siddhartha* and *Journey to the East* on the other. The heightened longing of Mahler's music as it reaches its most intense expression in "Farewell"—is it not cut from the same cloth as these words of the fictional Emil Sinclair?

> And all the pieces said the same thing, all expressed what the musician had in his soul: longing, a longing to identify oneself with the world and to tear oneself free again, listening to the workings of one's own dark soul . . .[8]

A MUSICAL CONTROVERSY: PROGRAM MUSIC VS. ABSOLUTE MUSIC

Great aesthetic debate has raged during the past 150 years over the question of musical meaning. Some have argued that nontexted music conveys verbal meaning, while others have just as roundly denied it. For some, music can tell a story without the aid of words; for others, music is absolute—it expresses nothing but itself. The former group subscribes to the belief—attributed to Schopenhauer—that music is

> the very image and incarnation of the innermost reality of the world, the immediate expression of the universal feelings and impulsions of life in concrete, definite form. That all music had transmusical content was one of the cherished, if not always acknowledged, beliefs of the nineteenth century.[9]

On the other hand, the "purist" group regards a piece of music as no more than a combination of sounds, timbres, rhythmic patterns, and the like, equivalent to the combination of colors, lines, and shapes in a non-objective painting. Any meaning that the listener receives is subjective—projected onto the music rather than induced from it.

> I consider that music is, by its very nature, essentially *powerless* to express anything at all, whether a feeling, an attitude of mind, a psychological mood, a phenomenon of nature, etc. . . . *Expression* has never been an inherent property of music. . . . If, as is nearly always the case, music appears to express something, this is only an illusion and not a reality. It is simply an additional attribute which, by tacit and inveterate agreement, we have lent it, thrust upon it, as a label, a convention—in short, an as-

pect unconsciously or by force of habit we have come to confuse with its essential being.[10]

The controversy over the nature of musical communication—is music a universal language, or any language at all?—became particularly acute toward the end of the last century. By that time the revolutionary new "program music" was the rage, competing with the absolute symphonic tradition established in the Classical period a hundred years earlier. (Short program pieces had been composed in the Baroque period, but program music did not have the clout then that it was to gain during the Romantic period.) Haydn, Mozart, and Beethoven had developed the four-movement symphony into a magnificent and enduring structure. Their symphonies for the most part were not *about* anything; they were simply superb musical structures. If occasionally a title became attached to a particular work, it was usually not the composer's choice (e.g., Beethoven's *Moonlight Sonata*) or else it was a little joke thought up by the composer, as in Haydn's *Surprise Symphony* (No. 94). In this work the very soft slow movement for strings alone suddenly explodes with a loud chord played by the full orchestra (including brass and tympani)—*that* is the surprise. Otherwise this work has no more verbal content than any other (untitled) Haydn symphony. A survey of Haydn's titled symphonies (and string quartets) reveals little of central programmatic significance in most examples.

Mozart, an expert opera composer (as we know from Chapter 13), also excelled in writing piano sonatas, chamber music, and symphonies—works still highly compelling two hundred years later despite the absence of programmatic subjects or titles. Beethoven broke the ice somewhat with his *Eroica* and *Pastoral* symphonies and added a chorus to the last movement of *Symphony No. 9* (see Chapters 15, 1, and 18, respectively). Before reaching the choral interpretation of Schiller's "Ode to Joy," however, *Symphony No. 9* proceeds at a leisurely pace through three sublime movements that relate to nothing that can be verbally translated. Like all great music, they pertain to thousands of little things and a few big things, but these "things" reach us via a direct, aural circuit. We "know" what the music is about when we find ourselves responding to it, but it is next to hopeless to try to express this experience or knowledge in words.

During the nineteenth century, many Romantic composers found themselves unable to sustain the great symphonic tradition passed down by their Classical forebears. Schubert composed outstanding symphonies, but he was as much a Classicist as Beethoven; only in his songs and short piano pieces can he be recognized as a true Romantic. Schumann and Mendelssohn made passable efforts, but their symphonies were no match for their predecessors', nor as good as their own character pieces for piano (usually titled), songs, and other short forms. Chopin concentrated on small forms almost exclusively. As the middle of the century approached, a new genre developed out of the symphonic vacuum—the tone poem, more or less created by Franz Liszt and carried to full splendor by the late Romantics—Tchaikovsky, Rimsky-Korsakov, Richard Strauss, Debussy, and Sibelius, among others. (Some of these composers lived well into the twentieth century.) A tone poem is essentially a one-movement symphony that describes a person, place, or event. Beethoven had already suggested the possibility of program music in the *Eroica's* funeral march (complete with solemn drum roll) and all throughout the *Pastoral*, with its babbling brook, singing birds, thunder storm, and dancing peasants. (Of course, these symphonies can be appreciated without knowing their programs; their musical quality is not a jot inferior to Beethoven's "pure" symphonies. But the incontrovertible fact is that these examples *are* programmatic.) Just after Beethoven's death (in 1827), Berlioz produced his five-movement hybrid, the *Symphonie fantastique* (see Chapter 28), a cross between standard symphonic construction and a suite of related tone poems. Berlioz actually printed a synopsis of the program of the *Symphonie fantastique* to be distributed to the audience. As in Beethoven's programmatic symphonies, Berlioz's music is good in and of itself (although few believe it matches the quality of Beethoven's major symphonic creations). But now the music is so highly descriptive that to ignore the program would be equivalent to viewing a Brueghel painting and seeing only lines, shapes, and colors instead of people, animals, buildings, and fields.*

Une Matinée chez Liszt, lithograph by Joseph Kriehuber, 1846. Like Chopin, Liszt epitomized the Romantic virtuoso/composer, enchanting his listeners with music full of sentiment and pathos.

So there was ample precedent for Liszt and his late Romantic descendants to focus on program music. If they could not succeed with full-scale absolute symphonies, they could handle more felicitously the shorter fifteen-to-twenty-minute tone poem.

*Brueghel was a sixteenth-century Flemish painter of panoramic scenes of peasant farm life.

The Romantic Composer/Philosopher

Correspondingly, in the realm of piano music they did better composing short program pieces rather than large nonprogrammatic sonatas. A great exception in their midst was Johannes Brahms (1833–1896), who composed four majestic symphonies, two piano concertos, a violin concerto, and a double concerto for violin and violoncello, along with numerous large works for piano and violin, piano and clarinet, piano and cello, piano trio, piano quartet, piano quintet, horn quintet, clarinet quintet, and string sextet. Brahms's enormous output of large-scale instrumental works makes him worthy of the accolade "successor to Beethoven." Not one of these sturdy and earnest works involves so much as a soprano soloist, nor has anyone thought up titles for them that have stuck. (Brahms's *Symphony No. 1* has sometimes been dubbed "Beethoven's Tenth," but this is purely tongue-in-cheek, based on a resemblance between the main theme of its finale and the "Ode to Joy" theme of Beethoven's *Symphony No. 9*.)

Adherents of the two kinds of instrumental music soon settled into opposing camps of "absolutists" versus "depictors." Great battles raged in the pages of music journals, with Brahms the "purist" pitted (more or less against his will) against the fiery Wagner (whose operatic integration of music and drama appealed to the program-music school). It seemed that you could like one kind of music or the other, but not both.*

In 1854 the absolutist cause was espoused by Edouard Hanslick in his book, *The Beautiful in Music,* which was regularly reprinted throughout the second half of the century. Hanslick became one of Brahms's most vociferous admirers, while Wagner was surrounded by a phalanx of adherents whose fanatical loyalty would have made Richard Nixon envious during his White House years. From our vantage point in the late twentieth century, the whole *contretemps* seems unnecessary. Wagner and Brahms were giants whose stature has long outlasted the petty bickering of their antagonistic contemporaries.

Caricature of Hanslick and Brahms. In his book, *The Beautiful in Music,* critic Hanslick championed Brahms, composer of "pure" absolute music, against Wagner, whose integration of music and drama appealed to the program music school.

*Curiously enough, Anton Bruckner (1824–1896), a composer of nine mammoth absolute symphonies, was allied to the Wagnerian camp.

Music and Ideas

It is now clear that both kinds of music have value and that the success of one is no threat to the long life of the other. Absolute music continues to be composed right alongside (and often by the same composers as) program music. And program music still breaks down into two types: (1) music which is so explicitly descriptive that the listener senses something missing if not given the title and/or accompanying verbal description and (2) music which seems absolute unless or until its programmatic content is specifically spelled out.

Today we have a new source of musical controversy: contemporary music, especially the atonal, electronic, aleatoric, and other experimental varieties. Many listeners are thrilled by the novel sounds of avant-garde music, while others cast aspersions on its very creditability as music. A survey of some of these new musical ventures is found at the end of Chapter 20.

20 THE TWENTIETH-CENTURY COMPOSER / PHILOSOPHER

In Chapter 19 we followed the integration of music and ideas through the end of the nineteenth century, focusing particularly on the music of Richard Strauss and Gustav Mahler. The last twenty years of Mahler's life can be regarded as a gestation period for the revolutionary changes that characterized the beginnings of modern music. The year of Mahler's death (1911) was marked by the premiere of Stravinsky's ballet *Petrouschka*, and by this time Bartók and Schoenberg in Europe and Charles Ives in America were experimenting with a variety of compositional techniques extending beyond the boundaries of traditional tonality. Before long, composers began also to experiment with musical sound itself. In this chapter we shall examine music by three notable American composer/philosophers—Charles Ives, John Cage, and George Crumb—and also survey some of the new kinds of sound which have emerged during the past fifty years.

CHARLES IVES

Perhaps no modern composer has been so overtly didactic as Charles Ives (1874–1954). As a young man he came under the influence of the transcendental movement, which propounded the view that one could rise above the problems of the mundane world by substituting exalted, even mystical conceptions of humanity and the universe for the coarse lessons of everyday experience. During the years 1909–1915 Ives composed his *Piano Sonata No. 2*, which is devoted to several of the principal philosopher/writers who lived in the transcendentalist stronghold of Concord, Massachusetts during the nineteenth century. Ives called his work, "Concord, Mass., 1840–1860," and named the four movements for Ralph Waldo Emerson, Nathaniel Hawthorne, the Alcott family, and Henry David Thoreau. The entire sonata is permeated by two principal motives, one of them the famous opening four-note motto of Beethoven's *Symphony No. 5*. For the third movement, "The Alcotts," Ives fashioned a characteristically "American" theme using the Beethoven motto as a starting point.

Example 114
IVES, *Concord Sonata*, "The Alcotts"

Still, Ives was uncertain that his music would say everything he had on his mind.

How far is anyone justified . . . in expressing or trying to express in terms of music (in sounds, if you like) the value of anything, material, moral, intellectual, or spiritual, which is usually expressed in terms other than music? How far afield can music go and keep honest as well as reasonable or artistic? . . . Can it be done by anything short of an act of mesmerism or an act of kindness on the part of the listener?[1]

Ives's solution to this conundrum was to write for the *Concord Sonata* a series of prefaces which he originally intended to publish jointly with the music. On second thought he decided the volume would be too cumbersome, so he printed the prefaces separately. The resulting *Essays Before a Sonata* represents probably the largest set of "program notes" ever prepared by a major composer. As is often the case with program notes, something may be said for listening to the music *first* and consulting the essays later.

Ives's philosophical interests were by no means limited to the transcendentalists. He was a social philosopher with strong views on how modern society and government should be reorganized. This is implicit in some of the titles of his numerous songs: "Immortality," "Lincoln, the Great Commoner," "Tolerance," and "An Election" (also called "It Strikes Me That" or "November 2, 1920"). In his song "The Majority (The Masses)" (also set as a choral work), Ives wrote a poem that casts him as a utopian visionary:

Thoreau and his circle. As a young man, Charles Ives came under the influence of the Transcendental Movement. Shown here are the movement's leading lights whom Ives depicted in his *Concord Sonata. Clockwise from upper left-hand corner:* Henry David Thoreau, Louisa M. Alcott, A. Bronson Alcott, Ralph Waldo Emerson, and Nathaniel Hawthorne.

Drawing by Elizabeth Shapiro

247

The Twentieth-Century Composer/Philosopher

The Masses are yearning, are yearning, are yearning.
Whence comes the hope of the World!

The Masses are as legion;
As the rain drops falling together make the Rivers and for a space become as one,
So men seeking common life together for a season become as one,
Whence come the nations of the World!

As the tribes of the ages wandered and followed the stars,
Whence come the many dwelling places of the World!

The Masses are dreaming, dreaming,
The Masses are dreaming,
Whence come the visions of God!

God's in His Heaven,
All will be well with the World!

In 1919 Ives wrote a long essay, "The Majority," in which he outlined his ideas for the reconstruction of democratic society.

> His plan was simplicity itself. Men were innately good; furthermore, "it must be assumed, in the final analysis and consideration of all social phenomena, that the Majority, right or wrong, are always right." Hence American democracy should be converted into one gigantic initiative and referendum. The people would vote directly on national laws, without regard to state lines. Political parties would be done away with, and all government officials would become "but an efficient clerical organization which shall carry out in detail the basic plans that the Majority propose." "Congress would become but a body of technical experts or specialists," preferably to be chosen through civil service examinations rather than by election; the president would be "executive head clerk." Elections would consist of two national ballots, separated by several months. On the first one, an initiative, the people would submit their suggestions for new laws. The "clerical machine" (Congress) would then select the most popular of these suggestions for inclusion on the second ballot and would make available to the people the "fundamental argument for and against each issue," avoiding unnecessary detail. The second vote would be a simple referendum on these issues. In discussing possible laws that the majority might approve under his scheme, Ives wrote favorably and in some detail of worker participation in the management of businesses, the nationalization of larger industries, and the imposition of limits on individual income and property. But his detailed plans show that he was principally interested in taking corrupting wealth away from the rich rather than in applying the surplus to the needs of the poor; and he tended to view all citizens, rich and poor alike, as good middle-class people like himself.[2]

JOHN CAGE

Another American composer who has turned to the written word as an adjunct to the sounded note is John Cage (b. 1912). Cage initially attracted attention with a variety of musical activities and experiments that led to his reputation as the "naughty boy" of American music. Perhaps emulating Ives's simultaneous mixture of different parade tunes in "Decoration Day" (see Chapter 8), Cage wrote a piece for twelve radios to be played simultaneously, each tuned to a different frequency. At the opposite end of the

American composer John Cage has more and more assumed the role of guru to avant-garde artists in music, dance, literature, and even the visual.

Richard Bunger, leading authority on the prepared piano, performs John Cage's *Suite for Toy Piano* at the Schoenhut 3-octave baby grand.

noise spectrum is his *4' 33"*, a work of total silence, albeit in three movements! (Cage's message is that absolute silence in concert halls is nonexistent, since airplanes fly overhead, the audience coughs and titters, etc.) Many of Cage's works are built on chance procedures, with the players controlling various aspects of the performance (so that no two performances are ever quite the same). Cage has also written innovative works for toy piano, prepared piano, and electronic instruments. (A *prepared piano* is a normal piano with various objects affixed to its strings to alter their timbre.) Many of these pieces display a charming naïveté that recalls the humor and dispassion of the French dadaist composer, Erik Satie (1866–1925). (For more on Satie, see Chapter 31.) Satie was one of the composers that Cage admired most during his formative years.

More and more since he first came to public notice, Cage has assumed the role of guru to avant-garde artists, both in and out of music. Gradually he has turned to lecturing and writing. His first book, published in 1961, is entitled—perhaps appropriately—*Silence*. More recently Cage brought out *A Year from Monday* (1967), in which—like Ives before him—he expresses concern for the moral reform of the world around him. The book is dedicated "To us and all those who hate us, that the U.S.A. may become just another part of the world, no more, no less." In his foreword, Cage says that he is "concerned with improving the world," and speaks of the importance of Marshall McLuhan and Buckminster Fuller. Three of the entries in the table of contents are excerpts from his diary, "How to Improve the World (You Will Only Make Matters Worse)." One must peruse the book oneself to taste its special flavor. Its typography was executed by an IBM Selectric typewriter with twelve different fonts, the selection of which (along with the margination on any given page) was determined by chance procedures. So even the book's appearance was directly influenced by Cage qua composer and aesthetician. The reader/listener is likely to be titillated at the very least, possibly genuinely amused, or even seriously engaged by Cage's musical output and graphic writings.

GEORGE CRUMB

One of the finest living American composers is George Crumb (b. 1929). Like Cage before him, he integrates chance procedures and novel sound sources into his music, yet achieves an artistic result which appears more substantial than Cage's. Crumb has demonstrated a great interest in the possibilities of philosophical expression in music. Many of his works are based on texts of Federico Garcia Lorca, one of the most important poets of the twentieth century. A characteristic work is Crumb's *Ancient Voices of Children* (1970), scored for mezzo-soprano, boy soprano, oboe, mandolin, harp, electric piano, toy piano, musical saw, harmonica, and percussion. Crumb tells us that in this work he has

> sought musical images that enhance and reinforce the powerful, yet strange haunting imagery of Garcia Lorca's poetry. I feel that the essential meaning of this poetry is concerned with the most primary things: life, death, love, the smell of the earth, the sounds of the wind and the sea.[3]

How does Crumb find the musical images he seeks? For one thing he constantly explores new sound effects and combinations.

> Perhaps the most characteristic vocal effect in *Ancient Voices* is produced by the mezzo-soprano singing a kind of fantastic vocalise (based on purely phonetic sounds) into an amplified piano, thereby producing a shimmering aura of echoes. ... Certain special instrumental effects are used to heighten the "expressive intensity"—e.g., "bending" the pitch of the piano by application of a chisel to the strings (second song); use of a paper-threaded harp (in "Dances of the Ancient Earth"). ... The mandolin has one set of strings tuned a quarter-tone low in order to give a special pungency to its tone. The three percussionists command a wide range of instruments, including Tibetan prayer stones, Japanese temple bells, and tuned tom-toms. The instrumentalists are frequently called upon to sing, shout, and whisper.[4]

Crumb goes on to quote Garcia Lorca, who speaks of a "mysterious power that everyone feels but that no philosopher has explained," but which is "in fact the spirit of the earth. . ." These last words recall Mahler's *Song of the Earth* (discussed in Chapter 19), and, indeed, Crumb acknowledges that his music includes a "reminiscence of Mahler with a breath of the Orient." As composer, Crumb has attempted to convey that which has escaped the pen of the philosopher. He is not alone in believing that music can delve into realms where words cannot penetrate. "What is too silly to be said may

Music and Ideas

be sung," . . . but what is too subtle to be said, or too deeply felt, or too revealing or too mysterious—these things can also be sung and only be sung."[5]

The artist speaks more clearly than the philosopher, and of all the arts, music is the clearest.

> All the things that are fundamental, all the things that, to the human spirit, are most profoundly significant, can only be experienced, not expressed. The rest is always and everywhere silence. After silence that which comes nearest to expressing the inexpressibile is music. . . . In a different mode, on another plane of being, music is the equivalent of some of man's most significant and inexpressible experiences.[6]

EXPANDING THE TONAL PALETTE

Twentieth-century music may be thought of as revolutionary in two senses. To begin, there is the structural sense. Music formerly was conceived in keys, now it frequently is not. For many composers *serialism*, and particularly the *twelve-tone system*, has replaced the conventional compositional strategies of tonality (Chapter 22). In recent decades many composers have dropped any kind of systematic approach to music, substituting free atonality or in some cases even random selection of pitches, rhythmic patterns, dynamics, and other compositional elements.

The second principal area of change in twentieth-century music has been the treatment of voices and instruments. Audiences have been subjected to a continuous barrage of new sounds—witness the music of Cage and Crumb described earlier in this chapter. Of course, not all sounds are new and unfamiliar, but—as in the case of the toy piano—they are often shockingly strange in the context of concert music. George Antheil (1900–1959) introduced modern technological noises into his music—for example, a recording of an airplaine engine in his *Ballet mécanique*. Percussion sections grew into enormous batteries with the introduction of such novelties as woodblocks, sleigh-bells, sirens, wind machines—"instruments" previously rare or unknown on the concert stage.

One of the most important composers to expand the tonal palette was Edgard Varèse (1883–1965). Varèse was a Frenchman who was influenced by the composer Ferrucio Busoni, an imposing intellectual figure, and author of a book called *Sketch of a New Aesthetic of Music* (1910). Busoni proclaimed that "the function of the creative artist consists in making laws, not in following laws already made"—which might be taken as the watchword of modern composers ever since. As early as 1908 Busoni told Varèse that he was convinced that "music machines" would soon be necessary in the quest for "new means of expression."

Music machines! How that idea must have fascinated the young Varèse. Later Varèse was to compose *Ionizations* (1931), a work scored for *thirty-seven* different percussion instruments (to be played by thirteen percussionists). And eventually, as the field of electronics burgeoned following World War II, the music machines predicted by Busoni came to pass. Now in his late sixties, Varèse joined the vanguard of those conducting the first experiments in electronic music. His *Deserts* (1954) became one of the first electronic "classics." Varèse defined music as "sound in space, breaking down the limitations set by tradition." He thought of himself as a musical scientist and preferred to speak of "organized sound" rather than simply of music; instead of describing

251

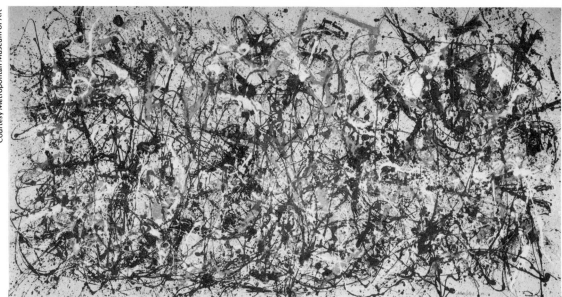

Jackson Pollock (1912–1956): *Autumn Rhythm.* Pollock's non-objective art style corresponds to the abstract character of much contemporary music.

himself as a musician, he would say he worked with "rhythms, frequencies, and intensities."[7]

Varèse was only one of many modern composers who have extended the traditional range of instrumental and vocal sounds. Some experimented with traditional instruments—as in the case of Alois Hába (1898–1972), whose string quartets include quarter tones and other microtonal subdivisions of the half step. Earlier we referred to Cage's experiments in altering the timbre of piano strings (*prepared piano*). Other composers, notably Henry Cowell (1897–1965), required pianists to reach inside their instrument to pluck and otherwise directly manipulate the strings, bypassing the regular hammer action of traditional piano music. Conlon Nancarrow (b. 1912) composed works of fascinating complexity to be performed exclusively on player pianos. Still other composers, such as Olivier Messiaen (b. 1908), scored music for newly invented instruments. Messiaen's *Turangalîla Symphony* features the *ondes martenot*, an electronic instrument that produces sounds like a female voice of enormous range. Indeed, during the past thirty years the principal innovation in sound sources has been the invention of electronic instruments. Shortly after World War II a new kind of music emanated from France called *musique concrète.* Basically this involved first making tape recordings of all types of natural, industrial, and other sounds, then subjecting them to changes of speed and other "sound effect" techniques; these novel sounds then served as a source for musical compositions. Gradually tape music spread to other countries, and the term *musique concrète* was dropped in favor of the more general term *electronic music.* In early tape works one might hear the sound of a flute transfered into the low range of a string bass, possibly sounding like a fog horn, while a genuine fog horn sound could be altered beyond recognition to produce still a different sound effect.

Music and Ideas

As remarkable as some of the early electronic music was, it was soon superseded by music generated from sound synthesizers. In effect a synthesizer is an instrument which can produce an infinite number of sounds selected and controlled by the composer. The special quality of these sounds is determined by various parameters, such as attack, decay, reverberation, envelope, and white noise. Traditional instrumental sounds consist of mixtures of these parameters; by altering them—for example, by changing the relative loudness of the overtones of a given pitch—new instrumental timbres can be created. Finally, in what has been described as the third generation of electronic music, digital computers have been programmed in connection with analog sound converters, as an alternative to costly synthesizers. Some composers have restricted their compositions to these new electronic sources exclusively, while others have combined them with live performers—for example, Milton Babbitt's (b. 1916) *Vision and Prayer* and *Philomel*, both for soprano accompanied by synthesized tape music. Some portable synthesizers are equipped for live performance—an effect utilized more and more in the popular music field. Even computers have been harnessed for live electronic musical performance. Gordon Mumma writes:

> One reason digital computers have found limited use in live performance is their unportable size. Either the live performance must be taken to the computer, or it must be connected to a remote computer by a data-link. A common data-link is a telephone line, with the computer at one end and a teletype among the live performers at the other.
>
> This procedure was used for my own work, *Conspiracy 8* (1970), which was performed live at the Guggenheim Museum in New York City, using a PDP-6 computer in Boston. Using a data-link, the remote computer received information about the performance, made decisions according to a basic program, and issued instructions to the performers. The computer participated as a decision-making member of the ensemble, and the ensemble accepted the sounds of its electronic decision-making—which were relayed to New York City by a second data-link—as a sonic contribution to the music.[8]

There seems to be no end to the innovations contemporary composers come up with. For example, Steve Reich (b. 1936) has made interesting experiments with *tape loops*. In works such as *It's Gonna Rain* (1965), he sets two tapes of the same sounds operating at first simultaneously, but then separated by ever so gradually widening time lapses. The effect is a "canon at the unison," but with the distance between entrances continually increasing. The constant repetition of just a single phrase results in a highly charged semihypnotic ostinato effect. Listeners may question whether works of this sort should be considered music in the first place. But, to the extent that we are dealing, in Varèse's words, with organized sound, it seems fair to call it music. By the same token, the school of *aleatoric* (random) composition is directly related to the Classical tradition of improvisation.

One other recent innovation is especially noteworthy with respect to the twentieth-century composer-qua-philosopher—namely, *collage music*. Collage works involve different kinds of music seemingly jumbled together into a patchwork quilt of unexpected sound combinations. Often there is an element of nostalgia, as in George Rochberg's (b. 1918) *Music for the Magic Theatre* (1965), which integrates generally

The Twentieth-Century Composer/Philosopher

atonal music of his own devising (played by conventional instruments) with Mozart's *Divertimento* K. 287, and other music of the past. Especially fascinating is Luciano Berio's (b. 1925) *Sinfonia*, which is scored for large orchestra and eight singers/speakers. The third movement is based on the "St. Anthony" movement of Mahler's *Symphony No. 2* (Chapter 19). Aside from the central Mahler work, *Sinfonia* includes brief excerpts from Beethoven's *Symphony No. 6* and *Symphony No. 9*, Stravinsky's *The Rite of Spring*, Strauss's *Der Rosenkavalier*, Debussy's *La Mer*, and Berg's *Wozzeck*, as well as passing references to music of Bach, Brahms, Wagner, Hindemith, Berlioz, Ravel, Schoenberg, Ives, Boulez, Stockhausen, and Pousseur. Furthermore, the performers recite a monologue from Samuel Beckett's *The Unnamable*, plus writings of James Joyce and Harvard undergraduates, Sorbonne wall slogans (from the uprisings of May 1968), recorded chatter of the composer's friends and family, and French solfège syllables (*do re mi fa sol*, etc.). Near the end of the movement the individual singers are introduced by name. Throughout all this adventuresome mixture of sounds and ideas, Mahler's music functions as a kind of anchor. The composer accounts for it this way:

> If I were to describe the presence of Mahler's "scherzo" in *Sinfonia*, the image that comes most spontaneously to mind is that of a river, going through a constantly changing landscape, sometimes going underground and emerging in another, altogether different, place, sometimes very evident in its journey, sometimes disappearing completely, present either as a fully recognizable form or as small details lost in the surrounding host of musical presences.[9]

MUSIC AND LITERATURE

Music and intellectual ideas interrelate in two ways: verbal ideas influence and are expressed in musical works (Beethoven's *Symphony No. 9*, Mahler's *The Song of the Earth*, Strauss's *Thus Spake Zarathustra*, etc.), and musical works influence literary thought. An example of music stimulating a literary work is Tolstoy's *Kreutzer Sonata*, the title of which is drawn from a violin sonata by Beethoven. (We shall consider Tolstoy's interpretation of Beethoven in another context, Chapter 27, *Music and Mood*.)

Mozart playing passages from his opera *Don Giovanni* for the first time before a select audience.

MOZART, DON GIOVANNI

The work most germane to a discussion of the influence of music on literature is Mozart's *Don Giovanni*. This opera is based on the adventures of a legendary Spanish nobleman, a "Don Juan" (the Spanish form of his name) obsessed—as we learn from the "Catalogue Aria" sung by his servant Leporello—by an uncontrollable lust for women of all descriptions (small and large, thin and fat, young and old, light and dark). On the face of it, this subject would seem of slight intrinsic merit, unlikely to cause much stir in literary intellectual circles. Yet in the nearly two hundred years since its premiere, *Don Giovanni* has been a source of inspiration to an impressive array of thinkers and writers. In this chapter we shall explore the powerful impact of Mozart's opera in the literary domain.

Don Giovanni alternates between episodes of woman chasing and scenes in which our hero is pursued by various outraged members of society. The latter include Donna Elvira, who claims that Don Giovanni legally married her before deserting her; Masetto, a young peasant resentful of the Don's attentions lavished on his fiancée, Zerlina; and Donna Anna, a noblewoman bent on avenging the death of her father, the Commander. The opera's first scene concerns the Commander's death. Don Giovanni, concealed by cloak and mask, has attempted to seduce Donna Anna, the fiancée of his friend, Don Ottavio, but without reckoning on her putting up a fierce defense. Donna Anna's screams wake her father, who appears sword in hand, ready to protect his daughter's honor. As an expert fencer, Don Giovanni warns the old man to stand back, but the Commander remains adamant. The Don accepts the challenge, easily dispatches his older opponent, and escapes. Despite having acted in self-defense, the masked intruder is dubbed a murderer by the grieving Donna Anna. Calling on Don Ottavio for assistance, she vows unrelenting pursuit of the unidentified assailant.

The remainder of Act I concerns Donna Anna's dogged efforts to seek redress for her father's death. In company with the meek Don Ottavio, she eventually allies herself with the excitable Donna Elvira. It is not long before they recognize Don Giovanni as the villain, but he easily eludes their grasp. In Act II it is still business as usual for Don Giovanni, whose roving eye takes in one woman after another. But now he must take care not to be outflanked by his pursuers. He does not object to being on the defensive—if anything he rather enjoys the challenge. And how do we, the members of the audience, respond to the Don's behavior? Shakespeare told us that all the world loves a lover, and in truth the dashing figure of Don Giovanni is one of the most popular of operatic heroes. Nevertheless, there is something disturbing about the Don's compulsive activity, his lack of remorse for killing the Commander, and his general flaunting of society's code of behavior. In the eyes of a moral and God-fearing society, the Don's amorous exploits are genuine crimes which demand real punishment. Sooner or later he must pay for the thousands of broken hearts, the unkept marriage vows, the death of a foolish old man determined to guard his daughter's reputation.

This brings us to the most fascinating part of the opera, where Don Juan's fate catches up with him. In what many music lovers regard as the single most brilliant scene in the entire operatic repertoire, Mozart—whom we often picture as slight, timid-looking, and innocent beneath his powdered wig—has portrayed the Don's comeuppance with astonishing musical/dramatic vigor and strength.

It is the middle of the night. Don Giovanni and Leporello find themselves hiding in the very cemetery where the Commander (Donna Anna's father) is buried. An impressive statue has been erected in the Commander's memory. The Don teases his servant with the news that his latest conquest was none other than Leporello's wife. As he is laughing at his servant's dismay, the Don is suddenly interrupted by the voice of the statue. In stately, rather lifeless tones the statue proclaims, "Your laughing will cease by morning." Sensing a new adventure at hand, Don Giovanni brashly invites the statue to supper. The statue readily assents and the two men head homeward. After an intervening aria sung by Donna Anna (unconnected to the exchange just described), the

Music and Ideas

scene changes to a room of magnificent splendor in Don Giovanni's palace. At first there is nothing amiss—the Don presides over a superb banquet, with music provided by a small stage band. There is much humor, as the master catches his servant sneaking food from the table; also, as the stage band plays an excerpt from Mozart's own *The Marriage of Figaro*, Leporello remarks caustically that "we've heard that tune once too often." A slight cloud is cast as Donna Elvira unexpectedly arrives, pleading with Don Giovanni to mend his ways. His reply is scornful laughter. Leaving, she screams as she sights the statue slowly advancing toward the door.

Somewhat surprised at the stone guest's appearance, Don Giovanni nevertheless remains cool and undaunted. The statue turns down offers of food and drink, and gets right down to business: Don Giovanni must repent his sinful ways. But this the Don will not do, lest it be regarded as a sign of cowardice, so he scoffingly rejects the Commander's admonishment. At this, the statue grasps Don Giovanni's hand, who is overcome with bodily shakings and terrors. Demons can be heard singing, and flames shoot out from below. With a fiery musical élan which even Wagner might well envy, Mozart consigned Don Giovanni to hell! What began as merely a series of amorous adventures has ended as a crackdown against moral delinquency. Any inclination we might have to laugh at justice being meted out by a statuesque ghost is squelched by the overwhelming force of Mozart's music. We in the audience get to slice the cake both ways. We can admire Don Giovanni's courageous disdain for social conventions, yet sit back and watch the miscreant receive his just deserts. The marvelous thing is that Don Giovanni never really loses his cool. Even under threat of the dancing flames he remains unyielding, unwilling to acknowledge the stern demands of religious rectitude. In the last scene of the opera, following Don Giovanni's damnation, the other characters appear in front of the curtain to sing the moral of the tale: "This is what happens to those who do wrong; those who are treacherous in this life are punished accordingly."

Giacomo Casanova (1725–1798). Casanova's amorous exploits earned him a reputation as a real-life Don Juan. He is thought to have attended the premiere of *Don Giovanni* in Prague (1787).

Music and Literature

Mozart has imbued the story of Don Juan with a level of meaning and importance quite beyond its limitations as a fairy tale. To confirm this, listen first to the Overture. The slow opening chords are more than somber; they are like strokes of fate.

Example 115
MOZART, *Don Giovanni*, Overture

Later we hear melodramatic rising and falling violin scales, which lead to the second, fast part of the Overture.

Example 116
Don Giovanni, Overture, Violin Scales

At the end of Act II the great confrontation scene between Don Giovanni and the statue brings back the slow part of the Overture—but now with a striking change in instrumentation, the addition of three trombones, which lend a new sinister quality to the music. (Mozart featured trombones in other works dealing with religion and the supernatural—e.g., *The Masonic Funeral Music, The Magic Flute,* and the *Requiem.* Regarding the *Requiem*, see Chapter 32.)

Example 117

Don Giovanni, Act II, Finale

a) The Statue's Entrance (cf. Example 115)

te — co   m'in - vi - ta - sti,   e   son ve - nu - to.
        you invited me,   and I am here.)

b) Continuation of the Statue's Scene (cf. Example 116)

Throughout the opera Mozart's musical tension highlights the dramatic content of the story; the music makes the drama *live*. Moreover, in view of its remarkable influence on future writers, we must accept *Don Giovanni* as a work of critical philosophical importance, quite aside from its purely musical value. The premiere took place in 1787. By 1813 E. T. A. Hoffmann (of *Tales of Hoffmann* fame) was writing *A Tale of Don Juan (as it happened to a traveling enthusiast)* about an operagoer's hallucinatory experience following a performance of *Don Giovanni*.[1] Somewhat later the Danish philosopher Søren Kierkegaard (1813–1855) based an entire chapter of his treatise *Either/Or* on *Don Giovanni*. The writer praised both Mozart and especially his *Don Giovanni* with unrestrained enthusiasm: "With his *Don Juan* Mozart enters the little immortal circle of those whose names, whose works, time will not forget, because eternity remembers them."[2] This sentiment need not be accepted as necessarily Kierkegaard's personal view, for he purposely took the stance of a young romanticist of overbrimming excitement. All the same, it is hard to think of any other musical work which has inspired speculative discourse of this order.

Hermann Hesse included Mozart as a character in the mystical novel *Steppen-wolf* (1927). He describes a strange puppet theatre in which the book's central figure, Harry Haller, hears

> the sound of music, a beautiful and awful music, that music from *Don Giovanni* that heralds the approach of the guest of stone. . . . "It is the last great music ever written," said I. . . . "A work of such plenitude and power as *Don Giovanni* has never since risen among men."[3]

Young George Bernard Shaw as the music critic, Corno di Bassetto. Shaw was a great admirer of Mozart. His penname means basset horn, an antiquated member of the clarinet family in common use during Mozart's lifetime. Shaw later achieved fame as a playwright and essayist and based part of one of his dramas *Man and Superman* (1903) on *Don Giovanni*.

GEORGE BERNARD SHAW

Of all modern thinkers, the one who has responded most extensively to *Don Giovanni* is George Bernard Shaw (1856–1950). Shaw's lengthy drama, *Man and Superman*, combines an updating of the Don Juan story with philosophical discourse centering on Nietzsche's theory of a superrace. The main characters are named after the principal figures of the opera: Don Juan Tenorio becomes John Tanner; Donna Anna is simply Anne; and Don Ottavio, her fiancé, turns into Tavvy. In his preface to the play, Shaw asserted that his hero, John Tanner, was not closely modeled after Don Juan, but Shaw also explained the insertion of a special scene featuring three characters borrowed directly from Mozart's opera: Don Giovanni, Donna Anna, and her father, the Commander/statue. These characters, along with the Devil himself, populate a dream experienced by John Tanner on a visit to Spain (which is also the locale of the opera). As Shaw explained, Tanner "has a dream in which his Mozartian ancestor appears and philosophizes at great length in a Shavio-Socratic dialogue with the lady, the statue, and the devil."[4] The scene, which is sometimes performed apart from the complete play and has been recorded as such, is known as *Don Juan in Hell*.

Much wit emanates from the talky goings-on in Shaw's Mozartian scene. To begin with, the righteous statue is so bored with the heavenly life that he has taken to visiting hell on a regular basis. Conversely, Don Juan finds hellish society tedious and is considering exchanging his abode for an eternity in heaven. Don Juan's dissatisfaction bruises the Devil's feelings, who regards the nether world as something like a fine social club. As for Anna, she is an old lady who has only just now expired, many years after the events occurring in the opera. Arriving in hell, Anna is greatly dismayed to discover that she has not been assigned to heaven. Much of the dialogue bears on the relative virtues of residing in heaven or hell. (It appears that either option is available to everyone!)

The stage directions and the dialogue contain numerous engaging references to the Mozart opera. At the very beginning of the scene Shaw explains that we are to hear "a faint throbbing buzz as of a ghostly violoncello." This turns into the opening of the allegro section of the overture. When Anna appears, we hear the lovely melody that introduces her Act II aria (sung just after the cemetery scene). (Shaw included some of the actual musical notation in his stage directions.) Later, the statue makes his entrance to "two great chords rolling on syncopated waves of sound . . . D minor and its dominant: a sound of dreadful joy to all musicians." This refers, of course, to the opening of the overture as well as to the statue's appearance at Don Giovanni's supper (see Examples 115 and 117a).

It soon becomes apparent that Don Giovanni and the statue have become good friends, despite their former mortal enmity. Don Giovanni chides the statue for not singing the music Mozart composed for him. The statue replies that unluckily he is a countertenor (i.e., a male singer with the high range of an alto), whereas Mozart's music was intended for a low bass. Then the statue takes his turn at twitting Don Giovanni, asking whether he has repented yet. Of course the statue knows the Don has no intention of repenting, and for that matter would himself like to join permanently the happy proceedings of the damned.

Although represented by a chorus of demons in the opera's finale, the Devil does not make a personal appearance in *Don Giovanni*. On the other hand, Mephistopheles is one of the principal characters of Gounod's *Faust*, a well-known nineteenth-century French opera. Therefore, for the Devil's entrance in the dream scene, Shaw calls for a musical background of Mozart mixed with Gounod.*

Complaining that Don Giovanni no longer sings Mozart's splendid lines, "Vivan le femmine! Viva il buon vino!" (Hurray for women, hurray for wine!), the Devil "begins to sing [these lines] in a nasal operatic baritone, tremulous from an eternity of misuse in the French manner." (As a Britisher Shaw enjoyed knocking the French style of singing.)

Shaw even included a reference to Mozart's personality. The Devil explains that, although Mozart was originally sent to hell, he did not like it there and moped so much that he was released and sent up to heaven. The Devil comments, "Curious how these clever men, whom you would have supposed born to be popular here, have turned out social failures. . . ."

*Goethe (1749–1832), the author of the Faust drama which served as the basis for operas by Gounod, Berlioz, Boito, Busoni, and others, was a great admirer of *Don Giovanni* and expressed the wish that Mozart might have lived long enough to have composed an opera based on *Faust*.

Some delightful banter transpires between Don Juan and the statue after the latter announces his intention of taking up permanent residence in hell.

> **Don Juan:** Audacious ribald: your laughter will finish in hideous boredom before morning.
>
> **Statue:** Ha ha! Do you remember how I frightened you when I said something like that to you from my pedestal in Seville? It sounds rather flat without my trombones. [See Examples 117a and b.]
>
> **Don Juan:** They tell me it generally sounds flat with them, Commander.

In view of his early distinguished career as a music critic, Shaw's intimate knowledge of Mozart's operatic music should come as no surprise.* An example of his critical skill is found in an essay written in 1887 on the occasion of the hundredth anniversary of the first performance of *Don Giovanni*. With biting sarcasm Shaw flouted the contemporary notion that Mozart was inferior to the reigning Romantic composers of the day. Assuming the position of devil's advocate, Shaw blithely asserted that "Mozart was a mere child in comparison with Schumann, Liszt, or Johannes Brahms." In the same vein he cast aspersions on those "claiming for Mozart powers simply impossible to a man who had never read a line of Hegel or a stave of Wagner."† From Shaw's remarks, it can be inferred that Victorian England regarded Mozart as a composer of pretty melodies but hardly a master in the same league as the illustrious Romantics listed above. That Shaw knew otherwise is clear from the final paragraph of his centennial essay, still cast in a tone of high sarcasm.

> I am bound to admit that the heat of the room produced a most extraordinary effect upon me. The commonplace melodies quite confounded me by acquiring subtlety, nobility, and dramatic truth of expression; the hackneyed diatonic harmonies reminded me of nothing I had ever heard before; the dominant discords had a poignant expression which I have failed in my own compositions to attain even by forcibly sounding all the twelve notes of the chromatic scale simultaneously; the ridiculous cadences and half-closes came sometimes like answers to unspoken questions of the heart, sometimes like ghostly echoes from another world; and the feeble instrumentation—but that was what warned me that my senses were astray. Otherwise I must have declared that here was a master compared to whom Berlioz was a musical pastrycook. From Beethoven and Wagner I have learned that the orchestra can paint every aspect of nature, and turn impersonal but specific emotion into exquisite sound. But an orchestra that creates men and women as Shakespeare and Molière did—that makes emotion not only specific but personal and characteristic (and this, mind, without clarionets, without trombones, without a second pair of horns): such a thing is madness: I must have been dreaming. When the trombones did come in for a while in a supernatural scene at the end, I felt more in my accustomed element; but presently they took an accent so inexpressibly awful, that I,

---

*He wrote under the pseudonym of Corno di Bassetto, which means "basset horn," a member of the clarinet family which Mozart was fond of using but which has since gone out of general use.

†Georg Wilhelm Friedrich Hegel was a German philosopher who lived from 1770 to 1831. Wagner was born in 1813, twenty-two years after Mozart's death.

who have sat and smiled through Liszt's *Inferno* with the keenest relish, felt forgotten superstitions reviving within me. The roots of my hair stirred; and I recoiled as from the actual presence of Hell. But enough of these delusions, which I have effectually dispelled by a dispassionate private performance at my own pianoforte.[5]

Shaw's views have long since triumphed. Today no composer is more revered than Mozart, and the awesome power of his music is understood and appreciated to the fullest extent.

The year 1887 was a busy Mozartian one for Shaw, for in addition to the essay quoted above he also wrote the delightful short story, *Don Giovanni Explains*. In this story he expressed some of the ideas he was to incorporate into *Man and Superman* some fifteen years later. The story concerns an independent young woman who has traveled by train to join some friends for a performance of *Don Giovanni*. She finds the performance a disaster—with some portions omitted, extraneous cadenzas added, and much poor singing and acting to boot. (Again we find Shaw the critic in action. Performance standards in the late nineteenth century were extremely low, especially with regard to Mozart.) The woman's opera companions respond to her jibes with annoyance and suggest that she would enjoy herself far more if she would just be less critical. She manages to stifle a reply that Mozart is too good for dolts like these!

Later, the woman dozes in her compartment on the late train back to her village. During the journey she awakens to find a traveler whom she had not previously noticed. (She is sure that she was alone when the train started.) The man is dressed in the gorgeous costume of the Renaissance Spanish nobility, and turns out to be no less than the ghost of Don Giovanni! When she cries out in dismay, he gallantly offers to leave her, but she prefers him to stay. (Even as a ghost Don Giovanni cannot help working his charms on the opposite sex!) He proceeds to relate *his* side of his famous story, which turns out much different from the Mozartian version. For one thing, he was not a pursuer of women, they always pursued him. What about the "Catalogue Aria," which lists country by country all the women whom the Don seduced (1003 in Spain alone)? All calumny, he insists; the list is a fabrication cooked up by Leporello to embarass him. Don Giovanni also explains that it was not his intention to compromise Donna Anna; it was she who mistook him in the dim light for Don Ottavio and embraced *him*. Her subsequent behavior was merely a cover-up!

The funniest part of the story concerns the statue's appearance at the Don's supper. With the statue demanding repentance and the Don refusing, the constant yelling back and forth of "Nay!" and "Aye!" makes Don Giovanni think momentarily he is attending a session of the House of Parliament. The end of the story recounts what happened to the opera's other characters *after* the curtain comes down. Donna Anna and Don Ottavio never did marry, for with the "help" of her nursing he died after a short illness. Later she married a Scotch Presbyterian and moved away from Spain. Donna Elvira went to live in a convent, resuming the life she had led prior to her "marriage" to the Don. Eventually she took up a career as a singing teacher. Another of Don Giovanni's conquests, the peasant girl Zerlina, achieved a reputation as an outstanding laundress.

The woman in the train then informs Don Giovanni that he is very famous, the subject of a play by Molière and an opera by Mozart. He asks whether he is fairly portrayed in the opera, to which she replies that he is cast as a libertine whom all women desire. He expresses disappointment that the opera does not corroborate his efforts to resist women.

> Strange! how slander clings to a man's reputation. And so I, of all men, am known and execrated as a libertine.

She replies:

> Oh, not execrated, I assure you. You are very popular. People would be greatly disappointed if they knew the truth.

Needless to say, if you are to appreciate Shaw's wit in his several writings on *Don Giovanni* you must first develop a close familiarity with the opera. Concentrate on the opening of the first act and the finales of both Acts I and II (a total of less than an hour's music). The coupling of Mozart and Shaw is one of the most felicitous intermarriages between the arts of music and literature. Enjoy both masters: listen to the glorious music of one, and read the sharply honed words of the other.

FAUST AND THE DILEMMA OF THE MODERN COMPOSER

Mozart's Don Giovanni goes to hell, but he does not actually meet the devil in person. (As noted in Chapter 21, we must consult Shaw's *Man and Superman* to discover the nature of that encounter.) However, the personage of the devil (Mephistopheles) does figure prominently in the centuries-old legend of Faust. As portrayed by the early English playwright, Christopher Marlowe (1590), and later by the early nineteenth-century German philosopher, Johann Wolfgang von Goethe, Faust is a thinker and striver, an old man who all his life has wrestled with the basic issues of philosophy. Of late he has taken up alchemy, the mystical "science" of converting base metals into gold, finding the key to exteneded longevity, and the like. Depressed, his energy ebbing, Faust senses approaching death, yet desperately longs to be young once again—to eat, drink, and be merry, to carouse and make love. Suddenly a strange dog appears in Faust's study. Faust's mystification deepens as the animal transforms itself into the Devil himself, who offers to restore Faust's youth. In exchange Faust must consign his soul to eternal damnation, foregoing heavenly redemption. Faust accepts the offer and is immediately rejuvenated.

Numerous distinguished composers have set all or parts of the Faust legend to music. Operas have been composed by Berlioz (1846), Gounod (1859), Boito (1868), and Busoni (1916–1924). Schubert set some of Goethe's verses (e.g., "Gretchen at the Spinning Wheel"); Schumann composed an oratorio, *Scenes from Faust*; Liszt wrote a *Faust Symphony*, and Wagner composed a *Faust Overture*. The finale of Mahler's monumental *Symphony No. 8* is a setting of the last scene from Part II of Goethe's drama. Stravinsky's opera, *The Rake's Progress* (1950), represents still another variant on the Faust theme (intermixed with the Don Juan legend.)*

THOMAS MANN

Perhaps the most important twentieth-century literary interpretation of the Faust legend is Thomas Mann's *Doctor Faustus*, subtitled "The Life of the German Composer Adrian Leverkühn as Told by a Friend." Mann's novel contains many varied and interesting references to music. He maintained a lifelong involvement with music and was friendly with many of the outstanding composers and performers of this century. Here is how he described his basic attitude toward music:

> Music has always had a strong formative influence upon the style of my writing. Writers are very often "really" something else; they are transplanted painters or

*A comparative survey of some or all these musical versions of *Faust* would make an excellent individual or group term project.

sculptors or architects or what not. To me the novel was always like a symphony; a work in counterpoint, a thematic fabric; the idea of the musical motif plays a great role in it.[1]

Mann wrote about music not only in *The Magic Mountain* (see the passage entitled "The Fullness of Harmony"), but also in his early stories *Tristan* and *Blood of the Walsungs*, built around two music dramas of Richard Wagner. His most voluminous musical study, the Faust novel (1947), was the product of his own old age, his interest in the subject stemming not only from his fascination with music and a possible wish to demonstrate his own continuing creative powers, but also from the idea of Faust as a symbol for the decadent "creativity" of the recently subdued Nazi Germany.

Unlike Goethe's elderly Faust, who seeks renewed youth and vigor, Mann's "Faust," Adrian Leverkühn, is still a young man when he encounters the devil. As a composer he has reached a plateau of artistic sterility and feels himself drained of creative inspiration. The devil promises renewed compositional vitality in exchange for the musician's soul.

Mephistopheles and Faust (nineteenth-century print).

Doctor Faustus is replete with musical details of Adrian's youthful attraction to music, his education, and the musical fruits of his mature years as a composer. Of special interest is Chapter 8, in which we meet Adrian's music teacher, Wendell Kretschmar. The highlight of this chapter is Kretschmar's analysis of Beethoven's *Piano Sonata in C Minor*, Op. 111. His last work in this genre, Beethoven's sonata is exceptional for its mere two movements, instead of the usual three or four. (Schubert's *Symphony in B Minor*, which also consists of just two movements, is known as the "Unfinished," the

Faust and the Dilemma of the Modern Composer

other two movements being either lost or never composed in the first place. But Beethoven's Op. 111 was from the first intended to comprise only the two extant movements.) The tempestuous first movement in sonata form is followed by a set of gentle variations. Kretschmar offers an amazing (for a work of fiction) description and interpretation of the variations movement.[2] He then inquires rhetorically why Beethoven failed to write at least a third movement, in accordance with sonata tradition, but promptly and imperiously demonstrates the absurdity of this idea. The second movement not only satisfactorily completes the sonata, it is also Beethoven's last word in the genre of the piano sonata. Kretschmar also discusses (and denounces) the view that Beethoven could not write a good fugue. Mann has provided a scintillating mixture of music theory, analysis, and biography, concluding the chapter with a particularly touching and amusing description of Beethoven's personal struggles while composing the "Credo" of his *Missa Solemnis*.[3]

Of even greater interest is Mann's depiction of the music ostensibly composed by Leverkühn while under Satanic influence. Mann later documented his effort "to build up the lifework of an important composer so that it seemed as if the compositions could be heard, so that they were absolutely believable."[4]

Here we have a paradox, since no amount of word painting can duplicate a genuine listening experience. Ultimately it is left to our own imaginations, albeit guided by the author's text, to determine what Adrian's music—for example, his cantata, *The Lamentation of Dr. Faustus* (Chapter 46)—might sound like. However, if Mann could only provide hints about Adrian's music, he could and did delineate with precision and vigor the compositional system purportedly discovered and developed by Adrian. Thus, in Chapter 22, Adrian comments upon a compositional technique in which a five-note figure determines both "horizontal melody" and "vertical harmony:"

> It is like a word, a key word, stamped on everything in the song, which it would like to determine entirely. But it is too short a word and in itself not flexible enough. The tonal space it affords is too limited. One would have to go on from here and make larger words out of the twelve letters, as it were, of the tempered semitone alphabet.* Words of twelve letters, certain combinations and interrelations of the twelve semitones, series of notes from which a piece and all the movements of a work must strictly derive. Every note of the whole composition, both melody and harmony, would have to show its relation to this fixed fundamental series. Not one might recur until the other notes have sounded. Not one might appear which did not fulfil its function in the whole structure.[5]

ARNOLD SCHOENBERG

The passage quoted led to one of the most remarkable artistic controversies of modern times. For Leverkühn's compositional system, devised in consequence of his devilish pact, is modeled after the actual twelve-tone compositional system invented by Arnold Schoenberg just after World War I. As refugees from Hitler, Schoenberg and Mann both emigrated to southern California, where they encountered one another frequently. Mann has recounted having "pumped S. [Schoenberg] a great deal on music and the life of a composer."[6]

*Mann is referring here to the *chromatic scale*, as represented by a succession of twelve adjacent black and white notes on a piano keyboard.

Music and Ideas

In other words, there was nothing secret about Mann's fictional appropriation of Schoenberg's compositional theories, and Mann undoubtedly regarded his supposed plagiarism as an act of homage to a great master. However, Schoenberg suffered during his lifetime from a lack of public acceptance of his musical importance, and particularly resented the unacknowledged infringement upon his ideas by a world-famous novelist. (Mann had won the Nobel Prize for Literature in 1929.) Moreover, Schoenberg may have been scandalized by the novel's climax, in which Leverkühn admits his twenty-four-year "marriage" with the devil and then collapses insane. In Mann's own words the central idea of the novel is "the flight from the difficulties of the cultural crisis into the pact with the devil, the craving of a proud mind, threatened by sterility, for an unblocking of inhibitions at any cost."[7] Was Mann implying that Schoenberg's great artistic achievement was the work of a satanically driven madman?

That Schoenberg found *Doctor Faustus* upsetting is hardly surprising in view of the fact that at one time he himself had been perplexed by a creative dilemma similar to Adrian's. Like many other post-Romantic composers at the end of the nineteenth century, Schoenberg recognized the apparent exhaustion of the tonal system—the ma-

Rembrandt: Faust in His Study

271

Faust and the Dilemma of the Modern Composer

jor and minor key system which had been developing during the previous four hundred years. The music of Wagner, Strauss, Bruckner, Mahler, and especially of early Schoenberg, tended to abandon a single controlling tonic note in favor of a state of continuous modulatory flux wherein all notes are structurally equal. A new kind of *atonality* arose in which harsh dissonances displaced the traditional domination of the consonant intervals of major and minor triads. Early atonal pieces were notable more for what they avoided (the tonal excesses of post-Romanticism) than for what they offered in exchange for the traditional sounds. As in the political arena at that time, the only worthwhile change seemed to be radical change. Music was suddenly plunged into a period of crisis (a crisis which has yet to be fully resolved).

Like many other early modern composers, Schoenberg was a fearless radical (Chapter 15), but more than any of the others he sought a positive compositional system to replace the outdated tonal system.* Like Adrian Leverkühn, Schoenberg went through several dry years during which he apparently produced no finished works. This difficult hiatus was brought to an end in 1923, when Schoenberg presented his first twelve-tone works to the public.

Let us move ahead to southern California in 1948. Legend has it that after the publication of *Doctor Faustus* Mann gratefully approached Schoenberg's house with a complimentary [sic!] copy in hand, only to have the angry composer turn the author from his door. Mann subsequently bowed to Schoenberg's ire by appending a note to all later printings, admitting that

> the form of musical composition delineated in Chapter XXII, known as the twelve-tone or row system, is in truth the intellectual property of a contemporary composer and theoretician, Arnold Schoenberg. I have transferred this technique in a certain ideational context to the fictitious figure of a musician, the tragic hero of my novel.[8]

A few years later, after Schoenberg's death, Mann had the last word on the matter:

> Ought I also to cite as an example of such an act of montage and theft from reality an element which many persons have found objectionable; namely, Adrian Leverkühn's appropriation of Schoenberg's concept of the twelve-tone or row system of music? I suppose I must, and from now on the book, at Schoenberg's request, is to carry a postscript spelling out the intellectual property rights for the uninformed. This is being done a bit against my own convictions—not so much because such an explanation knocks a small breach into the rounded, integral world of my novel, as because, within the sphere of the book, within this world of a pact with the devil and of black magic, the idea of the twelve-tone technique assumes a coloration and a character which it does not possess in its own right and which—is this not so?—in a sense make it really my property, or, rather, the property of the book. Schoenberg's idea and my *ad hoc* version of it differ so widely that, aside from the stylistic fault, it would have seemed almost insulting, to my mind, to have mentioned his name in the text.[9]

*It should be noted that the tonal system remains in constant use in many kinds of concert and church music, not to mention nearly all aspects of folk and popular music. The sense in which the tonal system was outdated is that almost all of the twentieth century's outstanding composers either modified it or abandoned it in striving to develop new and original compositional styles.

Music and Ideas

As in Mann's formulation cited earlier in this chapter, the gist of Schoenberg's approach is that within a given piece of music no single note is treated as preeminent with respect to any of the other notes. Instead, a composer arranges the twelve notes of the *chromatic scale* (*vide* the seven white and five black keys of the piano) into a specific ordering *prior* to the writing of the music. The particular row selected serves as source both of melodic and harmonic configurations. With regard to the former, the row rarely functions as melody in the generally accepted sense of the term. For since each of the twelve notes may appear as a pitch in any octave register (low, medium, or high) and with any durational value (short, medium, long), successive linear presentations of the row are likely to bear little overt resemblance to one another. (One need only disperse the notes of a familiar tune, such as "The Star Spangled Banner," among various registers, freely changing their rhythmic values, to discover that melodic identity depends heavily on the parameters of register and duration.)

Many people complain that twelve-tone music is cerebral and inaccessible, that one cannot listen and respond to it like more traditionally constructed music. Most of Schoenberg's atonal works have achieved little genuine popularity among music lovers, even among musicians, and his pedagogical and didactic writings are generally better known than his music. One of the few composers to exert a lasting influence on the development of twentieth-century music, Schoenberg's own music remains relatively unplayed, unheard, and unknown.* Schoenberg may yet have his day, however, for even Johann Sebastian Bach was appreciated in his lifetime mainly as a performer and teacher; his reputation as a master composer did not become established (due initially to assiduous efforts on the part of Felix Mendelssohn) until eighty years after his death.

At any rate, with reference to Schoenberg's relation to Mann's *Doctor Faustus*, one might suppose that the devil's music would be emotionally seductive rather than dryly intellectual. Indeed, on page 486, Mann asserts that the Faust cantata is "a work of expression . . . a work of liberation." Moreover, he goes on to claim for Leverkühn's [read Schoenberg's] compositional method that it allows for "change from the strictest constraint to the free language of feeling, the birth of freedom from bondage." Pehaps a day will come when the musical public will share Mann's estimation of the emotional range of twelve-tone music.

BASICS: TWELVE-TONE MUSIC

The student is invited to listen to Schoenberg's *Phantasy for Violin with Piano Accompaniment* as an introduction to his mature twelve-tone style. The term *phantasy* signifies a work in free form, somewhat akin to a rhapsody. Schoenberg's work was originally scored for solo violin, with the piano part added as an afterthought. The violin part is much more demanding than the relatively uncomplicated piano part; otherwise the

*Recently a French pianist played the complete piano works of Schoenberg in a New York recital (equivalent to about half a program). The local critics praised her performance, yet later a highly regarded New York pianist revealed his opinion that the performances were substandard. Her recordings substantiate this unhappy view. The critics, even in Gotham, simply have not heard enough of Schoenberg's music to reconize the difference between good and bad performances of it.

Faust and the Dilemma of the Modern Composer

work is a true duet in which the two instruments complement one another more or less equally, as in any piece of genuine chamber music.*

Question: How does one go about listening to twelve-tone music? *Answer:* The same way one listens to a Beethoven sonata or Brahms symphony. One need no more approach Schoenberg's music by tracking down its successive twelve-tone rows than one apprehends a tonal piece by labeling its chords or accounting for modulations from one key to another. In both types of music one simply listens to the music—period! Undoubtedly atonal music may be harder to get used to, but repeated listening can yield the same recognition and familiarity that are taken for granted with more traditional styles. Since the work at hand is a phantasy, the important thing is to listen for the sense of constantly changing moods. The work is a series of episodes, a small continuous *suite*. One can divide it into four large sections, each breaking down into a few smaller units.

The first few measures are characterized by bold, loud violin strokes, punctuated by crisp piano articulations. The two instruments rarely attack notes simultaneously; the piano enters either while the violin is sustaining a note or during a violin rest. So it is a special "event" when both instruments attack notes at the same time—just the opposite of traditional chamber music.

The harmonic effect of the opening measures is that of unremitting dissonance. To some extent this is a consequence of the row Schoenberg selected for this piece. Example 118 presents the first six notes of the row (i.e., its first *hexachord*). Each successive note pair forms an interval of one or two half steps (B♭–A, C♯–B♮, F–G), which when played jointly results in a procession of seconds and sevenths. In earlier styles these dissonant intervals would lead to almost immediate resolution to consonant thirds and sixths, but here the seconds and sevenths remain unresolved. Example 119 illustrates the first four measures of the *Phantasy*. Observe the dissonance of the first two piano notes, E–D♯, struck together. The next two notes, C–D, form an additional seventh, with one pitch following the other. Then the piano repeats both pairs of sevenths (the second pair simultaneously) and adds a third dissonant linear note pair, A♭–G♭. In both violin and piano parts we find dissonant intervals emphasized over traditional consonances. Observe the expression marking in the violin part—*passionato*. There is nothing dry and dispassionate about this opening!

Example 118
SCHOENBERG, *Phantasy for Violin with Piano Accompaniment*, Hexachord 1

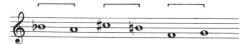

*In some earlier duets for violin and piano, such as the sonatas of Haydn and Mozart, the piano parts tended to overshadow the violin parts. By Beethoven's time, however, the allocation of musical materials between the two instruments was generally balanced, and since then the piano part has usually functioned as neither more nor less important than that of the "soloist."

Music and Ideas

Example 119
Violin Phantasy, Measures 1–4

Arnold Schoenberg (1874–1951) as drawn by Egon Schiele. Schoenberg's twelve-tone system of composition was appropriated by Thomas Mann in his novel *Doctor Faustus*.

Faust and the Dilemma of the Modern Composer

Schoenberg can also effect gentler intervals (thirds and sixths) by combining non-adjacent row notes. For example, in the piano part of measure 2, the dissonance, Bb–A, is partially mitigated by the consonant third, Bb–Db. (All three notes are sounded together.) And the second piano chord in that same measure is an incomplete dominant seventh chord, one of the most traditional of tonal harmonies. Note that the piano notes in measure 2 correspond to those of the violin part in measure 1; conversely, the violin part in measure 2 repeats the piano notes of measure 1. Observe, however, that *note* repetitions are not necessarily *pitch* repetitions, since the note repetitions are not limited to the same registers. Thus, the violin notes of measure 1, Bb–A–C#–Bb–F–G, are found in lower registers of the piano in measure 2.

A phantasy is a piece of many moods, and by measure 4 the loud passionate beginning turns into a mellow winding down, the violin eventually coming to rest on the same Bb which started the piece. The piano chords in these last three measures are lighter and less dissonant than before, sometimes sounding like incomplete (tonal) seventh chords. Measure 7 introduces a lush mixture of violin *glissando* (sliding) and piano *tremolando* (shaking) with soft pedal. In the next measure we hear the first of many violin *harmonics*—high pitches effected by gently pressing the strings at points which divide them by halves, thirds, fourths, etc. (Pressing the finger halfway down a string produces a pitch an octave higher than the open string. Dividing the string into thirds produces a pitch twelve notes higher, into fourths two octaves higher, and so forth.) This eerie effect is heard frequently throughout the piece.

Measure 10 marks an important structural juncture in the music. After slowing down in measure 9, the first tempo abruptly resumes in a rather jaunty manner. This is precisely where Schoenberg chose to introduce the second hexachord of his tone row. You may well wonder at the fact that only in measure 10 is the full tone row used for the first time. Certainly all the twelve available chormatic notes have been heard throughout the first ten measures, but always as permutations of the *first* hexachord of the row. Thus, all twelve notes are heard in the very first measure of the piece: the violin and piano each play six notes, with each instrument duplicating none of the other instrument's notes. However, the piano notes are merely a mirroring of the violin notes starting on a different pitch (see Example 120). The actual second hexachord—an independent formation with a different interval succession from that of the first hexachord—is first heard in the violin part of measures 10–11 (see Example 121).

Music and Ideas

Example 120
Violin Phantasy, Hexachord Mirror (M. 1)

Example 121
Hexachord 2, Mm. 10–11

Faust and the Dilemma of the Modern Composer

If this delayed presentation of the full row seems perplexing, remember that we are dealing here with a late work, Schoenberg's last major composition. His first twelve-tone pieces were much simpler, exhibiting considerably less sophisticated applications of the twelve-tone method (also known as *serialism*). The *Violin Phantasy* was selected to illustrate serial music less for its complex structure than for its masterful artistry. Apprehending the spirit of the music is much more important than uncovering its row technique. On the other hand, the spirit of the music is intimately related to its compositional structure, and for that reason a limited amount of structural information may be helpful to the listener.

A big mood change occurs in measure 25, which is marked faster and *furioso*. The violin part now becomes especially difficult, calling for numerous harmonics and *double stops* (playing two strings simultaneously). Then the music subsides, and in measure 32 we hear a gentle reprise of the opening violin melody of measure 1. This is one of the rare cases of the row being treated as a genuine melody, making it is easy to recognize the repetition of the opening of the piece. This completes the first principal section of the *Phantasy*. The elapsed time to this point is about two minutes.

After a gentle introduction, Part 2 continues with a very slow passage, the violin and piano each playing in extremely high registers (see Example 122). The next subsection is a waltzlike *grazioso* (cognate of the English *gracious*), after which the music turns heavy and earnest, with the two instruments now in very low registers (see Example 123). A cataclysmic dénouement leads to the beginning of Part 3, a sprightly *scherzando*. As in the traditional scherzo and trio of the Classical period, the structure is A–B–A, the middle B part somewhat slower and more tranquil than the outer A parts.

Photograph by G. W. Brewer

The sense of equality implied by a clock without hands corresponds to the spirit of structural equality inherent in twelve-tone music.

Music and Ideas

Example 122
Violin Phantasy, Slow Section, High Registers

Example 123
Slow Section, Low Registers

Faust and the Dilemma of the Modern Composer

The final section of the piece includes a gentle moderate passage with an engaging violin melody. Here the piano accompaniment is truly secondary.

Example 124
Phantasy, Violin Melody, Piano Accompaniment

The last thirteen measures of the piece commence with an imitation of the opening measures of the *Phantasy* and then develop into a spectacular display of violin pyrotechnics. The screeching final chord consists of eight different pitches: the piano plays the six violin pitches of measure 1, while the violin plays octave equivalents of the first two piano pitches of measure 1. So, although Schoenberg strictly avoided a sense of tonal centering, his concluding pitch configurations duplicate the pitch groupings which begin the piece. In other words, the piece is framed by the same notes at its beginning and ending; even avowedly atonal music may offer a sense of balanced repetition not unlike that of tonal music.

Listening to Schoenberg's *Phantasy* is one thing; appreciating it is another. The listening challenge is similar to the viewing challenge presented by the best modern non-objective paintings and sculptures. At first you may miss familiar tonal shapes and combinations, but eventually you will sense a value and immediacy in new formations of sound and color, formations which would be inconceivable within the traditional artistic constraints of the past. Try to regard listening to twelve-tone music as an adventure which may offer surprising rewards. Schoenberg's *Phantasy* is not only a masterpiece of twentieth-century music, it is one of the treasures of the entire chamber music repertoire.

Music and Ideas

CHECKLIST: CONCEPTS AND TERMS IN UNIT 4

Terms preceded by (•) are included in lists for previous units. Page numbers in parentheses indicate location of first and/or principal reference to each term within this unit.

General and Historical

Musique concrète (252)
"Ode to Joy" (217)
Transcendentalism (246)

Instrumental Music

double stops (278)
electronic music (252)
• glissando (276)
harmonics (276)
• overture (258)
phantasy (273)
• pizzicato (220)
prepared piano (249)
• program music (242)
• scherzo (220)
song symphony (236)
• staccato (220)
• suite (274)
synthesizer (253)
• tone poem (242)

Vocal Music

countertenor (264)
• recitative (220)

Theory

• atonality (272)
cadence (226)
• canon (253)
chance (249)
• chromatic scale (273)
• coda (225)
collage (253)
• counterpoint (220)
• dissonance (220)
• fugue (270)
hexachord (274)
• *Leitmotif* (234)
• major scale (240)
• meter (230)
• minor (229)
• ostinato (225)
• quarter tones (252)
serialism (278)
• theme and variations (225 ff)
twelve-tone system (270 ff)

Faust and the Dilemma of the Modern Composer

REVIEW: UNITS III AND IV

1. Make a list of the composers whose works are featured in Chapters 13–22, adding to it any other composers assigned for homework listening and/or presented in classroom discussion. Indicate the historical period of each composer, making your choices according to the historically associated styles of the compositions you have listened to. (Do not decide upon historical periods simply by correlating with raw dates; for example, even though J. S. Bach and his eldest son C. P. E. Bach were obviously contemporaries, the one was Baroque, the other Classical.) Also indicate the nationality of each composer, based on place of birth and ethnic heritage (usually the same as a composer's mother tongue).

2. Write a few sentences about your response to each work represented in your list of composers (Exercise 1). Try to indicate more than whether you like the music or not; tell *what* you do or do not appreciate in each piece individually. Feel free to make comparisons among these pieces and include comparisons also with the music of Units I and II, other music covered in class, outside concerts, and so on. (In this and other questions exclude the music of any chapter omitted by your instructor.)

3. Write a description of each of the genres listed below. Gear what you write for fellow students with little or no previous musical background. Be clear and precise, avoiding technical terms or other musical jargon whenever possible. Take pride in your prose.

chamber music
Broadway musical
music drama
operetta
phantasy
song symphony

4. In the same spirit, define the following terms:

absolute music
augmentation
collage
electronic music
fugue
Leitmotif
libretto
ostinato
overtone
recitative
serialism
theme and variations

5. Listen to and compare the first act of Wagner's *Tristan und Isolde* with the first act of Verdi's *La Traviata*. Each opera describes the beginning of a great love affair. Wagner's music drama represents a continuous musical/dramatic flow, whereas Verdi's opera sticks to tradition with a succession of more or less independent musical numbers. Write a two-page typed essay (600 words) on your response to these two opposing operatic styles. Be sure to follow a libretto when listening to the music.

6. Imagine an opera based on the Watergate/Nixon scandals. (You may wish to review these events in journalistic reports covering the period 1972–1974; consult *The New York Times, Time* and *Newsweek* magazines, etc.) Of all the composers of operas, operettas, and musicals discussed so far—Mozart, Wagner, Verdi, Strauss, Berg, Weill, Gilbert and Sullivan—who would you want to handle it? How would you construct the scenario—how many roles, acts, and so on? Would there be a chorus? (You may wish to save this question until you have studied Unit 5, and consider making the work an oratorio in the style of Handel, a passion of Bach, or a vocal symphony of Bernstein.) You needn't be too scholarly in your answer to this question—let your imagination roam!

7. Defend or attack the following statement:

Surface appearances to the contrary, the music of the twentieth century is by and large no more revolutionary than the music of the early Romantic period.

MUSIC AND RELIGION

The worship of a deity is one of humankind's preeminent concerns. In Western civilization, religious energy focuses on worship services conducted in sacred buildings and in which music is all but as important as the theological content itself.

> The Church knew what the Psalmist knew: music praises God. Music is as well or better able to praise Him than the building of the church and all its decoration; it is the Church's greatest ornament.[1]

Since ancient times Jews have obeyed the Biblical injunction to "make a joyful noise unto the Lord" (Psalm 100). The early Christians carried on the Jewish tradition of musical worship—in some cases keeping the same texts, as when the threefold Hebrew exclamation "Kodosh" became the threefold Latin "Sanctus," or "Holy, Holy, Holy." By the Middle Ages Roman Catholicism had developed its own fully standardized musical liturgy. Several centuries later music figured heavily in the Protestant Reformation, which among other things introduced congregational hymn singing as we know it today. At the same time, if music has supported the church, so likewise has the church supported music; nearly all important composers prior to the eighteenth century made their living working for the church.

Today, few of the various sects in America (for example, the Society of Friends) exclude music from worship services, but in earlier times music played only a minor role in all American churches. The Puritans deemed music fundamentally sinful and restricted the use of organs in church buildings, allowing only the sparsest unaccompanied hymn singing. Music was not to establish a secure foothold in American churches until Puritanism started to wane in the late eighteenth century and has only come into its own during the twentieth century. Hymn singing is now commonly accompanied by organ and supported by volunteer and/or professional choirs, which further enhance the service with anthems and responses. Solo organ music is performed at the beginning and ending of services (*prelude* and *postlude*), as well as at weddings and funerals. Larger churches present special music services, programing works considered too ambitious for regular worship services (for example, Bach cantatas, Handel oratorios, etc.). Jewish worship maintains its ancient tradition of congregational singing—unaccompanied in the more conservative synagogues, accompanied by organ at "reform" temples. All denominations have been experimenting with folk music, and guitars and other folk instruments are by no means unknown in American houses of worship. Spirituals, such as "Were You There?" and "Let Us Break Bread Together," have long functioned as hymns, so it is not so much that folk music is a new factor in worship as one newly emphasized. Even popular music is finding its way into worship, as in the vibrant songs from *Godspell* and the lovely "Sabbath Prayer" from *Fiddler on the Roof.*

Chapter 23 represents a survey of music of the Catholic Church. It includes excerpts for listening by Mozart, Bach, and Monteverdi, as well as a brief essay on passacaglia/chaconne form. Chapter 24 deals with the new musical forms which arose in conjunction with the Protestant Reformation. In Chapter 25 we turn to the dramatic side of religion—liturgical drama, the oratorio, the passion, and other genres such as opera and the Broadway show. Finally, Chapter 26 presents supplementary readings on religious music: a survey of Jewish worship music, a glance at music in American Protestant churches, and a brief discussion of the organ and its literature.

THE MUSIC
OF CATHOLICISM

23

The Christian era is fast approaching its two thousandth anniversary. From a musicological standpoint this period breaks down into two roughly equal subdivisions. The music of the first millenium is characterized by one-line melody without accompaniment (*monophony*), sung either solo or in choral unison. The great innovation of the second millenium was the rise of *polyphony*, or music in two or more parts to be sung or played at the same time.

The monophony of early Catholicism is called *plainchant*, or simply *chant*. The principal chants celebrate the Mass, as well as other worship services held throughout the day (Matins, Lauds, Vespers, etc.). Prior to 600 A. D., each European religious center cultivated its own independent collection of chants. Then under Pope Gregory a move was made to codify the liturgy throughout the entire Holy Roman Empire. This early

St. Stephen's church in Vienna. Stravinsky said, "Music is as well or better able to praise [God] than the building of the church and all its decoration."

repertoire is known as *Gregorian chant*. The melodies of plainchant are quite free rhythmically, following the natural inflections of the words, much as in modern vocal recitative. The contours of chant are gentle and soothing, consisting mainly of conjunct motion and repeated notes; large skips from one note to another are rare.

Example 125
Plainchant in Old Neumes and Modern Notation

After the invention of polyphony the new compositional styles still relied heavily on Gregorian chant, which was to remain the basis of polyphonic church music for several hundred years to come. The earliest form of polyphony was *organum*, consisting of a basic chant line coupled with a more or less exact replica pitched a few notes higher or lower than the model. Later came the Medieval *motet*, a multivoiced composition with one part featuring a particular chant. In some motets the chant notes are extremely slow and/or grouped in arbitrary rhythmic units, making it hard to perceive the chant line without recourse to the score; in other cases the chant can be heard easily. A chant or other melody used as the basis of a polyphonic composition is known as a *cantus firmus*.

The core of the Catholic liturgy is the Mass, a series of prayers culminating in the celebration of communion. Five sections of the Mass—the Ordinary—are unvarying in text: Kyrie, Gloria, Credo, Sanctus, and Agnus Dei. Other prayers change according to the season and church calendar. In the early days of polyphony—that is, after 1000 A. D.—a composer would write each section of the Ordinary separately, making no effort to combine all five sections into a unified musical compositon. Guillaume de Machaut is believed to have been the first composer to have fashioned a complete setting of the Mass. His *Messe de Notre Dame*, dating from the fourteenth century, displays an eerie quality that strikes many modern ears as decidedly foreign. (That Medieval music should sound strange to our ears is in itself hardly surprising. After all, the languages of those remote centuries differ enormously from their modern counterparts; for example, Chaucer's fourteenth-century English is so removed from ours as to require "translation" into intelligible modern English. Musical styles are likewise constantly changing, and the music of Chaucer's time is correspondingly distant from the musical styles we are accustomed to today.)

288

Giovanni Pierluigi de Palestrina (1525–1594). The Renaissance witnessed a great flowering of Mass composition by Palestrina, Dufay, Ockegehm, Obrecht, Josquin des Pres, Byrd, and Lassus.

PALESTRINA

During the Renaissance, 1400–1600, there was a great flowering of Mass composition, along with other kinds of church music, by Dufay, Ockegehm, Obrecht, Josquin des Pres, Byrd, Palestrina, Lassus, and other masters. Their works are generally in four to six parts (e.g., Soprano I, Soprano II, Alto, Tenor I, Tenor II, Bass) and are intended for performance by a small chamber chorus, generally unaccompanied by instruments. (Instrumentalists sometimes played along with the voice parts, but they were not supplied separate accompanying parts.) From the point of view of music history, considerable irony rests in the fact that Martin Luther's nailing of ninety-five theses on a church door in 1517—his great act of defiance against the Catholic hierarchy, instigating the Protestant Reformation—transpired only a few years before the death of one outstanding Catholic master, Josquin des Pres (1450–1521), and preceded by just a few years the birth of possibly the greatest composer of Catholic church music, Giovanni Pierluigi de Palestrina (1525–1594). This is to say that the Protestant religious insurgency began during one of the most fertile artistic periods of Catholic cultural development; despite the clerical corruptions which fueled the Reformation, the Church's music was ringing out in ever greater glory. By this time polyphonic music was no longer so intimately tied to Gregorian chant; indeed, earthy popular songs now sometimes functioned as the basis of the most profound liturgical compositions. Chant nevertheless remained prominent in much sixteenth-century music.

The principal structural feature of a Renaissance choral composition was *imitation*. One vocal section (i.e., sopranos, altos, tenors, or basses) would introduce a theme which the other sections would then successively imitate. Example 126 shows the opening Kyrie of William Byrd's *Five-Part Mass* (1588). The sopranos sing the theme first, quickly overlapped by the tenors, whose music imitates the soprano line but starts five notes lower. The imitation is not exact; only the general contour and rhyth-

The Music of Catholicism

mic structure are retained, as the imitation becomes progressively looser toward the end of the phrase. The baritones (second tenors) are next to enter, starting at the point at which the tenors reach their third note. The altos follow the baritones, and the basses enter last. Observe that the first bass note coincides with the final note of the sopranos' first phrase.

Example 126
BYRD, *Five-Part Mass*, Kyrie

Music and Religion

The complex imitative style just illustrated eventually provoked the anger of the church authorities, who complained that dense musical textures prevented clear projection of the texts. The issue was taken up by the Council of Trent, held during the sixteenth century. Legend has it that some members of the council wanted to destroy all existing polyphonic church music and ban any further polyphonic composition. The story culminates with a challenge accepted by the great master, Palestrina, who allegedly composed his *Pope Marcellus Mass* (1555) to prove to the church elders that musical beauty and clear text articulation could serve the Church jointly. Palestrina apparently succeeded, for the old scores were left unharmed. Furthermore, imitational techniques have remained a fixture of Mass and other prayer settings right up to the present day.

The Baroque period of music dates from approximately 1600. Up until this time instruments had played only a secondary role in the church, and for that matter vocal music had predominated in the secular sphere as well. But now the newer Baroque styles brought instruments to the fore, resulting in a new kind of accompanied vocal music. Two of the most significant Baroque innovations were the solo aria with keyboard accompaniment and the choral work with orchestral support. In comparing a 16th-century Palestrina mass with Monteverdi's *Vespers, 1610* (see below), one discovers that the former is *a cappella*, the latter accompanied by orchestra. Eventually the Baroque combination of voices and instruments led to the large-scale concert mass scored for vocal soloists, large chorus, and orchestra. One of the most famous settings is Bach's monumental *Mass in B Minor*, a work of some two and a half hours' duration. Among other concert masses, considerably shorter than Bach's but still overlong for actual church services, are numerous examples from the Classical period by Haydn, Mozart, and Schubert; Beethoven's *Mass in C* and his overpowering *Missa Solemnis;* Romantic settings by Anton Bruckner; and twentieth-century works by Jánaček, Poulenc, and Stravinsky. For a survey of musical interpretations of the special Mass for the Dead (Requiem Mass), see Chapter 32.

Quite independent of our particular religious heritages or interests, we are all subject to the cultural heritage of Judaic-Christianity, and particularly to the powerful impress of Christianity on Western civilization during the past millenium. A long time has passed and much ground has been covered since the Roman Church dominated the Western world; and so, since religious institutions now represent only one of many social forces, it is hard to appreciate the extent to which our cultural values originated in the bosom of the Church. Notwithstanding the rise in the sixteenth century of the powerful Protestant movement and its concomitant new forms of liturgical music (see Chapter 24), it should be noted that Western music as we know it today was established mainly under the aegis of the Roman Catholic Church. Every facet of contemporary music—popular and classical, secular and liturgical, vocal and instrumental—stems from musical/cultural traditions fostered by Catholicism; the structure of a Beethoven sonata, Bruckner symphony, Bartók quartet, or Beatles song is inherently derived from the Catholic polyphonic tradition, 1000–1600. All of us who listen to classical, and even popular, music are heirs to that tradition.

You are now invited to familiarize yourself with three important settings of Catholic liturgy. The first two are based on portions of the Credo of the Mass; the third is drawn from the Vespers service. The excerpts are presented in order of structural complexity, which happens to be the reverse of their chronology. The Classical period is represented by Mozart, the late Baroque by Bach, and the early Baroque by Monteverdi.

MOZART, ET INCARNATUS EST

This brief passage is taken from the Credo of Mozart's incomplete *Grand Mass in C Minor*, K. 427. Mozart began the work shortly after his marriage to Constanze Weber in August 1782. "For a considerable time before we were married we had always attended Mass and gone to confession and taken communion together; and I found that I never prayed so fervently or confessed and took communion so devoutly as by her side."[1] Mozart composed the mass as a token of his happiness in finding a wife whom he deeply loved.

The *Mass* is scored for soloists, chorus, and orchestra. "Et Incarnatus Est" is a soprano aria, accompanied by organ, strings, and three solo wind instruments: flute, oboe, and bassoon. The vocal writing is in the highly expressive lyrical style associated with Mozart's late operas (see Pamina's aria in the second act of *The Magic Flute*, 1791). The presence of the three solo winds makes this aria unique in the vocal literature—a cross betwen a solo vocal aria and chamber music (see Chapter 17).

The structure of the aria is *binary*, that is, twofold. After a brief orchestral introduction, the voice enters with a complete statement of the text: "And was born of the Holy Ghost from the Virgin Mary, and was made Man." At first the vocal part is extremely plain, but it becomes more ornate with the repetition of the final words, "et homo factus est." Then the oboe imitates the preceding soprano ornamentation, against a long-held high note in the voice. Eventually all three wind instruments are woven into the elaborate musical fabric.

The second part of the aria starts like the beginning but soon moves to different keys. Just when the aria appears about to conclude, Mozart inserts an astonishing *cadenza*. A cadenza is a solo passage, often associated with concertos, giving the soloist an opportunity to demonstrate virtuosity unimpeded by the orchestra. However, in this cadenza only the strings and organ drop out, leaving a quartet consisting of the soprano and the three wind instrumentalists. It is hardly an exaggeration to say that the purity of this page of music is unmatched in the entire repertoire of religious music. The cadenza is reproduced in its entirety in Example 127. The aria closes quietly soon after the cadenza ends.

Example 127
MOZART, "Et Incarnatus Est," Cadenza for Soprano, Flute, Oboe, & Bassoon

Music and Religion

ctus est.

The Music of Catholicism

Johann Sebastian Bach (1685–1750) earned his livelihood in the service of the Lutheran denomination but composed occasional works for the Catholic church as well. His *Mass in B Minor*, begun in 1733 but not completed until shortly before his death, is based in part on adaptations of music that Bach had previously used in Protestant cantatas (as described in Chapter 24). The setting, like Mozart's *Grand Mass*, is for soloists, chorus, and orchestra. It is a gargantuan work, the five parts of the Ordinary text being spread out through a total of twenty-four individual musical numbers.

After "Et Incarnatus Est," the Credo text continues with the "Crucifixus": "And was crucified for us under Pontius Pilate, died, and was buried." Bach scored this section for four-part chorus and, in keeping with its tragic text, cast the music in the minor mode. The form is that of a *chaconne*, a slow and stately dance (see the explanatory essay at the end of this chapter). The music consists of a constantly recurring bass line—called a *ground bass* or *ostinato*—over which Bach wove a fabric of continuous variations. The music opens with a statement of the ostinato for orchestra alone (flutes and strings). The sopranos enter in measure 5, followed successively by altos, tenors, and basses, each group enunciating the single word, "crucifixus." You will note that the altos' first syllable coincides with the sopranos' last syllable, and so forth with each new voice entrance. Most of these initial entrances begin on successively lower pitches, matching the descending motion of the bass line. In measure 9, the tenors commence a new four-measure section which exactly duplicates the previous four measures, except that the voice parts exchange the order of their entrances.

Example 128
BACH, *B Minor Mass*, "Crucifixus"

Ostinato Figure

continued

Example 128 *continued*

From this point on the vocal imitations are less literal, as new rising and descending motives are introduced. Notice that throughout the variations the orchestral bass part never changes. Although there is nothing inherently sad about the chaconne form, it admirably evokes the sadness of the Crucifixus text; the continuous varied repetition drives the message home over and over again. Altogether the bass ostinato is presented twelve times unaltered, followed by a thirteenth statement changed slightly to prepare for a modulatory ending in a brighter major key—signaling an ensuing change of mood anticipating the forthcoming words, "Et resurrexit tertia die" ("And was raised on the third day").

Listen carefully to the "Crucifixus" several times. Aside from its interesting motivic variations, the music abounds in luscious chord progressions. Few short pieces in the classical repertoire offer a comparable harmonic fascination.

Claudio Monteverdi (1567–1643). The creative life of Monteverdi spanned the end of the Renaissance period and the beginning of the Baroque in the same way that Beethoven bridged the Classic and Romantic periods.

MONTEVERDI, MAGNIFICAT

The creative life of Claudio Monteverdi (1567–1643) spanned the end of the Renaissance and the inception of the Baroque. We encountered Monteverdi previously in discussing the origins of opera (see Chapter 13); he was of no less stature in the field of religious music, displaying mastery in both the older a cappella choral styles and the newer accompanied styles. The *Vespers* of 1610 gives ample proof of his skill in the latter. A large opus for six- to eight-part chorus, the work also calls for an accompaniment of strings, cornetts, bassoons, trombones, flutes, recorders, and organ. (A *cornett* was a mild-toned wind instrument made of wood with a cupped mouthpiece—not to be confused with the modern trumpetlike cornet.) The concluding "Magnificat" is a compositional *tour de force* in which Monteverdi demonstrated the possibilities of continuous variation based on a simple plainchant theme. In some respects the "Magnificat" resembles Bach's "Crucifixus," in that its simple theme engenders a rich and complex series of variations. However, the compositional technique used here should not be confused with theme and variations form, as discussed in Chapter 18, for in this case the *theme itself* is not varied. It remains "firm" (in the sense of *cantus firmus*) while the other voices around it constantly change.

Example 129 presents the plainchant melody upon which Monteverdi constructed the "Magnificat." The music opens with a dramatic fanfare for seven-part chorus and orchestra. The cantus firmus is sung by the first sopranos.

Example 129
MONTEVERDI, *Vespers* (1610). "Magnificat," Cantus Firmus

Magnificat anima mea Dominum.   My soul doth magnify the Lord.

A succession of eleven sections follows, each consisting of the cantus firmus along with various combinations of vocal and instrumental lines. The following discussion will give you a detailed guide to the structure of the "Magnificat."

Section I

Et exultavit spiritus in Deo salutari   And my spirit hath rejoiced in God my
meo.   saviour.

Tenor I begins an ornate melodic line imitated a measure later by Tenor II. The cantus firmus is sung by the altos in long slow notes.

Example 130
Vespers, "Et Exúltavit"

Music and Religion

Section II

Qui respexit humilitatem ancillae suae; ecce enim ex hoc beatam me dicent omnes generationes.	For he hath regarded the lowliness of his handmaiden; for behold, from henceforth all generations shall call me blessed.

The orchestra commences an interlude in a cheerful fast tempo. Then one tenor soloist begins the cantus firmus in very long notes against complementary melodic lines (*descants*) played first by two flutes, then by two trombones, and finally by two recorders. After a return of the fast instrumental interlude, the last phrase of the cantus firmus is sung while the orchestral "jig" continues.

Section III

Quia fecit mihi magna qui potens est; et sanctum nomen ejus.	For he that is mighty hath magnified me, and holy is his Name.

As the altos sing the slow cantus firmus, two imitative descants are heard in the bass section of the chorus. Solo ornamental violin parts are also prominent.

Section IV

Et misericordia ejus a progenie in progenies timentibus ejum.	And his mercy is on them that fear him throughout all generations.

The chorus (in six parts) sings this variation supported by organ alone. This section represents the earlier Renaissance a cappella style, for the organ part merely duplicates the voice parts, adding nothing independent of its own. (Otherwise the "Magnificat" exemplifies the new kind of instrumental accompaniment associated with the rise of Baroque vocal styles.) First the lower three voices begin, with the slow cantus firmus carried by the tenor part. Then the upper three voices take over in a higher key, repeating the preceding text and melody of the lower parts. This alternation continues throughout the section, with all six voices interweaving only at the end.

Section V

Fecit potentiam in brachio suo; dispersit superbos mente cordis sui.	He hath showed his arm; he hath scattered the proud in the imagination of their hearts.

Another instrumental interlude, similar to that of Section II, leads to a solo alto statement of the cantus firmus.

Section VI

Deposuit potentes de sede, et exultavit humiles.	He hath put down the mighty from their seat, and hath exalted the humble and the meek.

Two cornetts commence a plaintive echoing duet, which counterpoints the cantus firmus as sung by the tenor soloist. The cornetts are replaced halfway by two violins, whose music calls for great agility.

Example 131
Vespers, "Deposuit"

Section VII

Esurientes implevit bonis, et divites dimisit inanes.	He hath filled the hungry with good things and the rich he hath sent empty away.

Another cheerful orchestral dance leads to a delicate soprano duet. The sopranos sing unsupported by instruments, but the jaunty orchestral part resumes in breaks between their phrases. The alternation of perky orchestra and poignant voices continues through the entire section, with the two groups combining only in the final measures.

Section VIII

Suscepit Israel puerum suum; recordatus misericordiae suae.	He remembering his mercy hath helped his servant Israel.

Again a soprano duet, but with the cantus firmus in the tenors (starting in measure 5). The ornate soprano parts offer contrast to the simple tenor line. The organ accompanies alone.

Section IX

Sicut locutus est ad patres nostros, Abraham et semini ejus in secula.	As he promised to our forefathers, Abraham and his seed forever.

Once again a cheerful orchestral passage starts things. The cantus firmus is sung by the altos.

Music and Religion

Gloria Patri, et Filio, et Spiritui Sancto.   Glory be to the Father and to the Son,
                                                and to the Holy Ghost.

A highly virtuoso tenor part commences this section, with the sopranos eventually entering with the cantus firmus. Just before the sopranos' entrance the second tenor sings a rising scale, echoing the first tenor's line in the preceding measure. Thereafter the echo principle prevails throughout the section.

Section XI

Sicut erat in principio, et nunc et   As it was in the beginning, is now and
semper et in secula seculorum. Amen.   ever shall be, world without end.
                                        Amen.

All singers and players participate in the grand final tutti. The first sopranos, first violins, and first cornett perform the cantus firmus, imitated in the style of a canon by the second sopranos, second violins, and second cornett. (You may find it difficult to single out the canon, so much else is going on at the same time.) To make things even more complicated, the time lapse between the cantus firmus and its canonic imitation changes from one measire at the beginning of the section to five measures in the middle. The "Magnificat" culminates in a stirring canonic "Amen" involving the choir and orchestra at their stentorian best.

BASICS: PASSACAGLIA/CHACONNE FORM

The *passacaglia* is a special type of variations form constructed over a *ground bass* (a melodic pattern repeated over and over, as in Bach's "Crucifixus"—see Example 128). Optionally there may be a soprano melody treated much like the theme in a regular set of variations, but, as in the "Crucifixus", there need be no consistent melodic pattern other than the repeated bass melody. Variations follow one after the other without pause, and the figuration in adjacent variations is often only slightly altered. The terms *chaconne* and *passacaglia* are closely related, and no significant structural difference can be attached to either term. Thus, the structure of the chaconne from Bach's *Partita in D Minor* for solo violin is virtually identical to that of Bach's *Passacaglia (and Fugue) in C Minor* for Organ. The latter starts with a solo statement of the ground bass, whereas the chaconne begins with a harmonically supported melody; otherwise, the patterns of the two works are extremely similar.

The final movement of Brahms's *Symphony No. 4 in E Minor* represents an excellent example of a passacaglia/chaconne from the late Romantic period. It commences with an eight-measure chord progression which serves as the underpinning of the entire movement. Each eight-measure variation begins immediately on the completion of the preceding variation, thereby lending the music a sense of large-scale continuity despite the brevity of each variation. Many of the variations, starting with the second, introduce melodic *descants* which submerge the top line of the basic chord progression. In variation 4 this top line is transferred to the bass part and remains there throughout much of the rest of the movement.

Example 132

BRAHMS, *Symphony No. 4 in E Minor*, Finale, Passacaglia Theme, (Reduced)

After a series of increasingly more complex variations, the tempo becomes twice as slow, and we hear four variations in this new solemn tempo. The first of these boasts one of the most beautiful flute solos in the orchestral repertoire. The second emphasizes other wind instruments, notably the oboe and clarinet, and at the same time the mode changes from minor to major. We then hear two final slow variations emphasizing trombones and French horns. The music becomes soft and mysterious, and with a descending scale in the solo flute it slows to a halt.

Suddenly the original tempo resumes, and we hear an approximation of the opening minor chord progression. After a series of exciting new variations we reach a loud section duplicating the first three variations of the movement, albeit with slight changes in ornamentation and played fortissimo by the entire orchestra. All in all, this gives us a sense of three-part (*ternary*) form, the slow middle section standing between the similar fast outer sections. The total of thirty-one eight-measure phrases breaks down as follows:

> *A* section - Opening theme and eleven variations (minor)
> *B* section - Four slow variations (three in major)
> *C* section - Opening theme and fourteen variations (minor)

As with other sets of variations, the movement ends with a coda, an exciting passage of increased tempo and intensity.

Other well-known examples of passacaglia and chaconne form, aside from the aforementioned three works of Bach, are Corelli's *La Follia* for violin, Beethoven's *Thirty-two Variations in C Minor* for piano, and the finale of Brahms's *Variations on a Theme of Haydn* (two versions, one for orchestra, one for two pianos). Also listen to Dido's "Lament" from Purcell's *Dido and Aeneas* (Chapter 31).

MUSIC AND THE PROTESTANT REFORMATION

24

Some four and a half centuries after its inception, it is difficult for us to appreciate the revolutionary nature of early Protestantism. The existence of Russian-Chinese communism looms no more menacing today than did the Reformation movement in the eyes of the sixteenth-century Catholic hierarchy. Catholics and Protestants now live peacefully side by side in most parts of the world (with the notable exception of Northern Ireland); in the 1500s and 1600s they were constantly at each others' throats. The Protestants restructured the liturgy, retaining some parts of the Mass while omitting others, and substituted for liturgical Latin the languages of those northern European countries (England, Germany, Holland, etc.) where the Reformation established a foothold. Music served an important function in this conflict, for Martin Luther (1483–1546) introduced a powerful new element into the liturgy—congregational singing. Prior to this, all worship music was performed by clerics; the laity merely sat back and listened. Luther changed this by requiring everyone to participate in the singing of *chorales* (hymns). He himself wrote the words and music to several chorales that have become hallmarks of the Protestant movement. His most famous hymn is "Ein feste Burg ist unser Gott," or "A Mighty Fortress Is Our God."

Example 133
LUTHER, Chorale, "Ein feste Burg 1st unser Gott"

Luther was a revolutionary, but not an incendiary. Nevertheless, his religious grievances soon fomented civil wars, spreading violence and brutality throughout Europe and resulting in widespread death and destruction. The following excerpt from Heinrich von Kleist's story, *Saint Cecilia, or the Power of Music* (written two and a half centuries after the onset of Protestantism) gives us a penetrating insight into the religious strife of the sixteenth century, as well as a hint of the mystical influence of music on men's minds and actions.

Around the end of the sixteenth century, when the religious riots were erupting in the Netherlands, three brothers—young men studying in Wittenberg—met in the city of Aachen with a fourth who was employed in Antwerp as a preacher. They were there to collect an inheritance which had been left them by an old uncle whom none of them had known and, since there was no one in the city to whom they could turn, they put up at an inn. After a few days, which they spent listening to

303

the preacher relate the curious events which had been taking place in the Netherlands, it came to pass that the nuns in the convent of St. Cecilia, which was located at the gates of this city at the time, were about to commence their solemn Corpus Christi Day celebration. As a result, the four brothers, roused by fanaticism, youth and the example of the Netherlanders, decided that they would present the city of Aachen with their own iconoclastic riot.

The preacher, who had more than once directed similar undertakings, convened the night before a number of merchants' sons and students—all young men dedicated to the new doctrine—who spent the night at the inn cursing the papacy amid food and drink; and when dawn broke over the summit of the city, they armed themselves with axes and every other means of destruction, ready to commence their unsavory work. Triumphantly, they agreed upon a signal with which they would begin to shatter the glass window panes adorned with biblical scenes; and, certain of a huge following among the people, they headed for the cathedral as the bells began to ring, determined not to leave a single stone unturned.

The Abbess, who had been informed at daybreak of the danger which hovered over the convent, sent word repeatedly and in vain to the Imperial Officer who had command of the city, imploring him to send a guard for the protection of the convent. The officer, himself an enemy of the papacy and consequently predisposed—at least unofficially—to the new doctrine, refused her the guard under the shrewd pretext that she must be seeing ghosts and that not even the shadow of a danger threatened her convent.

In the meantime, the hour arrived for the festivities to commence and the nuns, amid fear and prayers and grievous expectation of things to come, prepared for Mass. No one was there to protect them, save a 70-year-old parish officer and a few armed servants who had stationed themselves before the entrance to the church.

In convents, as is commonly known, the nuns perform their own music, being skilled in playing all sorts of instruments with a precision, understanding and sensitivity often unmatched in male orchestras (perhaps due to the feminine nature of this mysterious art). Now, to make matters worse than they were, it happened that Sister Antonia, who was accustomed to conducting the orchestra, had a few days earlier become seriously ill with a nervous fever; so that, aside from the four blasphemous brothers who were already visible huddling in their cloaks under the pillars of the church, the convent faced the further predicament of lacking an appropriate musical work to perform.

The Abbess, who had instructed the previous night that an ancient Italian mass by an unknown composer be performed—a mass which the orchestra had already performed with the greatest effect due to its special holiness and magnificence—sent once again with steadfast resolve to inquire how Sister Antonia was feeling. However, the nun who had been dispatched returned with the news that Sister Antonia was totally unconscious and that for her to conduct the intended music was completely out of the question.

In the meantime, a number of threatening events had already taken place in the cathedral, in which more than a hundred men of all ages and classes, armed with hatchets and crowbars and bent on destruction, had congregated. Several servants standing at the portals had been taunted in a most unbecoming manner, and the instigators had seen fit to utter the most brazen and impudent remarks about the nuns who, in carrying out their pious tasks, occasionally appeared in the corridors. As a result of all this, the parish officer retreated to the sacristy and begged the Abbess on his knees to call off the festival and retire to the city, under protection of the

Music and Religion

Commandant. But the Abbess was unshakable in her resolve that the festival in honor of God Almighty must take place. She reminded him of his duty to protect the Mass and the solemn procession held in the cathedral with life and limb; and, as the bell began to chime, she ordered the nuns, who formed a circle around her, shaking and shivering, to choose an oratorio—no matter which or how good it was—and to begin the performance of it immediately.

The nuns in the organ gallery were making preparations. The score of a composition that had already been performed frequently was being handed out, violins, oboes, and basses checked and tuned, when suddenly Sister Antonia appeared at the staircase, fresh and healthy, albeit somewhat pale. She was holding under her arm the score of the ancient Italian mass which the Abbess had so urgently insisted on performing. In reply to he astounded Sisters' question as to where she had come from and how she had so suddenly recovered, she answered, "No matter, friends, no matter," handed out the score she was carrying and, glowing with enthusiasm, seated herself at the organ to conduct the splendid piece of music.

A wonderful, heavenly feeling of consolation imbued the hearts of the Sisters. Immediately they took their places. Even the anxiety of their plight served to transport their souls, as if on wings, through all the heavens of euphony. The oratorio was executed with the greatest musical splendor. During the entire performance not a breath stirred in the pews. Especially during the Salve Regina, and even more so during the Gloria in Excelsis, the entire church assembly seemed stupefied. As a consequence, notwithstanding the four god-forsaken brothers and their followers, not even the dust on the plaster was scattered and the convent remained intact until the end of the Thirty Years' War, when it was secularized pursuant to an article in the Peace of Westphalia.

(translated by Gerald Romanow)

An important new musical form, the *cantata*, was created during the seventeenth century. The text of a cantata ties in closely with the church calendar, amplifying the theme for a given day's worship. For example, a cantata intended for the first Sunday of Advent would elaborate on the coming birth of Christ. Musically a cantata comprises choral sections alternating with solo arias, duets, and recitative-style narration. Often a composer would integrate the text and the music by basing part or all of a cantata on a familiar chorale melody. In this way a highly sophisticated compositional structure lasting thirty minutes or more could nevertheless be made intelligible to a lay congregation—the simple chorale tune cutting through the rest of the musical texture and reaching directly to the congregants. And the worshippers could sing along as the cantata concluded with a simple four-part version of the chorale. In one important respect the new musical practices of the Reformation duplicated an old Catholic tradition; for just as Gregorian chant was the backbone of Renaissance polyphony, the chorale was the foundation for numerous Baroque works.

BACH AND THE CANTATA

The best known composer of church cantatas is Johann Sebastian Bach (1685–1750). Bach was extraordinarily versatile, composing an enormous repertoire for keyboard (organ and harpsichord) and other instruments (solo partitas for violin, sonatas for violin and harpsichord, solo suites for cello, trio sonatas, orchestral works such as the six *Brandenburg Concerti*, etc.), as well as producing more than two hundred sacred cantatas and other major vocal works (e.g., *The Saint John Passion*—see Chapter 25). At the same time, he managed a busy home life, fathering twenty children by two wives. (Widowed at the age of 35, Bach married his former student, Anna Magdalena, for whose edification he composed the *Anna Magdalena Music Book*.)

Many of Bach's cantatas are based on familiar Lutheran hymns. *Cantata No. 80*, a celebration of Reformation Sunday, consists of eight independent movements, half of which feature Luther's chorale tune, "A Mighty Fortress Is Our God." (Compare Example 134 with Example 133.) The other voices follow suit, in the fugal style of Byrd's *Five-Part Mass* (see Example 126). The sopranos come in after the altos, with the tenors and basses entering last. A few measures later the trumpets and oboes play the first phrase of the chorale theme slow and unadorned. Each section of the chorale proceeds in similar fashion: all the voices take up one or two phrases of the chorale, followed by a slow and stately trumpet echo. The overall effect is truly grand.

Example 134
BACH, *Cantata No. 80*, "A Mighty Fortress Is Our God," Opening Tenor Line

Music and Religion

Johann Sebastian Bach, c. age 30. Bach was extraordinarily versatile, composing an enormous repertoire for keyboard and other instruments, as well as producing more than two hundred sacred cantatas and other major vocal works.

The second movement of the cantata presents an energetic violin passage as an introduction to a florid bass aria on a text commencing, "All, all that God endured . . ." Meanwhile the sopranos sing the chorale theme to words beginning, "No one can overpower us."

Movements 3 and 4 omit the chorale theme, which returns in movement 5. As opposed to the square-cut ⁴₄ meter of movements 1 and 2, the orchestra now introduces a surprising lilting ⁶₈ meter. Can you detect the chorale theme in its new rhythmic guise of three-note groupings? Eventually the chorus enters, singing the first phrase of the unelaborated chorale theme in simple octave doublings.

Example 135
BACH, *Cantata No. 80*, 5th Mvt.

The cantata concludes with a simple four-part congregational version of the chorale.

307

Another of Bach's chorale cantatas *Cantata No. 4*, "Christ Lay in the Bonds of Death," is analyzed in depth, below.

Bach was the last in a long line of distinguished German Baroque Protestant church composers. If you like his religious music, you may very well also enjoy some of the works of his predecessors, among the most illustrious of whom were Heinrich Schütz and Dietrich Buxtehude. Schütz was born one hundred years before Bach, Buxtehude half a century after Schütz. All three composers wrote stirring settings of the psalm text, "Singet dem Herrn ein neues Lied" (Sing unto the Lord a New Song"), the veritable "theme song" of the Reformation movement.

CANTATA NO. 4, "CHRIST LAG IN TODESBANDEN" ("CHRIST LAY IN THE BONDS OF DEATH")

Most chorale-derived cantatas feature the given chorale tune in only a few movements; *Cantata No. 4* is exceptional insofar as all of its eight movements are based on the chorale, "Christ Lay in the Bonds of Death," written by Martin Luther in 1524. The cantata unfolds a tale of the struggle between death and life, or evil and good, as symbolized by Jesus's crucifixion and subsequent resurrection. Structurally the work consists of an orchestral introduction, six movements based on the chorale, and a concluding four-part statement of the chorale. Despite the complexity of this cantata, its emphasis on the chorale theme offers even the inexperienced listener a firm auditory grip right from the outset. The following analysis explains the musical structure of *Cantata No. 4* with a view to underscoring the religious message which the music attempts to convey.

The chorale theme consists of six separate phrases which are grouped into two overall sections. The first section is made up of phrases 1 and 2, which are then repeated (with new words) as phrases 3 and 4.

Example 137
BACH, *Cantata No. 4*, "Christ Lay in the Bonds of Death," Sinfonia (Introduction)

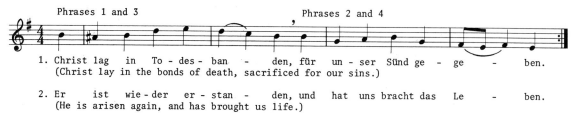

The second section is made up of the remaining four phrases sung in order and without repetition. Since the simplest version of the chorale melody comes at the end—in effect the "theme" appearing after the variations (see Chapter 18 re theme and variations form)—you should listen to the concluding choral before starting on the cantata as a whole.

Introduction

The brief orchestral introduction sets the tone of deep sadness associated with Christ's death. It is played by strings and organ, which are the sole accompanying forces in the work. The opening measures emphasize the first two notes of the chorale theme, the first full phrase of which is heard in measures 5–7. The repetition of the half-step interval between the first two notes establishes an effect of pathos, not unlike the initial choral utterances of Bach's "Crucifixus" (see Example 128). The remainder of the introduction maintains the same somber spirit, but is not otherwise derived from the chorale theme.

Example 136
Chorale (Traditional), "Christ Lay in the Bonds of Death"

Music and the Protestant Reformation

Verse 1

Although each verse of the chorale text consists of eight lines, Bach's musical settings of the verses vary considerably in size. Not surprisingly, the shortest is verse 7, the unadorned congregational version of the chorale, lasting about one minute. The most elaborate setting is verse 1, which runs to eight or nine minutes. The other verses take a few minutes each, with the complete cantata lasting about twenty-five minutes. How did Bach achieve these wide durational divergences, all the while using verse texts of exactly the same length? To begin with, in verse 1 Bach treats the chorale melody as a *cantus firmus*. (This term has already been encountered in the discussion of Monteverdi's "Magnificat"—see Chapter 23.) The sopranos sing the chorale melody in a slow dignified manner, while the other voices and the orchestra elaborate the melody at a faster pace. Bach's treble parts were sung by boys, and recordings of his cantatas are now available with boy sopranos and altos in place of their female counterparts. The musical value of boys' voices is related to Bach's habitual assignment of the cantus firmus to the soprano part; boys' voices are more effective than womens' voices in cutting through the thick mixture of voices and instruments. The clarity of the boys' sound is due to the relative lack in their singing of the pulsating effect known as *vibrato*.

At the opening of verse 1, the sopranos sing the chorale theme in *augmentation* (i.e., very slowly). Each note of the theme lasts approximately twice its normal length (at the basic tempo of verse 7, or as shown in Example 136). The very first note, on the word "Christ," is especially drawn out, eight times its normal duration. After completing phrase 1, the sopranos remain silent for two measures while the other vocal parts and the orchestra continue in the same energetic manner as before. When the sopranos finish phrase 2 there is a still longer break before they commence phrase 3 (a musical repetition of phrase 1). During this break the altos anticipate phrase 3, "Er ist wieder erstanden" ("He has risen") at the *normal* tempo. As the altos repeat these words to a subordinate melody, the tenors imitate the preceding alto entrance, the basses following with a similar imitation two measures later. Once the three lower voices have all had a crack at the new phrase, the sopranos return in the dignified slow manner established earlier—a procedure followed for each successive phrase of the chorale melody. The altos are not always the first to start, however, and sometimes a second part commences its imitation before the first part is finished. No matter how elaborate the other parts, the sopranos always patiently wait their turn, entering with long solemn notes.

Only at phrase 7 do the sopranos join the others in singing the theme at its regular tempo. To appreciate Bach's motivation for this change of pace, let us consider the text of verse 1.

> Christ lay in the bonds of death
> For our sins given,
> He is again arisen
> And has brought us life
> That we might be happy again.
> Praise God and be thankful to him,
> And sing hallelujah.
> Hallelujah!

The Entombment, fifteenth- century engraving by Andrea Mantegna.

Phrases 7 and 8 emphasize the word *hallelujah,* originally a Hebrew word signifying a glorified hurrah. Dignity must bend when it comes to singing this exciting word with suitable fervor. Thus, Bach not only reverted to normal tempo for the sopranos' entrance in phrase 7; in phrase 8 he devised an extensive fantasia in double time—twice as fast as the normal tempo—with all the voices exclaiming "hallelujah" over and over again. Bach even pepped things up by sometimes placing the first two syllables on syncopated offbeats, lending a distinctly jazzy touch to this triumphant finale. (For a discussion of *syncopation,* see Chapter 12.) Many of the "hallelujahs" are also set in quick eighth notes, some with pauses between the "halle" and "lujah." The musical tension increases until all the voices join for a final "hallelujah" in block chords, ending in a bright major triad. The effect is stunning.

Music and the Protestant Reformation

Verse 2

The message of verse 1 is essentially of good tidings: Christ's death is a victory for mankind. Verse 2 conveys a very different message: "Death gained strength due to mankind's sinfulness; therefore death came and assumed power over us, holding us prisoner within his realm." This gloomy text calls for a correspondingly morose musical setting; so Bach introduced a quiet recurring bass line (*ground bass*) which emphasizes the pathetic descending step motion of the chorale theme opening (and is also reminiscent of the orchestral prelude to verse 1—compare the bass line of Example 138 with the first violin part of Example 137). Only the sopranos and altos sing this verse, accompanied by a simple continuo mixture of cello, bass, and organ. The opening vocal phrase focuses on the descending half step between the first two notes of the chorale theme; the words "den Tod" ("O death") are repeated several times before the remainder of the phrase is sung.

Example 138
Cantata No. 4, Verse 2

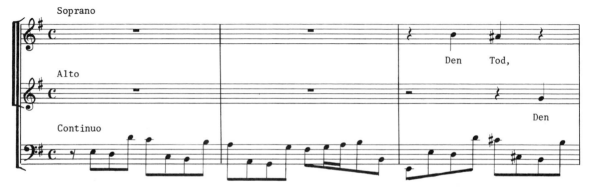

Music and Religion

Starting in measure 5 the sopranos present the chorale theme in full, while the altos supply imitative counterpoint. Phrases 3 and 4 correspond musically to phrases 1 and 2. The sad mood prevails throughout, culminating in four half-hearted hallelujahs, mildly spiced with off-beat accents.

Verse 3

At the start of this verse an energetic sixteenth-note figure in the violins betokens an abrupt change of mood. In this verse the tenors sing alone, declaring that "Jesus Christ, God's son, came to take our place, doing away with sin, and thereby removing from death its right and power—leaving nothing but the appearance (image) of death, which has lost its sting." Throughout this verse the violin figures express the valiant spirit of Christ. There is one exceptional moment, however. Line 6 asserts that nothing is left of death except its form or shape—"Da bleibet nichts denn Tod'sgestalt." This reference to the fearful image of death provokes a sudden slowing down, as if to acknowledge that even the *notion* of death is terrifying. But once the last syllable of this line is enunciated, the jaunty first tempo resumes. The music now regains its "up" feeling and the tenors proclaim, "Death has lost its sting." The tenors take over the fanciful violin figuration for their final hallelujahs.

Verse 4

Verse 4 returns to the complex counterpoint of verse 1. All four voice parts are present once again, although the accompaniment is reduced to simple continuo (as in verse 2). In this section we encounter the opposite of the augmentation found in verse 1; now we have *diminution*. First the tenors enter with phrase 1 twice as fast as normal. In measure 2 the sopranos enter at the same speed, and the basses follow suit in measure 3. The *absence* of an alto entrance in measure 4 is related to the fact that the alto part is to be differentiated from the other three parts throughout this verse. Indeed it is the alto part which will now carry the chorale theme, at its usual medium tempo (twice as slow as the other parts). Another special feature of the alto part is that it begins on F#, five notes higher than B, the first note of the chorale theme in the preceding verses. The altos actually sing the complete chorale theme in the secondary key of B minor (although Bach retained the written key signature—one sharp—of the original key of E minor). The polarity between the two keys of E minor and B minor continues throughout most of this verse. By phrase 6 all the parts imply B minor, and with the altos' final "hallelujah" the modulation to B minor seems complete. However, the chord supporting the altos' very last note (on the syllable "jah") is unexpectedly unstable, and, as the other voices sing their hallelujahs, the harmony reestablishes the principal key of E minor.

Why did Bach employ *two* keys in verse 4, instead of just the single E minor? The answer is to be found in the text, which tells us that "it was a wonderful battle between life and death; death was defeated and life carried the day. As the scriptures had foretold, one death consumed another (i.e., Christ's death overcame the general power of sin over mankind), and death has become a mockery. Hallelujah!" The violent struggle between life and death is symbolized by the competition between the keys of E and B minor. B minor nearly "consumes" E minor, but eventually E minor emerges triumphant. Bach's music deftly parallels the explicit conflict of the text.

Verse 5

A bass solo accompanied by the full orchestra now describes the Easter lamb that is "cooked in fervent love" on the Cross. The second half of the text refers to the "sign of blood over the door protecting us from death." The music here is equivalent to a slow waltz. Once again a conflict ensues between two keys, for the bass starts the chorale theme in A minor (beginning on E, five notes below the usual B), while the first violins respond with an elaborated version of the chorale theme in the original E minor. Line 6 is notable for the extremely low E# of the bass as he sings "dem Tode für," meaning "keeps death away." Also significant is the extremely high D at the beginning of line 7: "The slayer can do us no harm." At the end the bass solo gets carried away in a series of florid hallelujahs.

314

Verse 6

Next comes a duet for sopranos and tenors, with continuo accompaniment, telling us to "have a great celebration which will be lit up by the Lord, who is indeed the sun, giving light to our hearts as the dark sinful night disappears." As the voices sing the chorale theme, a martial countermelody in the continuo bass line helps express this cheerful message. You will also notice the voices expressing their happiness in several triplet *melismas*. (A melisma is a melodic configuration of several notes in conjunction with a single syllable of text.) The groups of evenly distributed triplets make for delightful contrast against the long-short rhythmic figures in the continuo.

Example 139
Cantata No. 4, Verse 6 (Line 2)

Verse 7

Verse 7 presents the simple chorale which is the source of *Cantata No. 4*. The text continues the food imagery of verse 5: "We live and eat well on the Passover bread; Christ will be our food, feeding the soul and supporting the faith." After all the telling effects of the preceding sections, the listener might expect this plain hymn setting to seem anticlimactic, but this is not the case. Its very simplicity is extremely moving, and no moment in the work is more effective than the single choral hallelujah which brings the cantata to a close.

Music and the Protestant Reformation

25   RELIGIOUS DRAMA

In Chapter 4 we encountered a musical setting of the primordial opening verses of Genesis—*The Creation*, by Franz Joseph Haydn. This is just one of many outstanding dramatic or semidramatic compositions based on the Old Testament. Other works recount the birth, life, and death of Jesus, as told in the several gospels of the New Testament. In more recent music we find operas and other stage works built around religious themes and/or characters. Chapter 25 examines (1) liturgical drama and the rise of the oratorio; (2) the most famous of oratorios, Handel's *Messiah*; (3) passion music by Bach and others; and (4) Romantic and modern examples of religious musical/dramatic works.

EARLY MUSIC

The earliest known form of music drama is *liturgical drama*, which is essentially an opera intended for performance within the confines of a church building. Spectacle accounts for a major part of its effect, with processionals and recessionals replacing the rising and falling of a proscenium curtain. Liturgical drama was popular in the medieval period, but few examples of it remain available to us today. Fortunately one complete work, *The Play of Daniel*, has been reconstructed for modern performance and is available on records.*

The play centers around the Biblical story of the prophet Daniel and his encounter in the lions' den. Daniel is a member of a group of Jewish exiles living in the ancient kingdom of Babylonia. Belshazzar, the son of Nebuchadnezzar and now the reigning king, gives a great feast at which a mysterious hand writes on the wall: "Mene, mene, tekel, peres." Belshazzar is greatly frightened by this strange occurrence, which none of his wise men can explain. Finally, the Queen intercedes, telling Belshazzar of Daniel's visionary powers. Daniel is called to the throne and interprets the words: Belshazzar has been found wanting by the Lord, and will be punished. Soon the prophecy is realized: the victorious army of King Darius appears, and Belshazzar is put to death. Daniel is greatly honored by Darius, causing resentment among the princes of the kingdom, who conspire to pass a decree, signed by Darius, that no one shall petition any lord save Darius during a period of thirty days. Shortly thereafter Daniel is discovered worshipping the God of Moses, and the envious princes demand his punishment. Darius loves Daniel, yet feels bound by the law he himself has approved. Daniel is cast into the lions' den, whereupon an angel of the Lord intercedes, protecting him. Seeing

*The performance is by the New York Pro Musica, a musical organization which pioneered the revival and performance of early music with authentic instruments and in correct performing styles. The group made numerous superb recordings during the 1950s and 1960s.

Music and Religion

Daniel raised up, Darius turns upon the envious counselors and orders *them* thrown to the lions. The counselors are consumed forthwith, and Daniel is reinstated to his high position.

The Play of Daniel was composed in the thirteenth century by an anonymous group of youths in Beauvais, France. The work is sung mainly in Latin, although there are brief phrases in French as well. Solo singers impersonate the principal roles, assisted by choruses of satraps, soldiers, counselors, attendants, and others. The music resembles Gregorian chant (Chapter 23) in its absence of vocal counterpoint or harmony (unlike Medieval and Renaissance polyphonic styles); that is, the vocal parts are exclusively monophonic, performed either by soloists or unison chorus. However, *The Play of Daniel* is scored for various instruments which double the voice parts and even sometimes play simple polyphonic sections alone. Percussion instruments provide timbral variety during the strictly monophonic vocal sections.

In light of this and similar medieval dramas, one might have expected liturgical drama to become a mainstay of modern Western musical culture. Instead, a new form, the oratorio, developed during the early Baroque period (commencing circa 1600), and the Church has not otherwise fostered more overtly dramatic forms.

An oratorio differs from a liturgical drama or opera in that it *tells* a story rather than enacts it. A narrator sings the basic plot, while commentary is interjected by other vocal soloists and the chorus. Frequently the soloists represent actual personages and sing in the first person, but even so they remain in a fixed location on stage and engage in no dramatic gestures or movements. The early oratorio literature abounds in colorful scenes drawn from the Old Testament. One of the finest early examples, *Jeptha*, by Giacomo Carissimi (1605–1674), tells the plight of a victorious commander who after promising God he will sacrifice the first person encountered on arriving home, discovers that person to be his own daughter. Besides Carissimi, other important Baroque oratorio composers include Antonio Vivaldi (1678–1741), Georg Philipp Telemann (1681–1767), and, undoubtedly the greatest of all oratorio composers, George Frideric Handel (1685–1759). Handel was born in Germany, traveled in Italy, and settled in England by the age of twenty-five. All his oratorios are settings of original English texts (unlike his operas in Italian). Most of them recount the lives of Old Testament figures, such as *Joshua* (who fought the battle of Jericho), Daniel (*Belshazzar*), *Saul, Solomon, Moses* (*Egypt in Israel*), and *Judas Maccabaeus*.

Gustave Doré: *Daniel in the Den of Lions.*

317

Handel's greatest oratorio, *Messiah*, has become one of the most universally famous compositions of all time. At the time he composed *Messiah* (1742), Handel had been living in London for about thirty years. Upon arriving in England he thrived as a composer of operas in the Italian style. Later, however, his success waned, as John Gay's enormously popular *Beggar's Opera* (1728)—a mixture of familiar ballad tunes and a comprehensible English libretto—displaced the archaically stylized Italian opera from its position of eminence on the British stage. At this point the ever practical Handel turned to the oratorio, a genre in which he is without peer among British composers. He composed *Messiah* in a mere twenty-four days, an astonishing feat in view of the work's duration (running to about three hours). It was premiered to great acclaim in Dublin, after which it was heard in London. At the first London performance King George II was apparently so powerfully moved by the "Hallelujah Chorus" that he jumped to his feet, whereupon the rest of the audience did likewise. To this day English and American audiences stand when this portion of the oratorio is performed.* Despite the King's enthusiasm, *Messiah* was slow to gain wide acceptance and was performed infrequently during Handel's lifetime. However, the composer's death (1759) sparked a Handel festival at which the oratorio was finally recognized as a masterpiece, and *Messiah* has maintained widespread popularity ever since.

Messiah is by no means a typical Handelian oratorio, for it avoids the narrative type of libretto characteristic of his other works in this genre. The second half of Part I—relating the story of the birth in the manger—is the only portion of the work conceived in narrative form. The remainder of the text, all drawn from Holy Writ without adaptation, consists of Old Testament prophecies of a coming messiah, lamentations concerning the crucifixion (Part II), and New Testament commentary on the redemptive meaning of the resurrection (Part III). The Biblical texts were selected for Handel's use by Charles Jennens.

> . . . It is fortunate that *Messiah* is based upon the wondrous poetry of the English Bible rather than upon some chain of rhymed nonsense pitched in a sanctimonious key. Happily for Handel and for *Messiah* Jennens realized that pregnant passages from the Prophets, the Gospel story, St. Paul's Epistles, and the Revelation of St. John would prove superior to any pedestrian versifying of his own, and one is therefore spared the miserable task of keeping his temper and restraining his guffaws at the well-intentioned absurdities of the usual Handelian libretto. Posterity has agreed that Jennens' masterly selection of texts constitutes a work of art in itself. Its rich imagery and concrete symbolism create a felicitous combination of the grand, the poetic, and the passionate upon a plane of almost prophetic elevation.
>
> For the first time in musical history the mighty drama of human redemption was treated as an epic poem in Handel's *Messiah*. Jennens' libretto is an epitome of Christian faith. It portrays in succession every shade of devotional sentiment from piety, resignation, and repentance to hope, faith, and exultation. While Handel's predecessors and contemporaries presented the mystery of Christ in human terms, Jennens translated the facts of Christ's life into exalted symbols of human destiny

---

*It is ironic that the "Hallelujah Chorus" is now so indelibly associated with the Christmas season. In Handel's oratorio it is sung not after the recounting of Jesus's birth, but in connection with his death. By all rights, then, this chorus should be sung only at Easter time.

and produced a Christian epic unfolding the moral autobiography of man. In displaying the character of Messiah he provided a comprehensive view of the divine scheme of Christian redemption through the Incarnation, Passion, and Resurrection, emphasizing the intense aspiration of each human soul, the promise and accomplishment of God's mercy, the apparent triumph of evil and destruction, and the final salvation of mankind through Christ's victory over Sin and Death. When viewed only as an historical fact the Crucifixion remains a tragic incident without deep significance, but Jennens transformed Christ's death into a universal experience occurring for the sake of the individual soul. Logically Handel's masterpiece should be called *Redemption,* for its author celebrates the *idea* of Redemption rather than the *personality* of Christ.

Hence *Messiah* is epic in content and theme, and since its appearance oratorios have hovered doubtfully between the epic and the dramatic. . . . The text of *Messiah* simply *indicates* events through a series of contemplative recitatives, arias, and choruses upon the "Messiah" theme. Undoubtedly Handel's pulsating dramatic sense guided his choice of subject and directed his striking effects, but in *Messiah* he largely abandoned theatrical means of expression and depicted his scenes with a degree of reserve generally suited to his theme.[1]

George Frideric Handel, German/English composer (1685–1759).

Baroque styles are noted for their rhythmic vitality, and Handel's music is no exception. Indeed, bouncy good cheer characterizes the greater part of *Messiah*, especially its choral sections, the most famous of which ("And the Glory of the Lord," "For unto Us a Child Is Born," and the "Hallelujah Chorus") boast a zest unmatched in the oratorio literature. By comparison, Bach's style in his passion settings (discussed below)—although also Baroque—is often heavy, even turgid. Bach dealt with misery by composing the misery directly into the music; not so with Handel. Even the settings of the darkest texts of *Messiah*, Part II ("Behold the Lamb of God," "Surely He Hath Borne Our Griefs," and "And with His Stripes We Are Healed") are nothing less than brightly inspirational in character. Some of Handel's solo arias are lyrical in their sadness ("He Was Despised"), but Bach's deep sense of tragedy is simply not to be found.

The lightness of Handel's music can be attributed partly to the fact that some movements of *Messiah* are borrowed from secular works (Handel's own) having to do with the joys of love. Oddly enough, Handel's self-plagiarisms work. Thus, in Part I, the stern choral text, "And He shall purify the sons of Levi" comes out sounding like a delightful idea; one gets here a sense of moral uplift rather than of simple punishment. In-

Example 140
HANDEL, *Messiah*, "All We Like Sheep"

Music and Religion

deed, uplift is essentially the musical message of the entire score. Nowhere in the score is this more apparent than in the choral setting of Isaiah 53:6, "All We Like Sheep Have Gone Astray." In Handel's music "sin glories in its shame with almost alcoholic exhilaration. . . . Handel invested his heartbreaking text with all the rollicking exuberance of a Gilbert and Sullivan comic opera."[2]

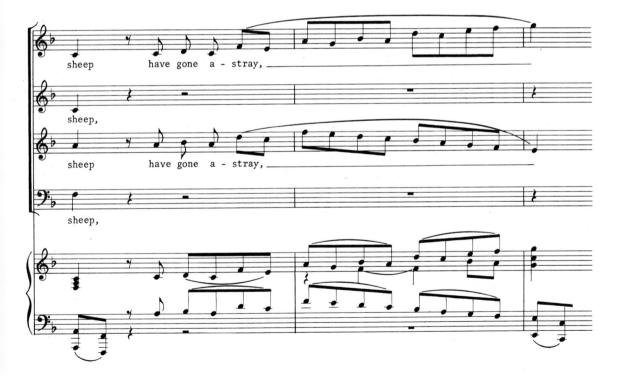

Although this music, too, was borrowed from an earlier secular source, Handel devised a new and wonderfully dignified ending for the final words, "and the Lord hath laid on Him the iniquity of us all." Perhaps what makes Handel's treatment so effective is the shock, after eight pages of jollity, of one final page of solemnity. Handel imbued his music with a combination of powerful significance and bountiful high spirits. No wonder *Messiah* is so popular!

Example 141
Messiah, "All We Like Sheep." Slow Conclusion

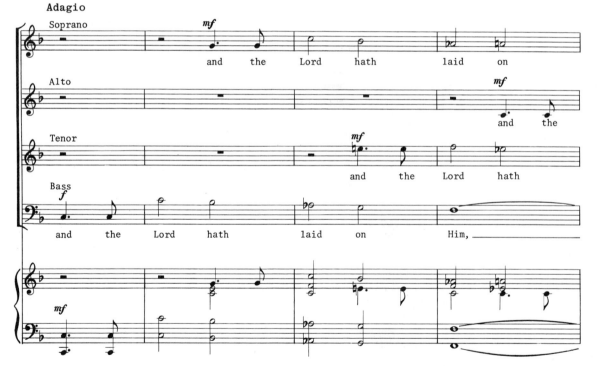

Hieronymus Bosch, *The Adoration of the Magi.* The second half of Part I of *Messiah* relates the story of the birth of Jesus.

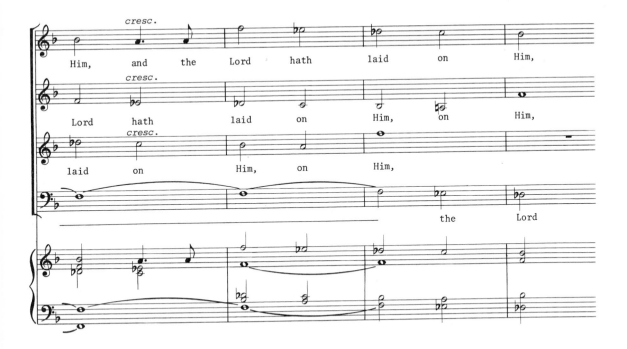

Religious Drama

Van Cleef, *The Crucifixion.*

PASSION MUSIC

Bach's dramatic treatment of the crucifixion story differs vastly from Handel's. Where Handel used the oratorio form, Bach turned to the *passion*, a special kind of oratorio relating the events leading to Christ's death. Bach left us two monumental works in this form, *The Passion According to Saint John* and *The Passion According to Saint Matthew*. Each consists of recitative narration sung by a high tenor (called the Evangelist); extensive arias by other soloists; first-person statements by Jesus, Peter, Pilate, and others; and exclamations and commentary by the chorus. Both passions conclude with the actions and sayings of those present at the Cross, as well as with the last words of Christ. The suspense builds continually until the dramatic climax, Christ's imminent death. For in-depth exposure to passion form, we will examine here the final portion of Bach's *Saint John Passion*.

Commencing at No. 56, the choir sings a verse of one of Bach's most beautiful passion chorales, "Jesus, Cross, Sorrows, and Pain." (This chorale is also heard earlier at the completion of Part I.)

324

Music and Religion

Example 142

BACH, *Passion according to Saint John*, No. 56, Chorale

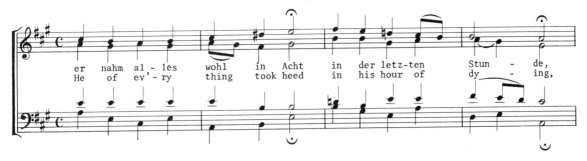

In No. 57 the Evangelist proceeds with the narration, describing the assemblage of Christ's mother and his disciples. Jesus, knowing that all the Biblical prophecies have been realized, speaks: "I am thirsty." A soldier offers him vinegar, and Jesus responds, "It is fulfilled."

Number 58 is a slow, mournful aria sung by the alto soloist: "It is fulfilled; console my aching soul. This night of sadness—let me count the final hours." Suddenly the tempo increases to a brilliant *vivace* as the alto proclaims, "Judah's hero fights mightily, and ends the strife!" The coda restores the original solemn tempo, and the alto twice repeats the opening words, "It is fulfilled."

Number 59 reports the climax of the entire story, the actuality of Christ's passing. It is a masterful stroke of musical understatement.

Example 143

St. John Passion, No. 59, Recitative

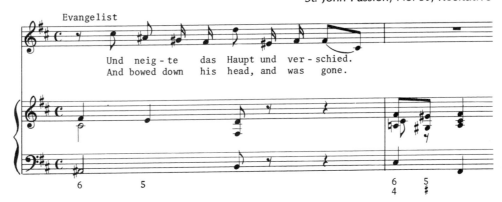

In No. 60 we hear a very complex musical passage in florid $^{12}_{8}$ meter, as the bass soloist comments on the fulfillment of the prophecies. At the same time, as background to the bass solo, the choir quietly intones the chorale melody we heard earlier (see Example 142).

Example 144
St. John Passion, No. 80, Bass Aria with Chorale Melody (See Example 142)

In No. 61 the Evangelist sings with great dramatic force: "And see, the curtain of the temple split in two . . . and the earth shook, and the mountains were destroyed, and the graves opened up, and many holy bodies arose." The orchestra punctuates this text with melodramatic scales and arpeggios. A brief tenor lament (No. 62) prepares us for one of the highlights of the oratorio literature, the soprano aria, "Zerfliesse, mein Herz, in Fluten der Zähren" ("Dissolve, O My Heart, in Cascading Tears") (No. 63). The instrumental accompaniment consists of an extraordinary blending of two transverse flutes (playing in *unison*), two oboes da caccia, and continuo (cello and organ). An oboe da caccia is a tenor oboe, the forerunner of today's English horn. The transverse flute was an early wooden version of our modern metal flute, and Bach used it here rather than its Baroque counterpart, the recorder. Frans Brueggen, a recorder virtuoso, believes that Bach selected the transverse flute for this aria because it is so hard to play.

> The text speaks of blood, guilt, and tears—the most miserable feelings you can possibly have—[and] Bach chooses the key of F minor. . . . If you realize that F minor—itself a solemn key—is amongst the most impossible, out-of-tune keys which exist for a one-keyed transverse flute, then it's clear why Bach chooses two flutes and not violins or oboes or recorders. Of course, it shouldn't *sound* out of tune, but Bach wanted a sense of strain and tragedy to pervade the music so he wrote for transverse flutes in F minor.[3]

Bach excelled especially in his treatment of the middle section of the aria: "Tell Heaven and earth [the news]: thy Jesus is dead." Take special heed of the voice's rendering of the work "tod" ("dead"). At this point the instruments return to the introductory material in the original key of F minor, leading us to expect a standard Baroque *da capo* repetition of the first section of the aria. (The *da capo aria* is the most common aria form of the Baroque period; it consists of three parts, the first and third being identical both in text and music.) Instead we are treated to a *false reprise*. The soprano avoids the opening text and instead reiterates the word "tod," as the music modulates to the secondary key of Bb minor. After this the instruments commence a genuine recapitulation in F minor, and the soprano repeats the first lines of the text. Even here we find no literal repetition of the first part, as in the conventional Baroque manner. Section 1 begins in F minor and ends in the *dominant* key, C minor, whereas section 3 is reworked so that it both starts *and* ends in the tonic key, F minor. The key relationships suggest incipient sonata form (see Chapter 12), a form mainly associated with the ensuing Classical and Romantic periods rather than the Baroque. Structural relationships aside, what counts most in the music is its extraordinary beauty.

Numbers 64 and 66 are recitative narrations of the events occurring after Christ expires, concluding with his burial in a freshly dug grave. There are also two final chorales, Nos. 65 and 68. In the principal concluding section, No. 67, the chorus sings "Rest in peace, you holy limbs . . . and bring me likewise to peace . . ." Note the peaceful effect which emanates from the recurring rhythmic motive of two brief eighth notes and a long half note (♪♫ | ♩ ♫ | ♩). The form of No. 67 is a five-part *rondo*, A-B-A-B-A, in which the second B is a *transposed* version of the first B, while the three A's are identical.

Bach's *Saint Matthew Passion* presents substantially the same account as the *Saint John*, but in a much more expansive version, running to nearly four hours in an uncut performance. Bach was by no means the first to chronicle the passion story in music. His predecessor Heinrich Schütz (born in 1585, exactly one hundred years before Bach), composed three passions and a shorter work entitled *The Seven Last Words of Christ*. This work consists of short opening and closing choruses which frame narration and a bass soloist's articulation of the actual words spoken by Christ—all (except for the choruses) in recitative style. The seven "words" are actually brief utterances drawn from the four gospels.

Composers have continued to set the passion story right up to the present time. In 1786 Haydn composed *The Seven Last Words*, a set of orchestral pieces to be played as interludes between sermons based on Jesus's last words. He later arranged them for string quartet and also as an oratorio with an added passion text. About a century later the English composer John Stainer (1840–1901) wrote an oratorio, *The Crucifixion*, which is still widely performed in churches today; an especially popular excerpt is the unaccompanied chorus, "God So Loved the World." And in this context we should not overlook the touching Negro spiritual, "Were You There?"

Example 145
Spiritual: "Were You There."

Were you there when they cru-ci-fied my Lord? Were you there when they cru-ci-fied my Lord?

Religious Drama

For a contemporary musical portrayal of the passion story, listen to the *Saint Luke Passion* by the Polish composer Krzystof Penderecki (pronounced Christoff Penderetski), born in 1933. While Penderecki's version is based mainly on Luke, it also includes quotations from John, along with various hymns, psalms, and other parts of the Roman missal. The text is in Latin. Composed between 1963 and 1966, the work is both *atonal* and *microtonal*, with much use of *quarter tones* in the string instruments.* Other special effects include vocal hissing, rubbing the back of the violin bow on a hard surface, and other such noises. The Evangelist intones his lines in speech rather than song.

Penderecki pays homage to the composer of the great *Saint John* and *Saint Matthew Passions* by introducing a theme based on the letters of Bach's name. (In German these letters represent the pitches Bb–A–C–Bb). Near the end of the work, when the Evangelist proclaims, "And it was the sixth hour; and there was darkness over all the earth . . . ," the music achieves a terrifying intensity leading into Jesus's final statement "Pater, in manus tuas commendo spiritum meo." ("Father, into Thy hands I commend my spirit.") Next we hear "Consummatum est" ("It is fulfilled") sung very softly, not by Jesus, but by a choir of boy sopranos. This brings us to the finale, sung by soloists and chorus, which is still atonal but concludes surprisingly with a loud major triad—"Thou hast redeemed me, O Lord, the God of Truth" (Psalm 30). (Penderecki employs traditional tonal materials earlier in the work, too.)

In 1970, the passion story crossed over the boundary that separates classical and popular music, and the musical world was "rocked" with *Jesus Christ Superstar.* Modeled loosely after passions by Bach and other "serious" composers, this remarkable rock opera was an instant hit first as a record album, then on the stage and finally as a movie. In the finale, the show's hit tune, "Jesus Christ Superstar," is sung by the voice of Judas (after his suicide) and the choir. This is followed by a four-minute vocal-instrumental number, simply called "The Crucifixion," that is reminiscent of some of the special effects in Penderecki's *Saint Luke Passion.* There are no words; the voices simply represent the catcalls of the onlookers mocking Christ. Then, against an orchestral background of the song "I Only Want to Say," Jesus calls out six of the traditional seven last words. (The second word is changed to "Who is my mother? Where is my mother?" and the third word is omitted.)

What is the relationship between *Jesus Christ Superstar* and the music of the past? According to composer-critic Ned Rorem, Andrew Lloyd Webber's score is almost totally derivative. In discussing the overture, Rorem says,

> Webber has treated his listener to a nearly indigestible stew of Hindu ragas, of Rodgers' *Slaughter on Tenth Avenue*, Prokofiev's *Age of Steel*, Strouse's *Bye Bye Birdie*, Honegger's *Pacific 231*, Bernstein's *Fancy Free*, Copland's *Rodeo*, Grieg's *Piano Concerto*, and the "heavenly choirs" of *Lost Horizon* which blur into Ligeti's choirs stolen for *2001*.[4]

Apparently Rorem's mind has room for more than one kind of originality, for he immediately goes on to defend Webber, allowing him "a personal energy . . . which will

---

*Quarter tones are pitches located halfway between the standard half steps which are the basis of the piano keyboard. For example, a quarter tone can be located equidistant between C and C#, another one between C# and D, etc. Penderecki's quarter-tone passages seem more vocal than instrumental, producing a curiously eerie effect.

Music and Religion

crackle for the next hour and a half." Notwithstanding Webber's dependence on a wide array of composers (Rorem also mentions Kurt Weill, Burt Bacharach, George Gershwin, Tchaikovsky, and Charles Ives), Rorem credits him with a wide measure of ability, even originality. "Where then lies Webber's originality? What is his 'color'?" Rorem asks.

> His originality, like anyone's, lies in the ability to take a chance and win. His color is the color of speed. The risk he ran here, whether by contrivance or by adrenergic dictates, was to use nearly all fast tempos. If one can assert that the most touching portions from the great classical cantatas are slow and introspective, then *Superstar's* grandeur owes nothing to the past. Webber's music loses effectiveness in proportion as it quiets down; the somber moments, few though they be, are the least compelling. Where the text would indicate to anyone but Webber a reflective pause, a hush, he goes hog-wild and chills us. His color then is the maintenance of fever pulse, a *trouvaille* utterly appropriate to the story's tension, and reminiscent only of itself.[5]

When one compares the popularity of *Jesus Christ Superstar*, the tunes of which have become known to millions of people, with the fame of the Bach passions, which are familiar to only the relatively small world of musical cognoscenti, one may be tempted to argue that Andrew Webber has outdone that grand old father figure of music, J. S. Bach. But here is a question to be answered some fifty years hence: Which of the two composers' music will endure? Perhaps both? Will *Webber* become a household name someday, just like *Bach* today? At his death in 1750 Bach's music was barely known—his fame rested mainly on his prodigious ability as an organist—and his passions gathered dust until Mendelssohn's great Bach revival in 1829. By our day, however, Bach's passions, along with his other extremely numerous works, have survived for some 250 years—an impressive record. This is not to knock *Jesus Christ Superstar*, a superb example of its genre, a really terrific rock opera. Rather, the issue hangs on whether rock opera has the survival power of the classical genres. Webber's music is highly enjoyable, even inspirational, but is it as moving as Bach's musical treatment of the crucifixion? Is not Bach's music more spiritually elevating, even if considerably less entertaining? Not that there is anything wrong with entertainment, per se, but immediate commercial success in a work of art is often—though not necessarily—a sign of brief staying power. Well, we'll just have to wait and see.

MODERN EXAMPLES

Leaving the passion form and returning to the oratorio proper, this genre went into a general decline during the nineteenth century. However, Mendelssohn composed some excellent oratorios, including *Elijah*, and Berlioz's *L'Enfance du Christ* (*The Childhood of Christ*) is a noteworthy—if atypical—example. (Berlioz's style is gutsier than the rather tame oratorio styles of Mendelssohn and other Romantics, but many people find Berlioz too idiosyncratic for their tastes.) The twentieth-century oratorio repertoire includes several excellent works, such as Arthur Honegger's *King David* and *Joan of Arc* and William Walton's *Belshazzar's Feast*.

As we suggested earlier, an oratorio is something like an unstaged opera, but with narration substituting for the stage action. The opera repertoire itself boasts relatively

329

few examples based on religious subjects. Mozart's *The Magic Flute* concerns the ancient Egyptian sect of Isis and Osiris, and is replete with Masonic ritual.[6] Several nineteenth-century operas bear witness to melodramatic persecutions of religious minorities (Bellini's *Norma*, Verdi's *Il Trovatore*, and Halevy's *The Jewess*), and Saint-Saëns's *Samson and Delilah* is based on an Old Testament story. Two of Wagner's music dramas feature morality stories: *Tannhäuser* and *Parsifal*.* More recent operas on religious themes are Puccini's one-act *Sister Angelica* and Poulenc's *Dialogues of the Carmélites*. A related form is Stravinsky's *Noah and the Flood*, a television ballet, and a popular short work, also composed originally for television, is Menotti's Christmas opera, *Amahl and the Night Visitors*.

In recent years, religion has invaded the Broadway stage. A black revivalist spirit pervades much of George Gershwin's *Porgy and Bess* (1935), an opera that has been performed on Broadway rather than in conventional opera houses. *Jesus Christ Superstar* is a rock version of the passion story, and *Godspell* is a cross between revival and rock. Jewish religious traditions, and the breaking of them, are explored in *Fiddler on the Roof*.

Another notable religious work which owes much to the Broadway musical theater is Leonard Bernstein's *Mass* (1972), written for the inaugural of the John F. Kennedy Performing Arts Center in Washington, D.C. The title of this work suggests a straightforward musical setting of the traditional Catholic Mass, but for Bernstein's fertile imagination the Roman liturgy is simply a point of departure. The work can only be described as a full-blown spectacle, complete with adult and boy choirs, a celebrant, rock and blues singers, ornate costumes and lighting, and a full complement of dancers. A dialogue is established between God and the people (somewhat in the spirit of Bernstein's *Kaddish Symphony*—see Chapter 26), and many important moral and theological issues of the day are brought right out into the open, without inhibition. Because of its complexity, the *Mass* is rarely seen on stage, but it sometimes appears on television. In any case one can absorb much of its excitement from the two-record album. The music swings all the way from hard rock on the one extreme to dissonant atonal and electronic textures on the other. The work is truly a synthesis of Bernstein's achievements as a composer of "classical" music (the *Jeremiah, Age of Anxiety*, and *Kaddish* symphonies) and Broadway musicals (*Wonderful Town, Candide*, and *West Side Story*).

---

*The noted American critic H. L. Mencken described *Parsifal* as an "elaborate and outrageous burlesque of Christianity." He dismissed the Act III *Good Friday Music* "as so downright lascivious and indecent that even I, who am almost anesthetic to such provocations, blush every time I hear it. . . . All my Freudian suppressions begin groaning and stretching their legs in the dungeons of my unconscious." See "More of the Same," in *Reflections on Human Monogamy, Prejudices: Fourth Series*, New York, 1924, pp. 107–108.

Music and Religion

BASICS: RELIGION AND MUSIC HISTORY

JEWISH WORSHIP

Up to now we have been dealing exclusively with music of the two principal Christian faiths in America, the Roman Catholic and Protestant, but Christianity itself is derived from an even older religion, Judaism. In this essay we shall survey the function of music in Jewish worship and then examine an important symphonic composition based on Jewish liturgy.

Traditional Jewish worship entails two leaders, a rabbi and a cantor. The rabbi is the "minister" of the congregation; the cantor leads much of the actual services in song. (*Cantor* is derived from the Latin root, *cantare*—to sing.) An important aspect of Jewish worship is the reading from the Torah (Old Testament), which is recorded on large parchment scrolls kept in a central location on the temple pulpit. The cantor intones the weekly Torah excerpt in an improvisatory style based on traditional cantorial *modes* (i.e., scales) and melodic patterns derived from these modes. The modern "reformed" practice of Judaism relies much less on the cantorial art than the older, more orthodox side, but many reform temples still employ cantors, even if in a lesser role. In reform services, the cantor sings a few solos and otherwise simply leads the congregation in traditional responses.

Knath's *Day of Atonement.* The musical highpoint of the Jewish calendar comes on the eve of Yom Kippur (Day of Atonement) with the chanting of "Kol Nidrei." Several important twentieth-century musicians have composed settings of Jewish liturgical texts.

Courtesy Museum of Fine Arts, Boston

For example, near the beginning of a service the congregation stands and recites "Bor'chu," a short response which glorifies God. The cantor sings the first line, and the congregation responds with the second line.

Bor'chu es adonoy ham'voroch.	Praise ye the Lord, to whom all praise is due.
Boruch adonoy ham'voroch l'olom voed.	Praised be the Lord, to whom all praise is due forever and ever.

The numerous musical settings of this simple text are mostly characterized by simple melodies which the congregants can learn to sing with ease. Shortly after the "Bor'chu" comes the "Sh'ma," which is something like a Hebrew doxology. The best known setting of this prayer is by the nineteenth-century Jewish composer, Solomon Sulzer.

Example 146
SULZER, "Sh'ma Yisroel"

Sh'ma   Yis-ro - el   A - do - noy   E - lo - he - nu,   A - do - noy   E - chod!
(Hear, O Israel: The Lord our God, the Lord is One!)

You will note that these responses are sung in Hebrew, although they may be spoken first in English. (Practice varies from synagogue to synagogue.) Many of the responses sung in a Jewish service have a conventional nineteenth-century flavor, but others exhibit a distinctly Eastern European folk character.

Example 147
"Mee Chomocho"

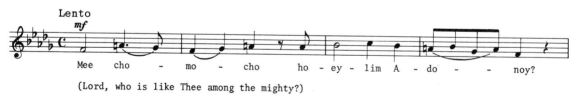

Mee   cho - mo - cho   ho - ey - lim   A - do - - noy?
(Lord, who is like Thee among the mighty?)

Music takes on special importance in the celebration of the chief holy days of the Jewish liturgical year. Choirs are augmented and extra services are scheduled. The chants and responses of the regular sabbath services are replaced by special melodies associated with the different holy days—one melody for Rosh Hashanah (New Year), another for Succos (harvest), and still another for Pesach (Passover). The musical high point of the Jewish calendar comes on the eve of Yom Kippur, the Day of Atonement, with the chanting of "Kol Nidrei."

Example 148
"Kol Nidrei." Arranged by Arnold Schoenberg

All vows and oaths, and prom-is-es, and plights of an-y kind, where-with we

Several twentieth-century musicians have composed complete musical settings of the Jewish reform service, notably Ernest Bloch and Darius Milhaud. However, these works are little known among temple congregations and are rarely heard outside the temple (unlike many Christian works performed in concert halls). Arnold Schoenberg included the "Sh'ma" text in his *Survivor from Warsaw*, a dramatic piece for narrator, chorus, and orchestra. This work was inspired by the heroic Warsaw ghetto uprising (1942), as personally described to the composer by one of its survivors. The severely atonal style makes appreciating this work difficult, but the sound of the men's chorus reciting the "Sh'ma" text is in itself extremely moving. Although Schoenberg avoids the familiar Sulzer melody (Example 146), the simple recitation of this traditional prayer—often called the watchword of the Jewish faith—makes for powerful and stirring "counterpoint" against the musical dissonance. Schoenberg made use of the tradition-al "Kol Nidrei" theme in his choral setting of that prayer (see Example 148).

Another contemporary composition based on Jewish liturgy is Leonard Bern-stein's *Kaddish Symphony* (1963). Bernstein has achieved great success as concert pian-ist, conductor, lecturer, author, and composer of both concert music and music for the Broadway theater. (Bernstein's most recent major religious work, *Mass*, is discussed at the end of the preceding chapter.) The *Kaddish Symphony* is scored for soprano solo, chorus, boys' choir, narrator, and orchestra. It reveals Bernstein not only as composer, but also as author of an extended spoken text framing the sung text of the "Kaddish," a Hebrew-Aramaic prayer which expresses glorification of the Lord. Although this prayer is traditionally recited as a memorial for the dead, the text itself makes no reference to death, but testifies rather to an appreciation of life.

Bernstein's spoken commentary is striking in its direct personal approach to God. It is delivered by a female speaker who probes various issues in varying moods, some-times addressing God in great anger—complaining that He has let humankind down—only to switch suddenly to a spirit of forgiveness and sympathy with the plight of the Lord. The text bears a strong existentialist flavor, implying that God exists only to the extent that we conceive of Him and, indeed, that God is made in our human image. At one point Heaven is inspected and found wanting. But later, in a lighter mood, the nar-rator depicts Heaven as a paradise of happiness and delight.

Despite its derivation from a prayer for the dead, the *Kaddish Symphony* itself is in no way doleful; indeed, it offers many extended passages of joyful, even manic, mu-sic. Despite the ominous quality of the introduction, much of the first movement dis-plays a jazzy, exciting quality, especially during the actual singing of "Kaddish" (in con-tradistinction to the music which highlights the spoken text). The core of the second movement is a touching soprano solo, a lyrical melody in $\frac{3}{8}$ meter, more in keeping with the mournful aspect of "Kaddish." The last movement achieves a wild, almost orgiastic effect. The boys' choir sings a melody reminiscent of "There's a Place for Us,'" from

West Side Story (composed several years earlier). The boys sound like cherubim, flitting about the heavenly scene. The final orchestral meditation introduces a transformation of a theme first heard in the second movement, but which now sounds like a motive from Alban Berg's expressionistic opera, *Wozzeck* (Chapter 15). This section also includes a cyclic theme heard in each of the movements and the "pop" melody mentioned above. The work closes with a great choral-orchestral *fugue* (see Chapter 16)— the soloist reappears at one point as well—in the exciting lopsided $\frac{7}{8}$ meter Bernstein has so often employed in his works.

Example 149a
BERNSTEIN Theme from *Kaddish Symphony* (Final Orchestral Meditation)

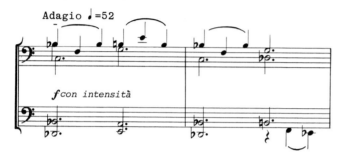

Example 149b
BERG, Theme from *Wozzeck*, Act 1, Scene 3

PROTESTANT MUSIC IN AMERICAN CHURCHES

In the United States there are many different Protestant denominations, each with its own musical tradition. The lengthy cantata, discussed in Chapter 24, has never taken hold as an integral part of American Sunday worship. Typically a church choir will sing an *introit* (introductory prayer greeting), one or two short *anthems*, and a few prayer responses. The church anthem is an English form, of about five minutes' duration, which reached full flower in the music of Henry Purcell at the end of the seventeenth century. Purcell's stirring anthem, "Lord, How Long Wilt Thou Be Angry?" is a fine example of this form. The first part is in fugal style, much like the Kyrie from Byrd's *Five-Part Mass* (see Example 126). This means that all the vocal parts are more or less independent and equally important. However, there are also several "block-chord" (*homophonic*) passages in which the soprano melody takes precedence over the other parts.

Music and Religion

Example 150
PURCELL, "How Long, O Lord?"

Anthem writing continues as an important part of the church music scene today. Randall Thompson's "Allelujah" is a classic among twentieth-century American anthems.

Example 151
THOMPSON, "Allelujah"

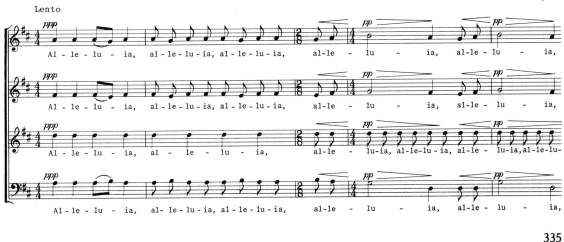

The fundamentalist or revival service, which has long been popular in the South, involves much greater congregational participation than usually occurs in more staid northern areas. And the southern black gospel movement has now spread far and wide throughout America. The following two quotations give testimony to the importance of gospel music in contemporary American popular culture:

> The gospel sound . . . is everywhere. All rock's most resilient features, the beat, the drama, the group vibrations derive from gospel. From rock symphonies to detergent commercials, from Aretha Franklin's pyrotechnique to the Beatles' harmonics, gospel has simply reformed all our listening expectations. The very tension betweeen beats, the climax we anticipate almost subliminally, is straight out of the church.[1]

> Music, to begin with, came from the Pentacostal First Assembly of God Church. "Since I was two years old all I knew was gospel music; that was music to me. We borrowed the style of our psalm singing from the early Negroes. The preachers cut up all over the place, jumping on the piano, moving every which way. The audience liked them. I guess I learned from them. It became such a part of my life it was as natural as dancing, a way to escape from problems and my way of release."[2]

The new popularity of gospel music is reflected in the great success of the recent Broadway musical, *Godspell*. Blacks and whites alike can relish hits like "Day by Day" and "Prepare Ye the Way of the Lord." But in the black community the significance of gospel music goes much further than simple enjoyment.

> Black music is unity music. It unites the joy and the sorrow, the love and the hate, the hope and the despair of black people; and it moves the people toward the direction of total liberation. It shapes and defines black being and creates cultural structures for black expression.[3]

All told, music plays a far bigger role in American churches today than it did two hundred years ago (see the introduction to Unit V), but a lesser role than in the two-hundred-year heyday of German Protestantism between Luther and Bach. Bach's congregations accepted his lengthy cantatas, despite durations of thirty minutes and more. American congregations expect music merely to spice their worship services; if the musical selections last too long complaints may be heard from the parishioners or even from the minister.

John Updike, the noted American writer, recognized this aspect of the American religious tradition in his recent novel, *A Month of Sundays*.[4] In Chapter 9 a parishioner complains to the minister, Tom Marshfield, that an offertory anthem by Praetorious had lasted so long (seven minutes) that one of the ushers holding the collection plate felt his arm go to sleep. Tom broaches the matter to Alicia, the organist and music director, asking how much of the music budget was spent for a performance of a Handel concerto grosso (a work for string orchestra). She replies that all the performers were friends who played gratis, to which he counters the fear that the church might be turning into a concert hall. Eventually the conflict comes to a head after a church service in which Tom prematurely spoke the words, "God be with you," when the anthem was only half over. He defends himself, saying that there was a silence. Alicia retorts that it was just a two-beat rest and that a recorder duet which two little girls had practiced for weeks got left out. Later Tom decides to fire Alicia, ostensibly on the grounds that her

Music and Religion

musical activities strain the congregation's receptivity. All in all, Updike demonstrates a witty and realistic awareness of the restraints placed on music in many American churches.

In connection with Protestant music it should be noted that the Catholic church has traditionally rejected many of the finest "modern" musical settings of the Mass, including masterpieces by Bach and various Classical composers (see Chapter 23). But these works are frequently performed by university and community choral societies, often in conjunction with major symphony orchestras, and they may also be heard in special music programs offered by Protestant churches. Thus, we have an ironic situation in which Catholic masses are offered in the original Latin by Protestant or secular choirs, while Catholic churches have now dropped Latin and regularly present their liturgy in English.

ORGAN MUSIC

A special category of religious music is the literature for organ. Although organs are found in theaters, museums, concert halls, and school auditoriums, the principal location of organs is houses of worship. Even when one hears *absolute* (i.e., secular) organ music—such as Bach's famous *Toccata and Fugue in G Minor*—there is an almost inescapable religious aura surrounding the music. Early forms of the organ have existed since antiquity, but the keyboard-type instrument we know today dates only from the thirteenth century. As we have already observed, one of the principal novelties of the Baroque period was an emphasis on instrumental music for its own sake (as opposed to functioning as a mere appendage to vocal music). Church composers now began to take special interest in the organ, creating a brand-new solo repertoire which culminated in the magnificent works of J. S. Bach. In his own lifetime Bach was actually better known as an organist than as a composer. Like his fellow organists, his repertoire consisted mainly of works he himself had composed. With the church as their principal employer, most organists composed music suitable for use in actual worship services.

Picture a congregation assembling for worship in an early eighteenth-century North German church. The organist attempts to engage the attention of the congregants by playing music of a spiritual nature; better yet, the organist tries to provide a hint of the content of the forthcoming service. In this connection chorale melodies play an extremely important role. You will recall from Chapter 24 that the congregants are familiar with a large repertoire of chorales dating back to Luther and are used to singing these chorales and to hearing cantatas based on them. So it makes good sense for the organist to play a prelude based on the chorale of the day. For example, if the period is Advent (the month preceding Christmas), the organist may play a timely piece based on Luther's chorale, "From Heaven Above I Come to Earth." Example 152a presents the first phrase of this chorale (harmonized by Bach), while Example 152b shows the opening of the chorale prelude which Bach derived from it. The latter is included in his organ collection, *The Liturgical Year.**

---

*As another example of the same tradition, the second piece of Debussy's two-piano suite, *En blanc et noir* (In Black and White), contains strains of Luther's hymn, "A Mighty Fortress Is Our God," in the manner of a chorale prelude. Debussy included this chorale tune as an expression of indignation over the death of a friend killed in World War I.

Baroque composers took special interest in the organ, creating a solo repertoire which culminated in the magnificent works of J. S. Bach. Right, the keyboard and pedals of Bach's organ in Arnstadt.

Example 152

a) BACH, *Chorale,* "Vom Himmel Hoch"

Vom Him - mel hoch, da komm ich her!

(From Heaven above, I come to Thee!)

b) BACH, *Chorale Prelude,* "Vom Himmel Hoch" (For Organ)

(Vom Him - mel hoch da komm ich her!)

Music and Religion

What actually is an organ?

To some the organ is known as the "King of Instruments," the largest of all musical instruments, commanding the widest pitch and dynamic range, and by others derided as the most mechanical, costly and unexpressive means of music-making.[5]

To begin, imagine the construction of a harmonica, also known as a mouth organ. Each slot into which you blow produces a single pitch. Now think instead of a series of metal pipes stacked side by side—as organists say, in a *rank*. Instead of blowing into each pipe by mouth, a blowing mechanism operated electrically does the job. The longest and largest pipes produce the lowest pitches, and conversely the smallest pipes produce the highest pitches. One can select specific pitches by depressing keys on a *manual*, similar to a piano keyboard. However, the pipe organ is more versatile than the piano, for, whereas the piano has just one set of strings, the organ can have numerous sets of pipes. (These are often hidden from sight, so that only the organist's console remains visible. The discussion here applies only to pipe organs; the modern electronic organ is at best a pale imitation of the pipe organ.) Each set of pipes displays an individual tone color. The organist can select sounds resembling those of a flute, string, double reed, or brass instrument. Aside from these imitative timbres, there is also a basic organ sound, known as *diapason*. The organ console is provided with *stop* buttons or levers, by means of which the organist can select one or more sets of pipes at any particular time. In a sense it is like having an orchestra at one's finger tips.

But that is not all. Many organs have two, three, or even four manuals. The organist can set up one manual to sound like flutes, a second manual to imitate strings, and a third to resemble reeds (oboe or bassoon). Thus, one might play a melody with a flute

A modern Holtkamp organ, most of which is shown behind the choir seats, in St. Paul's Lutheran Church, Cleveland, Ohio.

339

stop in the right hand and accompany it with a string stop in the left hand. Modern organs provide couplers which allow stops from one manual to be combined with stops from another; for that matter, stops can be combined on a single manual as well, so that the organist is truly in the position of an orchestrator who can pick and choose from a whole palette of sounds at any given time. This means that two different renditions of a given organ piece may represent two completely different "orchestrations." (Only in recent times have organ composers begun indicating stop requirements in their scores; these specifications are known as *registrations*.)

There are many other fascinating aspects of organ sound. Low sounds are produced by means of a pedal board played by the feet. For most of the pitches available on the keyboard there are *couplings* which duplicate them at higher or lower octaves, allowing the organist to depress a single key yet produce octave doublings or more distant equivalents. Not all of these reinforcement stops need be at the octave; a whole range of the *harmonic series* is available, meaning that a pitch can be augmented with its overtone pitches at the twelfth, seventeenth, and so on. (see Example 153). The aural effect of these overtones is the peculiar *mixture* effect which accounts for many of the special acoustical effects of organ music.

Example 153
Organ Mixture

4th overtones of pitches shown below

2nd overtones of pitches shown below

Organist plays three fundamental pitches, but overtone couplings result in additional six pitches shown above.

With this remarkable array of timbres, harmonics, and couplings, the organ represents a veritable kaleidoscope of sonorities. Among single instruments, only the modern electronic synthesizer can compete with it (Chapter 20).

An organ score resembles a piano score, but with two important differences. To begin with, to the pianist's two five-line staves (one for each hand) the organ score adds a third staff for the feet. And in modern scores the composer adds registrations directing the performer to produce the precise sounds the composer wishes (see Example 154). However, the actual effect of a given registration depends on the quality of a particular instrument and the acoustical properties of the building in which it is housed. The performer must therefore always exercise personal judgment as to how best to achieve the composer's intended effects.

Music and Religion

Example 154
MESSIAEN, *The Nativity of the Lord*

Many musicians regard the Baroque organ literature as the finest yet composed for this instrument. After Bach's death (1750), organ composition declined, and the organ remained more or less neglected for the next hundred years. Although Mendelssohn and other early Romantics composed some music for organ, it was not until the last part of the nineteenth century that the organ literature began a resurgence. A whole new school of organ composers arose, notably, César Franck (1822–1890) in France and Anton Bruckner (1824–1896) in Austria. Johannes Brahms, a composer not primarily associated with church music, composed several chorale preludes for organ shortly before his death in 1897. During the nineteenth and early twentieth centuries the organ was enlarged from its modest Baroque size to mammoths with three or more keyboards. French composers have taken a particular fancy to the organ during the past century. The contemporary French master, Olivier Messiaen, is among those who have written significant works for this instrument. Among them is a series of nine meditations on the Christmas story, *The Nativity of the Lord* (see Example 154).

Organists not uncommonly program contemporary works (along with those of Baroque and nineteenth-century masters) in churches and university chapels; these recitals are generally open to the public and offer the student a convenient opportunity to sample a variety of organ music styles.

Terms preceded by (•) are included in lists for previous units. Page numbers in parentheses indicate location of first and/or principal reference to each term within this unit.

General and Historical

- Baroque period (291)
  Council of Trent (291)
  Kaddish (333)
  liturgy (287)
  Mass (287)
  Medieval (288)
  Reformation (303)
  Renaissance period (289)
  vespers (287, 297)

Instrumental Music

chorale prelude (337)
cornett (297)
couplings (340)
manual (339)
pipe organ (337 ff)
registration (340)
stops (339)

Vocal Music

a cappella (291)
anthem (334)
- aria (291)
  cantata (305)
  cantor (331)
  chorale (303)
  da capo aria (327)
  gospel singing (336)
  Gregorian chant (288)
  liturgical drama (316)
  melisma (315)
  motet (288)
- oratorio (317)
  passion music (324 ff)
  plainchant (287)
- recitative (288)

Theory

- augmentation (310)
  binary (292)
- cadenza (292)
  cantus firmus (288, 297, 310)
  chaconne (294, 301)
- coda (302)
- continuo (312)
  descant (299)
- diminution (314)
  false reprise (327)
  ground bass (294, 312)
  harmonic series (340)
  imitation (289)
  microtonal (328)
  monophony (287)
  organum (288)
- ostinato (294)
  passacaglia (301)
- polyphony (287)
- quarter tones (328)
  rondo (327)
- syncopated (311)
- transposed (327)
- variations (294, 302)

UNIT VI

MUSIC AND EMOTION

The feelings that Beethoven put into his music were the feelings of a god. There was something Olympian in his snarls and rages, and there was a touch of hell-fire in his mirth.[1]

The human personality enjoys the capacity for a wide range of emotional states. Music, of all the arts, is supreme in depicting variations of feeling. Emotion characterizes our responses to all aspects of life, and therefore every chapter of this book contains music reflective of human emotion. In this unit we shall focus initially on the musical expression of two emotional polarities—mania and depression (Chapters 27 and 28); then we shall consider the music of the most popular emotion of all—love (Chapter 29). The first two chapters feature music of Beethoven, Schubert, and Berlioz; the third begins with various works about Romeo and Juliet and concludes with love duets by Verdi, Wagner, and Puccini.

MUSIC AND MOOD

MAJOR VERSUS MINOR

There is a widely held notion that the major and minor modes of the tonal system represent two opposing emotional states, happiness and sadness (or solemnity). This is a gross oversimplification. We can easily find examples of cheerful major-mode music and somber minor-mode music, but there are plenty of contrary examples as well. Consider the vivacious opening and closing movements of Mozart's *Piano Sonata in A Minor* and the inexpressibly wistful Adagietto in F major from Mahler's *Fifth Symphony.* Franz Schubert had a great knack for composing sad songs in *major* keys.

> What distinguishes [*Winterreise*] is not so much the preponderance of minor keys . . .
> as the capacity to invest the tonic major with the color, the very glow, of desolation
> and disillusion. No other composer has quite the same power to make the major
> mode sound even sadder and more poignant than the minor . . .[1]

This is not to deny that the major triad, in and of itself, is brighter than the minor triad. Go to a piano and compare the major and minor triads for yourself. It is easy to construct a major triad. Pick any note as bass note of your prospective three-note chord. Add a note four half steps above the bass note, counting each successive black and white key as a half step. Then add a third note three half steps above the second. To convert this into a minor triad, simply move the middle note down one half step.

Example 155
Constructing Major and Minor Triads

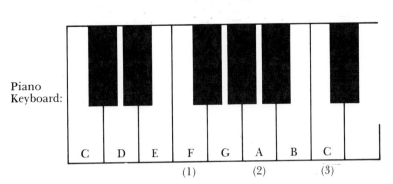

Piano Keyboard:

C D E F G A B C
        (1)   (2)   (3)

Major Triad
{ 1) Pick any pitch — e.g., F
{ 2) Add a note 4 half-steps higher (A)
{ 3) Add a third note 3 half-steps higher (C)

For minor triad, substitute A♭ for A♮.

When we speak of a composition in the key of x major or y minor, we mean that the entire composition is based on a given triad. You can think of that triad, the *tonic triad*, as the *core* of the musical superstructure. In addition a tonal composition consists of myriad other chords; all but the most simple-minded pieces (such as nursery rhymes) present a constantly changing succession of major and minor triads and more complex chords as well (see Chapter 9). Furthermore, the emotional character of a piece derives from a wide variety of factors—melody, rhythm, phrasing, and tempo, among others—beyond the single element we have been considering—namely, harmony.

Children's songs mainly consist of major triads. "Frère Jacques" is a good example, for in its normal format (as a round) it does not contain a single minor triad. Now try thinking of "Frère Jacques" in the minor mode. Flat the third note, so that the first and third notes form a minor third—the bottom interval of a minor triad—instead of a major third. It seems reasonable to claim that the minor version of "Frère Jacques" sounds at least moderately sad, certainly less cheerful than its standard major version. Yet if you listen to the third movement of Mahler's *First Symphony* you will hear a mock-serious variant of "Frère Jacques" (the Germans call it "Bruder Martin"), a zany funeral march played initially by a solo string bass in an uncharacteristically high register. The humor of this passage derives in part from the surprise of hearing a familiar folk song played in a different mode. By switching from major to minor Mahler did not exchange happy for sad; rather he exchanged the commonplace for the amusingly unexpected. Incidentally, it is not difficult to make "Frère Jacques" sound sad in the *major* mode—all you have to do is play it very slow and *legato* (smooth and connected), or for that matter, sing it in a slow and moody manner.

Example 156
"Frère Jacques" in Minor

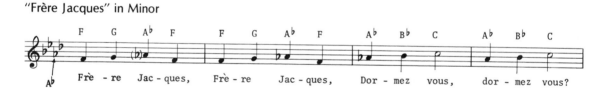

In Chapter 6 you read about Smetana's majestic *Moldau* theme. Smetana presented this theme in three different versions: (1) exclusively minor, (2) partially minor and partially major, and (3) all major (see Example 15). The modal changes make for great expressive contrast, but the differences are not simply a matter of upbeat versus downcast. All three versions of the melody are more "up" than "down."

What it really comes down to is that a lot of music is intrinsically neither happy nor sad; one needs a much wider descriptive vocabulary to account for all the varying moods one finds in music. For example, the slow movement of Beethoven's *Symphony No. 5* opens with a lovely lyrical theme cast in A♭ major. Then later in the same movement we hear this melody converted into A♭ minor. But that is not the only change, for instead of long sweeping cello and viola lines, we now hear soft disconnected (*staccato*) notes played by the oboe. The effect is unequivocally lighthearted.

Music and Emotion

Example 157
BEETHOVEN, *Symphony No. 5*, 2nd Mvt. (Opening)

Example 158
Symphony No. 5, 2nd Mvt., Minor Version of Main Theme

Major and minor versions of a theme often occur within the same piece. (Listen again to the *C Minor Fugue* from Bach's *Well-Tempered Clavier*, Vol. 1—see Chapter 16.) Sometimes this produces a definite correlation between happy and sad—for example, compare the morose minor incipit of the finale of Brahms's *Symphony No. 1* with the good-natured major main theme of that movement. On the other hand, in Mozart's *Piano Concerto in D Minor* the minor finale brims over with good cheer from the outset; it simply becomes still more joyous in its major-mode version.

CLASSICAL VERSUS ROMANTIC

Consider one of the greatest Romantic orchestral works, Tchaikovsky's *Symphony No. 6*, subtitled *Pathétique*. Although given to moods of grief and despair, Tchaikovsky nevertheless felt great excitement over this work, especially its slow finale. In a letter to his nephew he described the new work:

> Just as I was starting on my trip, the idea for a new symphony came to me. This time with a program, but a program of a sort that remains enigmatic to everyone—let them guess it who can. . . . The program is full of subjective emotion. While I was composing it during my trip, I frequently cried. . . . There will be much in the work that is novel as regards form. For example, the Finale will be, not a great allegro, but an adagio of considerable dimensions. You cannot imagine what happiness I experience at the conviction that my time is not yet over.[2]

Ironically, Tchaikovsky suffered a horrible attack of cholera and died shortly after the first performance of the *Pathétique* (1893).

The *Pathétique* ends with one of the most beautiful slow movements in the Romantic orchestral repertoire. The music starts out in a mood of unrelenting despair (minor mode). Later it changes to a mood of gentle resignation (major mode). The ending, like virtually no other Romantic symphony (such as Dvořák's *New World Symphony*—see Chapter 12), eschews a thrilling orchestral fanfare in favor of the quietest possible murmuring in the low range of the cellos and basses. The closing feeling of desolate melancholy is unique in the symphonic literature.

Example 159

TCHAIKOVSKY, *Symphony No. 6*, Finale, Opening

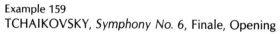

Example 160
Symphony No. 6, Finale, Second Theme

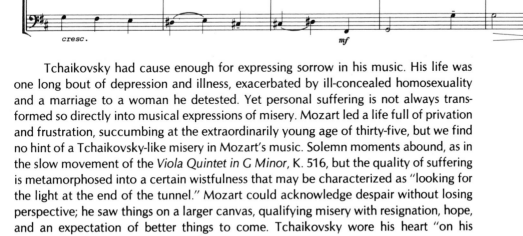

Tchaikovsky had cause enough for expressing sorrow in his music. His life was one long bout of depression and illness, exacerbated by ill-concealed homosexuality and a marriage to a woman he detested. Yet personal suffering is not always transformed so directly into musical expressions of misery. Mozart led a life full of privation and frustration, succumbing at the extraordinarily young age of thirty-five, but we find no hint of a Tchaikovsky-like misery in Mozart's music. Solemn moments abound, as in the slow movement of the *Viola Quintet in G Minor*, K. 516, but the quality of suffering is metamorphosed into a certain wistfulness that may be characterized as "looking for the light at the end of the tunnel." Mozart could acknowledge despair without losing perspective; he saw things on a larger canvas, qualifying misery with resignation, hope, and an expectation of better things to come. Tchaikovsky wore his heart "on his sleeve"; Mozart kept a "stiff upper lip."

Quite aside from differences in their musical personalities, Mozart and Tchaikovsky were representatives of vastly different style periods. Mozart was Classical, Tchaikovsky was Romantic. As a true Romantic, Tchaikovsky indulged himself in a level of

Peter Ilich Tchaikovsky
(1840–1893), age 34.

emotional self-expression which the Classical period would never have tolerated. Musical Romanticism virtually required composers to open up their souls, pouring everything forth—especially feelings of longing, sadness, and despair.

The composer whose music bridged the gap between the values of Classicism and Romanticism was Ludwig van Beethoven (1770–1827). He matured during the last quarter of the eighteenth century, a time when the Classical masters, Mozart and Haydn, were at their zenith. Beethoven, just fourteen years younger than Mozart and a student of Haydn, started out in their image but soon broke through the bonds of Classicism and developed into a genuinely Romantic composer. During the first quarter of the nineteenth century, Beethoven's music acquired a range of expressive possibilities

Music and Emotion

hitherto unimaginable. Eventually, in his very last years, Beethoven was to create a series of works that for depth of musical expressivity stand unrivaled in the history of music.

Beethoven lived a life of great loneliness, dogged by his inability to form an enduring and satisfying love relationship and suffering the torment of increasing and finally total deafness. Like Tchaikovsky, Beethoven also composed a work labeled "Pathétique," but the opening page of the first movement (to which the title mainly refers) conveys a sense of majestic solemnity quite unrelated to Tchaikovsky's expression of personal misery.

Example 161
BEETHOVEN, *"Pathetique"* Sonata, Opus 13, 1st Mvt., Introduction

Beethoven's musical output is usually categorized as early, middle, or late. The expressive power exhibited in the early *Pathétique Sonata* intensified during the middle and late periods. By the third period Beethoven's deafness had isolated him from his fellows and was causing him great bitterness. Many people feel that his late works—*Symphony No. 9*, the last five or six piano sonatas, the *Missa Solemnis*, and most especially the last string quartets—represent a powerful transfiguration of the composer's great suffering into a beatific mystical experience transcending mere emotional pain. "The last quartets testify to a veritable growth of consciousness, to a higher degree of consciousness probably than is manifested anywhere else in art."[3]

We know . . . that Beethoven was a man who experienced all that we can experience, who suffered all that we can suffer. If, in the end, he seems to reach a state "above the battle" we also know that no man ever knew more bitterly what the battle is.[4]

Listening to a late Beethoven quartet is a very special experience. Unlike his earlier music, most of which gained easy public acceptance, the late works mystified and disturbed Beethoven's audiences. Even today these works are hard to comprehend at first hearing.

Small wonder . . . that only decades later these works began to meet not with understanding but at least with some measure of respect from laymen and professional musicians. There is in them so much that is new and unusual, even strange, as regards form, style, and expression, as to explain the lack of understanding on the part of Beethoven's contemporaries toward these quartets, which demand the utmost concentration and receptivity even from hearers of our [own] era. . . .[5]

Music and Mood

Beethoven's *String Quartet in A Minor*, Op. 132, is said to have been composed under stress of severe illness. Or so much can be infered from Beethoven's heading for the third movement: "Holy Song of Thanks to the Divine One from One Restored to Health, in the Lydian Mode" ("Heiliger Dankgesang eines Genesenen an die Gottheit, in der lydischen Tonart"). J. W. N. Sullivan writes:

> Of the three great last quartets . . . the A minor is the least mystical and the one most full of human pain. . . . The normal Beethoven of those days [was] poor, ill, stone-deaf, wretchedly housed, utterly alone, betrayed and abandoned by the one human being whose love he so desperately and pitifully craved [his nephew's]. . . . The yearning and the pain of the first movement . . . is but little lightened in the second movement, where there reigns a spiritual weariness which is quite unmistakable. . . . From this matrix rises the slow movement, the most heartfelt prayer from the most manly soul that has expressed itself in music.[6]

Listen to each movement of Op. 132 and compare your own responses to Sullivan's. The first movement begins with a subdued slow introduction. The ensuing allegro proceeds just two measures before the first principal motive is introduced, a figure of longing and pathos (cf. cello part, measure II).

Example 162
BEETHOVEN, *String Quartet in A Minor*, Opus 132, 1st Mvt., Introduction

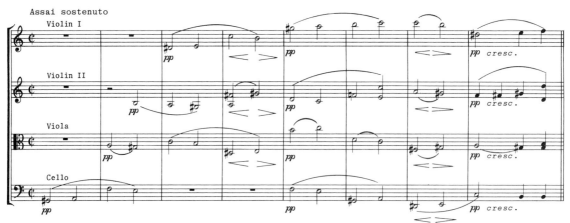

Music and Emotion

Example 163

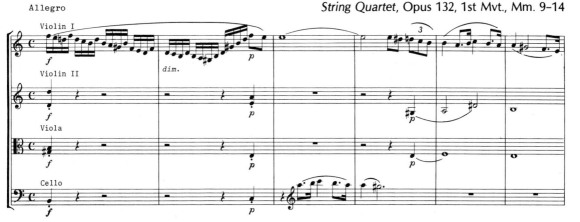

To this writer Sullivan's idea of the first movement seems more apt than his notion of the "spiritual weariness" of the second movement. Moreover, we take exception to his view of the finale as a "victory so hard-won that we are left with . . . a feeling . . . of thankfulness . . . tinged with doubt," finding in it rather the transfigured suffering that Sullivan has described elsewhere (quoted above).

BASICS: CHURCH MODES

Let us take a closer look at the slow movement of Op. 132, one of the most remarkable of Beethoven's creations. First, with regard to its title, what did Beethoven mean by the "Lydian mode"? In the first part of this chapter we inquired into the emotional qualities of the major and minor modes as if no other modes existed. Yet now we encounter a third mode, the Lydian; for that matter there are other modes as well, such as the Dorian, Phrygian, and Mixolydian. These modes, along with the Ionian and Aeolian (the old names for major and minor), comprise the *church modes* of the Medieval period (roughly 600–1400).*

In the distinction we made earlier between the major and minor modes we stressed the significance of the major and minor triads. That is, the major triad is the principal chord of the major mode, and correspondingly the minor triad is the tonic sonority of the minor mode. But we cannot proceed in the same manner in the case of the remaining church modes, for there exists no chord such as a Dorian or Lydian triad. Rather, the major triad is the principal chord of the Lydian and Mixolydian modes, and the minor triad functions similarly in the Dorian and Phrygian modes. Nonetheless we can easily identify the differences among these modes simply by comparing their scales.

At a piano or other keyboard instrument, locate middle C and then play seven successive white keys in either direction; this is the scale of C major. Now start on A,

---

*These modes also figured in Renaissance compositional practice for about a century after 1400. But in actuality performers during that period tended to add flats or sharps of their own volition, thereby converting the six ostensible church modes into the two "modern" ones, the Ionian and Aeolian. Eventually theory took notice of practice, and the old church names were replaced by our present terms, *major* and *minor*.

two white keys below C, and proceed seven keys in either direction; this the A minor scale. You will notice that A minor sounds different from C major, despite the fact that both scales contain exactly the same notes—thus demonstrating that the *ordering* of scale notes is one of the determining factors in the way a scale sounds. To put it another way, the identity of a scale is partially established by the order of its intervals; if you change the interval succession, you change the scale—even if all the notes are left intact. The major scale consists of an ascending succession of whole (W) and half (H) steps—W W H W W W H—that differs from the intervalic ordering of the natural minor scale (W H W W H W W).

A white-key scale can begin on any white key. Starting on D will give you the Dorian mode. (For all practical purposes the terms *mode* and *scale* are interchangeable in this discussion.) Starting on E will produce the Phrygian mode, F the Lydian, and G the Mixolydian. All these scales sound peculiar to us, as if there were something wrong with them, for we are accustomed only to the major and minor scales.* So, in constructing a slow movement of *Op. 132* in the Lydian mode, Beethoven was intentionally seeking a strange, archaic effect. By a curious anachronism, his simple but severe Lydian harmonic progressions strike some listeners as remarkably modern, as if composed within the past century. Much early music sounds modernistic in this sense, mainly due to "outmoded" modes and other stylistic characteristics. (See the discussion of Machaut's *Notre Dame Mass* in Chapter 23.)

In any case, in the pure Medieval sense Beethoven's music is not strictly Lydian; it would be more accurate to describe it as "crypto-Lydian." True, the note F functions as tonic, and Beethoven assiduously avoided the note Bb (which would make the music sound major). However, he also tended to stay clear of B♮, which would make the music sound outright Lydian. (The first B♮ occurs only in measure 6, and by this point the music sounds if anything more Dorian than Lydian.)

Example 164
Opus 132, 3rd Mvt.

*An illustration of the Dorian mode is found in Example 18 above. In this case, the Dorian scale is transposed down a perfect fifth, the key signature contains one flat, and the key may be said to be "G Dorian."

Music and Emotion

In truth there is no adequate terminology for what happens in the first section of this movement; the music is unique. At the onset of the second section, marked "Feeling of new power," Beethoven switched abruptly to D major, in a faster, loud triple meter. There are five sections in all, the second and fourth in D major, the first, third, and fifth in F Lydian. The fifth section, marked "With most intimate feeling," is the longest and most ethereal part of the movement. The final ten measures, like the opening, are notable for the mutual absence of the notes B♭ and B♮.

HUXLEY, POINT COUNTER POINT

Having acquainted yourself with Beethoven's Lydian movement from his *Op. 132*, you are now in a position to appreciate its function in Aldous Huxley's *Point Counter Point*. Music figures prominently in this novel, both as subject matter and in a structural sense. As an example of the former, an important event in the novel is a musical party featuring a performance of Bach's *Suite in B Minor* for flute and strings; with regard to the latter, Huxley introduced ideas and characters like musical themes, combining and offsetting one against the other in the manner of musical counterpoint. Undoubtedly the most crucial musical reference occurs in the final chapter, which intermixes the explosive culmination of the main plot theme with a detailed account of the music we have been considering—the slow movement of Beethoven's *String Quartet in A Minor*.

One of the principal characters is Spandrell, a nihilist who has secretly murdered the fascistic political leader, Eberhard Webley. Spandrell has decided to end his own life by inviting Webley's cohorts to his apartment, having warned them that they will find the assassin, armed and highly dangerous. Spandrell prearranges an audience for his execution/suicide by inviting his artist friend, Mark Rampion, and Rampion's wife for a visit. (Rampion is said to be modeled after the novelist D. H. Lawrence, a close friend of Huxley's.) The bewildered Spandrell, somewhat like Roskolnikov in Dostoyevsky's existentialist novel, *Crime and Punishment*, is intent on affirming the existence of God—but not by means of theological arguments. Instead he simply points to the evidence of Beethoven's *String Quartet in A minor*. "It's the only proof that exists; the only one, because Beethoven was the only man who could get his knowledge over into expression."[7]

The period of the novel is the late 1920s. Spandrell is excited over having just purchased a recording of Beethoven's *Op. 132*. His phonograph is primitive and nonelectrified; it has to be rewound every few minutes, and, because the records are (of course) 78 RPMs, there are constant interruptions as the disks are changed. After the Rampions arrive, Spandrell puts on a record, skipping over the first two movements to the slow movement. This is the *Heilige Dankgesang*, the *Holy Song of Thanks*, which is crucial to his thesis. As the music begins, the narrative provides us with a highly detailed account of the placing of the record on the turntable, the lowering of the needle, and finally of the music itself.

> A single violin gave out a long note, then another a sixth above, dropped to the fifth (while the second violin began where the first had started), then leapt to the octave and hung there suspended through two long beats.[8]

(An examination of the score—see Example 164—confirms the accuracy of Huxley's description of the music.) The Rampions and Spandrell argue over the music and what

355

it signifies. Rampion cannot accept Spandrell's manic enthusiasm and complains of the music's "spiritual abstraction from reality . . . why couldn't he [Beethoven] be content to be a man and not an abstract soul?" Rampion's words disappoint Spandrell horribly, but he consoles himself with the thought that his friend may be mistaken. Spandrell's response to the music is ever increasingly ecstatic:

> It was as though heaven had suddenly and impossibly become more heavenly, had passed from achieved perfection into perfection yet deeper and more absolute. . . . The miraculous paradox of eternal life and eternal repose was musically realized.

The approach of the musical climax of the slow movement merges with the dramatic climax of the novel. A knock is heard. Spandrell, who unknown to the Rampions is armed, leaves his visitors, goes to the door, and pulls out his gun. After an exchange of fire he falls dead. As the astonished Rampions run to Spandrell's side the scene is accompanied by the unearthly final strains of Beethoven's music: "the passion had begun to fade from the celestial melody. . . . And then suddenly there was no more music; only the scratching of the needle on the revolving disc." For Spandrell, Beethoven's music represented life; the ensuing silence symbolizes his sudden death.

As with any piece of fiction, you may well wonder to what extent Spandrell's ideas are an expression of Huxley's personal beliefs. A partial answer is found in an essay he wrote concerning a dramatized version of the novel. Recounting his experience of the last act, during which a recording of the slow movement of *Op. 132* is played, Huxley wrote,

> The play, as a whole, was curiously hard and brutal. Bursting suddenly into this world of almost unmitigated harshness, the *Heilige Dankgesang* seemed like the manifestation of something supernatural. It was as though a god had really and visibly descended, awful and yet reassuring, mysteriously wrapped in the peace that passes all understanding, divinely beautiful. . . . Whatever pains we [the author and the adapter] might have taken, we should have found it absolutely impossible to express by means of words or dramatic action what those three or four minutes of violin playing made somehow so luminously manifest to any sensitive listener.[9]

Incidentally, Huxley/Spandrell's ecstatic perception of Beethoven's quartet recalls the views of J. W. N. Sullivan, as discussed above. This is hardly a coincidence, for the two writers were close friends who saw each other frequently while Huxley was writing *Point Counter Point*.

The power which music wields over men is not a new idea, either in literature or philosophy; in his interpretation of Beethoven's Lydian elegy, Huxley joined a procession of writers encompassing Plato, Kleist, and Tolstoy. In the hey-day of ancient Greece, Plato argued that music was greatly influential in the education of youths.* Kleist wrote of the demonic power of music in his story, *Saint Cecilia, or the Power of Music* (see Chapter 24). And in his short novel, *The Kreutzer Sonata,* the great Russian fundamentalist Leo Tolstoy (1828–1910) went so far as to attribute a murderous act to the destructive power of music.

*Plato specifically warned against listening to Phrygian and Lydian music (the Phrygians and Lydians were defeated peoples brought back to Greece as slaves) because these modes tended to make men effeminate and depraved.

Music and Emotion

Tolstoy's novella is named after the *Sonata in A Major*, Op. 47, Beethoven's grandest and possibly greatest contribution to the literature for violin and piano. (The work was dedicated to one of Beethoven's patrons, Rudolphe Kreutzer.) Tolstoy's story tells of a purported love affair between the wife of one Pozdnuishef and a male acquaintance by the name of Trukhachevsky. She is a pianist, he a violinist, and their musical communion irritates the unmusical Pozdnuishef. At one point he returns home unexpectedly to find his wife performing with her friend. It was one thing to play sonatas in the husband's presence, quite another to do it behind his back! Enraged, he attacks the two musicians and stabs his wife to death. Later Pozdnuishef recounts the situation which lead to the tragic dénouement:

"They played Beethoven's *Kreutzer Sonata*," he finally went on to say. "Do you know the first *presto*—You know it?" he cried. "U! U! U! . . . That sonata is a terrible thing. And especially that movement. And music in general is a terrible thing. I cannot comprehend it. What is music? What does it do? And why does it have the effect it has? They say music has the effect of elevating the soul—rubbish! falsehood! It has its effect, it has a terrible effect—I am speaking about its effect on me—but not at all by elevating the soul. Its effect is neither to elevate nor to degrade, but to excite. How can I explain it to you? Music makes me forget myself, my actual position; it transports me into another state not my natural one; under the influence of music it seems to me that I feel what I do not really feel, that I understand what I do not really understand, that I can do what I can't do.[10]

In this chapter we have seen how music is held to wield a powerful influence over personal actions. In the next chapter we shall examine music which itself is an expression of two of the most intense emotional states—mania and despair.

MUSIC OF MANIA AND DESPAIR

Franz Schubert and Hector Berlioz were two of the most important composers of the early Romantic period. Born respectively in 1797 and 1803, they received their musical tutelage during Beethoven's later years. Despite the closeness of their birth dates it is hard to think of them as contemporaries, for Schubert grew to musical maturity and *died* before Berlioz had completed his first major work. (Dying at the age of thirty-one, Schubert outlived Beethoven by only one year, whereas Berlioz lived into well beyond the middle of the nineteenth century.) Schubert's instrumental music, like Beethoven's, can be categorized as Classical, with Romantic leanings. However, in the field of vocal music Schubert was a full-fledged Romantic who single-handedly established the *lied* (song) as a principal genre of German Romanticism. Berlioz was a Romantic from the very outset—not one phrase of his music sounds the least bit Classical. The works featured in this chapter represent two of the major expressions of early nineteenth-century Romanticism.

SCHUBERT, WINTERREISE

Franz Schubert possessed probably the least imposing personality among the entire gamut of great composers. One contemporary source confirms what many others have written: "One thing I ought to add for the sake of truth, though I do not like doing it; Schubert was as undistinguished as a man as he was distinguished as a composer."[1]

Schubert was an extremely shy man, lacking in self-confidence and barely capable of making the musical world aware of his remarkable creative gifts. His main pleasures were playing music in casual gatherings of friends and carousing in Viennese night spots. He was so unimposing that Beethoven hardly knew of his existence, although they long lived in the same city and knew the same fellow musicians. Today we see both composers as musical giants; in Schubert's time the disparity in their reputations was enormous. Beethoven's death in 1827 was a monumental loss, mourned by the entire civilized world. (Schubert was a torch bearer at the funeral proceedings.) Schubert's death was ignored by all but a small band of loyal friends. The better part of the nineteenth century was to pass before the magnitude of Schubert's genius was fully appreciated.

Prior to the nineteenth century, opera was the chief secular vocal medium. The song genre was not taken very seriously by Baroque and Classical composers, who seem to have regarded songs as too short to be worthy of their best creative energies. Then Schubert came along and developed the song into an art form—not merely composing a large number of individual gems, but also elevating the new *song cycle* to a position of eminence, lavishing on this genre the same high degree of inspiration that earlier composers had invested in the cantata, oratorio, and opera. The very first song

A contemporary of Beethoven, Franz Schubert was an unimposing little man whose music was virtually unrecognized during his brief lifetime (1797–1828). Today he is regarded as a musical giant, master of the art song and one of the harbingers of the Romantic era in music.

cycle had come from Beethoven's pen (*An die ferne Geliebte*); it is a lovely work, but hardly his best (compared with his many concertos, symphonies, sonatas, and quartets). Schubert, already a master song composer before he reached the age of twenty, was the first to create a song cycle masterpiece, *Die schöne Müllerin* (The Lovely Maid of the Mill) (1823). This is a substantial work, a cycle of twenty songs which fills an entire song program. Each song manifests its own individual *Geist* (spirit), yet achieves its full meaning only within the context of the other songs. The cycle also projects a dramatic element. The poems relate a story progressing from a youth's first hopeful glimpse of a beautiful young woman, through the ecstasies and pains of infatuation, to growing despair as she rejects him for another. With this composition Schubert unveiled the song cycle as an ideal vehicle for the expression of romantic feelings— longing, sentiment, love, hopelessness, and so on.

One of Schubert's last compositions is a setting of twenty-four poems by Wilhelm Müller, *Winterreise* (Winter's Journey). Müller's poetry represents a monumental expression of alienation and despair. Each poem details the increasing woes of a young man spurned by the woman he adores. He vows to take leave of his friends, relations, and, most important, his beloved. He will abandon his personal world, wandering to distant places where his fate concerns no one, where he can blend anonymously into the larger impersonal world of the living, perhaps finding solace among the dead. We know of Schubert's frequent bouts of depression from contemporary accounts; his musical settings of these poems demonstrate all too clearly his familiarity with despair.

The very first song, "Gute Nacht" ("Good Night") establishes a mood of dejection that is maintained throughout most of the work. The opening melodic line in the piano introduction expresses an exquisite poignancy, preparing us for the first lines, "I came as a stranger, as a stranger I shall depart." The poem compares the hopefulness of the previous spring with the despair of the present winter. Like many of Schubert's songs, "Gute Nacht" is *strophic*; that is, it repeats the same music for successive verses. The first three verses are fittingly in the minor mode, but Schubert changed the fourth verse to major. Compare the similar melodic lines of verses 1 and 4. Do not be deceived by the notion that the major mode signifies any upgrading of our hero's spirits. Quite the contrary! "I'll no longer disturb your dreams, I'll bother you no longer . . .," he intones. Here we have but the first of many instances of Schubert's touching application of the major mode (referred to in Chapter 27). Listen for the final words, "On your door I've written 'good night,' so that you will know that I was thinking of you." At this point the major mode is still in force, but then the singer—as if as an afterthought—repeats "I was thinking of you" in the minor mode, and the last few piano measures restore the gloom of the song's minor opening.

Example 165
SCHUBERT, *Winterreise*
a) "Gute Nacht," Verse 1 (Minor)

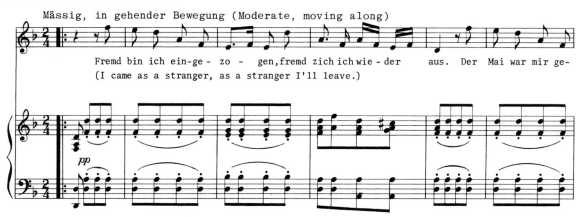

Music and Emotion

b) Verse 4 (Major)

Songs 2, 3, and 4 are also minor, as the sad traveler muses over many things—the weather vane on his beloved's house, tears found coursing down his cheeks, the cold of winter—all interpreted in terms of his lost love. Song 5, "Der Lindenbaum" ("The Linden Tree"), is well known outside the cycle; like several other Schubert songs it has achieved the status of a German folk song. Once again we have the major-minor polarity—the first part in major, the second briefly in minor, the remainder in major. The setting of the fifth stanza (there are six altogether) is especially evocative: "The cold wintry winds blew right into my face . . .". Listen expecially to the broken sixths and octaves in the accompaniment. The final page recalls the song's calm sweet opening, as our youth again reminisces about happy days spent beneath the linden tree, days now lost forever.

Example 166
SCHUBERT, "Der Lindenbaum," Verse 5

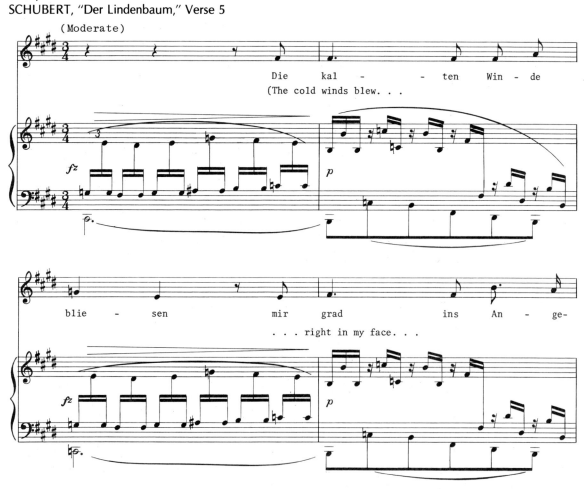

Music and Emotion

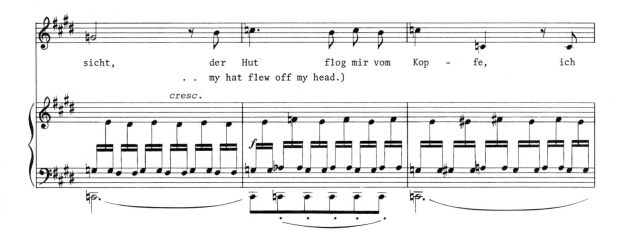

Song 9, "Irrlicht" ("Will-o'-the-Wisp"), is unremittingly minor and despondent. The poem mentions a phosphorescent light caused by swamp gases—a deceptive light which leads us, with all our sorrows and all our joys, astray. The singer's voice becomes ever more plaintive as he declaims, "Every stream finds the sea, every sorrow its grave."

Example 167

SCHUBERT, "Auf dem Flusse," Verse 3 (Melody in Piano Part)

Song 8, "Rückblick" ("Looking Back"), switches from minor to major, back to minor, then ends in major. Each of these modal switches signifies a change in the youth's feelings. First he angrily sings his desire to leave the town behind him; then he recalls how happy he was there earlier; then how he mournfully wishes he could return—as expressed first in the minor mode, later even more sadly in the bittersweet major mode.

Songs 6–10 are all in the minor mode. In the wistful Song 7 the youth addresses a stream: "You used to rustle so cheerfully . . . now you are so quiet." The middle of the song changes to major, but this time with a melody different from the opening minor phrases. When the minor mode returns, the piano takes up the melody as the singer reaches the emotional climax, "Oh my heart, do you see your reflection in this stream?"

Example 168
SCHUBERT, "Irrlicht," Ending

At last there is relief from the all-pervading gloom. In Song 11, "Frühlingstraum" ("Spring Dream"), the lover imagines the joy of springtime, contrasted with the reality of winter. But the happy dream is short lived, and Song 12, "Einsamkeit" ("Loneliness"), brings us back to the stark present reality.

Winterreise was originally published in two sets of twelve poems each. Schubert had encountered the first set in a periodical and finished composing them before discovering the existence of the second set. As it turns out, the poems were not published in proper order. For example, Song 13, "Die Post" ("The Mail Coach"), should appear as Song 6 instead of at the opening of Part II. Musically we can enjoy Schubert's error, for

Music and Emotion

the galloping horses and the cheery coach bell provided him an opportunity to recharge the musical energy at the beginning of Part II. The text remains sad, however, as the forlorn wanderer vainly looks for mail from those he has left behind.

Example 169
SCHUBERT, "Die Post"

Etwas geschwind (Quite fast)

Von der Stras - se her ein Post - horn klingt.
(The mail coach rings along the road. [Is there mail for me?])

After the bright Eb major of "Die Post," the brooding C minor of Song 14 seems particularly ominous. Entitled "Der greise Kopf" ("The Grey Head"), it presents an image of the falling snow transforming our sad youth into a white-haired old man. This idea appeals to him: once he is old, death cannot be far behind! But then the snow thaws, and hope of an early death vanishes. Listen for the melancholy piano interludes, echoing the singer's phrases.

Next comes the beautiful song, "Die Krähe" ("The Crow"). After a wistful piano introduction the voice enters, speaking to the bird of carrion as if addressing a friend: "I won't keep you waiting much longer . . . soon I'll be dead, just trust me." On and on our antihero trudges, singing of lost hopes, storms, and disappointments. Song 20 once again starts in the minor, changes in the middle to major, and then returns to minor. Do not be fooled by the warm opening of Song 21, "Das Wirtshaus" ("The Inn"). It sounds so pleasant and inviting—would it not be a good thing for our traveler to rest? But the opening words give away the secret: the inn is in reality a graveyard where the youth would gladly find eternal repose. Even this wish is not to be granted; there is no room at the "inn." The weary wanderer must forge ahead.

Example 170
SCHUBERT, "Das Wirthshaus"

Song 22, "Mut" ("Courage"), for the last time offers us contrast between minor and major sections. It starts in a loud brash minor, as the man tries to keep his spirits up, brushing snow from his face. By the end of the second verse the music becomes brighter, modulating to a new major key. The singer is positively happy:

Example 171
SCHUBERT, "Mut," Verse 3

Lu-stig in die Welt hin-ein ge - gen— Wind und— Wet-ter!
([I go] cheerful into the world, despite wind and weather.)

Then comes a statement the content of which is astonishingly modern, to wit, "God is dead." We hear, "We'll go out in the world cheerfully. If we find no god on earth, then we'll be gods ourselves."

The last two songs are among the most moving in the repertoire of German lieder. "Die Nebensonnen" ("The Mock Suns") starts with a warm piano phrase in A major. The singer repeats this music in his opening lines: "I saw three suns standing in the heavens, and looked at them long and hard." At this point Schubert ingeniously repeats the voice part, pitch for pitch, but alters the piano accompaniment to give us a phrase in F# minor: "And they also stood so fixed, as if they did not want to take leave of me."

Example 172
SCHUBERT, "Die Nebensonnen"

Music and Emotion

an - ge-sehn.   Und sie auch stan - den da so stier, als
... And they stood so still there, as if they would

wol - len sie___ nicht weg von mir.
not leave me.)

Finally we come to Song 24, "Der Leiermann," about the old man standing out in the cold playing his hurdy-gurdy (barrel organ). Through the musical device of the organ grinder's drone (an open fifth, B-F♯, played in every measure by the left hand), the accompaniment achieves a sense of near-perfect stillness, of eternal quiet. The right hand gently plays a simple tune, repeating it often throughout the song. The text depicts the old man's destitution, his empty plate, the dogs growling, with no one to hear his plaintive music. In what must surely stand as the most touching moment in the German lied repertoire, the youth concludes with the query, "Wonderful old man, shall I go with you? Will you accompany my songs?" (See Example 173.)

Example 173
SCHUBERT, "Der Leiermann," Ending

(Slow)

Wun-der-licher Al-ter,   soll ich mit dir   gehn?   Willst du meinen Liedern
(Wonderful old man, shall I go with you?)   Will you play my songs

(Drone)

dei - ne Lei-er drehn?___
on your organ?)

BERLIOZ, SYMPHONIE FANTASTIQUE

Hector Berlioz represents the image of the Romantic composer *par excellence*. Everything about him seems unique, even his Basque name (pronounced, surprisingly, just the way it looks—i.e., sounding the z). In 1827, at the age of twenty-four, Berlioz fell in love with a Shakespearean actress, Henrietta Simpson, then appearing with an English troupe performing in Paris. Berlioz first glimpsed Henrietta as Ophelia, the mad anti-heroine of *Hamlet*; he then saw her portray Juliet. Their subsequent courtship is possibly the most romantic in the history of Western music. Smitten by Henrietta, but too shy to meet her, Berlioz sublimated his intense passion through composing. The result was the semiautobiographical *Symphonie fantastique*, literally a symphony of fantasies, the work by which Berlioz is best known today. The structure of the *fantastique* represents a radical departure from the Classical orchestral tradition. Each of its five movements presents a recurring melody, an *idée fixe*, which symbolizes a beloved woman who always remains beyond the man's reach. Berlioz conceived of himself as the lover, Henrietta as the unattainable beloved. After the first performance in 1830 Berlioz revised the work, presenting it again two years later. All this time Hector and Henrietta had still not met, but by 1832 she was back in Paris and actually attended the

Hector Berlioz (1803–1869) represents the image of the Romantic composer *par excellence*. The structure of his *Symphonie fantastique* departs radically from the Classical orchestral tradition. Photograph by Felix Nadar.

first performance of the revised symphony—although barely aware, if at all, of her identification with the woman of Berlioz's imagination. The composer and actress were finally introduced the following day and were married the next year. Ironically, they had a terrible life together—she is said to have turned into a "dumpy, pedestrian wife, nagging, complaining, indulging in fits of jealousy"[2]—and they eventually separated.

Berlioz was a great admirer of Beethoven and knew the *Pastoral Symphony* well. From Chapter 1 you may recollect that Beethoven provided a title for each of his five *Pastoral* movements. Berlioz went a big step further. In addition to titles, he wrote a paragraph explaining the meaning of each movement. This "program" was published in a Paris newspaper as an advertisement for the première, and it was also distributed to members of the audience. Unlike those who believe music expresses what words cannot (see Chapter 20), Berlioz's purpose in distributing the program was to say in prose what he had left unsaid in the music. Later, however, he decided that the program was unnecessary to an appreciation of the symphony, that the titles alone would suffice.

For several reasons the *Symphonie fantastique* was in its time a work of revolutionary importance. For one thing it was a purely instrumental work which nevertheless focused on the volatile subject of a deranged human personality. The symphony is a medley of the fantasies and nightmares of a distraught lover sky-high on drugs, with each of its five movements detailing a different episode in the meanderings of the man's imagination. Then too the symphony as a whole is the progenitor of the program symphonies composed later in the nineteenth century by Liszt, Mahler, and Richard Strauss, while its individual movements are models for the tone poem, soon to become one of the principal Romantic orchestral genres. With the inclusion of the *idée fixe* in each movement, Berlioz created the first fully cyclic symphony (see Chapter 12). Still another factor is Berlioz's huge orchestra of ten winds, thirteen brass, five percussion, two harps, and a minimum of sixty strings. (Today we take this size for granted, but we should remember that just sixty years prior to Berlioz Mozart took delight in an ensemble less than half as large.) Finally, and perhaps most important, the *Fantastique* is a prototype for the new Romantic ethic according to which a composer poured forth his deepest feelings, painting his life and personality in music.

Listen to each movement of the symphony, guided by the descriptions presented below.

Movement 1

The first movement, entitled "Reveries, Passions," alternates between quiet reveries and fitful passions. The beginning is especially gentle and soft, seemingly coming out of nowhere, as if the "hero" had suddenly awakened from a drug-induced stupor. This section serves as a long, slow introduction to the fast principal subject to come. As the tempo quickens, the *idée fixe* is heard for the first time. It is played quietly by flute and violins, the rest of the strings accompanying them with a subdued galloping figure. This rather ungainly melody can hardly be described as pretty. Does it imply that for all the intensity of the man's desires, he finds his unrequited feelings painful and awkward?

Example 174
BERLIOZ, *Symphonie fantastique*, 1st Mvt., *Idée fixe*

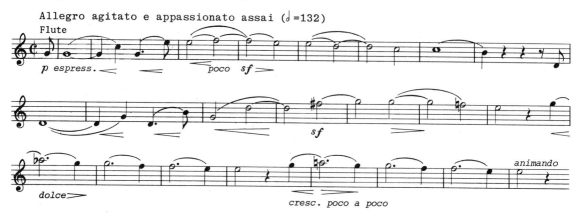

Music and Emotion

The Classical first movement tradition calls for at least one contrasting theme after the exposition of the first theme. But apparently Berlioz wanted to emphasize his *idée fixe*, for his second theme adds merely a single new phrase to the short first phrase of the main theme. Both these themes are heard prominently throughout the remainder of the movement. After a loud syncopated statement of the main theme the movement closes with soft chords suggesting an amen. (Berlioz added the word "religiose" to the score.)

Example 175
Symphonie fantastique, 1st Mvt., 2nd Theme

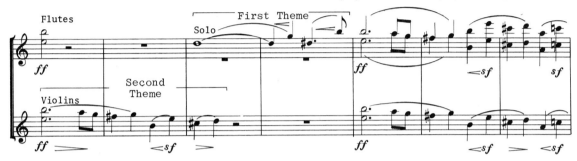

Movement 2

This movement is called "A Ball." After a brief introduction played by strings and harps (the harp being one of Berlioz's many additions to the orchestra), the music proceeds with a lovely waltz theme—representing still another Berliozian innovation, the waltz replacing the traditional Classical minuet or scherzo. Of course this waltz tune is in triple meter, whereas the *idée fixe* of the first movement is in $\frac{4}{4}$; but when the lover sees his beloved at the ball, her theme becomes transformed into a waltz, too. It is played by flute and oboe. After the return of the main waltz theme, the music works up to a climax, again interrupted by the *idée fixe*, which is now played by clarinet. After a few notes of the *idée fixe* the movement concludes with a loud coda in the style of the principal waltz theme.

Example 176
Symphonie fantastique, 2nd Mvt., "The Ball," *Idée fixe*

Movement 3

The third movement, the tranquil "Scene in the Country," begins with shepherd calls (like those of Beethoven's *Pastoral* finale) played by oboe and echoed by English horn (a symphonic instrument rarely used before Berlioz). Much of this movement resembles the *Pastoral* second movement, "At the Brook." A gentle rustic theme is played by flute and violins; then, taken over by violas and cellos, the theme is punctuated by winds and horn playing a repeated-note figure not unlike the bird calls which

Music of Mania and Despair

conclude Beethoven's portrait of the brook. Next there is a stormy warning by low strings and bassoon, followed directly by the *idée fixe* played by oboe and flute. The *idée fixe* is now irregular—jerky and syncopated. Subsequently a new theme is introduced by the clarinet, after which the second violins repeat the main theme of the movement with the new theme as counterpoint in the winds and the first violins providing a busy thirty-second-note figure as well. Toward the end the flute and clarinet hint at the *idée fixe* as the violins and violas play the main theme. Then the violins and clarinet similarly take up the *idée fixe* motive, answered by French horn and violas. The movement winds down with a repetition of the shepherds' tune from the beginning, but now accompanied by tympani rolls. These are meant to suggest thunder, another obvious reference to Beethoven's *Pastoral* (fourth movement).

Example 177
Symphonie fantastique, 3rd Mvt., *Idée fixe*

Movement 4

In the last two movements of the *Fantastique* Berlioz really allowed his imagination to soar. First he gave us the grandiose "March to the Scaffold." The introduction starts with horns, tympani, and pizzicato cellos and basses. A somber but loud minor theme is heard in the low strings. Finally the main theme of the movement is heard, a march played as if by a band—i.e., without strings. (The key is B♭ major, which happens also to be the key of the "band" variation in the finale of Beethoven's *Symphony No. 9*—see Chapter 18. B♭ major is the most convenient key for wind instruments to play in.) The rest of the movement is based on these two themes, one earnest and declamatory, the other a blaring march. Just before the end, after a roaring orchestral tutti, the clarinet plays the first phrase of the *idée fixe*, very soft and delicate and once again in ⁴₄, as in the opening movement. The orchestra responds with a deafening G minor triad—signifying the death blow, the chopping off of our hero's head. Resounding G major chords bring the movement to a close.

374

Music and Emotion

Movement 5

The Finale is entitled "Dream of a Witches' Sabbath." Here Berlioz devised genuine "spook music," setting the precedent for other Romantic examples such as Mussorgsky's *Night on Bald Mountain*, Saint-Saëns's *Dance macabre*, and Dukas's *Sorcerer's
Apprentice*. The violins are now divided into six distinct groups instead of the usual
two. The violas are also divided, and all the strings play with mutes to emphasize the
spooky effect. After an atmospheric beginning the first theme to be heard is a cackling
version of the *idée fixe*—in a fast ⁶⁄₈, with grace notes added for extra effect. The *idée
fixe* has hardly begun when there is a tremendous tutti outburst, and then the *idée fixe*
starts up once again.

Example 178

Symphonie fantastique, Finale, *Idée fixe*

We next hear a section which combines the sounding of the ghostly knell with
the first phrase of an important new theme, the witches' round dance. This is interrupted by the intoning of the Gregorian chant, "Dies Irae," by tubas and bassoon. (For
more on "Dies Irae," see Chapter 30.) As soon as the tubas are finished the knell recom-
mences, and the horns and trombones play the "Dies Irae" at twice the preceding tempo. Finally, the "Dies Irae" changes again, as the winds and pizzicato strings play it in
the mocking rhythmic pattern of the preceding version of the *idée fixe* (see Example
180). Eventually the round dance theme starts again, at first in fits and starts, but finally
getting fully under way played by cellos and basses (see Example 181). The remaining
strings accompany from above.

Example 179

Symphonie fantastique, Finale, "Dies Irae,"

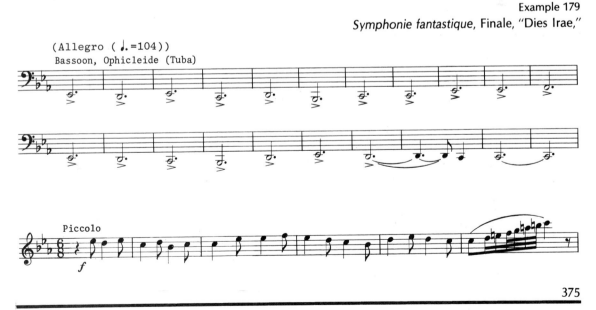

Music of Mania and Despair

Example 181
Round Dance

We have now reached the orgiastic climax of the movement. After "Dies Irae" quietly recurs, we hear an intense build-up leading to a stunning combination of "Dies Irae" and the round dance—all in all, a magnificent conclusion to a spectacular milestone in the development of orchestral music.

Example 182
Round Dance & "Dies Irae" Combined

Berlioz was an orchestral genius, producing dazzling effects never before attempted. Shown here, a caricature of Berlioz conducting one of his orchestral works.

Music and Emotion

The *Symphonie fantastique* is an astonishing work. It broke through many of the barriers imposed by Classical form, telling a story in music that anticipated Freud's stream-of-consciousness by nearly a century. Berlioz was also a genius of orchestration, producing dazzling effects never before attempted. His experiments and innovations presaged the great strides in orchestral tone painting soon to be taken by Richard Wagner (1813–1883). One might fairly describe Wagner as Berlioz's disciple (even if Wagner would have hated the notion of his indebtedness to a non-German composer!). Note the recurrent image of drug-induced perceptions in the following commentary from the pen of the great French poet-critic, Charles Baudelaire.

> No musician excels as Wagner does in *painting* space and depth, both material and spiritual. . . . He possesses the art of translating, by means of the subtlest shades, all that is excessive, immense and ambitious in spiritual and natural man. One seems sometimes, when listening to this fiery and peremptory music, to recapture the dizzy perceptions of an opium-dream, painted upon a backcloth of darkness.[3]

Another important Romantic artist was Frédéric Chopin (1809–1849). No two contemporary composers seem more opposite than Chopin and Wagner. Chopin was a miniaturist, composing mainly for the piano; Wagner was a "monumentalist," writing almost exclusively for heroic voices and a gigantic orchestra. Yet Chopin wielded an important influence on Wagner through his explorations into the world of tonal *chromaticism*. Chopin would often pass through several different key areas within a relatively brief span of musical time, the sense of key constantly fluctuating. (Later, after Chopin's premature death, Wagner was to exhibit a similar high-powered chromaticism.) Listen to Chopin's brief *Prelude in E Minor* (one of the pieces "played" by Jack Nicholson in the film, *Five Easy Pieces*), the extended ballades in G Minor and F Minor, the exquisite *Nocturne in C Minor*, the stormy *Fantasy in F Minor*—all highly charged with intense feeling. Within the limited confines of Chopin's perfumed chromaticism (few of his works last more than ten minutes), one encounters an emotional gamut comparable to the expressive range of the boldest Wagnerian music dramas.

A spiritual descendant of Chopin was the Russian Impressionist composer, Alexander Scriabin (1872–1915). Scriabin composed many volumes of highly sensitized piano music. He also wrote five symphonies. *Symphony No. 3*, subtitled *Divine Poem*, comprises movements labeled "Struggles," "Sensual Delights," and "Divine Play." According to the composer's program notes, the symphony concerns the division of the ego into Man-God and Slave-Man.

> They struggle with each other, and proceeding though the total concord and discord of human experience, finally reach unity and that longed-for divine freedom which enables man to exist playfully as god himself in the sky of other worlds in blissful ecstasy.[4]

"Ecstasy" was a key word for Scriabin. His next symphony is entitled *Poem of Ecstasy*. Again the composer indulges in mystical imagery, as the "Man-God arrives at release through love and sex, creation and procreation. The freedom of untrammeled action . . . would suffuse the entire world, dissolving it into ecstasy."[5] The music delves into a

> gamut of emotions and experiences — delicious excitement followed by soothing languor, terror, doubt, "the maggot of satiety . . . the bite of hyenas . . . sting of serpent," intoxication, burning kisses, spiritual and temporal love-making, and ultimately, ecstasy.[6]

Scriabin's last symphony, *Poem of Fire*, calls for the projection of color patterns in coordination with the musical flow. Scriabin may well have created the first multimedia extravaganza!

To complete our survey of emotion in music we turn to a vocal work based on words of Christopher Smart, an English poet of the eighteenth century. Smart was given to madness, and wrote his lengthy poem, *Rejoice in the Lamb*, while committed in an insane asylum. In 1943 Benjamin Britten selected portions of this work to serve as the text of a cantata of the same name. Although Britten's selections emphasize various aspects of worship (and therefore more properly fit Unit 5), his fifth section belongs in this discussion as a powerful expression of personal despair.

> For I am under the same accusation with my Saviour —
> For they said, he is besides himself.
> For the officers of the peace are at variance with me, and the watchman smites me with his staff.
> For Silly fellow! Silly fellow! is against me and belongeth neither to me nor to my family.
> For I am in twelve HARDSHIPS, but he that was born of a virgin shall deliver me out of all.

Britten's music starts out in great simplicity, as the chorus sings spare unaccompanied perfect fifths. At the words, "Silly fellow!" Britten introduces a syncopated rhythmic figure, with the entire choir singing in octaves. (For a review of the concept of *syncopation*, see Chapter 12.) "For I am in twelve HARDSHIPS" is presented as a free *canon* — starting in the altos with each subsequent part entering two beats later. After the climax in the sixth measure, the music gradually dies down to *ppp*. The hopefulness of the final phrase of text is undermined as the organ plays a brief melodic *obbligato* (contrapuntal line) coupled with the voices' despairing E minor triad.

Example 183
BRITTEN, *Rejoice in the Lamb*, Section 5, "For I Am Under the Same Accusation"

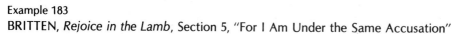

Music and Emotion

From the minstrel songs of the Middle Ages to the latest hit from Tin Pan Alley, the subject of love has commanded composers' attentions like few others. We shall begin this chapter by looking into musical treatments of the star-crossed lovers, Romeo and Juliet, and follow with an examination of love duets by Puccini, Wagner, and Verdi.

Albrecht Dürer, *Adam and Eve*. The subject of love has commanded composers' attention like few others.

ROMEO AND JULIET

Few dramas are as well known as Shakespeare's *Romeo and Juliet*. With its many famous lines (e.g., "A rose by any other name would smell as sweet"), the play boasts hopeful scenes of romance and courtship culminating in scenes of death and despair. Three important films of *Romeo and Juliet* have been produced: one directed in the 1930s by George Cukor, with Leslie Howard and Norma Shearer; a second made in the 1950s with Laurence Harvey and Susan Shentall; and Franco Zeffirelli's great box-office hit of the late 1960s, with the previously unknown Leonard Whiting and Olivia Hussey (who have since returned to relative obscurity). And, of course, the original Shakespeare drama is performed frequently on stages throughout the world.

In view of its steady popularity it should occasion little surprise that *Romeo and Juliet* has stirred considerable interest among composers. The list of works inspired by this play includes operas by Bellini, Gounod, and Delius; a dramatic symphony by Berlioz; a tone poem by Tchaikovsky; a ballet by Prokofiev; and a Broadway musical by Leonard Bernstein. The next pages are devoted to a consideration of these last four works.

Berlioz, Romeo and Juliet

The dramatic symphony, *Romeo and Juliet* (1839), is one of Berlioz's masterpieces. Unlike his earlier *Symphonie fantastique* (Chapter 28), this work is scored not only for orchestra, but also for three vocal soloists and chorus. It falls short of an opera, however, for of the three soloists only one represents a protagonist. (The bass soloist impersonates Friar Laurence.) Moreover, Berlioz related only certain parts of the drama in his music—he only gave us part of the story.

Berlioz was an inveterate Romantic. In his own words, he approached his new symphony, "floating into a halcyon sea of poetry, wafted onward by the sweet, soft breeze of imagination; warmed by the golden sun of love unveiled by Shakespeare."[1] One of the finest passages is the "Scène d'amour" (Love Scene); Berlioz himself regarded it as his favorite original work. Except for a brief mens' chorus, the music is scored for orchestra alone. About twenty minutes' long, it depicts the great declaration of love which takes place on Juliet's balcony shortly after the Capulet's ball.

We are in the Shakespeare play, Act II, Scene 2. Juliet, musing over the unbreachable enmity between her own Capulet family and Romeo's family, the Montagues, declaims,

> O Romeo, Romeo! wherefore art thou Romeo?
> Deny thy father and refuse thy name;
> Or, if thou wilt not, be but sworn my love,
> And I'll no longer be a Capulet.

Suddenly Romeo speaks out from the darkness below, and she asks how he gained entrance to the Capulet's well-guarded grounds. He replies,

> With love's light wings did I o'erperch these walls,
> For stony limits cannot hold love out;
> And what love can do, that dares love attempt.
> Therefore thy kinsmen are no stop to me.

Declaring their common passion, the two youthful lovers vow to be married as soon as possible.

Berlioz's "Love Scene" is the third movement of his symphony, located about halfway through the work. At first one hears extremely soft (*pppp*) orchestral chords depicting—in Berlioz's own words—"the deserted and quiet garden of the Capulets." We then hear a soft men's chorus, as if at a distance, representing the revelers departing from the ball. They sing (in French), "Capulets, good night; ah, what a night, what festivities . . . what lovely girls of Verona . . . let's go home and dream of love."

With the dying out of the voices, the orchestra takes over again, initially with the strings muted. (*Mutes* considerably reduce the resonance and carrying power of stringed instruments.) Other instruments are added very gradually. The violas play a typically slow angular Berliozian melody. A second, more conventional theme, one of

Music and Emotion

Aristide Maillol, *Desire*.

the most memorable in the "Love Scene," is introduced by the cellos and French horn. The tempo is now a little faster. Theme 1 returns at the original slow tempo, again played by violas accompanied mainly by other strings. A sudden rushed transition—*animato*—brings back Theme 2 in full force, *appassionato* and *fortissimo*.

Example 184

BERLIOZ, *Romeo and Juliet*, Love Scene, Second Theme

A still longer and faster transitional passage, marked *agitato*, features a solo cello recitative which seemingly suggests Romeo's imploring voice. A new section commences very slowly. The first flute plays Theme 3, doubled an octave below by the English horn. This leads directly into one of the most beautiful themes in all Romantic music, played by the first violins. This fourth theme, a variant of Theme 2, dominates during the rest of the movement. Gradually the music becomes more excited, pushing toward a climactic restatement of the second part of Theme 2 (Example 184) now transposed to another key and played in three octaves by violins, violas, and cellos. Then the slow tempo resumes, the original key returns, we hear snatches of Theme 4, and the movement is over.

381

Music and Love

Example 185
Romeo and Juliet, Love Scene, Fourth Theme

Tchaikovsky, Romeo and Juliet

Another musical interpretation of Shakespeare's romantic drama, composed some thirty years after Berlioz's symphony, is Tchaikovsky's tone poem of the same name (1869). This composition is comparatively brief, equivalent in duration to a single movement of a late Romantic symphony. The key word here is *concise*, for Tchaikovsky managed to pack several diverse elements of the story into his musical narrative. Notable sections include the sword fight between the Capulets and Montagues, and the remarkable love theme. Especially lovely is the "mood music" which opens the piece, somewhat reminiscent of the soft introduction to Berlioz's "Love Scene."

Example 186
TCHAIKOVSKY, *Romeo and Juliet*, Love Theme

*Notated at sounding pitch- see Example 63

Sergei Prokofiev
(1891–1953).

Prokofiev, Romeo and Juliet

In 1935 another Russian, Sergei Prokofiev, composed a full-length ballet based on Shakespeare's play. This ballet can often be seen in live productions, and it has been filmed by the Bolshoi Ballet (1956) and the Royal Ballet of England, starring Dame Margot Fonteyn and Rudolf Nureyev (1966). It has long been the practice of bal-

Music and Emotion

let composers to carve orchestral *suites* from the music of full-length ballets. Prokofiev fashioned two such orchestral suites from *Romeo and Juliet*. (Several different recordings of these suites are available. At least one conductor, Charles Münch, recorded a third suite of his own devising.) Suite 1 includes the Balcony Scene (No. 6). It starts with muted strings and harp and features two important lyrical themes. Suite 2 depicts the night shared by the lovers before parting (No. 5)—equivalent to the nude scene in the Zeffirelli movie, but not actually found in the Shakespeare play (where the lovers part on Juliet's balcony). Perhaps the finest music is in No. 7 of Suite 2, "Romeo at Juliet's Tomb," a passage of extreme emotional intensity. Prokofiev's music will appeal to anyone with a taste for the astringent; it is much "gutsier" than the prettier Romantic styles of Berlioz and Tchaikovsky.

Bernstein, West Side Story

Of all the lovers of the recent Broadway stage, probably none are better known than those of *West Side Story* (1957). Tony and Maria are star-crossed lovers who are burdened by conflicting ethnic backgrounds (rather than kinship ties). The entire plot of Bernstein's musical is loosely analogous to Shakespeare's *Romeo and Juliet*, including the lovers' first meeting at a dance, the violent rumbles, and—following Tony's death—the reconciliation of the indigenous American versus immigrant Puerto Rican gangs. Tony and Maria's initial love scene displays the excitement and anticipation found in Shakespeare's balcony scene. With a sure hand Bernstein mixed popular and classical styles—the latter influenced by Stravinsky (see Chapters 30 and 31) and Prokofiev.*

Example 187
BERNSTEIN, *West Side Story*, Love Duet

To-night, to-night, won't be just a-ny night, to-night there will be no morn-ing star.

LOVE DUETS FROM ROMANTIC OPERAS

Puccini, La Bohème

The "Love Scene" from Berlioz's *Romeo and Juliet* is the orchestral equivalent of an operatic *love duet*. The love duet is a traditional element in nineteenth- and twentieth-century operas, most of which are populated by lovers who—like Romeo and Juliet—fall in love at first sight, but almost never live happily ever after. As it happens, none of the operas based on the Romeo and Juliet legend is highly popular with the general music public, but a comparable example derived from a more recent love story is Puccini's *La Bohème*. Composed in 1896, this opera is based on Henri Mürger's *The Bohemian Life*, a French novel published in 1851, and it has since become one of the most popular Italian operas in the Romantic repertoire. The story concerns Rudolfo, a young and starving poet, and Mimi, an equally down-and-out flower vendor. They

*For more on *West Side Story*, see "Death Scenes," Chapter 31.

reside on different floors of a cheap rooming house in the Latin Quarter of Paris—a section roughly comparable to the "Bohemian" Greenwich Village of New York City.

The Act I Love Duet begins just after Rudolfo's roommates have left for a nearby café. He has remained behind in an effort to do some writing—work before pleasure! A tapping on the door reveals Mimi, asking for a light for her candle. The two have never seen each other before, and she is very shy. Gasping at her pale beauty (for she is not in good health), Rudolfo insists that she step in, drink a bit of wine, and rest a little. It is clearly love at first sight. She drops her key and he adroitly blows out his own candle, providing an excuse for her to remain longer. It is a simple but touching scene for which Puccini created a lavish musical setting. First Rudolfo sings an aria identifying himself as a young, idealistic, but not very successful poet. In response Mimi sings an aria describing her simple and lonely life. Finally the two join together to express their longing and newly found delight in each other. So ends the first act.

Here is a more detailed guide to the music of this scene.

Just after the roommates have left, the orchestra plays a light-hearted tune and Rudolfo takes out pen and paper. When Mimi enters, breathless from the exertion of the stairs, the orchestra introduces her special theme:

Example 188
PUCCINI, *La Bohème*, Act I, Mimi's Theme

Mimi nearly faints, and the orchestra presents a theme reflecting Rudolfo's anxiety. (Like Wagner's *Leitmotifs*—see Chapter 14—many of these themes return throughout the opera, as, for example, when Mimi is near death in Act IV.) As Mimi revives and appears to feel better, the orchestra resumes its previous jaunty style. A new and beautiful theme—Puccini's operas are noted for their abundance of lovely melodies—is now heard as Mimi discovers she has dropped her key. Example 189 commences a complete A–B–A section in the music, accompanying her apology for troubling Rudolfo while he (supposedly) hunts for her key.

Example 189
La Bohème, Act I, Mimi's Aria

Un poco più mosso (♩=126)

Mimi

Oh! sven - ta - ta, sven - ta - ta! La chia - ve del - la stan - za do - ve l'ho la - scia - ta?
(Oh! How dreadful, how dreadful, I cannot find my door-key, I am so forgetful!)

384

Rudolfo now sings his aria, commenting on Mimi's tiny frozen hands* and then launching into a forthright description of himself. The second part of Rudolfo's aria introduces still another gorgeous melody, the "hit tune" of the opera.

Example 190
La Bohème, Act I, Rudolfo's Aria

Mimi now sings her aria, answering Rudolfo's questions about her. "Mimi" is just a nickname, a substitute for her real name, Lucia. She sews enough to earn a meager living and also makes artifical flowers. Her aria consists of no less than three superb themes. When it is over we hear Rudolfo's roommates calling from below, urging him to hurry along and join them. This interruption is followed by a reprise of the mellow "hit tune" (Example 190), and then their duet commences. During a recitative passage in the middle of the duet the new lovers agree that Mimi will accompany Rudolfo to the café. When he asks, "And after that?" she coyly responds, "We'll see." The opening theme of Rudolfo's aria brings the duet to a close.

As in *Romeo and Juliet*, the happiness of the young lovers of *La Bohème* lasts but a short time. At first no genuine tragedy intrudes; the infatuation simply wears off and

*Legend has it that at one performance at the Metropolitan Opera House, the irrepressible Enrico Caruso, then the world's leading Italian tenor, pressed an ice cube into the hands of his leading lady at this point in the opera.

Music and Love

the lovers "split" (in Act III).* But Mimi turns out to be a good deal sicker than she first appeared, and in Act IV she is discovered to be near death. This brings about a romantic reconciliation of the lovers, and Mimi dies resignedly in Rudolfo's arms.

Wagner, Die Walküre

Adultery and incest alike are combined in the second music drama of Wagner's *Ring* cycle, *Die Walküre* (*The Valkyrie*). (The *Ring* was introduced in Chapter 14.) The title refers to Brünnhilde, one of the heroic daughters of Wotan, king of the Gods. Acts II and III are primarily involved with struggles and machinations among the Gods, but Act I concerns the problems of two mortals, Siegmund and Sieglinde. A strong bond is implied by the similarity of their names. Although ostensibly meeting one another for the first time, they are in fact long-lost twin siblings. Through a forced marriage Sieglinde is the wife of the gloomy Hunding, a hunter. As the curtain rises, Siegmund rushes into Hunding's house from the stormy outside. Here he seeks protection from his enemies, and the lonely, unhappy Sieglinde is only too willing to give him succor. Upon Hunding's return it develops that Siegmund's pursuers are Hunding's own kinsmen; granting his unwelcome (and unarmed) guest a night of rest and haven, he nevertheless challenges him to a duel the next morning. Hunding and Sieglinde then retire for the night, but, having given her husband a sleeping potion, Sieglinde soon reappears to carry on her conversation with Siegmund. Gradually their discussion leads to familial recognition. Long separation and hunger for renewal of family ties fuels their infatuation, and love proceeds unrestrained.

The musical format of the last part of Act I of *Die Walküre* is similar to that of Act I of *La Bohème*. Each protagonist sings an independent aria, and then the two join in a glorious (but in this case much lengthier) duet.

First Siegmund sings his "Spring Song" (Winter Storms Have Given Way to the Month of May). Siegmund rhapsodizes about spring replacing winter, voicing thoughts of warmth and new growth. The orchestra then plays a love motive which has been hinted at since early in the act. This phrase leads directly into the melody which Sieglinde will later sing near the beginning of her aria. He concludes with the words, "United are love and spring!" The orchestra presses on with Example 191, and Sieglinde bursts in with her first theme. She immediately proceeds with Example 192, which recurs several times during her aria.

With Siegmund rejoining Sieglinde, each presents a motive expressing the driving emotions within them. Sieglinde speculates on the feeling of recognition which welled up inside her upon first seeing Siegmund. The orchestra plays a *Leitmotif* associated with their father, Wotan, and their clan, the Walsungs (see Example 68 above). Example 193 returns, as Siegmund declares "You are the image I have always carried within me." Example 194 accompanies Sieglinde's query regarding his real name. Earlier, in Hunding's presence, he had answered vaguely, "Well, you cannot call me 'Joyful' or

---

*In Mürger's novel an overt connection between Rudolfo and Romeo is established when Rudolfo, on the rebound from Mimi, falls for a young lady named Juliet. He vows to change his own name to Romeo, and purchases a rope-ladder for climbing her balcony, along with a pigeon as a stand-in for Shakespeare's "lark that pierced the fearful hollow of thine ear." The pigeon faithfully performs its task of waking the lovers, but the larder being empty, they end up cooking the bird for breakfast.

Music and Emotion

'Peaceful'; better to call me 'Woeful'!" Now he exclaims, "No longer call me 'Woeful';
I'm too happy now."

Example 191

WAGNER, *Die Walküre*, Act I, Siegmund's Aria

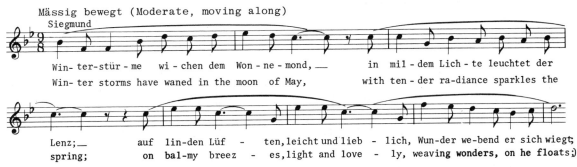

Mässig bewegt (Moderate, moving along)

Siegmund

Win- ter-stür- me wi - chen dem Won- ne-mond, __ in mil - dem Lich - te leuchtet der
Win- ter storms have waned in the moon of May, with ten - der ra-diance sparkles the

Lenz; __ auf lin-den Lüf - ten, leicht und lieb - lich, Wun-der we-bend er sich wiegt;
spring; on bal-my breez - es, light and love - ly, weaving **wonders, on he floats;)**

Example 192

Die Walküre, Love Motive

Mässig bewegt

Example 193

Die Walküre, Sieglinde's Aria

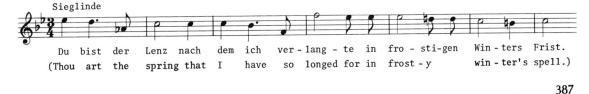

Sieglinde

Du bist der Lenz nach dem ich ver - lang - te in fro - sti-gen Win - ters Frist.
(Thou art the spring that I have so longed for in frost - y win - ter's spell.)

387

Music and Love

Example 194

Die Walküre, Leitmotif Associated with Wotan and the Walsung Clan (see Example 68)

(Moderate)

Siegmund *p*

Ein Wun - der will mich ge - mah - nen:
(A mar - vel wakes my re - mem - brance:

più p

"And your name isn't 'Peaceful', either?"
"Call me whatever you wish!"
"Well then, I'll call you 'Victorious' ('Siegmund')!"

The orchestra plays an electrifying motive heard earlier as Siegmund shouts his response,

"Call me 'Siegmund', for I *am* Siegmund!"

He explains that he has always known that a sword would appear to him when he needed it most. Earlier Sieglinde had shown him the handle of a sword implanted in a tree stump (located in a corner of the hut). A stranger had left it there long before, at her wedding, and the strongest men present had been unable to pull it out. Now, in a burst of passionate energy, Siegmund grasps the handle and frees the sword. The Sword motive wells up in the orchestra. Once again the music becomes passionate, replaying Siegmund's love theme (Example 191). Finally, Sieglinde cries out,

"You're Siegmund? Well, I am your long lost sister, Sieglinde!"

He replies,

"Sister and bride all in one; let the blood of the Walsung clan live on!"

The lovers rush out into the moonlight, while the orchestra plays feverish versions of Examples 192, 195, and 193, in that order.

Example 195

Die Walküre, Sword Motive

ff *f marcato*

Music and Emotion

In a scene from *Die Walküre*, Wotan takes leave of Brünnhilde.

Having listened to the *Walküre* Love Duet, you may now wish to examine a remarkable short story by the great German writer, Thomas Mann (whose novel *Doctor Faustus* is discussed in Chapter 22).

Blood of the Walsungs recounts the doings of a pair of twins named after the *Walküre* twins, Siegmund and Sieglinde. (The title is derived straight from Siegmund's last words in Act I, just quoted.) Mann's twins are a pair of highly attractive young adults who are passionately attached to each other, a spoiled lot living a luxurious life in the Germany of an earlier day. Sieglinde is engaged to marry the older and ineffectual Herr von Beckerath (her parents' choice), but she vastly prefers the companionship of her twin brother. (The name von Beckerath suggests Beckmesser, Wagner's comic villain in *Die Meistersinger*.) The wedding is soon to take place. As a special privilege the twins request their parents' permission to attend one last performance of their favorite opera, *Die Walküre*. Herr von Beckerath readily supports the parents' assent, only to discover that he has not been invited along. It is to be a tête-à-tête of the siblings alone.

The twins arrive at the opera house. Mann has framed a rather straighforward account of the trials of the operatic twins with a humorous but scathing portrayal of their decadent namesakes sitting out in the audience. The performance is described as

389

Music and Love

mediocre. At the point where, at Hunding's behest, the on-stage Sieglinde leaves Sieg-mund alone on stage, Mann wrote,

> [Siegmund's] brows made two black furrows, and one foot, resting on the heel of his patent-leather shoe, was in constant nervous motion. But it stopped as he heard a whisper close to him.
>
> "Gigi!"
>
> His mouth, as he turned, had an insolent line. Sieglinde was holding out to him a mother-of-pearl box with mara-schino cherries.
>
> "The brandy chocolates are underneath," she whis-pered. But he accepted only a cherry, and as he took it out of the waxed paper she said in his ear [referring to Sieglinde's departure with Hunding]:
>
> "She will come back to him again at once."
>
> "I am not entirely unaware of the fact," he said so loud that several heads were jerked angrily in his direction . . ."[2]

At the end of Act I Mann's narrative continues:

> Siegmund pushed back his chair and stood up. He was hot; little red patches showed on his cheek-bones, above the lean, sallow, shaven cheeks.
>
> "For my part," said he, "what I want now is a breath of fresh air. Siegmund was pretty feeble, wasn't he?"
>
> "Yes," answered Sieglinde, "and the orchestra saw fit to drag abominably in the *Spring Song*."
>
> "Frightfully sentimental," said Siegmund, shrugging his narrow shoulders in his dress coat. "Are you coming out?"

Verdi, Otello

Most operatic lovers die soon after their first meeting, and therefore few operas feature love duets sung by married couples. An exception to this rule is found in Act I of Verdi's *Otello*. This Italian opera is based on a Shakespearean tragedy, in which Othello (spelled with an *h* in English, without the *h* in Italian) is led by Iago's imputa-tions to doubt the fidelity of his new wife, Desdemona. The climax of the plot finds Othello murdering Desdemona, only to learn immediately of the falseness of Iago's ac-cusations. In Act I of the opera Otello has not yet been infected by Iago's venom; hav-ing just returned from a victorious battle, Otello is delighted to embrace Desdemona. In their love scene they reminisce about their first meeting and how they fell in love. Their mood gradually becomes more romantic, until he passionately calls for a kiss (*un bacio*) and still another kiss (*encore un bacio*). This same love music recurs at the end of the opera, just after Otello learns of his wife's unblemished virtue.

> I kissed thee ere I killed thee. No way but this,
> Killing myself, to die upon a kiss.

In the opera, as in the play, Otello kisses Desdemona one last time, then stabs himself to death. Verdi adds extra pathos to this death scene by reintroducing the "bacio" mu-sic from the finale of Act I.

Example 196

VERDI, *Otello*, Act I, Finale, (Love Duet)

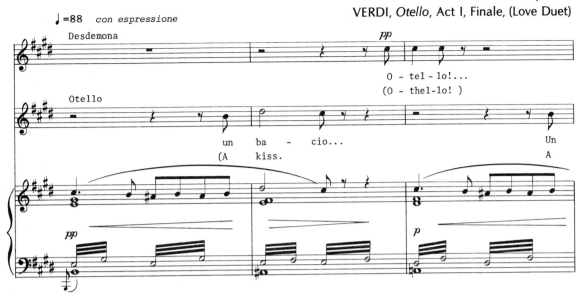

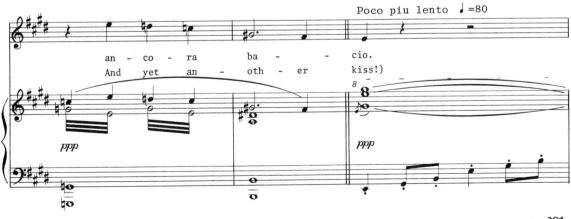

Terms preceded by (•) are included in lists for previous units.

General
- • Classical (349, 358)
- • Romantic (349, 358)
- "Dies Irae" (375)

Vocal Music
- • aria (385)
- • canon (378)
- lied (358)
- • song cycle (358)
- strophic (359)

Instrumental Music
- • cyclic form (372)
- English horn (373)
- *idée fixe* (370)
- mute (380)
- obbligato (378)
- • staccato (346)
- • suite (382)
- • symphony (370)

Theory
- chromaticism (377)
- church modes (353)
- • coda (373)
- • counterpoint (355)
- • half step (354)
- • legato (346)
- • *Leitmotif* (384)
- Lydian mode (353)
- major triad (345)
- minor triad (345)
- • mode (354)
- • scale (354)
- • syncopated (373)
- tonic triad (346)
- • whole step (354)

REVIEW: UNITS V AND VI

1. The four historical periods of the first four units have now been expanded to six. List them with approximate dates.

2. Make a list of the composers whose music is featured in Units V and VI, adding any other composers assigned for homework listening and/or discussed in class. Indicate the historical period of each composer, based on the stylistic characteristics of the music rather than merely on dates of birth and death. Also indicate the nationality of each composer in your list.

3. Write a simple, nontechnical definition of each genre listed below. Your answers should be comprehensible to your fellow students.

anthem
cantata
chorale prelude
Lied
liturgical drama
mass
passion

4. Explain the following technical terms:

binary form
cadenza
canon
continuo
cyclic form
ground bass
monophony
organ stop
organum
recitative
strophic form

5. Compare a Roman Catholic worship service of the seventeenth century with a Lutheran (Protestant) service of the same period with regard to the musical content typical of those services.

6. List briefly the differences between a standard set of variations and a passacaglia/chaconne. How do the structures of Monteverdi's *Vespers* (1610) and Bach's *Cantata No. 4* represent variational techniques?

7. Write a brief commentary on Aldous Huxley's use of music in the final chapter of *Point Counter Point*. Can you relate to his choice of music as an affirmation of

God's existence? Looking back on the music you have come to know this semester, can you select a composition suitable for having a literary work built around it? Give an outline of the kind of verbal context you imagine.

8. Compare the first movement of a late Tchaikovsky symphony (Nos. 4–6) with his tone poem *Romeo and Juliet* to determine the differences between a symphonic movement and a tone poem. Also, with regard to Berlioz's *Symphonie fantastique*, does this work seem to you more a coherent symphony or a loose set of tone poems?

MUSIC AND DEATH

Death engages our attention as does almost no other life experience. The cessation of life intrigues us even more than its inception, for although birth establishes us as living creatures, personal self-awareness itself comes only long after the act of birth is completed. Death, on the other hand, looms vividly ahead of us all through life. We read of the deaths of others, we live through the personal loss of loved ones, and, most important, we anticipate our own death. What will it be like—sudden or drawn out, painful

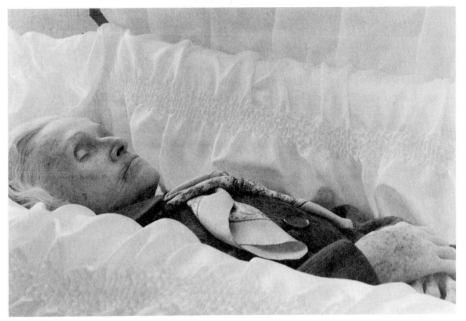

Photograph by Caldwell Colt

or merely gentle? Will we die young or live out a long and full life? And then what? The question of life after death has occupied people's minds since time immemorial. (By comparison, few concern themselves with the question of reincarnation from previous existences.) So, in a purely egoistic sense, death rates higher than birth and possibly represents the single most fascinating issue of our entire lives.

A powerful bond links the subject of death and the art of music. Death has consistently occupied the great composers, and the literature of death music is superlative both in its range and quality. Chapter 30 presents instrumental music of death, drawn mainly from the repertory of the dance and the tone poem. Chapter 31 takes up vocal music, including death songs for voice and piano, and death scenes from operas and musicals (the latter being excerpted mainly from works composed in English). Chapter 32 deals with memorial music of a liturgical nature. Finally, Chapter 33 considers the music of composers nearing death, and concludes with three works based on the concept of death transcended.

Much of the music of Unit VII is tinged with sadness, even despair. But you will also find signs of hope, faith, and even triumph. Death is a loss, and yet each death participates in the succession of generations, the procession of life. For without death there could be no life; death ultimately symbolizes less the denial of life than its affirmation. In keeping with this view, much of the music of death is inspirational in character. Some death music may bring you down, but more of it will lift you up. Explore the music of death in good cheer!

Music and Death

"DIES IRAE"

At the beginning of Kurt Weill's opera, *Mahagonny*, one of the characters steps up to the audience and announces, "What you are about to see is a dance of death." To which another character responds dubiously, "What in hell is a dance of death?" We find one answer to this enigmatic question in a recent study of the French author, Louis-Ferdinand Céline.

> Death [is] a kind of dancing master without whose tapping foot the round falters and halts, a piano tuner without whose intervention the music falls flat and has no tone . . . an ever-present factor in human existence, its contemplation constituting [in Céline's own words] "the primary concern of man." . . . It becomes a *leitmotif* which predominates, accompanies, disappears only to assert itself again, is always part of the orchestration.[1]

In other words, the dance of death is nothing less than life itself. Hans Holbein, the sixteenth-century German painter, created a series of engravings entitled "The Dance of Death" depicting skeletons, corpses, and other figures in a grim series of death images. Numerous musical compositions have taken up the same theme, literally setting the beat and calling the tune of death. The tune most commonly used is the ominous "Dies Irae," the Gregorian liturgical chant ("Day of wrath, that day when the ages shall vanish in ashes . . .") which Berlioz wove so effectively into his *Symphonie fantastique* (see Example 179). Other composers have created their own dances of death without borrowing from external sources. We shall examine a variety of these works, including the special music designed for death processionals, the funeral march. Then we shall explore one of the masterpieces of modern music, Stravinsky's *The Rite of Spring*, a ballet which culminates in the sacrifical death of a young virgin.

Franz Liszt, born in 1811, was one of the founders of the Romantic movement. He greatly admired Berlioz and dedicated his *Faust Symphony* to him. (Berlioz dedicated his opera, *Damnation of Faust*, to Liszt.) Liszt was undoubtedly impressed by the presence of "Dies Irae" in the *Symphonie fantastique*, for he subsequently composed a work based in its entirety on this medieval theme. The complete title is *Totentanz (Danse macabre)—Paraphrase on "Dies Irae."* The work was inspired by Andrea Orcagna's painting, *The Triumph of Death*.

> The fresco portrays a series of ghastly scenes. Death is flying towards her victims swinging a scythe. A heap of corpses lie at her feet. Souls are rising to heaven while others are being dragged down to the flames of hell. There are open graves containing decaying bodies.[2]

Totentanz is a concerto in one large movement for piano and orchestra. It begins as a set of variations on "Dies Irae." The theme is first presented by winds, brass. and lower strings, with the piano pounding out a clangorous accented *ostinato* (repeated figure). Over and over we hear the famous melody, sometimes for piano alone, but mostly for piano with orchestral support. Eventually a second Gregorian-style theme is introduced. Liszt was perhaps the greatest piano virtuoso of the nineteenth century, and in much of his piano music he devised previously unheard-of technical challenges. All throughout *Totentanz* we hear superb cadenzas running up and down the keyboard in the great Lisztian tradition (see Example 198).

Example 197
LISZT, *Totentanz*, Opening

Example 198
Totentanz, Piano Cadenza (Orchestra Tacit)

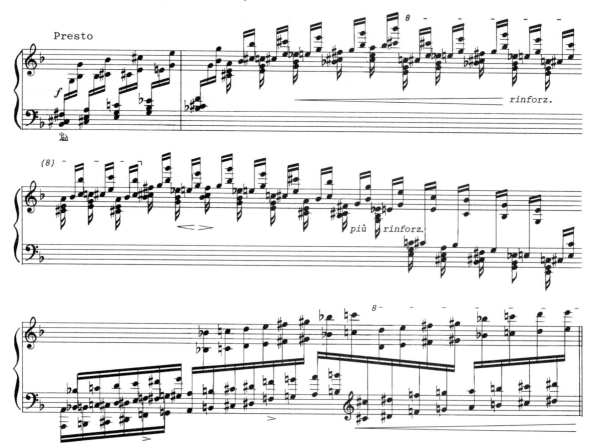

Sergei Rachmaninoff (1873–1943) was in many respects a musical descendant of Liszt. Both were outstanding concert pianists who left a large repertoire of virtuoso music for their chosen instrument. Rachmaninoff's *Rhapsody on a Theme of Paganini* is especially indebted to Liszt, who had earlier composed variations on the same theme (Paganini's familiar *Caprice in A Minor*).* Rachmaninoff's *Rhapsody* is a piano concerto of similar proportions to Liszt's *Totentanz*. Despite its title, it is essentially a set of variations (one of them is discussed in the essay on fugue, Chapter 16) which at one point introduces the "Dies Irae" as a secondary theme. In Variation 7 cellos and bassoons play the Paganini theme while the piano plays a gentle version of "Dies Irae."

*Brahms also composed two sets of pyrotechnical variations on Paganini's theme.

Music and Death

Example 199
RACHMANINOFF, *Rhapsody on a Theme of Paganini,*
Variation VII ("Dies Irae" in Piano Part)

Like *Totentanz*, Rachmaninoff's tone poem, *The Isle of the Dead*, was inspired by a painting of death—in this case, Arnold Böcklin's work of the same name. Once again Rachmaninoff exploited the medieval "Dies Irae" theme, mainly utilizing short fragments and providing a more complete verson thereof only in the very last measures of the work.

Arnold Böcklin's painting *Isle of the Dead*, which inspired Rachmaninoff's tone poem.

Courtesy Metropolitan Museum of Art

The Dance of Death

Probably the most famous short work containing the "Dies Irae" theme is Camille Saint-Saëns's tone poem, *Danse macabre*, composed in 1874. The piece is based on a poem by Henry Cazalis.

Zig, zig, zig, Death in cadence,
Striking with his hell a tomb,
Death at midnight plays a dance-tune,
Zig, zig, zig, on his violin.
The winter wind blows and the night is dark;
Moans are heard in the linden-trees.
Through the gloom, white skeletons pass,
Running and leaping in their shrouds.
Zig, zig, zig, each one is frisking,
The bones of the dancers are heard to crack —
But hsst! of a sudden they quit the round,
They push forward, they fly; the cock has crowed.

Saint-Saëns's music features two original themes and eventually also brings in "Dies Irae" in a mocking triple-meter version reminiscent of Berlioz's $\frac{6}{8}$ treatment in the finale of the *Symphonie fantastique* (see Example 180).

Example 200
Saint-Saëns, *Danse macabre* (*Dies Irae*)

A relatively recent instance of "Dies Irae" in an orchestral work is Ottorino Respighi's *Brazilian Impressions* (1929). Respighi had traveled to Brazil, visiting Butantan, a snake garden outside São Paolo. Here a wide assortment of poisonous snakes and vipers was housed as a source for antitoxin serums. The composer was so strongly impressed by this collection of death-dealing creatures that he worked the "Dies Irae" theme into his otherwise lyrical description of the lush tropical scene. A much more recent citation of this venerable medieval theme is found in George Crumb's *Black Angels for Electric String Quartet* (*Thirteen Images from the Dark Land*), composed in 1970. "Dies Irae" is heard in the fifth image, which is entitled "Dance Macabre."

The late Italian master, Luigi Dallapiccola, employed the "Dies Irae" theme in all three of his semi-twelve-tone *Prisoners' Songs* for chorus (1939–1941). This is a rare instance of our theme in a vocal, as opposed to purely instrumental work. (Strangely, none of the great musical settings of the Catholic Requiem liturgy include this theme as a setting of the "Dies Irae, Dies Illa" text — see Chapter 32.)

As one last example of a dance of death, we cite the second movement of Mahler's *Symphony No. 4*. Redlich describes it as follows:

The *Totentanz* of the second movement has the form of a scherzo, regularly alternating between "Maggiore" (Major) and "Minore" (Minor) sections, [with] two trios intersecting the returns of the scherzo. Its spectral climate is determined by the ghostly Solo-Violin asked to play "like an ancient fiddle" on specially retuned strings . . . [and] also by the devilish cackle of the chattering woodwinds.[3]

Music and Death

The writer also describes the "spookish Coda introduced by the kettledrums . . ., in which all the motifs reappear, as it were, at the wrong turning, only to disintegrate in broken fragments, ending disconsolately in the groans and hiccupping cello, blotted out by the heartless cackle of the woodwinds."

FUNERAL MARCHES

The music of the second movement of Mahler's *Symphony No. 4* owes nothing to borrowed traditional themes, but his *Symphony No. 1* presents a minor-mode version of "Frère Jacques" as a mock *funeral march*. This form has aroused the interest of numerous composers. Handel's *Saul* is noteworthy for a funeral march in the *major* mode. Beethoven composed a "Funeral March on the Death of a Hero" as the middle movement of his *Piano Sonata in A♭*, Op. 26, although he is much better known for the funeral march which constitutes the second movement of his *Eroica Symphony* (Chapter 15). The opening somber theme in the violins is accompanied by a "drum roll" in the contrabasses, unassisted by the cellos. (In Classical symphonies the basses usually simply double the cello part an octave lower; here is a rare case of the basses playing an independent part of their own.) Curiously, the tympani do not join the "drum roll." The melody is repeated by the oboe, accompanied by all the strings playing the drum roll figure, with the tympani now finally playing single notes at the end of each roll. The movement as a whole is a large-scale A–B–A, with a pensive theme in the B section, and a coda at the end of the second A section.

Example 201
BEETHOVEN, *Symphony No. 3,* "Eroica," 2nd Mvt. (Funeral March)

The Dance of Death

By tradition, the *Eroica* second movement is performed at public orchestra concerts following the death of a famous personage. Harry Ellis Dickson, in his otherwise merry summation of thirty-five years as a member of the Boston Symphony Orchestra, relates the following poignant episode concerning President John F. Kennedy:

> The Beethoven *Eroica Symphony* is carried automatically on all tours of the orchestra, to be played in case of the death of a famous person. When F.D.R. died in April, 1945, we got word on the train to Philadelphia and that night we played a memorial concert for the late President, including, of course, the Funeral March of the *Eroica*. As a matter of fact, this Beethoven *Third Symphony* has become a kind of symbol of sadness for us in the orchestra. The day J.F.K. was assassinated we had had word just before our Friday afternoon concert that he had been shot; how seriously we did not know until, after the first piece on the program, our two librarians suddenly appeared on the stage to hand out the music for the *Eroica*. Then we knew.[4]

Of all funeral marches, undoubtedly the best known is the third movement of Chopin's *Piano Sonata in B♭ Minor*. At one time people thought that Chopin had composed this piece just shortly before his death, as if to provide music for his own funeral. In fact, he wrote the piece in 1836 or 1837, some dozen years before he succumbed to tuberculosis, and just after starting his long-term liason with Baroness Aurore Dudevant, otherwise known as the writer, George Sand. As it happens, his funeral march did serve as the processional at Chopin's funeral, but the principal work performed—at his prior request—was Mozart's *Requiem*. (The bass soloist in this work had the remarkable distinction of having sung the same music twenty-two years earlier on the occasion of Beethoven's death.) The lovely less familiar *B* theme (in the major mode) should not be overlooked. Is it meant to suggest paradise? (See Example 203.)

Example 202
CHOPIN, *Piano Sonata in B♭ Minor, 3rd Mvt. (Funeral March)*

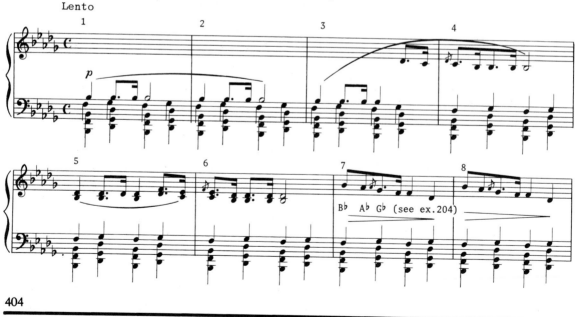

Music and Death

Example 203
Funeral March, Part 2

The last movement of the sonata is an extraordinary Presto, consisting exclusively of triplet octaves until a resounding tonic chord occurs in the last measure. A title, not Chopin's, has come to be associated with this brief movement: "Winds of Night Sweeping over Churchyard Graves."[5]

Jean Genet's existentialist brothel drama, *The Balcony* (1958) is the basis of Robert DiDomenica's opera of the same name (1972). At the end of scene 3 Genet calls for Chopin's *Funeral March* to be heard as one of Madame Irma's clients assumes the role of a glorious but dead general. In the spirit of Alban Berg, who worked the first four notes of Bach's "Es Ist Genug" into the tone row of his *Violin Concerto* (see Chapter 33 for a detailed analysis of this work), DiDomenica has used for Scene 3 a tone row which includes a three-note segment of the Chopin melody. That is, the first three notes of his row duplicate the first three melodic notes of the seventh measure of the Chopin march. (Compare Examples 202 and 204.) DiDomenica presents four measures of the funeral march in the orchestra alone. In measure 5, one of Irma's girls sings the first ten notes of the row as the orchestra continues with the unaltered Chopin extract. Three final measures of orchestra combine the funeral march in the trombones, the last two notes of the (girl's) row in the high harp, and other segments of the row in the upper strings. The tympani maintain a steady ostinato of a two-note figure, F-Gb. These two notes are featured throughout the first section of Chopin's march.

Example 204
ROBERT DIDOMENICA, *The Balcony,* Scene 3, Tone Row

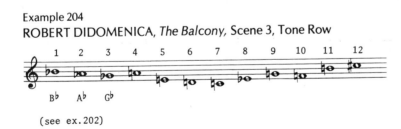

(see ex. 202)

The Dance of Death

Example 205

The Balcony, Scene 3, Ending

As we have noted, many examples of death music exhibit distinct traces of humor. This is certainly the case in Rachmaninoff's *Rhapsody*, Saint-Saëns's *Danse macabre*, and Mahler's *Symphony No. 1*. Two other instrumental works which treat death from a humorous standpoint are Richard Strauss's tone poem, *Till Eulenspiegel's Merry Pranks* (1895) and Michael Sahl's *A Mitzvah for the Dead* (1966). The former illustrates various adventures in the life of a German folk villain. Near the end of the work Till is sentenced to be hanged, and we hear the clarinet depict his climb up the ladder to the gallows. Oboes and English horn join the clarinet for the quiet descent. We hear Till's last gasp in the flute (a fortissimo *trill*); pizzicato strings over muted horns signify that he is dead.

Sahl's work is scored for solo violin accompanied by tape recording. The work consists of four movements, the first two for solo violin with a background of taped violin, the third for tape alone, and the fourth for unaccompanied violin. In view of its recent origin, as well as the inclusion of electronically generated sound, one might surmise that Sahl's music would exhibit modernistic atonal sounds to the exclusion of more traditional tonal configurations. However, quite to the contrary, the first movement opens with a Paganini-like *cadenza* (reminiscent of the midnineteenth century) with occasional superimposed electronic distortions that produce an effect of increased virtuosity. The whole thing is distinctly "schmaltzy," in a very supersentimental Romantic style. The tape accompaniment periodically interpolates strange noisy patches, but the solo violin proceeds undisturbed—thereby creating an extra dimension of manic humor. The music is exasperating, yet somehow enjoyable. The first movement ends with cascading major triads, followed by a coda which consistently repeats a phrase that sounds like a beginning rather than an ending.

The second movement is a lyrical—and again schmaltzy—solo played against a tape background of soft violin pyrotechnics. The third movement is a mish-mash of military band music, exploding guns, blaring trumpets, a tavern accordian—it's really nutty! The last movement is the strangest of all: a set of unaccompanied variations on the romantic song, "The Last Rose of Summer."

Music and Death

What was Sahl's purpose in writing this piece, and to what does the title refer? (*Mitzvah* is the Hebrew word for *blessing*.) To begin, the music originated as incidental music for a play about two men longing for the good old days in a little Polish town —

> its beauties, its culture, its cuisine, its women. So I decided to produce a larger-than-life violin sound, playing material they [the two men] might actually have heard, but in the grand, not to say, grandiose, manner, the way they imagined it sounded. This was broken into by all sorts of disorientating modernisms and distortion, much in the manner of a bad dream.[6]

The work pays homage to the sentimental past, and that is where the title comes in.

> The sense in which this piece is a mitzvah for the dead . . . is that it is an attempt to come to terms with the music of the dead and to write the kind of music that might have gratified them, had they heard it.[7]

STRAVINSKY, LE SACRE DU PRINTEMPS (THE RITE OF SPRING)

Who are the most important composers of the twentieth century? If we pass over Ravel, Debussy, Sibelius, and Richard Strauss — composers who had already achieved maturity and fame by the end of the nineteenth century — then we are likely to select three names: Schoenberg, Bartók, and Stravinsky. Since Bartók was a retiring personality whose music went almost unnoticed until after his death in 1946, we can safely state that Schoenberg and Stravinsky were the composers who wielded the greatest musical influence during the first half of this century. Although born within a few years of each other (Schoenberg in 1874, Stravinsky in 1882), these two musical giants nevertheless differed from one another in many important respects. Schoenberg was an Austrian Jewish intellectual who had to struggle to gain recognition from a begrudging musical public. Stravinsky belonged to the Russian upper class, subscribed to the Russian Orthodox faith, and easily rode to fame and fortune on the coattails of the great opera/ballet impresario, Sergei Diaghilev. Most significantly Schoenberg and Stravinsky — while both revolutionaries who helped tear down the previously secure fortress of tonal music — approached the problem of modernity in diametrically opposite ways. Schoenberg opted for *serialism* (i.e., the twelve-tone method — see Chapter 22), whereas Stravinsky turned to *neoclassicism* (see Chapter 31). (In his very last years Stravinsky also adopted serialism, but this was after the greater bulk of his music was already composed.) Finally, Schoenberg remained to the end a difficult, disgruntled, even unpopular personage in the musical world, whereas Stravinsky reached a position of eminence, love, and admiration. At his death Stravinsky was possibly the most popular musical figure of his time.

The Rite of Spring was composed by a man who studied with Rimsky-Korsakov, who loved the music of Mussorgsky, whose family was personally acquainted with Tchaikovsky, and who was devoted to the folklore of his native Russia. One might therefore reason that Stravinsky's music would carry on the Russian nationalist tradition of the nineteenth century (discussed in Chapter 7). Quite to the contrary, Stravinsky broke away from the prevaling musical traditions of his childhood, developing instead a unique approach to composition that appears to have had no antecedents in

The Dance of Death

Igor Stravinsky (1882–1971) developed a unique compositional approach that appears to have had minimal roots in the Romantic period. Photograph by Alvin Langdon Coburn.

the Romantic period. This is not to suggest that Stravinsky's music is totally disconnected from the past—in his neoclassical music there is very strong connection indeed —but it is to say that the originality of Stravinsky's music, even more than Schoenberg's (who started out, after all, as a post-Wagnerian, like Strauss and Mahler), created its own ambience, its own special niche.

The Rite of Spring seems to have sprung from nowhere, an intentional effect, no doubt, for Stravinsky wished to create an atmosphere of primitive paganism. The music was composed as a ballet, the scenario of which starts with the reawakening of the earth, the stirring of sonambulent forces. It then moves on to pagan worship. A young virgin is chosen to be sacrificed to the gods, and in the final scene the girl dances herself to death. To suggest a time long past, a primordial community living in a hazy Russian setting, Stravinsky needed to abandon as many characteristics of the Western musical tradition as possible. This meant the surrender of melody in the Classical-Romantic tradition, replacing it with short motivic phrases characteristic of ancient Russian folksong. It also required a new treatment of motivic ideas; by constructing melodic phrases which recur over and over again without alteration, Stravinsky avoided the kind of transformational development associated with the Classical-Romantic symphonic style. Traditional triadic harmony is not so much abandoned as restructured;

Music and Death

many of Stravinsky's dissonant chords are actually polytonal combinations of familiar triads and seventh chords. Thus, the second section of Part I, the "Dance of the Adolescents," is based on a single dissonant chord which breaks down into an E♭ dominant seventh chord superimposed over an F♭(E♮) major triad.

Example 206
STRAVINSKY, *The Rite of Spring*, "Dance of the Adolescents"

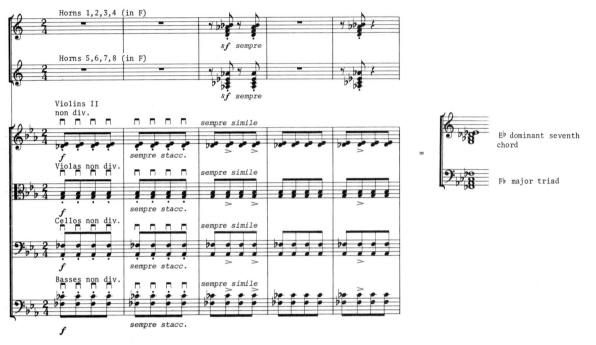

Undoubtedly the most important feature of Stravinsky's new style was its emancipation of rhythm. Rhythm took over, becoming almost the most important ingredient of his musical mix. The musical texture is replete with ostinatos—repeated patterns of chords, motives, and accompanimental figures. The complexity of the music shows little evidence of the developmental techniques used by Bach, Beethoven, Brahms, and others; rather the texture is effected through a process of musical *addition*. That is, Stravinsky would gradually accumulate as many as a dozen different rhythmic figures, eventually combining them into one simultaneous outburst. One need only listen to the Introduction to Part I to perceive this effect. Initially one hears a lone high bassoon, playing a simple motive in conjunction with contrapuntal lines scored for French horn, two clarinets, and bass clarinet. Other instruments gradually join in, suggesting the sounds of slowly awakening animals, birds, and other creatures. There is a vast and varied array of instruments, many of which repeat the same melodic patterns over and over, but always in different timbral and rhythmic combinations. Eventually a state of harmonic stasis is reached, a panoramic accumulation of nature sounds.

Example 207
The Rite of Spring, Part 1, Opening

Example 208
Part 1, Grand Tutti, "a panoramic accumulation of nature sounds"
Facing Page

Music and Death

(Lento)

411

The Dance of Death

Stravinsky was a genius of rhythmic ingenuity. Repeating part or all of the chord illustrated in Example 206, he could produce an exciting sense of natural urgency, introducing hardly any other musical components—as if the entire orchestra were a percussion section, generating constant energy, churning up an ever-changing kaleidoscope of musical evocations. It has been said of *The Rite of Spring* that its musical power is so great that it hampers the creation of balletic choreography good enough to match it. (And Stravinsky himself was extremely critical of Njinsky's original choreographic conceptions.) At any rate, *The Rite* is now mainly a concert piece, one that holds a position of preeminence among twentieth-century compositions for orchestra.

Some of the maidens in a scene from the first performance (1913) of *The Rite of Spring*.

This makes all the more fascinating the fact that at its première in Paris (1913), a riot brought the performance to a virtual standstill. The noise from the audience was so loud that the dancers could barely hear the orchestra. Of course, a musical public raised on the niceties of nineteenth-century ballet—with fairy tales prettily danced to sweet, often innocuous melodies—could hardly be blamed for reacting in shock to music of such extreme novelty.

> No one had ever heard music like it before; it seemed to violate all the most hallowed concepts of beauty, harmony, tone, and expression. Never had an audience heard music so brutal, savage, aggressive, and apparently chaotic; it hit the public like a hurricane, like some uncontrolled primeval force.[8]

Those present at this tumultuous occasion were witnessing a fundamental breakdown of the old musical order, a true beginning of modern musical culture. The world of music was never to be the same again.

In physical stature Stravinsky was diminutive; all others towered over him. Yet in musical terms he was a giant. In 1965, as a renowned master, Stravinsky returned to the *pension* in Vevey, Switzerland, where he had composed *Le Sacre*. Amazingly a Madame Rumpert was still there some fifty-four years after the Stravinsky family had resided there. She recalled that the other residents complained that the young composer "played only wrong notes." To this Stravinsky replied, "They were the wrong notes for them but the right ones for me."[9] Stravinsky eventually lived to see the world accept his notes as the right ones for them too. His ballet was even featured in one of the most popular films of all time, Walt Disney's *Fantasia* (1940).

Part II of *The Rite of Spring* is called "The Sacrifice," and it is this portion of the work which pertains specifically to the music of death. It begins with a pensive introduction, which then leads into the "Mysterious Circle of the Adolescents," a relatively

Example 209
The Rite of Spring, "Glorification
of the Chosen Victim"

The Dance of Death

slow section, followed in turn by the wild syncopated glorification of the chosen victim. After "Evocation of the Ancestors" and further ritualistic dancing, we come to the finale, the "Danse sacrale" ("Sacrificial Dance"). This passage is famous for its repetitive irregularity—a paradoxical description, no doubt, yet accurate, for Stravinsky brilliantly combined metrical unpredictability with constantly recurring ostinato motives.

Example 210
"Danse sacrale"

Music and Death

This final portion of *Le Sacre* represents a *rondo*, a form in which contrasting episodes alternate with a steady refrain. The preceding example represents the beginning of the refrain, or *A* section. A mysterious pianissimo figure introduces the first episode, or *B* section—a set of variations on a pair of motives, but with no genuine theme. The refrain (*A*) returns, followed by an even more tumultuous *C* section. The remainder of the "Sacrificial Dance" combines elements of sections *A* and *C*, the *C* motive sounding out ever more forcefully. The dance reaches a state of frenzy; finally, after a brief pause in all the instruments, it climaxes with a crashing knell. The demands of nature's annual cycle have been fulfilled—the chosen one has completed her dance of death.

Example 211

"Danse sacrale," C Section

Music and Death

The Dance of Death

31 THE VOICE OF DEATH

The subject of death has engendered a large repertoire of vocal music. Dividing this repertoire into two categories, staged and unstaged, we shall be dealing in this chapter primarily with (1) scenes from operas and musicals and (2) solo songs accompanied by piano. Taking up the latter category first, we will encounter songs in German, Russian, and English. The second part of the chapter presents five death scenes, three from opera and two from the Broadway stage.

SONGS OF DEATH

One of the more popular types of death song presents a dialogue between Death (personified) and a human being on the verge of dying. A well-known example is Schubert's "Der Tod und das Mädchen" ("Death and the Maiden"). The form of the song is a simple A–B–A; that is, the first and last sections are similar, whereas the middle section is based on a different melody and faster tempo. The opening A section—a slow piano introduction—embodies the solemn overtones of death. In the second section, the girl anxiously addresses Death: "Pass me by . . . I am still young." The tempo picks up accordingly. In the final section, Death replies in the dirgelike mood of the piano introduction, soothingly inviting the girl to cease resisting his charms. (Schubert used the principal musical material of this song as the theme of the second movement of his *String Quartet in D Minor*. The quartet is generally known by the title of the song. George Crumb also used the same material in one section of his electrified string quartet, *Black Angels*.)

Example 212
SCHUBERT, "Death and the Maiden," Piano Introduction

Perhaps the single best known German *lied* is Schubert's "Erlkönig" ("Erlking") (1814). Schubert was just seventeen years old when he composed this setting of Goethe's poem. The text involves a three-way conversation among a child, his father, and the erlking. The American Heritage Dictionary defines *erlking* as "an evil spirit of Germanic mythology and folklore, typically represented as a perpetrator of cruel tricks

William Strang's *Death and the Ploughman's Wife* (1894) illustrates the spirit of dialogue songs of death such as Schubert's "Erlkönig" and the second of Mussorgsky's *Songs and Dances of Death*.

on children." As the song begins, the father and his son are riding toward home late at night. The child tells his father he sees and hears the erlking, but the father repeatedly tries to calm the boy, insisting it is merely fog, wind, or rustling trees. As in many poems of this kind, Death (or his surrogate) is presented as considerate and thoughtful, winning "converts" by spinning attractive tales of peaceful happiness. In this case the erlking promises to play games with the child and commands his daughters to dance and sing for him. Only once does the erlking threaten force. The child cries out in pain, and, as they finally arrive at home, the boy is dead.

The piano introduction of "Erlkönig" projects a rushing effect arising from repeated triplet octaves in the right hand over an energetic "motion" figure in the left hand.*

Example 213
SCHUBERT, "Erlkönig," Opening

*The "Erlkönig" accompaniment is one of the most difficult in the song literature. Liszt made a piano transcription of the song which is even harder to play. The Liszt transcription is one of several pieces referred to in George Bernard Shaw's little known but extremely witty one-act play, *The Music Cure—A Piece of Utter Nonsense* (1913).

419

The Voice of Death

Key changes occur frequently, as the father (singing in a low range) reassures the child, and the child (in a high range) continually expresses fear. Like the child, the erlking also sings in high tones, but with a slightly different accompaniment figure. After the erlking's first ingratiating speech, the right-hand octaves return, as the child anxiously inquires, "Father, father, don't you hear what the erlking is promising me?" At the same time the left hand plays a menacing figure. This figure recurs twice, each time at the words, "Mein Vater, mein Vater" ("Father, oh Father") and a step higher in the scale. The dramatic climax of the poem—the boy's death—occasions a new element in the music: the piano pauses, and the last line of the vocal text is sung as recitative.

Example 214
"Erlkönig," The Fearful Child, Accompanied by Menacing Piano Octaves

Music and Death

Example 215
"Erlkönig," Conclusion

Another remarkable dialogue song of death is Mahler's "Das irdische Leben" ("The Earthly Life"), its text drawn from the German folk collection, *The Youth's Magic Horn*. Mahler left us two versions of this song, one with simple piano accompaniment, the other with orchestra. The song deals with no imaginary perpetrator of cruel tricks, as in Schubert's "Erlkönig"; rather, it confronts the very real specter of starvation, which is all too familiar today in large sections of Asia and Africa. The song opens with a child begging his mother for food: "Give me bread, or surely I shall die!" The mother assures the boy that he need only wait one more day for the harvest to commence. After the corn has been brought in, the child again implores his mother for bread. Again she puts him off, saying that they will thresh the corn tomorrow. Again the child's warning lament, and again the mother's reassuring response: "Tomorrow we shall bake." The song ends abruptly as the bread at last is ready—but too late, for the child is dead. Although the words were recorded nearly two hundred years ago, they tell a story that is happening right now with ever greater frequency throughout the third world.

Modeste Mussorgsky composed a wonderful cycle of four *Songs and Dances of Death*. Stylistically these songs bear a strong resemblance to the composer's Russian nationalist opera, *Boris Godunov* (see Chapter 7). The second song is a dialogue between Death and the mother of a small child. Over and over you hear Death's soothing lullaby, "Bayushki, bayu, bayu" ("Hush, baby, hush, hush"). As in other songs of this type, Death claims to be more healing, more comforting than the mother: "You have failed to comfort your little one; I can do it better." The mother begs Death to leave off his infernal singing; he assents, but only after the child is truly and eternally asleep.

The other three songs in this set are monologues sung by Death. In the first and third songs Death displays a soothing, inviting demeanor—assuaging fears, comforting the wounded. But in Song 4, "The Commander," Death appears in all his ferocious splendor, bragging of his power and spreading a message which should be the watchword of all opponents of war: "The battle is over, and I alone am the winner. I have defeated *both* sides, for all you enemies in life are now united in *my* army. And when everyone else has forgotten you, I shall still remember." This is certainly one of the most thrilling songs ever written.

Other death songs of the military/battle type are Schumann's "The Two Grenadiers" and Mahler's "Reveille" and "The Drummer Boy." The farewell of the drummer boy, about to be executed, is especially moving. "Reveille" is a macabre song about a dead soldier who returns to visit his sweetheart. Both of these Mahler songs are based on the *Youth's Magic Horn* poetry collection. Schumann's *The Two Grenadiers*, based on a poem by Heine, is a dialogue between two soldiers returning to France after being captured in Russia during the Napoleonic invasion. Feeling that he is about to die, one of the soldiers asks the other to carry his corpse back to France and bury him armed with sword and rifle—so as to be ready to rise from the grave to fight again whenever his emperor might need him. The opening of the song creates a heavy minor atmosphere, catching the swagger of the grenadiers. The last two verses introduce the French national anthem, the "Marseillaise":

Example 216

SCHUMANN, "The Two Grenadiers" ("Marseillaise")

Till the roar of can-non re-sounds thro' the gloom, And
bis einst ich hö-re Ka-no-nen-ge-brüll und

tramp of the horse-men spur-ring. Then o-ver my grave will my
wie-hern-der Ros-se Ge-tra-be. Dann rei-tet mein Kai-ser wohl

Em-per-or ride, While swords with clash are de-scen-ding,
ü-ber mein Grab, viel Schwer-ter klir-ren und bli-tzen,

We move now into the twentieth century. An unusual vocal work in a contemporary idiom is J. K. Randall's *Mudgett: Monologues of a Mass Murderer* for soprano and electronic tape (1965). This piece presents episodes in the career of a mass murderer, Herman Webster Mudgett, who was executed in 1896. After an intense "Electronic Prelude," the soprano commences a simple ballad in English. But later the same performer, while still singing on one track, recites on another track excerpts from the libretto of Wagner's *Tristan und Isolde* (in German). (Since the work is scored for only one solo singer, it can obviously be performed only on a recording.) Randall has skillfully combined the speaking and singing voice, constructing a bizarre "dialogue" out of Mudgett's monologues and Wagner's poetry. The work is available on the recording *Computer Music*, Nonesuch Records H-71245.

While all the songs described above are typical in their serious depiction of death, not all songs of death radiate lugubrious overtones. A good case in point is "Charlie Rutlage," by the pioneer American composer, Charles Ives (see Chapter 8). This delightful good-natured song is about a cowboy who takes a bad fall, is killed, and (it is hoped) goes to heaven. The song starts out innocently like a folk-song, with an easy-going cowboy rhythm in the piano part and a simple swaggering tune for the singer:

Example 217
IVES, "Charlie Rutlage"

424

Music and Death

(Ives found the text in a collection called *Cowboy Songs and Frontier Ballads*, edited by John A. Lomax and published by The Macmillan Company.)

In the second part of the song, the singer *speaks* the text in rhythmic patterns (indicated by the composer), while the piano creates a suspenseful background of steadily increasing intensity. At the words "Caused by a cowhorse falling, while running after stock," the piano part adds the traditional cowboy melody "Whoopee ti yi yo, git along little dogies" above the noisy background. The pianist plays progressively louder and wilder until reaching a climax on the words "Another turned; at that moment his horse the creature spied and turned and fell with him." The accompaniment explodes into *chord clusters* effected by the pounding of both fists on the keyboard. With the words "Beneath poor Charlie died . . ." the soloist switches back to singing, and suddenly the original tune resumes: "His relations in Texas never more will see, But I hope he'll meet his loved ones beyond in eternity . . ." As the soloist sings, "[at] the shining throne of grace," the song breaks off — as if in musical midsentence, and concludes with a traditional I-IV-I Amen cadence as at the end of a hymn.

DEATH SCENES

In the realm of music theater, two subjects contend the most for composers' attentions — love and death. Indeed, these two subjects are virtually inseparable, as countless examples from opera attest: *Tristan und Isolde, La Traviata, La Bohème, Salome,* and *Otello,* among others. It is almost as if love were a guarantee that death, like Mary's proverbial lamb, was sure to follow. We shall now examine five death scenes, four of which are based on original English texts. Henry Purcell's *Dido and Aeneas,* composed in 1689, represents the oldest English opera still in regular production. By contrast, Igor Stravinsky's *The Rake's Progress* (1951) is one of the most recent additions to the roster of widely sung English-language operas. Dating from 1920, Erik Satie's *Socrate* is a unique French blend lying somewhere between opera, oratorio, and solo song. Leonard Bernstein's *West Side Story* (1956) is a musical adapted from the Romeo and Juliet legend, and Mitch Leigh's Broadway show, *Man of La Mancha* (1965), is derived from the ancient Spanish legend of Don Quixote.

Purcell, Dido and Aeneas

Henry Purcell (1659–1695) was the finest English composer of the second half of the seventeenth century. His output consisted mainly of instrumental chamber music, religious and secular vocal music, and incidental music for masques and other theater pieces. Without doubt the jewel of his musical creation was the short opera, *Dido and Aeneas.* Composed for a girls' school, the opera's three acts last barely an hour in performance. The story is based on events occurring after the fall of Troy. Aeneas, a survivor of the Trojan Wars, has arrived in Carthage intending to found a dynasty with Dido, the beautiful Queen of Carthage. Dignified and imperious, she hesitatingly accepts Aeneas's declarations of love. Fate intervenes, however, in the form of a mischievous sorceress and her covy of witches who connive to persuade Aeneas to leave Carthage for Italy (where he is destined to found the city of Rome). Aeneas unsuspectingly accepts the mission (ostensibly delivered by the god Mercury, but actually by a witch in disguise), planning an early return to pursue his nuptial goals. But the wound to Dido's vanity and honor are too serious; she not only dismisses him forever, but vows to die ignominiously by suicide. He offers to cancel his trip, but to no avail. The more he insists on staying, the more determinedly she bades him be off. Eventually she gets the last word, and he departs.

The synopsis just given suggests a mixture of theatrical and psychological nonsensicality compared to which a typical Gilbert and Sullivan plot might seem pretentious. Nevertheless, Purcell's treatment of Dido's approaching death represents one of the most beautiful and moving of operatic scenes. The text, by Nahum Tate, is both quaint and touching. In an opening recitative, Dido sings

Thy hand, Belinda! Darkness shades me,
On thy bosom let me rest.
More I would, but death invades me.
Death is now a welcome guest.

Coming directly after the lovers' parting "I'll stay/No go!" exchange, this brief passage is a marvel of musical sleight-of-hand, preparing us for Dido's final aria. This is a solemn lament constructed over a ground bass, a descending bass line that is repeated continuously throughout the aria (see Bach's "Crucifixus" from the *Mass in B Minor*, Chapter 24). Above the ground bass, a stately melody expresses Dido's bruised feelings. The opera concludes as the chorus sings, "With drooping wings, ye Cupids, come and scatter roses on her tomb . . ." Appropriately, by way of "drooping," the music proceeds through a descending minor scale.

Example 218
PURCELL, *Dido and Aeneas*, Dido's Lament

(Numerals represent *figured bass* notation. The keyboard player "realizes" chords above the given bass line, in accordance with the numerals; e.g., $^6_5$ below F♯ specifies a chord with F♯ in the bass, and also containing a C and a D, five and six notes above F♯.)

Music and Death

Stravinsky, The Rake's Progress

No name looms larger in the history of twentiety-century music than Igor Stravinsky. Born in 1882, this native Russian moved to France and created a sensation with his early ballets, *Firebird*, *Petrouschka*, and *The Rite of Spring* (see Chapter 30). These works are essentially atonal, consistent with the experiments being made at the same time by the Austrian Arnold Schoenberg, the American Charles Ives, and others. Subsequently Stravinsky joined the vanguard of *neoclassical* composers; starting with his chamber ballet, *Histoire du soldat* (The Soldier's Tale) (1917), he returned to tonality, albeit in a distinctly modern manner. *Neoclassicism* was a movement, essentially framed in time by the two world wars, in which composers freely adapted Classical formulae —melodic patterns, rhythmic devices, major and minor keys, and tonal gestures of all sorts—in such a way that their music sounded simultaneously old and new. From the standpoint of the past, much of the neoclassical output sounds like Classical music with wrong notes. Compared with other twentieth-century movements, neoclassical music often sounds downright old-fashioned.

Stravinsky retained his commitment to Neoclassicism until about 1950, at which time he switched to the twelve-tone system (see Chapter 22). His last major neoclassical work was the opera, *The Rake's Progress*. Stravinsky composed this work in collaboration with the Nobel poet laureate, W. H. Auden, assisted by Chester Kallmann; it is the only opera he set originally in English.

The setting of the drama is eighteenth-century (Classical) England, making it entirely fitting for the composer to have framed it in a quasi-Classical style. The story of *The Rake's Progress* was immortalized in a series of prints (of the same title) by the emi-

The story of Stravinsky's *The Rake's Progress* had been immortalized in a series of prints by the eighteenth-century English engraver, William Hogarth. Right, *Bedlam*, the London insane asylum where Tom Rakewell ends his days.

nent English painter and engraver, William Hogarth (1697–1764). The opera concerns the adventures of one Tom Rakewell, whose personality represents a cross between Faust and Don Giovanni. Tom unwittingly sells his soul to the devil, in the personage of his servant, Nick Shadow. In keeping with the names of the main characters—Tom's faithful fiancée is Anne Truelove and the madame of a London brothel is Mother Goose—this morality tale is told with amusing flair, but nothing could be sadder than Tom's end. Under the terms of their agreement, Tom is granted all his wishes for a year and a day, after which he must pay Nick's wages. Tom has naïvely assumed that the wages were to be paid in the coin of the realm, but Nick now lays claim to Tom's soul. Standing by an open grave, Nick offers Tom a choice of weapons with which to do himself in before midnight. Ominously the clock begins to strike twelve times. At the stroke of nine, however, time stops and Nick offers a game: Tom shall live if he can guess three cards Nick has selected from a deck. Amazingly Tom guesses all three cards correctly; thereafter, having lost his power over Tom's soul, Nick himself sinks grumbling into the grave. As a last evil trick, however, Nick robs Tom of his sanity. As the last scene of the opera opens, poor demented Tom is found in Bedlam, a London insane asylum, surrounded by others of like affliction.

As is characteristic of neoclassical music, the opening measures of this scene offer Classical styles (à la Gluck and Mozart) mixed with a certain dissonant modernity. The orchestra is of Classical proportions, consisting merely of pairs of winds and brass, plus tympani and strings, with harpsichord for the recitative passages. Some of the tunes are even suggestive of Classical models—for example, Anne's Act I aria recalls her namesake's (Donna Anna's) aria from Act I of Mozart's *Don Giovanni*.

At the opening of the Bedlam scene, Tom, believing himself to be Adonis (a legendary Greek youth of extraordinary beauty), announces the impending arrival of "Venus, the Queen of Love, who will pay a visit to her unworthy Adonis." The chorus of madpeople (sanely) protests that he is crazy and then proceeds to chant a jaunty minuet equating Bedlam with Hell. (Paraphrasing a line from Dante's *Inferno*, "Abandon all hope, ye who enter here," they sing, "Leave all hope and love behind.") As the keeper approaches, the chorus runs offstage in fear. Anne Truelove enters, but Tom ignores her when she calls him by name. Only when she gently calls out (at the Keeper's suggestion), "Adonis," does Tom respond, exclaiming, "Venus, my queen, my bride. At last." He then sings a truly Mozartian *arioso* (usually a cross between a recitative and an aria but in this case simply a brief aria).

Example 219
STRAVINSKY, *The Rake's Progress*, Act III, Tom's Arioso

I have wai - ted, I have wai - ted for thee so long, till ___

Music and Death

Sitting at Anne's feet, Tom confesses his sins (one of them being that he had abandoned Anne and married a bearded circus lady, Baba the Turk) over an accompaniment that recalls Bach's passion music (see Chapter 25). Anne generously insists that there is nothing to forgive, and the piece ends as a sweetly ornamented duet.

Example 220
The Rake's Progress, Final Duet

Tom is now exhausted, and Anne sings him a folksong-like lullaby. It is in three verses, with interspersed commentary from the offstage chorus of madpersons. As Tom sleeps, Anne's father, Mr. Truelove, enters and tells her to come home with him. After they leave, Tom awakes, panicked by the absence of his Venus. The madpeople deny anyone has been there. With allusions to the song of the dying swan, the laments of Orpheus, and the death of Adonis, Tom—broken in mind and spirit—dies. The scene closes with a simple, stark dirge sung by the chorus.

Satie, Socrate

Erik Satie (1866–1925) was a French composer whose name is now linked with the ideals of the Dada movement. The American Heritage Dictionary defines *Dada* as

a Western European artistic and literary movement (1916–1923) having as its program the discovery of authentic reality through the abolition of traditional cultural and aesthetic forms by a technique of comic derision in which irrationality, chance, and intuition were the guiding principles.

Satie was undoubtedly a comic genius, as one can infer from the titles of his pieces—for example, *Three Flabby Pieces for a Dog* and *Dessicated Embryos*. His *Troix Morceaux en forme de Poire* (*Three Pieces in the Shape of a Pear*) for piano four-hands was a response to Debussy's complaint that his music lacked form. (The French word *forme* translates into English either as *form* or *shape*.) Ironically, the work consists of not just three pieces, but seven, and aside from the humorous title, the music itself is gently amusing. As a composer, Satie had little direct impact on musical culture, and today his music is probably more discussed than played. He seems most important as a progenitor of the modern "Dada" movement, as represented by John Cage and others (Chapter 20).

Given this background, Satie's *Socrate* (1920) stands out as a beautiful and serious work. Based on dialogues of Plato, the ancient Greek philosopher, the text consists of discussions between Socrates and his disciples (in French). The roles and narration are sung by female voices exclusively. The musical style of *Socrate* recalls the monodic recitative championed in early Baroque opera (e.g., Monteverdi's *Combattimento di Tancredi e Clorinda*). The music is extremely simple and direct, emphasizing the words (which are never repeated for the sake of musical design) and avoiding melody for its own sake. Even harmony seems unimportant, and the orchestra always plays discreetly "under" the singers. Composer Ned Rorem has aptly described Satie's approach:

> The words of Plato are not illustrated, not interpreted, by the music: they are framed by the music, and the frame is not a period piece; rather, it is from all periods. Which is what makes the music so difficult to identify. Is it from modern France? Ancient Greece? or from the time of Pope Gregory?[1]

Or, as suggested, from the time of early Baroque opera? Rorem goes on to speak of Satie's "absolutely original way with the tried and true. . . . The music is not 'ahead' of its time, but rather . . . outside of time, allowing the old, old dialogues of Plato to sound so always new."[2]

The last section describes Socrates' stoical acceptance of his death sentence. Having challenged and affronted the governmental authorities, he is required to drink the fatal hemlock—a situation with obvious parallels to the crucifixion of Christ. (But

Jacques Louis David (1748–1825), *The Death of Socrates*. Based on Plato, Erik Satie's *Socrates* stands out as a beautiful work. The music is extremely simple and direct, "outside of time, allowing the old dialogues of Plato to sound so always new" (Ned Rorem).

no greater musical contrast will be found than between Satie's bare style and Bach's elaborate passion music.) With regard to the death of Socrates, the historian Grout has written: "*Socrate* . . ., particularly in the last scene . . . attains a poignancy which is intensified by the very monotony of the style and studied avoidance of direct emotional appeal."[3]

Although *Socrate* is occasionally mounted as a stage production, it is basically a concert piece—one that is performed all too rarely.

430

Music and Death

Bernstein, West Side Story

In the history of music few individuals can match the versatility of Leonard Bernstein (b. 1918). Concert pianist, virtuoso conductor, brilliant lecturer, and television personality, he is also a composer equally deft in the worlds of classical and popular music. We have already encountered his *Kaddish Symphony* (Chapter 26), and in Chapter 29 we touched upon *West Side Story*. Arthur Laurent's stageplay for this Broadway hit is an ingenious adaptation (perhaps we should say "derivation") of Shakespeare's *Romeo and Juliet*. Here we have two rival gangs (instead of two rival families), the "Jets"—an American melting-pot mixture of Italian, Polish, and other ethnic backgrounds—and the newly arrived, unassimilated Puerto Rican "Sharks." Tony (short for Anton, a Polish name) and the Puerto Rican Maria represent the roles of Romeo and Juliet. They fall in love at first sight at a community center dance. The two gangs agree to a "rumble." Maria's brother, Bernardo (Tybalt), kills Tony's best friend, Riff (Mercutio); Tony, like Romeo originally a peacemaker, avenges Mercutio's death by killing Bernardo. All the violence notwithstanding, the love between Tony and Maria grows strong and holds fast. Tony hides out in the basement of Doc the druggist (Friar Laurence), who lends him money to escape. But a misunderstanding arises: Doc gives Tony a message from Anita saying that Maria's ex-boyfriend has killed her. Bereft, Tony runs into the street inviting his death at the hands of Chico, Maria's supposed killer. Suddenly he sees Maria, who is unharmed. As they run toward each other a gun fires, and Tony falls mortally wounded. At this point, the entire company assembles, and Maria (assuming the role of Shakespeare's Prince of Verona) demands that the warring gangs make peace. Sheakespeare's lines

> Where be these enemies? Capulet, Montague,
> See what a scourge is laid upon your hate,
> That heaven finds means to kill your joys with love!
> And I, for winking at your discords too,
> Have lost a brace of kinsmen. All are punish'd.

are transformed into Maria's simple shout, "We all killed him!"

The deaths of Riff and Bernardo occur in the musical number, "Rumble," which concludes Act I. The chaotic music matches the shouting of the boys, with snatches of the earlier Jets' music. Tony's death comes just before the end of Act II, preceded by Maria's song, "I Have a Love." This song quotes (perhaps unintentionally) the "Redemption through Love" *Leitmotif* from Wagner's *Ring* cycle.

Example 221a

WAGNER, *Götterdämmerung* (*Twilight of the Gods*), Conclusion, "Redemption Through Love" *Leitmotif*

The Voice of Death

Example 221b
BERNSTEIN, *West Side Story*, "I Have a Love"

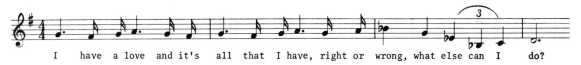

I have a love and it's all that I have, right or wrong, what else can I do?

After Tony is shot, Maria comforts him in her arms and reprises the *Dream Scene* with its message of hope, "There's a Place for Us." At the line "Hold my hand and we're halfway there," Tony starts to sing, but he cannot go on. The chorus completes the passage with "Somehow, somehow," and the orchestra concludes with a mixture of the two notes of "somehow" (an ascending major second), the minor seventh of "There's a," and the "Redemption Theme" from Maria's last song (Example 221b). Bernstein has upheld the long-standing operatic tradition of accompanying the actuality of death with a reprise of music of love and hope. (Earlier models include Verdi's *La Traviata* and *Otello*, Wagner's *Tristan und Isolde* and *Götterdämmerung*, and Puccini's *La Bohème*.)

Leigh, Man of La Mancha

The subject of death ordinarily receives little attention in popular music, and Broadway musicals generally feature happy endings. Thus, with its exceptional tragic dénouement, *West Side Story* was something of a landmark on the Broadway stage. A Broadway show with a very different kind of death scene is Mitch Leigh's *Man of La Mancha* (1965). This is the story of the foolhardy knight of chivalry, Don Quixote, and his creator, Don Miguel de Cervantes (1547–1616). Cervantes, having been imprisoned by the Spanish Inquisition, spends his time in jail enacting for his fellow prisoners scenes from his novel, *Don Quixote*. After numerous misadventures, the old knight lies dying, barely able to remember the words of his quest, "The Impossible Dream." Just as Mussorgsky's Boris Godunov cries out at his impending death, "I still am Tsar!" (Chapter 7), Don Quixote temporarily regains his strength and repeats his song, "Man of La Mancha." Finally the end is at hand, and a priest intones in Latin the opening of Psalm 130, "Out of the Depths I Cry to Thee, O Lord." (These words have also been set by numerous classical composers, such as Bach and Schoenberg.)

All along we have been witnessing a play within a play, with Cervantes himself enacting the role of his muddle-headed hero. After Don Quixote expires, Cervantes removes his knightly costume, resumes his own personality, and cheerfully goes off to face his inquisition.

Gustave Doré: *Don Quixote in his Library*, dreaming of great adventures and his quest for "The Impossible Dream."

The Voice of Death

MEMORIAL MUSIC

The event of death ordinarily brings forth surviving friends and family for some sort of gathering—if not a religious funeral, then at least a nonreligious memorial meeting. Memorial services provide us with an opportunity to acknowledge the extraordinary fact of death (extraordinary despite its commonness), its unremedial, unrelenting reality. To many mourners funeral ceremonies are still more important for the sake of the deceased. For example, in the Roman Catholic liturgy, funeral rites send off the departed in peace, to seek everlasting rest amidst the blessings of Heaven. The Requiem text (*requiem* means *rest*) includes some terrifying warnings about the Day of Judgment ("Dies Irae"), along with portions of the ordinary Mass for the Living (the "Kyrie," "Sanctus," and "Agnus Dei").

The devout of earlier times believed in the efficacy of these rites. In 1474, the composer Guillaume Dufay wrote a will decreeing that his motet, "Ave Regina Coelorum," be performed immediately upon his death. The text is a traditional Latin anthem, addressed to the Virgin Mary: "Hail, Queen of Heaven, Hail, Mistress of the Angels." Dufay added several extra lines of text, including "Miserere tui labentis Dufay, Peccatorum ruat in ignem fervorum," which means "Have pity on thy dying Dufay, Cast into the burning fire." Dufay also requested that a Requiem Mass be performed later at his funeral.[1]

Most composers have not gone as far as Dufay in personalizing their mourning music; even the dying Mozart, working feverishly on his *Requiem*, did not insert his own name into the text. But over the centuries composers have produced a great body of music generally applicable to those who have died. For example, Mozart's *Requiem* was performed at the interments of Beethoven and Chopin, and it was sung more recently at Boston's Cathedral of the Holy Cross at a Solemn Pontifical Mass celebrated shortly after the assassination of John F. Kennedy. (This performance featured the Boston Symphony Orchestra under the direction of Erich Leinsdorf, with the late Richard Cardinal Cushing officiating. The recording of the entire ceremony [RCA Victor LM-7030] can still be found in many record libraries.)

In the early years of Catholicism, the Requiem, like all other parts of the liturgy, was set as monophonic chant—as unaccompanied melody sung by individuals or by groups in unison. (See the discussion of Gregorian chant in Chapter 23.) Following the initiation of polyphony in the twelfth century, multipart choral writing as we now know it gradually developed. Polyphonic settings of the Requiem Mass originated as early as the fifteenth century, but the musical requiems that are most familiar today were composed only during the last two hundred years. The first of these is by Mozart, who died while attempting to finish it (in 1791). An apprentice, Franz Süssmayr, completed the work after Mozart's death (prodded by his widow who was anxious to collect payment from the patron who had commissioned the work), adding orchestration and even composing original sections which Mozart had left unsketched. (Although it is currently fashionable to downgrade Süssmayr's contribution, his accomplishment should be regarded as nothing less than heroic—look whose shoes he was expected to fill!)

Next comes Berlioz's *Requiem* (1837), a monumental work scored for mammoth chorus and orchestra, the latter featuring ten pairs of cymbals, four tam-tams (large gongs), sixteen kettle drums, and four extra brass ensembles. Although based on essentially the same Latin text, the Mozart and Berlioz works are as different as two Classical and Romantic works can be. In contrast to both of them, Brahms's *A German Requiem* (1868) abandons the Roman liturgy in favor of a compilation of Biblical passages translated into German. Brahms's compositional style reflects some of the Romantic innovations of Berlioz's music, but it also carries forward the spirit of the late Classicism of Beethoven and Schubert.

Example 222
Monophonic Gregorian Chant, "Requiem Aeternam"

Giuseppe Verdi's *Requiem* (1873) is overtly operatic in style. Although it sets the traditional Latin texts, the work was conceived for the concert hall rather than for performance in church. Gabriel Fauré's *Requiem* (1887) is a lovely work, but rather small-scale compared with the works already mentioned here. Finally, the outstanding requiem of recent years is Benjamin Britten's *War Requiem* (1962), which combines traditional Latin texts with antiwar poems of Wilfred Owen, an English poet who died at the age of twenty-five just one week before the Armistice of November 1918.

Not all memorial music is based on liturgical or even Biblical texts; indeed, some memorial music has no vocal text whatsoever. Leonard Bernstein's *Kaddish Symphony* (Chapter 26) was commissioned by the Boston Symphony Orchestra on the occasion of its seventy-fifth anniversary in 1955. However, the work was not begun until 1961 and was in the very last stages of completion on November 22, 1963, the day of President Kennedy's assassination. Therefore, Bernstein inscribed the work "to the beloved memory of John F. Kennedy." Some fifty years earlier, Arnold Schoenberg is reputed to have composed the last of his *Six Piano Pieces*, Op. 19, immediately after learning of Mahler's death (1911). In both cases, a composer was moved to devote a work to the memory of a specific personage, but the compositions involved were not originally conceived as memorials. However, there are numerous other compositions intended to honor the memory of specific dead persons, musicians or otherwise. Alec Robertson tells of several examples in his chapter, "Memorial Music and Laments."[2] In the fifteenth century it was common practice for composers to honor recently deceased colleagues. Thus, Johannes Ockegehm (born circa 1430) composed a lament on the death of Gilles Binchois (died 1460), while Josquin des Pres in turn wrote his *Lament on the*

Memorial Music

Passing of Jean Ockegehm in 1497. Part of the latter is based on the opening of the Gregorian chant introit, "Requiem aeternam" (see Example 222).

Franz Liszt reacted to the death of his friend Chopin (1849) by writing *Funerailles*, a piano work that opens with simulated bells tolling in the left hand and a solemn figure in the right hand. The principal thematic material is in the style of a funeral march. Secondary themes are introduced, and one gets a taste of Liszt's most sturdy bravura "big-piano" style. All in all, the work is similar in style to Chopin's larger polonaises.

In this century Paul Hindemith (1895–1963) composed memorial music for King George V, the grandfather of the present Queen (*Trauermusik* for strings), and for Franklin Delano Roosevelt (*When Lilacs Last in the Door-Yard Bloomed*, an oratorio based on Walt Whitman's homage to the memory of Abraham Lincoln). Igor Stravinsky composed a setting of Dylan Thomas's *Do Not Go Gentle into That Good Night* in memory of the poet and *Elegy for J.F.K.* in honor of the late president (who had honored Stravinsky at the White House). Probably the most important piece of nonreligious memorial music composed in the twentieth century is Alban Berg's *Violin Concerto* (1935). The work was dedicated to the memory of Manon Gropius, who succumbed at the age of eighteen to polio.* The concerto is analyzed in part in Chapter 33.

We shall now consider in detail the requiems of Fauré, Mozart, and Brahms.

Gabriel Fauré (1845–1924).
Photograph by Felix Nadar.

FAURÉ, REQUIEM

Gabriel Fauré was an influential French composer who lived from 1854 to 1924. He received his musical education during the heyday of Romanticism, yet lived to partake in Impressionism (circa 1890–1925), the movement which ushered in the modern period in France. Fauré's own music played a seminal role in the development of the two most important Impressionist composers, Debussy and Ravel—especially the latter, who was Fauré's student for a time. Fauré contributed abundantly to the song repertoire, and can be thought of as the French equivalent of the great Austrian song com-

*Manon's parents were Alma Mahler, widow of Gustav Mahler, and her second husband, Walter Gropius, the Bauhaus architect.

Music and Death

poser, Franz Schubert (see Chapter 28). The earmark of Fauré's songs is subtle nuance; he was a master interpreter of poetic sentiments. Even in his setting of the Roman liturgy Fauré emphasized the humanistic elements of the text. Charles Koechlin has pointed out that in his *Requiem* Fauré had no desire to portray hell,[3] and indeed Fauré omitted the threatening poem, "Dies Irae" ("Day of Wrath"), which follows the opening portions of the modern Roman Requiem (or Mass for the Dead). (The "Dies Irae" is thought to have been inserted into the liturgy in the thirteenth century. Fauré took for his text the earlier form of the Requiem liturgy, as codified during the Middle Ages.)

The *Requiem* is a poignant, lyrical work. It projects a feeling of personal intimacy rather than a large-scale grappling with the forces of life and death. Of all the famous requiems, Fauré's is the gentlest, the most delicate.

> It might be said that he understood religion more after the fashion of the tender passages in the Gospel according to Saint John, following Saint Francis of Assisi. . . . His voice seems to interpose itself between heaven and men; usually peaceful, quiet and fervent, sometimes grave and sad, but never menacing or dramatic.[4]

The omission of "Dies Irae" makes Fauré's the shortest of the famous requiems of the past two hundred years. It is also the simplest with respect to choral writing. For example, in many passages we hear just one vocal part (sopranos alone or tenors alone) or the entire chorus singing in unison or octave doublings. The work calls for soprano and baritone soloists.

Let us examine the opening of the Requiem liturgy, the "Introit," as set by Fauré.

Requiem aeternam dona eis, Domine, et lux perpetua luceat eis. Te decet hymnus, Deus, in Sion, et tibi reddetur votum in Jerusalem. Exaudi orationem meam, ad te omnis caro veniet. Requiem aeternam . . .	Eternal rest grant them, O Lord, and let perpetual light shine upon them. Thou shalt have praise, O God, in Sion, and to Thee let the vow be paid in Jerusalem. Heed my prayer! All flesh must come before thy judgment seat. Eternal rest . . .[5]

The music begins with the full chorus solemnly intoning the opening words in pianissimo block chords. Everyone sings the same words at the same time (as differentiated from imitative passages in which the separate vocal sections of the chorus sing independent textual and melodic lines simultaneously). Simplicity reigns: the orchestra is reticent, the harmonies are simple, there is barely even a sense of melody. Only at the end of the introduction, at the words "luceat eis," does Fauré permit himself one of the luscious harmonic progressions for which he is noted. (Fauré anticipated the harmonic daring of the Impressionist styles of Debussy and Ravel. His *Requiem* must have sounded very modern indeed to nineteenth-century ears.)

We now hear a repetition of the opening words, this time sung by the tenors alone in a lovely melody with simple string accompaniment. The delicacy of these pages is quite different from the relatively grandiose settings of other composers. The tenors' solo is followed by a similar one for sopranos. (Do not confuse a "solo" for the entire soprano section with the aria for soprano solo, "Piu Jesu," which comes much later in the work.) At the words, "Exaudi orationem meam!" ("Heed my prayer!"), the entire chorus sings resounding block chords. These stirring measures resemble the "big" sound of the other requiems referred to above, but they remain atypical in this work.

Example 223
FAURÉ, *Requiem*, "Introit"

The final part of the "Introit" repeats the preceding tenor melody (Example 223). At this point Fauré makes a textual elision by introducing the words of the ensuing Kyrie, thereby omitting an independent musical setting of this part of the liturgy. The full chorus quietly sings these words which commence the Mass for the Living (Chapter 23), "Kyrie eleison" ("Lord have mercy"). Then there is a brief loud shout, "Christe eleison" ("Christ have mercy"). After this the music resumes its subdued character as the chorus whispers the final "eleisons." (Fauré made still another elision by leaving out the final "Kyries" which normally follow "Christe eleison.")

A Romantic view of Mozart on
his deathbed with friends and
students performing the finished
sections of the *Requiem*. In the
"Lacrimosa" ("Weeping"), the
rising soprano line superbly illustrates humankind's aspiration
for heavenly grace. This is the
last passage Mozart composed
before his death.

Freunde und Schuler W.A.Mozarts spielen den vollendeten Theil des Requiem am Krankenbette vor

MOZART, REQUIEM

The second principal musical section of Fauré's *Requiem*, the "Offertory," follows the
early form of the Requiem liturgy. This is the point at which the Mozart, Berlioz, Verdi,
and Britten requiems proceed to the "Dies Irae," a poem consisting of seventeen three-
line verses, followed by a single four-line verse and a closing sentence. The Gregorian
chant setting of this text is well known from numerous citations in instrumental works,
such as Berlioz's *Fantastic Symphony*. (See Example 179. Others instances are discussed in Chapter 30.) However, none of the famous choral requiems utilize this chant
melody. Because of its length the "Dies Irae" text is usually divided into several subsections, each with its own musical setting. Mozart's version entails six individual musical subsections. The first of these never fails to thrill, as the chorus barks out the text in
vibrant block chords. This initial section covers the first two verses of "Dies Irae" (see
Example 224). Mozart passes straight through the two verses twice in a row, then pits
the basses' tremulous "Quantus tremor est futurus" ("How people will tremble and
grow pale") against the opening of verse 1 in the upper parts (see Example 225).

439

Memorial Music

Example 224

MOZART, *Requiem*, "Dies Irae," Opening

Music and Death

Example 225
"Dies Irae," Mm. 40–44

Mozart next presents a remarkable trombone solo, which accompanies the bass solo "Tuba mirum spargens sonum per sepulchra regionem" ("A trumpet first shall sound a mighty blast through all the regions of the dead"). Each of the other three soloists sings briefly, and then all four join for the last line of verse 7. Compare this gentle setting of the "Tuba mirum" with Berlioz's stupendous version, which emphasizes the text with four extra brass bands sounding over and above the mixture of oversize orchestra, inflated percussion section, and huge chorus. (If Berlioz were alive today he would undoubtedly use slide projections, strobe lights, and the like for a thoroughly mixed media presentation of the "Dies Irae" text.)

Although Mozart chose to project the "Tuba mirum" quietly, we already know that he had big guns available when he wanted them, and he brought out the whole arsenal for verse 8, "Rex tremendae majestatis" ("King of tremendous majesty"). This begins with three massed choral exclamations, "Rex," over an insistent dotted rhythmic pattern in the orchestra (see Example 226). Another stirring section is No. 6, which opens with verse 16, "Confutatis maledictus, Flammis accribus addictus" ("When sentence on the damned is passed, and all consigned to piercing flames"). These lines are sung by the men, after which the music melts into a gentle treble imploration of the third line, "Voca me cum benedictus" ("Call my name among the blessed"). We then arrive at an especially wonderful passage, the setting of verse 17.

Oro supplex et acclinis,
Cor contritum quasi cinis,
Gere curam mei finis.

441

Memorial Music

These words have been rendered into English by an anonymous seventeenth-century poet:

> Lord, this I beg on bended knee,
> With heart contrite as ashes be—
> That thou take care both of my end and me.[6]

A mysterious haze envelops this passage. Chorus and orchestra alike perform as if muted, in a spirit of absolute contrition. Modulating through a sequence of descending half steps, Mozart utilized chromatic harmonies that anticipate the music of Romantics like Chopin and Brahms. (A *sequence* is a succession of more or less verbatim repetitions of an inital phrase, but starting in each instance on a different pitch.)

Example 226
Requiem, "Rex Tremendae"

We have now reached the final section of the "Dies Irae," the "Lacrimosa" ("Weeping"). The violins play two-note bowed groupings (*slurs*) illustrative of the title of this section. The text relates the soul rising to heaven to face the hour of final judgment, and the music matches it with a stunning depiction of the idea of ascending, as the sopranos sing fifteen successive scale notes rising from a low D to a high A. The violins continue their weeping slurs throughout. This superb illustration of humankind's aspiration for heavenly grace is the last phrase of music that Mozart composed before his death. (Everything following it is the work of his apprentice, Franz Süssmayr.)

Music and Death

Example 227

La - cri - mo - sa di - es il - la,
(There will be a great day of weeping

qua re - sur - get ex fa - vil - la ju - di - can - dus ho - mo re - us
when man arises from earth to face his judgement)

The power, beauty, and serenity of Mozart's *Requiem* reflect the composer's essentially positive attitude toward death. Mozart expressed his feelings on death in a letter written to his father during the latter's final illness (1787):

> As death, when we come to consider it closely, is the true goal of our existence, I have formed during the last few years such close relations with this best and truest friend of mankind, that his image is not only no longer terrifying to me, but is indeed very soothing and consoling! And I thank my God for graciously granting me the opportunity . . . of learning that death is the *key* which unlocks the door to our true happiness. I never lie down at night without reflecting that—young as I am—I may not live to see another day. Yet no one of all my acquaintances could say that in company I am morose or disgruntled. For this blessing I daily thank my Creator and wish with all my heart that each one of my fellow creatures could enjoy it.[7]

BRAHMS, A GERMAN REQUIEM

Johannes Brahms was born in 1833 in the northern German metropolis of Hamburg. Like Beethoven, Brahms was the son of a small-time musician. The younger Brahms's first "gigs" were in rather low-class dives in Hamburg's red-light district, but eventually he rose to a position of great distinction in German/Austrian musical circles. As a young man Brahms was befriended by Robert and Clara Schumann, two musicians who wielded enormous influence during the midnineteenth century. It is possible that Robert Schumann's death in 1856 may have first suggested to Brahms the idea of composing a requiem.

Brahms was noted for his gruff temper and sarcastic wit, but he exhibited many signs of a warm heart as well. Nowhere is this clearer than in his response to the death of his life-long friend, Clara Schumann, shortly before his own death in 1897. He had recently completed his *Four Serious Songs*, Op. 121, on texts drawn from the Bible. After the funeral services, Brahms went to the home of friends, where he sang and played through his four Biblical songs. A young lawyer present at the scene recorded the event:

> [Brahms] was so deeply moved during the rendering of the third song, "O Tod, wie bitter bist du" ["O death, how bitter you are"], . . . that great tears rolled down his cheeks, and the pathetic end, "O Tod, wie wohl bist du" ["O death, how welcome you are"], he almost murmured to himself in a voice choked with emotion. I shall never forget the tremendous effect of this song. It was characteristic of Brahms, who disguised a very tender heart with an armor of outer roughness, that he turned to me, sitting on his left, and with a heavy slap on my leg, said, "Young man, this is not for you; you must not think of these things at all."[8]

Clara Schumann, shortly before her death in 1896. After her funeral, Brahms went to the home of friends, where he sang and played through his *Four Serious Songs*.

Music and Death

Johannes Brahms (1883– 1897). Many of his contemporaries regarded Brahms as the successor to Beethoven. The *German Requiem* stands comparison to Beethoven's *Missa Solemnis* in the sense that both are majestic masterpieces of the religious choral repertoire.

Many musicians, including the Schumanns, regarded Brahms as the "true" successor to Beethoven, a composer who could properly tread in the latter's gigantic footsteps. Certainly *A German Requiem* stands comparison to Beethoven's majestic *Missa Solemnis*—both are masterpieces of the religious choral repertoire. But an important distinction must be drawn between these two colossal works. Beethoven's setting is of the traditional Roman Catholic liturgy, the Mass for the Living, whereas Brahms's texts bear little resemblance to the Catholic liturgy of the Mozart, Berlioz, Verdi, and Fauré requiems. Unlike these other composers, Brahms was a Protestant and wished to compose a requiem in terms acceptable to *all* Christians, indeed to all humankind. (At one point he considered entitling the work, *A Human Requiem*.) By selecting a German text, in place of the traditional Latin, Brahms endeavored to communicate directly to all German-tongued listeners.

From Chapter 24 you will recall that one of the aims of the Protestant Reformation was the translation of the liturgy into the various languages spoken throughout Europe. These linguistic changes accompanied a restructuring of the liturgy, and, although the Mass was not dropped entirely, the Requiem service was not maintained as before. Consequently we do not find literal renderings of the Requiem liturgy in languages other than Latin. When Brahms decided to compose a requiem, he compiled his own text drawing upon the Old and New Testaments. The opening chorus consists of a quotation of Jesus, "Blessed are they that mourn: for they shall be comforted" (Matthew 5:4), coupled with Verses 5 and 6 of Psalm 126, "They that sow in tears shall reap in joy. He that goeth forth and weepeth, bearing precious seed, shall doubtless come again with rejoicing, bringing his sheaves with him."

Like the Fauré *Requiem*, *A German Requiem* is scored for soprano and baritone soloists. It is hard to single out any one of its special movements for commendation; the work is a sturdy masterpiece throughout. The opening number is remarkable for its somber orchestral coloring, achieved through the *absence* of violins. (One must search far and wide to find pre-twentieth-century orchestral examples which omit violins. Bach's *Brandenburg Concerto No. 6* and the second movement of Vivaldi's *Spring Concerto* [see Chapter 1] are among the best known examples.) Its tone is elegiac—combining a feeling of resignation with a longing for peace and hope.

Example 228
BRAHMS, *A German Requiem*, 1st Mvt., Opening

The somber second movement is tantamount to a funeral march, albeit in *triple* meter—a paradox, since marches are normally in duple meter (to accommodate the regular alternation of left/right, left/right). First we hear an opening orchestral melody—a complete introductory "paragraph"; then the voices enter with a countermelody accompanied by a repetition of the orchestral introduction. As in several passages in Fauré's *Requiem*, the chorus sings in octave doublings.

Music and Death

Example 229
A German Requiem, 2nd Mvt.

Altogether Movement 2 breaks down into four sections. After the funereal opening, the music changes to a cheerful Gb major for the text, "So seid nun geduldig, lieben Brüder" ("Be patient, brethren"). This is followed by a reprise of the opening section, in the original key of Bb minor. Finally, the music switches to the bright key of Bb major for the last portion of the text, "Aber des Herrn Wort bleibet in Ewigkeit" ("But the Lord's word remains forever"). This is only the first of several brilliant passages in which a belief in the positive power of faith replaces the pessimism often associated with the concept of death. Over and over Brahms hammers away at the Biblical injunction, "Die Erlöseten des Herrn werden wieder kommen" ("Those redeemed by the Lord will come again"). First the basses proclaim this message, then the rest of the choir sings it. Next, to the text "Freude and Wonne werden sie ergriefen" ("Joy and gladness shall be theirs"), the sopranos sing a cheerful melody while the tenors simultaneously imitate it in *augmentation* (twice as slow) an octave lower. The movement ends quietly with the words "ewige Freude" ("eternal joy").

Example 230
A German Requiem, 2nd Mvt., Mm. 233–237 (Soprano Melody in Quarter-Notes with Tenor Augmentation in Half-Notes)

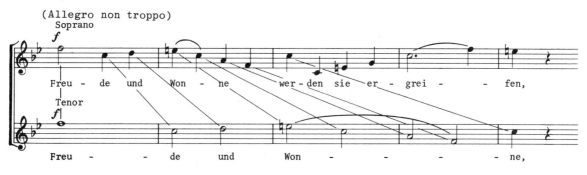

Movement 3 offers the first of two powerful baritone solos. The choir repeats several of the baritone's themes, producing a dialogue effect between the one and the many. The movement concludes with a stirring fugue on the text, "Der Gerechten Seelen sind in Gottes Hand" ("The souls of the righteous are in God's hands"). The entire fugue (thirty-six measures long) is constructed over a single bass note, which makes it one of the longest and most impressive *pedal points* in tonal music.

Movement 4 is a gentle chorus on the text, "Wie lieblich sind deine Wohnungen" ("How lovely are thy dwelling places"). The opening melody is one of the most beautiful that Brahms ever composed. Movement 5 presents the exquisite soprano solo, "Ihr habt nun Traurigkeit" ("Ye now are sorrowful"). The soft sustained beginning solo phrase lies very high in the soprano range, suggesting the flutelike sounds of an angel. In this and other passages the solo lines rise in graceful arches, reminiscent of the soprano solo, "Et Incarnatus Est," from Mozart's *Grand Mass in C Minor* (Chapter 23). The choir sings during most of this movement, but always in a subdued manner. Listen to the choral parts for augmentation of the first theme.

Music and Death

Example 231

A German Requiem, 5th Mvt., Mm. 62–66 (8th Note Melody [Soprano Solo] Imitated in Augmentation by Tenors, Then Chorus Sopranos)

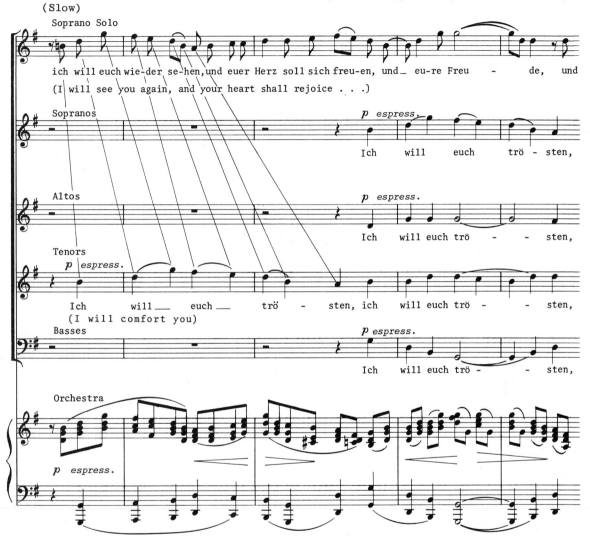

Movement 6 starts quietly with the choir singing, "Denn wir haben keinen blei-bende Statt" ("Here on earth we have no continuing place"). Then the baritone soloist enters with the text, "Lo, I unfold unto you a mystery. We shall not all sleep when He cometh, but we shall all be changed in a moment, in a twinkling of an eye, at the sound of the trumpet." Here we encounter once again the resounding trumpet of the "Dies Irae" (see the discussion of "Tuba mirum" in the Mozart and Berlioz requiems). The music becomes increasingly animated, culminating in a brilliant choral proclamation: "For the trumpet shall sound, and the dead shall be raised" (see Example 232).

Example 232

A German Requiem, 6th Mvt., Mm. 82–93, Finale

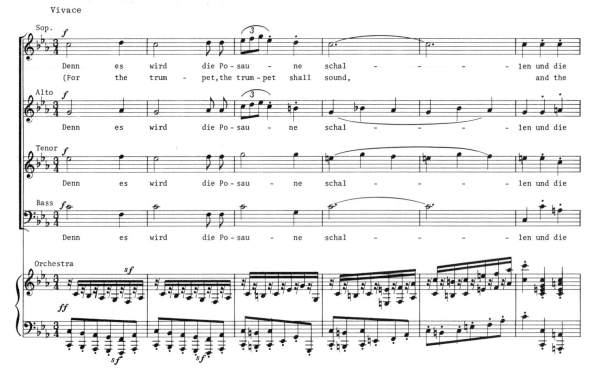

Music and Death

After another brief baritone solo, the choir returns with the same melody for the text, "For death shall be swallowed in victory! Grave, where is thy triumph? Death, where is thy sting?" Each of these textual phrases is repeated many times, culminating in a long fortissimo "Where?" before the final "Where is thy sting?" This magnificent passage represents the climax of the entire *Requiem* in both a musical and religious sense.

The idea of death defeated is one found throughout the musical repertoire of Christianity. Bach announced it in Verse 3 of his *Cantata No. 4* (Chapter 24); Handel proclaimed it in Part 3 of *Messiah*. (In view of his penchant for bright resounding choruses—for example, the *Hallelujah Chorus*—Handel's treatment of this message is surprisingly a subdued and lyrical alto-tenor duet.) Musical settings of these inspiring Biblical words help us buttress our spirits against the awful certainty that each and every one of us will eventually die. The music helps us cope with our anxiety, helps us anticipate the inevitability of death in a spirit of victory rather than defeat. The noblest artistic formulations show humankind confronting death with equanimity, sometimes even with enthusiasm. Perhaps the finest English-language statement of this philosophy is found in the poem, *Death, Be Not Proud* by John Donne (1573–1631).

Death, be not proud, though some have called thee
Mighty and dreadful, for thou art not so:
For those whom thou think'st thou dost overthrow
Die not, poor Death; nor yet canst thou kill me.
From Rest and Sleep, which but thy picture be,
Much pleasure, then from thee much more must flow;
And soonest our best men with thee do go—
Rest of their bones and souls' delivery!
Thou'rt slave to fate, chance, kings and desperate men,
And dost with poison, war, and sickness dwell;
And poppy or charms can make us sleep as well
And better than thy stroke. Why swell'st thou then?
One short sleep past, we wake eternally,
And Death shall be no more: Death, thou shalt die!

As you listen to Movement 6, try to correlate Donne's purely poetic expression of the "death of Death" with Brahms's musical setting of the equivalent Biblical words. In so doing, you will be entering into the universal spirit of Brahms's music.

Movement 6 concludes with an awe-inspiring fugue praising the power and virtue of God. The seventh and last movement begins with a gentle setting of the text, "Selig sind die Toten, die in dem Herren Sterben" ("Blessed be those who die in the Lord"). The key is F major, as in the opening of Movement 1, giving us a sense of returning to the point from which we started. Eventually Brahms confirms this feeling by repeating the thematic-harmonic opening of the *Requiem*; the final twelve measures of Movement 7 virtually duplicate the ending of Movement 1. "Selig sind . . ." ("Blessed be . . .") we hear, as the work winds down to a pianissimo conclusion, with the harp (as before) emerging as the principal accompanying instrument, the instrument of angels.

FINALITY—MUST IT BE?

The finale of Beethoven's last string quartet, the F Major, Op. 135—his last major work—bears the following paradoxical inscription: "The Difficult Resolution: Must It Be? Yes, It Must Be!" Beethoven converted this verbal conundrum into a three-note musical motive which in its original form sounds like a question, but in its inverted form sounds like an answer. The cello and viola "ask" the question five times during the slow introduction; the violins repeatedly "answer" it in the ensuing *allegro* section.

Example 233

BEETHOVEN, *String Quartet in F Major*, Opus 135, Finale, "The Difficult Resolution—Must It Be? It Must Be! It Must Be!"

In posing this riddle, what did Beethoven have in mind? Was he thinking of his own impending death? (He died less than six months after completing the quartet.) Since there is no documentation in this matter, the whole thing must remain moot. In any case, the question and its resolution pertain to everyone. We may all ask, "Must it be?" And eventually the same reply resounds, "Yes, it must be!"

There are two ways to confront the reality of death. We may (in Kierkegaard's words) cower in fear and trembling, or we may approach the end of life in a spirit of confidence and hope. Several of Bach's church cantatas concern death. One of these, *Cantata No. 60*, "O Ewigkeit, Du Donnerwort" (O Eternity, Thou Word of Thunder), consists of a dialogue on death between alto and tenor soloists. The alto represents Fear, the tenor Hope. The alto exclaims, "As I approach death I am terrified," to which the tenor replies "My saviour's hand will protect me." Fear declares that "the open grave looks gruesome," and Hope replies, "For me it will be a house of peace," and later (as at the end of Brahms's *A German Requiem*), "Blessed are the dead who die in the Lord." The final chorale, "Es Ist Genug," completes Hope's thoughts:

It is enough; Lord, whenever it pleases you, release me; my Jesus comes, so good-night, world. I'm traveling to the dwelling above; I go there in peace, leaving my great cares below. It is enough, it is enough. [Paraphrase by the author]

To what extent do these words reflect Bach's personal attitude toward death? Albert Schweitzer, the great humanitarian-philosopher-musician, wrote eloquently on this matter:

> In his innermost essence [Bach] belongs to the history of German mysticism. . . . His whole thought was transfigured by a wonderful, serene longing for death. Again and again, whenever the text affords the least pretext for it, he gives voice to this longing in his music; and nowhere is his speech so moving as in the cantatas in which he discourses on the release from the body of this death. . . . Sometimes it is a sorrowful and weary longing that the music expresses; at others, a glad, serene desire . . . then again a passionate, ecstatic longing, that calls death to it jubilantly, and goes forth in rapture to meet it. . . . This is Bach's religion as it appears in the cantatas. It transfigures his life.[1]

In Chapter 32, we took note of the fifteenth-century Burgundian composer, Guillaume Dufay, who inserted into his motet "Ave Regina Coelorum" the line, "Take pity on your dying Dufay." In his own way, Bach also composed his name into his "swan song," *Art of the Fugue*. But, where Dufay's words suggest trepidation, Bach's music represents his usual calm and methodical way of handling things. *Art of the Fugue* is a collection of canons and fugues designed to instruct an apprentice composer in the various types of polyphonic imitation. (Bach did not specify instrumentation. The work is usually performed by string quartet or organ.) One principal theme serves as subject throughout, but in some of the more elaborate sections Bach introduced secondary subjects as well. (See the discussion of fugue, Chapter 16.) As he approached his final moments on earth, the blind old composer, recently operated on for cataracts, was dictating a quadruple fugue (based on four subjects). He never made it to the fourth subject. The third subject was a four-note figure based on his own name: B A C H (i.e., in the German system of note names, Bb A C Bl). Tradition has it that his eldest son, Carl Philipp Emanuel Bach, wrote the following note on the last page of the manuscript: "With this fugue, where the name B. A. C. H. is brought into the counterpoint, the author died."[2] The grand old master went out with a sure unhesitating hand, doing what he knew how to do best—compose and teach. The mystical religious philosophy which Schweitzer has described stood Bach in good stead at the end. "Must it be?" "It certainly *must* be!" Bach might have answered. Yet there was also a fearful side of Bach, and one of his last works is a four-part arrangement of the chorale tune, "When We Are in Utmost Need" (which was originally appended to the first edition of *Art of the Fugue*).

For the final listening assignment of this book, three compositions have been selected which project a positive attitude toward death. The first of these integrates the final chorale of Bach's *Cantata No. 60* into its own finale; the other two deal explicitly with the concept of transfiguration. It is hard to put into simple terms the meaning of *transfiguration*. Literally it signifies a change of figure or form, but its application to the soul after death is paradoxical, since the soul has no concrete form. The sense of the word may perhaps be explained by equating death with defeat, and transfiguration with glorification or redemption. (See the last sentence of the Schweitzer excerpt earlier.) This is the spiritual concept underlying Bach's *Cantata No. 4* and Movement 6 of Brahms's *A German Requiem*. Ultimately these works express triumph over death—in

Finality—Must It Be?

Donne's words, "Death shall be no more; Death, thou shalt die!" It is an important message, one many pieces of music offer to comfort us when faced with the primary fact of the human condition: Yes, it must be that we shall all die!

BERG, VIOLIN CONCERTO

As indicated in Chapter 32, Berg composed the *Violin Concerto* as a memorial to his young friend, Manon Gropius. (Berg himself died in 1935, shortly after completing the concerto.) It is a twelve-tone work that also includes elements of earlier tonal styles. Its *tone row* (the term is explained in Chapter 22) alternates triadic major and minor thirds, ending with a four-note segment of the whole-tone scale. This final four-note segment coincides with the opening four notes of Bach's chorale, "Es Ist Genug," from *Cantata No. 60*. The tune is unique in its incipit (beginning) of three rising whole steps. The chromatic chords with which Bach spiced the melody are no less remarkable.

Example 234
BERG, *Violin Concerto*, Tone Row

Example 235
BACH, *Cantata No. 60*, "Es Ist Genug," Chorale

Music and Death

Because of the overlap between the last four notes of Berg's tone row and the first four notes of Bach's chorale, the subsequent entrance of the chorale in the concerto is implied from the very first statement of the row in the first movement. However, the full chorale appears only in the final section of the work—that is, in the second half of the second movement.* The tempo of this finale is very slow. Listen to it several times through, to develop a familiarity with its overall effect. Then focus on the successive variations on the chorale theme, as described in the following paragraphs. (Warning: Since the finale proceeds without interruption from the preceding part of the second movement, you may require assistance in locating the precise point at which the chorale treatment commences.)

At first the solo violin plays the chorale melody against one dissonant contrapuntal line in the bassoon and contrabassoon and another line in the violas. Then the original Bach harmonization of his first phrase is played by three clarinets and a bass clarinet—an ironic twist, since these modern instruments did not exist in Bach's time. During long notes of this phrase the muted second violins play ascending and descending whole-tone lines. This leads to the next phrase of the chorale tune, played by the solo violin in Berg's nontraditional harmonization. The same phrase is then echoed by the Bach version, again with clarinets. The solo violin returns for the first of the two final "Est ist genug" statements, again echoed by the Bach original, and the whole passage concludes with a drawn-out repetition of this last phrase by both solo violin, playing rolled (*arpeggiated*) chords, and clarinets (see Example 236).

The next section features the chorale theme played as a *canon* (round) by cellos and harp, accompanied mainly by a quartet of horns. As the solo violin reenters, the trombone section picks up the chorale melody, and the canonic treatment is dropped. For the last two phrases, the trombones are joined first by cellos, then by violas, with an echo of the cellos in the high violins.

The horns then immediately commence an *inverted* (upside down) statement of the chorale theme, against a triplet figure in the violins (see Example 237). The trumpets join in the repetition of the first phrase, in canon with the basses, cellos, and contrabassoon, as the music pushes toward a climactic grand fortissimo *tutti*. As quiet is restored, the chorale inversion continues in the brass and cellos, with the solo responding in a peaceful descending scale. Shortly after this the violins repeat a bit of a folk tune from the first movement, leading to the coda of the concerto.

*According to Douglass Green, Berg designed his tone row without reference to Bach's "Es Ist Genug." Only after the *Violin Concerto* was well under way did he begin searching for a Bach chorale suitable for inclusion in the second movement. By a curious coincidence, Robert DiDomenica similarly selected the tone row of Scene 3 of his opera, *The Balcony*, unaware of the overlap between his row and Chopin's *Funeral March*. See Examples 202, 204, and 205.

Finality—Must It Be?

Example 236
BERG, Violin Concerto, Finale, End of Variation I

·Music and Death

Example 237

Violin Concerto, Finale, Var. III, Horn Inversion of Chorale Theme

In the coda the flutes play the chorale theme accompanied by solo violin and woodwinds; as the third phrase begins, pizzicato strings join the winds. The solo violin then plays the last chorale phrase against the full twelve-tone row as played by solo string bass and successively imitated by solo cello, solo viola, solo orchestral violin, and finally the concerto soloist. By this time the last "Es ist genug" phrases are being played at a slow pace in the brass. As the violin soloist sustains the last note of the row, a high G, two muted horns play the first four notes of the chorale tune in a low inversion, also ending on G (C♯-B-A-G).

In accordance with the composer's notation, "as from a distance," the muted first violins gently remind us of the concerto's initial open fifths (representing the four strings of the violin). Just prior to these fifths, harp, horns, and winds play a chord consisting of four notes, B♭, D, F, and G, a mixture of the G minor and B♭ major triads. The perfect fifth, B♭–F, repeats the first two notes of the concerto, as well as reflecting the key (B♭ major) of Bach's harmonization of "Es Ist Genug." So, despite its basically atonal structure, the concerto both opens and closes with strong hints of triadic keys (G minor and B♭ major). Also the two individual notes G and B♭ are partially treated as tonics—particularly G. The gentle tonal consonance of the last measure makes for a truly heavenly ending, befitting the dedication "to the memory of an angel."

STRAUSS, DEATH AND TRANSFIGURATION

Richard Strauss (1864–1949), one of the three most important post-Wagnerian composers (along with Mahler and Schoenberg), devoted much of his composing career to opera and songs, but first achieved fame through his tone poems. Even now his tone poems remain his most frequently performed works. Strauss was just twenty-five when he wrote *Tod und Verklärung* (*Death and Transfiguration*). The score recreates the sufferings of a dying man—his violent struggle with death, his actual expiring, and finally the transfiguration of his soul. The musical idea which Strauss used to represent transfiguration delineates an overt heavenly ascent—listen for the octave leap between the fourth and fifth notes.

457

Example 238
STRAUSS, *Death and Transfiguration*, Transfiguration Theme

At the beginning of the work there is no portent of heaven. All is dark and somber. A little later, two short but important melodic figures are introduced by flute and oboe, accompanied by harp. These cheerful figures depict happier days long before. After a return of the first somber material, a longer theme in the oboe (again with harp background) suggests pleasant thoughts of childhood. The mood here is idyllic, with the two shorter motives being interpolated between statements of the "childhood" theme (which is to become one of the main themes of the piece). Again the somber material returns, bringing the first part of the work to a soft close.

Music and Death

Example 239

Death and Transfiguration, Oboe Theme (Childhood)

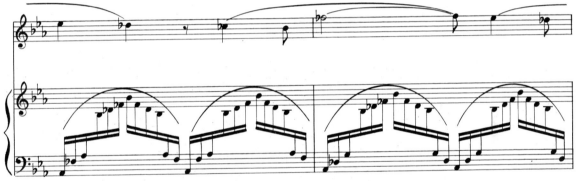

After Strauss completed *Death and Transfiguration*, his friend Alexander Ritter wrote a poem expressing the content of the music. The following is a prose translation by Gerald Romanow:

> In his pitifully small chamber lit only by the feeble light of a candle stump, lies the sick man in bed. He has been fighting a desperate battle with death and now, exhausted, he sinks back into slumber; the gentle ticking of the wall clock punctuates the room's awesome silence, foreshadowing death's approach. A melancholy smile forms across the man's pallid features. Now, in life's final hour, does he perchance dream of childhood's golden age?

The music now changes radically, as for the first time we hear the entire grand orchestra, fortissimo, at twice the previous tempo. This is overt "struggle music," full of brilliant orchestral figures and dissonant chords. The music reaches a *furioso* climax, with the whole orchestra playing the principal struggle theme. This theme, along with

459

other subsidiary motives, dominates the musical fabric for several minutes. At the end of this section we hear the first full statement of the transfiguration theme (see Example 238). After another similar statement the music subsides into a quiet passage.

> But not for long will death grant its victim slumber and dreams. Cruelly it rouses him to resume the battle anew. The drive to live versus the power of death! A ghastly struggle! Yet neither is the victor and once again stillness rules.

Part 3 brings back the relaxed childhood theme (Example 239), played by flutes and accompanied by light strings. After a brief interpolation of the struggle theme, *un poco agitato* (a little agitated), the music presents a military figure combining one of the short motives of Part 1 with the childhood theme. Next comes a passage marked *appassionato*, which mixes some of the preceding themes with a new motive, leading eventually to another climactic section in which the struggle theme figures prominently in the trombones. After still more intensive building, the radiant transfiguration theme emerges triumphantly. The childhood theme is featured here as well.

Example 240
Death and Transfiguration, Part 3, Military Figure with Childhood Motive

There is now a brief repetition of the slow introduction, with its somber hues, followed by a short recapitulation of the struggle music from Part 2. A rising chromatic scale in the violins and winds portrays the man giving up the ghost. At the sound of a gong, he dies.

> Weary of the battle, sleepless and delirious, he sees now his life unfold before him, scene after scene. First the dawn of childhood, gleaming in pure innocence. Next the reckless playfulness of youth, testing and probing its strength, gradually ripening into manhood's struggle for life's highest achievement—to recognize the exalted and to exalt it still further—this alone being the noble goal that leads him through life. . . . Then the final blow from death's iron hammer reverberates, shattering the earthly hull in two, surrounding the eye with the [eternal] night of death.

Music and Death

Richard Strauss (1864–1949), who first achieved fame as a composer of tone poems, was just twenty-five when he wrote *Death and Transfiguration*. The score recreates a man's violent struggle with death and the final transfiguration of his soul.

Part 4 opens mysteriously as the horn and then the winds herald the transfiguration, while the strings nestle the childhood theme into the last notes of the transfiguration theme. After another impressive climax, based on the same material, the music gently dies away.

But what so longingly he sought here on earth resounds mightily from heaven: deliverance, transfiguration!

Although still very young when he composed *Death and Transfiguration*, Strauss returned to it shortly before his death nearly sixty years later. In 1948 he composed the *Four Last Songs* for soprano and orchestra. As the soprano sings the last line of "Im Abendroth" ("At Sunset")—"Ist dies etwa der Tod?" ("Is this then really death?")—the orchestra plays the transfiguration theme from the tone poem (Example 238). In this way Strauss joined Dufay and Bach in inserting a personal reference to himself in his final work. Having composed his "swan song," Strauss slipped gently into death a year later.

Finality—Must It Be?

Wagner's romantic masterpiece, *Tristan und Isolde*, concerns a man and a woman whose love both originates in death and is eventually consummated in death. Probably the most intense lovers in the entire operatic repertoire, Tristan and Isolde long for death from the moment their love begins. Earlier Tristan had killed Isolde's fiancé in battle, and himself nearly succumbed to his own wounds. Unaware of his identity, Isolde nursed Tristan back to health, and now in Act I he is escorting her from Ireland, against her will, to become the bride of old King Marke of Cornwall. Isolde bitterly conspires to bring about her own and Tristan's deaths by demanding that Brangäne, her lady-in-waiting, concoct a death potion. But Brangäne instead substitutes a love potion, a potion so overwhelmingly powerful that upon drinking it Tristan and Isolde immediately fall into a trance, unaware of their surroundings, conscious only of each other. The depth of their feelings is boundless, unbearable; only death can release them from their intense suffering. One critic has related the situation of Wagner's lovers to these classic lines of poetry:

> One Heaven, one Hell, one immortality,
> And one annihilation. Woe is me!
> The winged words on which my soul would pierce
> Into the height of Love's rare Universe,
> Are chains of lead around its flight of fire—
> I pant. I sink. I tremble. I expire![3]

In Act II, Tristan and Isolde meet secretly and sing the longest and probably greatest love duet ever composed. Again and again they yearn for death, which they regard as a blissful and eternal fulfillment of their passion.

> Tristan and Isolde simply could not expose their searing, utterly exclusive passion for each other to an everyday world. There was no place in the world for such a love. Death, I agreed with Wagner, was their only possible future.[4]

The love duet culminates in disaster as the lovers are discovered by King Marke. Badly wounded by one of Marke's lieutenants, Tristan is taken to a lonely island. Here (in Act III) he awaits Isolde, in the hope she will nurse him back to health as she had done once before. After a period of seemingly interminable suspense Isolde arrives, but only moments before Tristan expires. She accuses him of betrayal, of passing on without her to the death they have together so ardently longed for. The music drama concludes as Isolde, transfixed, gazes at her dead lover, in whom she mysteriously detects signs of life. She now commences her great aria, "Liebestod," which at first repeats a theme from the Act II love duet. Earlier they had sung, "So let us die that we may remain unseparated, eternally united, without end, without waking, without fear, bound together in a love that cannot be named, completely given over unto ourselves, only our love still living." While they lived the lovers sought death; now, with Tristan dead, Isolde paradoxically imagines him alive.

Example 241
WAGNER, *Tristan und Isolde*, Act III, Finale, "Love–Death"

Sehr mässig beginnend (Starting moderately)

Mild und lei-se / wie er lä-chelt, / wie das Au - ge / hold er öff-net / seht ihr, Freun-de,
(Fair and gently / he is smiling; / see, his eyes he / soft - ly o - pens! / See, my friends, ah!)

Despite the extreme poignancy of this scene, it also affords an alternate interpretation. Recalling Olive Fremstad's performance of Isolde at the Metropolitan Opera, Samuel Chotzinoff has written

> The "Liebestod" was its crown. This . . . was no dirge, no farewell, no submission to fate. It was a hymn of gratitude to death for fulfilling the lovers' true destiny. . . . The "Liebestod" as Fremstad sang it was a paean to Annihilation. No Isolde before Fremstad had been aware of this joyful implication of the "Liebestod." . . . By her rapturous, other-worldly smile as she gazed at her dead lover, she illuminated the hidden idea of the story—that it was not King Marke who had stood between her and Tristan, but life itself.[5]

The end of the "Liebestod" recapitulates the last pages of the Act II love duet and then proceeds to a grand *plagal cadence* (like the IV-I "Amen" chord progression at the end of a hymn). This occurs first in two-measure sections, then in an expanded grouping of ten measures, five measures each for the successive IV and I chords. The opera concludes with a final orchestral reference to the longing motive which opens the Prelude to Act I.*

---

*The complete longing motive shown in Example 242a is quoted in the sixth movement of Alban Berg's *Lyric Suite* for string quartet (1927). The entirety of this work has recently been revealed as a declaration of love by Berg for a married woman whom he secretly adored. See George Perle, "The Secret Program of the *Lyric Suite*," in the *Newsletter of the International Alban Berg Society*, no. 5, June 1977, pp. 4ff.

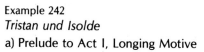

Example 242

Tristan und Isolde

a) Prelude to Act I, Longing Motive

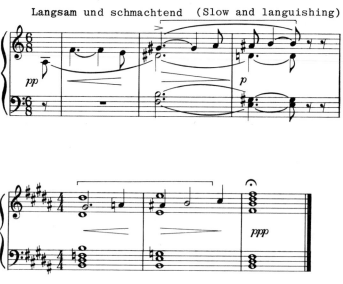

Here again we encounter the idea of transfiguration: Wagner's stage directions at the end of "Liebestod" read, "Isolde sink, wie verklärt" ("Isolde collapses, as if transfigured"). Thomas Mann has movingly described this passage in his story, *Tristan*:

> Followed the immeasurable plenitude of that vast redemption and fulfillment; it was repeated, swelled into a deafening, unquenchable tumult of immense appeasement that wove and welled and seemed about to die away, only to swell again and weave the *Sehnsuchtsmotiv* [longing motive] into its harmony; at length to breathe an outward breath and die, faint on the air, and soar away. Profound stillness.[6]

CHECKLIST: CONCEPTS AND TERMS IN UNIT 7

General and Historical
Dada (429)
Dance of Death (397)
erlking (418)
Gregorian chant (439)
Reformation (445)
transfiguration (453)

Vocal Music
chorale (454)
"Dies Irae" (397)
lied (418)
recitative (420)
requiem (434ff)

Instrumental Music
arpeggiated (455)
cadenza (398)
chord cluster (425)
coda (403)
concerto (398)
funeral march (403)
pizzicato (406)
slur (442)
trill (406)

Theory
atonal (406, 427)
augmentation (448)
block chord (437)
cadence (425)
canon (455)
chromatic scale (460)
fugue (448)
ground bass (426)
inverted (452, 455)
monophonic (434)
neoclassicism (407, 427)
octave (405)
ostinato (398)
pedal point (418)
plagal cadence (463)
polyphonic (434)
rondo (415)
sequence (442)
serialism (407)
syncopated (414)
tape music (406)
tone row (405)
triple meter (446)
triplets (405)
tutti (455)
twelve-tone music (454)
variations (406)
whole-tone scale (454)

Finality—Must It Be?

REVIEW: UNIT VII

1. In your own words, explain the following terms:

Dada
inversion
neoclassicism
pedal point
requiem
serialism

2. Write a brief historical summary of "Dies Irae" as text and chant melody in modern orchestral works and requiems. Base your report on information (and listening) provided in Chapters 30 and 32.

3. The "Danse sacrale" from Stravinsky's *The Rite of Spring* is an example of rondo form. Give a brief explanation of this form and show how it differs from sonata form.

4. With regard to the discussion of triumph over death (Chapter 32), what is your own position with regard to the role of music? Does it help (has it helped) you sustain a more positive attitude toward life (and death)? What compositions that you have heard (within the compass of this book or elsewhere) have been most inspiring to you?

5. Looking back over *Music and Human Experience*, Units II–VI, cite examples of music which touch upon death and which therefore might have been included in Unit VII.

NOTE TO READER

Having covered parts or all of *Music and Human Experience* you are now faced with the question, "What next?" Because this book was organized on the assumption that the novice listener will respond more readily to music through the conduit of external subject matter than via historical or technical routes, its coverage of the music repertoire has been correspondingly restricted. Whole areas of music have been left virtually untouched, especially in the realm of absolute music. Vast amounts of instrumental music have been excluded—the symphonies of Haydn, Mozart's piano concertos, the chamber music literature, much of the solo piano repertoire—altogether an enormous stockpile of potential listening challenge and enjoyment. The Medieval and Renaissance periods have received relatively little attention, and here too wonderful treasures await you. Even in the stressed areas, numerous works had to be passed over lest the book reach an unconscionable length.

The suggested projects and assignments (Appendix I) are designed to assist your exploration of the areas of music which have been relegated to the sidelines in this volume. Suggestions are given for correlating absolute works—symphonies, sonatas, and so on—with the program and vocal works you have been studying. As you listen to absolute music you may at first feel at a loss in the absence of a story or subject. You will soon realize, however, that listening to music of all kinds is fundamentally *one* experience. The material already covered has given you a chance to get your feet (ears) wet, in a musical sense. If your response to these varied musical stimuli has been positive, then you will soon find you no longer need the "crutch" of extramusical content. The biggest challenge is to get past the feeling of unfamiliarity, to feel *assimilated* in the world of music. Having come this far, you are no longer a novice; if only for a short distance, you have started on the connoiseur's path. The first stretch is the hardest. From now on you can take various side paths, exploring some areas in depth, skipping others, following your own musical impulses.

Another thought: Have you attended any *live* concerts? Undoubtedly you have been relying heavily on records and tapes for your listening assignments; recordings are an essential aid to the introductory music teacher and student alike. However, no matter how good the reproduction system, recordings miss all sorts of basic musical elements, one of them being simply the possibility of error on the part of the performer. In other words, recordings sacrifice spontaneity and suspense. (Engineering techniques are now so highly developed that small patches of music can be re-recorded separately and then spliced in without the listener noticing. Recorded performances tend to be conglomerations of oft-repeated-until-perfect sections.) Perhaps the most important aspect of live performance is communication. Music is a communicatory art, a language of expression. Have you ever conversed with a robot? Listening to a recorded performance is analogous to carrying on a dialogue with a machine. Communication ought to take place between two *live* entities, and that is what happens in a live performance. It is like an intricate conversation (admittedly one way, except for the audience's applause) between the performers and listeners, with the players' telling the audience what the composer thinks. Yes, *thinks*. For a musical composition represents the formulation of a musical thinking process. It may be impossible to see the composer in person—there really is no need to—but the performer(s) should be visible in all three dimensions. Attend some concerts, and your listening experiences will be both accentuated and intensified.

Of course, this advice is based on the assumption that you will hear good—if not great—performers. Depending on how close you live to a major cultural center—usually located in a big city—you will have varying opportunities to hear good live concerts. Large cities offer great musical variety, sometimes making it hard to know what to select. The small town or rural college with a single concert series makes things simpler—there are few programs to choose from. If you plan to visit a large city, check tourist information centers and local newspapers for guidance in selecting concerts. Or you might call a local university music department and ask a faculty member or music major for suggestions.

Do not worry about what to wear at a concert. Informality is the rule these days, even in major concert halls, opera houses, and churches. Go backstage after the performance, and talk with the artists. You may be surprised to find that even the most famous performers like to chat with members of the audience after a concert. The next day, look for a review of the concert in the arts section of the newspaper; it is fun to find out whether the music critic felt the same way you did.

The whole point is to make listening an active experience. Records are fine when all you want is a passive musical experience, perhaps as background to some other higher-priority activity. But, when music itself is to be the central focus, records can be a disappointment. For one thing, the acoustics are rarely right; recording engineers almost always tamper with the microphones, play with the dynamics, and so on. Moreover, you are likely to listen to records in a poor location, such as a music library or your own room. Beautiful music is meant to be heard in spacious, high-ceilinged halls, with decor and adornments to match. There should be an absence of annoying distractions, such as phones ringing or people talking. Still more important, one should be able to *see* the facial expressions of the musicians. Also, many contemporary works involve unusual sights, such as electrified instruments, synthesizers, and the ever-expanding battery of percussion instruments. When it comes to operas, listening to records is like listening to a recorded drama—satisfactory, perhaps, but not nearly as good as the real live play.

If you can, take up singing or playing an instrument yourself. Short of composing, this is the ultimate musical activity. Whether you perform or just go to concerts, or simply stay at home listening to records or tapes, the point is to really get out there and relate to music actively. Find what you like and stick to it. Music is a gift to treasure for the rest of your life. This book is about music and the human experience. Make music *your* human experience. Enjoy it as much as you can!

468

APPENDICES

APPENDIX I
PROJECTS AND ASSIGNMENTS

1. The most obvious day-to-day assignment is to listen thoroughly to the music you have read about. Even if your instructor plays some of the music in class, you should listen to it again outside of class. You will not have time to listen to all the pieces of each chapter, but you (and/or the teacher) can select a representative number of works for *repeated* listening. Then, perhaps, you might select one work for intensive listening. It would seem that a minimum of two listenings should be necessary with regard to any piece you are seriously interested in, with extra attention being paid to special sections that are underscored in the book or that you or your teacher find especially interesting. Consider keeping a diary of your listening experiences. It will come in handy: your teacher may want to see it, and you can consult it when preparing for reports or examinations.

2. Take some of the pieces *not* emphasized in a particular unit—the ones just mentioned in passing—and research them. Listen to them first, so that you can make comments about your personal responses. Then look up the composers, the periods, the genres, even the particular works—in a music encyclopedia, music history, or biography. Write a brief commentary on the pieces as a supplement to what you have found in this book. Your instructor may wish to reproduce your commentary for distribution among the other students, or may ask you to read it in class.

3. Supplement a particular chapter by finding extra works to add to it. Then write a commentary on them as in Project 2. For example, you might pick Vaughan Williams's *Sea Symphony* for Chapter 1, Wagner's *Siegfried's Rhine Journey* for Chapter 11, Messiaen's *Quartet for the End of Time* for Chapter 20, or Penderecki's *Auschwitz Oratorio* for Chapter 31. The best way to find suitable pieces is to consult the index of a music history textbook (looking for titles listed independently or under composers' names) or check the title headings in a record catalogue.

4. Select works by three different composers in a given chapter. Then find three nonprogrammatic pieces by the same composers and compare the pieces in the book with the absolute pieces you have selected. For example, compare Schubert's *String Quartet in D Minor*, "Death and the Maiden," with another string quartet by Schubert. Discuss similarities and differences among the paired works.

5. Select several works from the book, all by the same composer. Aside from differences in subject matter, are the works basically quite similar? Amplify.

6. Pick a piece you have enjoyed from the book, and find two or three other pieces outside the book in the same genre but by other composers (a) of the same period, (b) from an earlier period, or (c) from a later period. For example, you might select Beethoven's *String Quartet in A Minor*, Op. 132 (Chapter 27) and then listen to some other *absolute* string quartets. From your listening can you generalize about historical developments vis-à-vis the genre you are considering?

7. Pick a piece, as in Project 6, and then pick two other pieces by the same composer but in different genres. Do you find that you have a particular preference for one genre over another, and/or is your appreciation of music influenced by other factors?

8. Compare any two or more works discussed in the book which seem related to one another in any way that seems interesting to you. Are there chapter headings that have been left out that you would like to see included (e.g., Music of the Occult and Supernatural)?

9. Match composers omitted from the book with contemporaries from the same part of the world (e.g., Kodály with Bartók, Jánacek with Dvořák, Krenek with Berg). Choose a representative number of works by each composer for your comparison.

10. Write an essay on what kind of music you like best and least. Support your statements with examples drawn from the book.

11. Write a review of a live concert. Describe everything relevant about the concert—the audience, the performers, the music—in your *own* terms. Emphasize your personal response to the music. Do not try to write as an authority or professional critic; rather, write your review much as if you were writing a letter to a friend who had expressed an interest in what you have been doing lately.

12. Research the subject of folk music as a source for concert works. Use your research to supplement the information on folk music in Chapters 6–8. This assignment will give you a good opportunity to look further into the music of Bartók and other Eastern European composers, as well as music of American composers like Copland and Ives. Check out Mahler's *Symphony No. 1*, Movement 3, and Schoenberg's *String Quartet No. 2*, Movement 2.

13. In Chapter 29 we surveyed various works revolving around the subject of Romeo and Juliet. All this music was written long after Shakespeare's death. What about the music of Shakespeare's time—what was it like? Research and describe.

14. Research and listen to music on the subject of Don Quixote: Strauss's tone poem, songs by Ravel and Ibert, *Man of La Mancha*, others?

15. Listen to John Gay's *The Beggar's Opera* and compare it with *The Threepenny Opera* by Brecht and Weill (Chapter 15).

16. Write a minichapter on any one of the subjects listed below. Suggested pieces for listening are included.

Clowns and commedia del arte figures
Stravinsky, *Petrouschka*
Schoenberg, *Pierrot Lunaire*
Leoncavallo, *I Pagliacci (The Clowns)*
Busoni, *Arlecchino (Harlequin)*
Schumann, *Carnaval*

Drinking songs
Verdi, *Otello*, Act I
Berlioz, *The Damnation of Faust*, Act I
Orff, *Carmina Burana*
Mahler, *The Song of the Earth* (I)
Verdi, *La Traviata*, Act I
Mozart, *Abduction from the Seraglio*, "Vivat Bacchus"
Strauss (Johann), *Wine, Women and Song*

Farewell
Massenet, *Manon*, "Adieu, ma petite table"
Schubert, *Winterreise*, "Gute Nacht"
Schubert, "Der Wanderer"
Schubert, "Taubenpost"
Beethoven, *Piano Sonata in E♭ Major*, Op. 81a
Verdi, *La Traviata*, Act III, "Addio del passato"
Leadbelly, "Good Night, Irene"
(Traditional), "So Long, It's Been Good to Know You"
Mahler, *Songs of a Wayfarer*

Pomp and grandeur
Wagner, Overture to *Die Meistersinger*
Berlioz, *Requiem*, "Tuba Mirum"
Mussorgsky, *Boris Godunov*, "Coronation Scene"
Elgar, *Pomp and Circumstance March, No. 1*
Mozart, *Magic Flute*, Act I, entrance of Sarastro
Gilbert and Sullivan, *Iolanthe*, Entrance of the Peers

Humor (a subject so extensive it could be shared by a group of students working together)
Mozart, *A Musical Joke*
Haydn, *Joke Quartet* (strings)
Satie, *Three Pieces in the Shape of a Pear*
Debussy, *Children's Corner*, "Golliwogg's Cake-Walk"
Debussy, *Preludes*, "S. S. Pickwick, P.P.M.P.C."
Beethoven, *Rage over a Lost Penny* (piano)
Beethoven, *Piano Sonata in E♭ Major*, Op. 31, No. 3, Movement 2
Telemann, *Funeral Music for an Aesthetic Canary* (cantata)

Bach, *Coffee Cantata*
Rossini, *The Italian Woman in Algiers*, sneezing scene
Puccini, *Gianni Schicchi* (opera in one act)
Prokofiev, *Love for Three Oranges* (opera)
Ravel, *L'Heure espagnole* (opera)
Ives, *Three-Page Sonata* (a burlesque of sonata form)
Johann Strauss, *Die Fledermaus* (operetta)
Gilbert and Sullivan, *Patience*
Bernstein, *Candide* (Broadway musical)
Bernstein, *Trouble in Tahiti* (short opera)
Wolf, Hugo, "Mousetrap Incantation" (song)
Brahms, "Vergebliches Ständchen" (song)
P.D.Q. Bach, *Concerto for Horn and Hardart*, etc.

Dance (another group project)
Renaissance and other early dances
Bach, *English* and *French Suites*
Schubert, *Valses nobles et sentimentales* (piano)
The minuet in the Classical symphony
Couperin and other French Baroque keyboard composers
Bartók, *Dance Suite*
Piano music of Chopin: mazurkas, waltzes, polonaises
Polkas, waltzes and other central European dances by Liszt, Dvořák, Brahms, Johann Strauss
Ravel, *Rhapsodie espagnole, La Valse, Pavane for a Dead Infante, Bolero*
Popular American and Latin American dances: waltz, rhumba, tango; Weill, *Threepenny Opera*; Stravinsky, *L'Histoire du soldat*
Schoenberg, *Piano Suite*, Op. 25
Massenet, *Manon*, "Gavotte" (aria)
Mozart, *Don Giovanni*, Act I Finale, Minuet

17. Defend or attack the following argument: There are vast amounts of music in which composers make various statements on their views of life. Much of this music involves a verbal text or (in the case of purely instrumental music) program. Kierkegaard thought that the combination of music and language was superior to music alone. But not everyone holds that view. Indeed, there are many who feel that the mixture of words and music makes for a kind of bastardization—thus, according to this view a song is neither as good as a poem nor as a purely instrumental piece. For some opera is the finest of musical arts, for others the lowest. . . . There are many who consider the late string quartets of Beethoven the most sublime music ever written. Presumably this sublime quality has something to do with the content of these works—their messages. Is it possible to think of an instrumental composition as a wordless statement, much like an abstract painting or sculpture? If so, then perhaps music left entirely to itself, uncombined with other media, has the best chance of reaching its zenith. A great composer is perforce a great thinker, but one whose language is music and whose ideas are *musical* ideas. As fascinating as philosophical messages in music may be, it is probably true that composers can best express their philosophies nonverbally.

18. Write a short paper on revolutionaries in music. Not political revolutionaries, like Wagner, but composers responsible for effecting revolutionary changes in the sphere of music (like Wagner!). Other suitable composers would be Monteverdi, Carl Philipp Emanuel Bach (J.S.B.'s eldest son), Beethoven, Debussy, and Schoenberg.

19. Make a survey of electronically produced music. Is the synthesizer a new kind of orchestra? Is the computer taking over the role of the composer? Amplify.

20. Write a report on musical transcriptions. Some of these involve concert arrangements of classical music—for example, Stokowski's orchestrations of Bach, Busoni's piano arrangements of Bach, Bach's arrangements of Vivaldi, and Stravinsky's transcriptions of Pergolesi (*Pulcinella*). Others include popular transcriptions of classics, as in the Swingle Singers' recordings; synthesized versions of Bach, Ravel, and Bizet (*The Well-Tempered Synthesizer* or *Everything You Always Wanted to Hear on the Moog*); Broadway shows based on Grieg and Borodin; popular songs based on Tchaikovsky, Chopin, and Rachmaninoff; Emerson, Lake, and Palmer's adaptation of Mussorgsky's *Pictures at an Exhibition* (originally for piano, later orchestrated by Ravel); and popular songs converted for classical use, as in Bach chorales, Dufay and Palestrina masses, and the *Baroque Beatles Book* recording.

21. Write a paper on unusual instruments and combinations thereof. Mozart composed music for glass harmonica, other pieces for basset horns. Look into the heckelphone (a giant oboe) and various forms of percussion instruments. What is a krumhorn or a sackbut? Bach's *Brandenburg Concerto No. 6* is for strings, but calls for no violins. Stravinsky's *Les Noces* (*The Wedding*) is scored for four pianos and percussion (and no other instruments). Contemporary composers, such as John Cage, George Crumb, and Karlheinz Stockhausen, use a wide variety of unusual instruments and/or call for unconventional use of traditional instruments (electrified violin, etc.). Also, there are some unusual combinations of traditional instruments and/or voices with electronically produced tapes (e.g., Milton Babbitt's *Philomel*).

22. Write a report on composers who have bridged the gap between the worlds of classical and popular music: Kurt Weill, George Gershwin, and Leonard Bernstein. Others? What is *Third Stream*?

23. Prepare an introduction to the music of neglected composers of the past—for example, Gesualdo (Italian), Elgar (English), and Nielsen (Danish). Who was John Field? What about some of the Bachs besides Johann Sebastian?

24. Regarding early music, pick a country (European) and examine its music prior to 1700. Or pick a century before the eighteenth and examine music from several countries.

25. Write a historical survey of a form or genre from the following list: madrigal, motet, anthem, operetta, song, string quartet, concerto, symphony, opera, theme and

Projects and Assignments

variations, sonata, secular keyboard music, organ music for the church, mass, other Catholic liturgical music (vespers, te deum, etc.).

26. Research classical music as used in films. This project may include films of operas (Bergman's *Magic Flute* by Mozart), operettas, and ballets; films on musical subjects (*Song to Remember*, starring Cornell Wilde as Chopin); and films in which the music functions primarily as background (*Elvira Madigan*, Mozart; *The Seventh Veil*, Beethoven; *The Great Lie*, Tchaikovsky; *Alexander Nevsky*, Prokofiev; *Sunday, Bloody Sunday*, Mozart; *Clockwork Orange*, Beethoven; Cocteau's *The Strange Ones*, Vivaldi/ Bach).

27. Discuss the conversion of a play, novel, or legend into an opera. Compare the original version with the libretto of the opera and comment on the dramatic function of the music in support of the libretto. Examples: Shakespeare's *Macbeth, Othello*, and *Falstaff* turned into operas by Verdi; Dumas's *Lady of the Camelias* into Verdi's *La Traviata*; the legend of Tristan and Isolde into the opera by Wagner; Beaumarchais's comic masterpieces into Rossini's *The Barber of Seville* and Mozart's *The Marriage of Figaro*; Maeterlinck's *Pelléas et Mélisande* into the opera by Debussy; and Molière's *Le Bourgeois Gentilhomme* into Richard Strauss's *Ariadne auf Naxos*.

28. Make a study of modern operas in English. Consider the operas of the English composer Benjamin Britten, as well as American operas by Virgil Thomson (*The Mother of Us All, Four Saints in Three Acts*), Samuel Barber (*Vanessa*), Douglas Moore (*The Devil and Daniel Webster, The Ballad of Baby Doe*), Gian-Carlo Menotti (*The Medium, The Saint of Bleecker Street*, etc.), and others.

29. Make a study of musical interpretations of astrology. Start with Gustav Holst's orchestral suite *The Planets*, and then proceed to George Crumb's *Makrokosmos*, Volumes I and II, each a series of "twelve fantasy-pieces after the zodiac for amplified piano." Can you locate other relevant examples?

GLOSSARY OF TERMS

Absolute: nonprogrammatic music, i.e., music with no apparent extramusical content.

A Cappella: vocal music unaccompanied by instruments.

Accelerando: a gradual increase in tempo. Abbreviation: *accel.* (Ital.)

Accent: an emphasis on a note due to sharp attack or strong rhythmic pulse.

Accompaniment: music which is subsidiary to some other principal musical component, as in the piano *accompaniment* of a vocal work.

Adagio: very slow (Ital.).

Agitato: agitated (Ital.).

Aleatoric: indicates music composed by random methods of selecting pitches, rhythms, instrumentation, etc.

Allegretto: moderately fast (Ital.).

Allegro: fast (Ital.).

Alto: A woman's low voice, also known as *contralto*. Alto parts in early music may also be sung by high male voices (countertenors). Also the second part of a four-voiced texture, lower than the soprano part, but higher than the tenor and bass parts.

Alto Clef: a symbol locating middle C on the third line of a five-line staff. In modern scores used principally in viola parts.

Andante: moderately slow (Ital.).

Animato: animated (Ital.).

Answer: a version of a fugue subject usually starting a perfect fifth higher or a perfect fourth lower than the original subject.

Anthem: a relatively brief choral work, usually religious.

Anticipation: the early entrance of a chord note, usually a dissonance against the notes of the preceding chord with which it appears.

Appassionato: passionately (Ital.).

Arco: indicates string music to be played with the bow (after a *pizzicato* passage) (Ital.).

Aria: a song for solo voice in a cantata, oratorio, opera, etc., usually accompanied by orchestra.

Arioso: a passage partly in recitative style, partly like an aria.

Arpeggio: a series of notes generally belonging to a single chord, wherein the chord notes are sounded one at a time. A linear version of a *block chord*.

A Tempo: indicates a return to the original tempo of a piece of music, or section thereof (Ital.).

Atonality: music in which no single pitch or class of pitches predominates; music which avoids the traditional characteristics of tonal music, i.e., a sense of key.

Attacca: immediately attacking the next movement or other section of a large work, as opposed to proceeding after a pause (Ital.).

Augmentation: the presentation of a musical passage in longer note values than in its previous statement.

Augmented: indicating a large-size interval or chord; e.g., a sixth larger than a major sixth is an *augmented sixth*. In an *augmented triad* the top note of a major triad is raised a half step.

Ballet Suite: a collection of excerpts from the music composed for a ballet, designed to be played in an orchestral concert.

Bar: a unit of measure. See *measure*.

Baritone: a man's voice range, lower than a tenor, higher than a bass.

Bar Line: a vertical line demarcating the end of one measure and the beginning of the next.

Baroque: a period in music history extending from roughly 1600 to 1760.

Baroque concerto: see *concerto grosso*.

Bass: the lowest notes in a multivoiced texture, as in a *bass line*. Also a man's low voice and the lowest part in a multi-voiced texture, as in a *bass part*.

Bass Clef: a symbol locating F below middle C on the second highest line of a five-line staff.

Basset Horn: a middle-register member of the clarinet family, found in scores by Mozart and other eighteenth-century composers

Basso Continuo: see *continuo*.

Beat: a rhythmic pulse, typically an equal subdivision of a measure.

Bel Canto: the smooth vocal style of Italian opera of the eighteenth and nineteenth centuries (Ital.).

Binary Form: the structural division of a work into two principal sections.

Bitonality: the simultaneous presence in a piece of music of two keys. See *polytonality*.

Block Chord: the simultaneous sounding of all the notes of a chord (as opposed to an *arpeggiation*).

Blue Note: a slightly flattened seventh (e.g., a low B♭ above C) associated with jazz styles.

Broadway Musical: an operetta or comic opera in the style of American popular music.

Cadence: the conclusion of a phrase, providing a sense of articulation or breath (or final completion).

Cadenza: a showy passage in an instrumental or vocal work, usually performed by a single musician; typically a solo passage in a concerto (with the orchestra silent).

Canon: a piece in which an initial melodic line is exactly imitated in one or more succeeding melodic lines. The imitation may start on the same note as the model, or it may be transposed. Simple canons at the unison are called *rounds*.

Cantata: an extensive vocal work in several movements, often with religious text, usually with soloists and chorus accompanied by orchestra. See *chorale cantata*.

Cantor: a liturgical singer and leader of congregational singing in Jewish worship services.

Cantus Firmus: a melodic line which serves as the basis for a musical work (*chorale prelude, chorale cantata*, etc.), frequently borrowed from an earlier source, such as Gregorian chant or Lutheran chorales (Lat.).

C Clef: a clef which locates middle C on one of the five lines of a staff—e.g., *alto clef, tenor clef*.

Chaconne: a dance form in slow triple meter in which an original passage of four or eight measures is followed by a series of variations of similar length. Similar to a *passacaglia* (Fr.).

Chamber Concerto: a concerto for one or more soloists accompanied by a small orchestra.

Chamber Music: music for small ensemble, usually performed without conductor.

Chamber Orchestra: the small orchestra of the eighteenth century and revived in the twentieth century.

Chance Music: see *aleatoric*.

Chanson: a Renaissance part song, similar to a *madrigal* (Fr.).

Chant: a simple melody. See *Gregorian chant*.

Chorale: a German hymn.

Chorale Cantata: a cantata in which one or more movements are based on a chorale melody. See *cantata*.

Chorale Prelude: a keyboard work based on a chorale.

Chord: a collection of notes which are conceived as sounding simultaneously, but which can also be linearized as in an *arpeggio*.

Chord Cluster: in modern music the sounding of many contiguous pitches, usually performed (on the piano) by using the hand, fist, and/or arm to depress several keys simultaneously.

Chromaticism: refers to music with frequent key changes or accidentals from secondary keys, also to music in which the chromatic scale figures so strongly as to deny the predominance of any single key.

Chromatic Scale: the succession of twelve notes equally subdividing an octave. Twelve or more successive black and white notes on the piano keyboard.

Church Modes: see *mode*.

Classical: refers to serious or concert music, as opposed to folk or popular music. With an upper-case C, refers to the period of music history starting in roughly 1730 and ending about 1820.

Clef: a notational symbol which specifies locations of pitches. See *alto clef, bass clef, treble clef*, etc.

Coda: the final section of a movement or work.

Collage: a type of composition which provides a "multitrack" texture of old and new music, speech, random sounds, etc.

Coloratura Soprano: a very high soprano.

Compound Meter: meter in which the number of beats per measure exceeds four, e.g., $\frac{6}{8}$, which represents two groupings of three beats each.

Concerto: a work scored for one or more soloists accompanied by orchestra.

Concerto Grosso: a Baroque work usually scored for a few soloists accompanied by a small string ensemble. The soloists rarely play alone, but rather stand out as a solo group differentiated from the accompanying group. In a concerto grosso the soloists generally participate in the ensemble during nonsolo passages (Ital.).

Glossary of Terms

Consonance: the quality of sounds in harmonious combinations; and of intervals belonging to the major and minor triads, as opposed to stepwise intervals and the tritone (augmented fourth/diminished fifth).

Con Sordino: with mute (Ital.).

Contemporary: indicating the music of the most recent past, especially the music composed since World War II.

Continuo: in Baroque music the bass line of a composition, as played by cello, bass, or bassoon, and chords and other notes played above the bass line, as played by a keyboard instrument. Continuo parts may be figured or unfigured, the former a numerical shorthand for informing the keyboard performer how to construct the necessary chords. (Only rarely did Baroque composers write out a complete keyboard continuo part.)

Contralto: a low woman's voice type. See *alto*.

Cornett: an early instrument made of wood, combining qualities of the later oboe and trumpet. (Not to be confused with the modern cornet, which is similar to a trumpet.)

Counterpoint: the intermixing of two or more independent melodic lines.

Countersubject: a contrapuntal melody which accompanies the (principal) subject of a fugue.

Countertenor: a high male voice, equivalent in range to an alto.

Coupling: a device on harpsichords and organs whereby the performer depresses a single key but produces doublings, usually at the octave.

Crescendo: get louder gradually. Abbreviation: *cresc.* (Ital.).

Cyclic Form: a type of instrumental structure in which one or more themes are heard in two or more movements.

Da Capo Aria: a Baroque form in which a contrasting middle section is followed by an exact duplication of the first section; an A-B-A form (Ital.).

Decrescendo: see *diminuendo* (Ital.).

Descant: a subsidiary melodic line, often lying in a higher register than the principal melody.

Development: a passage in which previously stated material is repeated in various forms and guises, extensions, transformations, etc. The middle of the three principal sections of *sonata form*.

Diapason: a much-used organ stop which imitates neither a vocal nor orchestral timbre.

Diatonic Scale: the notes belonging to a given key, as indicated by its key signature, as opposed to external (i.e., chromatic) notes.

Diminished: an interval or chord smaller than some standard size (e.g., reducing a minor third by a half step results in a diminished third; similarly a diminished seventh is a half step smaller than a minor seventh). A diminished seventh chord consists of two kinds of diminished intervals, a diminished fifth and a diminished seventh. A diminished triad is one in which the top note of a minor triad is lowered by a half step.

Diminuendo (Dim.): get softer gradually (Ital.).

Dissonance: the opposite of consonance. Often signifies discordant sounds, but also in tonal music simply characterizes any interval not belonging to the major or minor triads — e.g., seconds and sevenths.

Divertimento: a Classical suite of a light, diverting nature for chamber ensemble or orchestra (Ital.).

Dolce: gently or sweetly (Ital.).

Dominant: the fifth scale degree of a diatonic scale. Also the chord or triad built on that note as root.

Dominant Seventh: a chord built on the fifth scale degree of a diatonic scale, consisting of a major triad with a minor third superimposed, e.g., in C major, the chord consisting of the notes B, D, and F above the root G.

Dorian Mode: an early church mode with the step succession W H W W W H W. See *mode*.

Dot: a rhythmic marking indicating the extension of a note duration (or rest) by half.

Double Flat: signifies lowering a pitch by two half steps (♭♭).

Double Sharp: signifies raising a pitch by two half steps (×).

Double Stop: the simultaneous bowing of two or more strings of a string instrument.

Doubling: an accompanying pitch, usually a higher or lower octave equivalent.

Downbeat: the first beat of a measure.

Drone: a continuous sounding of one or more pitches, producing a mild bagpipe effect.

Duet (or Duo): a piece or passage featuring two singers or instrumentalists.

Duple Meter: successive measures of two or multiples of two beats: ⅔, ⅘, etc.

Dynamics: pertaining to gradations of loudness and softness; volume.

Eighth Note: one half of a quarter note; an eighth subdivision of a complete measure in ⁴₄ time.

Electronic Music: music generated by means of electronic instruments, such as tape recorders and synthesizers, sometimes aided by computers.

English Horn: a tenor-range member of the oboe family.

Enharmonic Equivalents: two pitches with different diatonic names that occupy the same position in the chromatic scale — e.g., C# and Db.

Ensemble Scene: a passage of theater music involving several singing participants.

Episode: a contrasting section of a rondo or fugue.

Exposition: the opening section of a *fugue* or *sonata-form*.

Expressionism: bold and stark atonal music of Schoenberg, Stravinsky, Hindemith, and their contemporaries, dating from the early and mid twentieth century.

F: abbreviation of *forte* (loud).

False Reprise: a passage which commences deceptively as if duplicating an earlier section, but moves into new areas before the inception of the genuine reprise.

Fantasy: a work in free form, usually consisting of several sections each of which introduces new thematic material.

Figure: a rhythmic/pitch pattern.

Five, The: a group of nationalist Russian composers during the latter part of the nineteenth century.

Flat: a symbol (♭) which lowers a pitch a half step.

Form: the structure of a piece, as in *sonata form, theme and variations, rondo, fantasy.* Sometimes also a synonym for *genre.*

Forte: loud (Ital.).

Fortissimo: very loud (Ital.).

Fret: a metal bar which indicates the location of specific pitches on the fingerboard of string instruments such as guitar, banjo, and dulcimer.

Fugato: a passage in fugal style (Ital.).

Fugue: a polyphonic work in which all linear parts are structurally equal; generally based on a single melody or *fugue subject.*

Fugue Subject: the main theme of a fugue.

Funeral March: slow, solemn processional music.

Genre: a category of composition, such as opera, symphony, or concerto.

Glissando: sliding up or down a scale without articulation of individual pitches (Ital.).

Grace Note: a note of very brief approximate duration which immediately precedes a note of more substantial duration. Grace notes are indicated by noteheads and stems of subnormal size.

Gregorian Chant: the musical liturgy of the Roman Catholic Church as codified under the edict of Pope Gregory (sixth century).

Ground Bass: a bass melody which is repeated over and over throughout a given piece or passage, as in a *chaconne* or *passacaglia.*

Half Note: the durational equivalent of two quarter notes; one half of a complete measure in ¢ meter.

Half Step: the smallest *interval* of the chromatic scale.

Harmonic: a tone specially produced on stringed and other instruments equivalent to an *overtone* of a given (fundamental) pitch. See *overtone series.*

Harmonic Minor: a minor scale in which the seventh degree is raised by a half step, thereby converting the interval between the seventh and eighth scale degrees to a half step, and the interval between the sixth and seventh degrees to an augmented second (three half steps).

Harmonic Series: see *overtone series.*

Harmony: the vertical or chordal aspect of music, in contradistinction to its melodic contrapuntal aspects.

Hexachord: a six-note collection. In twelve-tone composition the first or second half of a *tone row.*

Homophonic: indicates a musical texture of a single melody with simple chordal accompaniment.

Idée Fixe: a theme which recurs in various movements of a large instrumental work (Fr.).

Imitation: exact or approximate repetitions of melodic lines and motives, starting on the same or different pitches; also replicating by means of reversal (retrograde) or mirroring (inversion).

Impressionism: a musical movement, 1890–1925, centered in France, inspired by Impressionist painters.

Interval: the tonal space between two pitches.

Intonation: the state of playing or singing in exact tune, referring especially to non-keyboard instruments and voices.

Inversion: with regard to intervals, a complement of an interval with respect to the octave, i.e., the distance remaining in an octave after "subtracting" the given interval. For example, the inversion of a major third is a minor sixth (four half steps subtracted from twelve equals eight half steps). A perfect fourth (five half steps) inverts to a perfect fifth (seven half steps), and an augmented fourth (six) inverts to a diminished fifth (six). With regard to chords, *inversion* refers to a position of a chord in which its root is located outside the bass part. With regard to melodies, *inversion* means mirroring of the intervallic contour of a melody. Thus, if a given melody rises a fifth and drops a third, its inversion drops a fifth and rises a third, etc.

Jew's Harp: a metal instrument of lyre shape, with a projecting steel tongue that is held between the teeth as the instrument is played.

Key: the tonal organization of a composition. The key of a piece is the same as its *tonic* note, as when one speaks of a piece in C major or B minor. Note that the specification of key also includes an indication of *mode* (major, minor).

Key Signature: the sharps or flats (or absence thereof) notated at the beginning of each staff of a tonal piece, indicating its diatonic pitches.

Köchel Number: the *opus number* assigned to a composition by Mozart. (Köchel definitively catalogued Mozart's music during the nineteenth century.)

Largo: a slow stately tempo. Also a work in that tempo and character (Ital.).

Leading Tone: the seventh degree of the major scale, one half step below the tonic.

Legato: playing or singing in a manner in which one note is connected to the next smoothly without interruption (Ital.).

Leger Line: an extra line (or lines) extending above or below a five-line staff. For example, middle C is located on the first leger line above the bass staff, also the first leger line below the treble staff.

Leitmotif: as conceived by Wagner, a musical motive signifying a character, object, idea, etc.; used in operas to support the dramatic narrative (Ger.).

Lento: slow (Ital.).

Libretto: the text of an opera, operetta, or other dramatic musical work.

Lied (Lieder): a German song (songs) (Ger.).

Liturgical Drama: a Medieval music drama or pageant designed as a church festivity.

Lydian Mode: an early church mode with the step succession W W W H W W H. See *mode.*

Madrigal: an English or Italian secular part song of the Renaissance period, usually unaccompanied.

Maestoso: majestic (Ital.).

Major Mode: the modern successor of the early Ionian mode, consisting of the scalar succession: W W H W W W H. To say that a piece is in the major mode is to assert that it is based structurally on the major scale. (The two terms are essentially synonymous.)

Major Scale: see *major mode.*

Major Triad: a three-note chord consisting of the first, third, and fifth scale degrees of the major scale.

Manual: a keyboard, as in a "two-manual organ."

Marcato: in a marked or accented style (Ital.).

Mass: a musical setting of the Roman Catholic Mass. It consists of the five parts of the Ordinary: Kyrie, Gloria, Credo, Sanctus, and Agnus Dei.

Mazurka: a Polish national dance in triple meter, often with accented third beats.

Measure: a time unit—a grouping of beats demarcated by bar lines. E.g., a piece in ¾ meter consists of successive measures of three quarter-note beats.

Medieval: signifying the period in music history from the Dark Ages to roughly the beginning of the fifteenth century.

Melisma: the singing of two or more pitches for a single syllable of text.

Melodic Minor: an alteration in the standard natural minor scale in which the sixth and seventh notes are raised a half step. The intervallic succession proceeds W H W W W W H.

Meter: pertaining to the organization of music into groups of pulses or beats. See *measure.*

Mezzo Forte: medium loud (Ital.).

Mezzo Piano: medium soft (Ital.).

Mezzo-Soprano: a woman's voice range somewhat lower than a soprano's, but not as low as an alto's. A medium-range voice.

Microtonal: refers to intervals smaller than a half step. The most commonly used microtones are *quarter tones.*

Mighty Handful: see *The Five.*

Minor Mode: one of the two principal modes of tonal music, based primarily on the natural minor scale W H W W H W W. Commonly the seventh degree (sometimes also the sixth degree) is raised a half step. See *harmonic minor* and *melodic minor.*

Minor Scale: see *minor mode.*

Minor Triad: a three-note chord consisting of the first, third, and fifth scale degrees of a minor scale.

Minuet: a moderate tempo dance in triple meter; also a piece in this style.

Minuet and Trio: a symphony or sonata movement in three parts, the first in minuet style, the second equivalent to a contrasting minuet—usually somewhat subdued as compared with the first minuet, and the third a literal or varied repetition of the first minuet.

Mixolydian Mode: an early church mode with the step succession W W H W W H W. See *mode.*

Mixture: certain organ registrations in which a fundamental tone is combined with pitches duplicating some of its overtones. See *overtone series.*

Glossary of Terms

Mode: a scale. In early music one of several scales used in musical composition, each starting on a different note of the diatonic scale, and known as *church modes* (Dorian, Phrygian, Lydian, Mixolydian, etc.). In music of the last four hundred years two principal modes have assumed predominance, the major (formerly Ionian) and minor (formerly Aeolian). In Jewish liturgical music, *mode* signifies melodic patterns and scales of traditional cantorial vocal styles.

Modern: indicating the music of the twentieth century, particularly compositions of adventurous and innovative character. See *contemporary*.

Modulation: a change from one key to another within a given piece; also a transitional passage accomplishing a change of key.

Monody: a spare melodic style of composition with simple accompaniment, as in the operatic style of the early Baroque period.

Monophonic: one-voiced music, as in Gregorian chant, as opposed to *polyphony*.

Motet: a work for several singers or chorus, often unaccompanied. A principal vocal form of the Medieval and Renaissance periods.

Motive: a melodic and/or rhythmic pattern. See also *Leitmotif*.

Movement: an independent section of an instrumental or vocal work.

Musical: see *Broadway musical*.

Music Drama: an opera which emphasizes a realistic dramatic flow (as opposed to a stylized series of independent musical numbers), associated primarily with the operas of Wagner.

Musique Concrète: an early form of electronic music (1950s) originating in France (Fr.).

Nationalism: a musical movement in which composers have asserted their national autonomy by emphasizing folk melodies and other indigenous characteristics in opposition to mainstream classical styles.

Natural Minor: the unaltered diatonic minor scale, W H W W H W W.

Natural Sign: an accidental (♮) which cancels out a flat or sharp.

Neighbor Note: a relatively ornamental note which is a scalar adjacency to a structurally superior note. (In the configuration 8-7-8—the numbers representing scale degrees—8 is the main note, 7 the neighbor note.)

Neoclassicism: a movement starting during World War I and lasting until about 1950 in which composers

integrated aspects of earlier Classical, Baroque, and Romantic styles into newer musical gestures.

Neumes: the noteheads-cum-stems used in the notation of Gregorian chant and other Medieval music.

Obbligato: a secondary melodic line (Ital.).

Oboe Da Caccia: literally "oboe of the hunt," an early member of the oboe family but with a lower (tenor) range. Music for this instrument is now often played on the English horn (Ital.).

Octave: a distance of eight diatonic notes, as from one C to the next higher or lower C. Also, a span of twelve half steps.

Octave Equivalent: a pitch located at an interval of one or more octaves from a given pitch.

Ondes Martenot: an electronic instrument used in certain orchestral works by the modern French composer Olivier Messiaen. It sounds somewhat like a female voice of very extensive range (Fr.).

Opera: a stage drama enacted by singers, accompanied by orchestra.

Operetta: a light opera, usually with spoken dialogue, rather than sung recitative, between musical numbers.

Ophicleide: a low-register brass instrument found in scores by Berlioz and other nineteenth-century composers. In today's orchestra it is normally replaced by the tuba.

Opus Number: a number assigned by a composer or publisher, signifying the publishing chronology of a work with respect to the composer's previous publications.

Oratorio: a large-scale semi-dramatic work for soloists, chorus, and orchestra, frequently on a religious subject. Although the soloists may impersonate roles, the main elements of the drama are unfolded through sung narration.

Organum: the earliest form of polyphony, in which a chant is accompanied by an imitating voice at the distance of a perfect fourth or fifth.

Ornamentation: the decoration of structurally important notes with subsidiary notes, as in a *trill, gracenote*, etc.

Ostinato: a continuously repeated pitch and/or rhythmic motive, often in the bass. See *ground bass*.

Overtone Series: an infinite collection of tones which accompany a given tone (*fundamental*) as produced by most voices and instruments. Although separate overtones are not easily distinguishable by human ears, their presence contributes to our perception of the timbral qualities of different voices and instruments. For

Glossary of Terms

a given fundamental the lowest and most audible overtones are the octave, perfect twelfth, double octave (fifteenth), and major seventeenth (comprising a *major triad*); the fifth overtone is equivalent to a slightly flattened minor seventh (similar to a *blue note*).

Overture: the prelude to an opera or other music drama, often incorporating musical material to be heard later in the work.

P: abbreviation for *piano* (soft).

Passacaglia: like the chaconne, a stately dance-form in triple meter. In instrumental music a composition in this style consisting of a brief theme (often in the bass part) and numerous variations (Ital.).

Passing Tone: in structural terms, a subsidiary note which connects two notes of greater structural weight. E.g., in the first phrase of "Three Blind Mice," the first and third notes, members of the tonic chord, are the main structural notes and the second note is a passing tone.

Passion: an oratorio based on the events leading to the crucifixion of Christ.

Pedal: a foot device associated with keyboard and other instruments (harp). A pedal may produce a pitch, modify a pitch, or produce other effects, such as muting, sustaining, octave coupling, etc.

Pedal Point: a note sustained beneath a chord progression. In tonal music this note is usually the dominant or tonic scale degree.

Pentatonic: refers to a five-note scale found in music of the Orient and other parts of the world. The five black notes of a piano keyboard represent the pentatonic scale; its intervals are two and three half steps in size.

Phantasy: alternate spelling of *fantasy*.

Phrase: a musical clause, such as a line of song punctuated by a breath, or the instrumental equivalent thereof.

Phrygian Mode: an early church mode with the step succession H W W W H W W. See *mode*.

Pianissimo: very soft (Ital.)

Piano: soft. Also the modern keyboard instrument, the full name of which, *pianoforte*, signifies its capability in differentiating among various degrees of volume (Ital.).

Pizzicato (Pizz.): indicates string music to be plucked instead of bowed (Ital.). See *arco*.

Plagal Cadence: a cadence consisting of the progression IV-I or I-IV-I (where IV represents the triad built on the fourth degree of a diatonic scale, and I signifies the tonic) which normally serves to confirm a standard V–I cadence. Associated with the "A-men" chord progression found at the end of hymns.

Plainchant: the unaccompanied Catholic chant repertoire which came into full flower during the Medieval period.

Polonaise: a Polish national dance in triple meter. Also, a musical work in this form, usually of a brilliant and flamboyant nature.

Polyphony: music consisting of two or more coexisting voices of equal structural weight; opposite of *homophony*.

Polytonality: the simultaneous occurrence of two or more keys, a special effect often associated with a sense of two or more separate pieces being played at the same time.

Prepared Piano: as devised initially by John Cage, the attachment of various objects to the strings of a piano to effect unusual timbres.

Presto: extremely fast (Ital.).

Program Music: instrumental music which represents extramusical subject matter, as in a *tone poem*. Program music may attempt to narrate a story, project an abstract or intellectual idea, set a mood, and so on.

Quarter Note: a basic metrical unit in music of the past several hundred years. Four quarter notes represent a whole note. The most commonly used *time signatures* are expressed as groupings of quarter note beats.

Quarter Tone: one half of a half step, the most common subdivision in *microtonal* music.

Quartet: a work for four instrumentalists or vocalists, or a group of four performers of such a work.

Range: the distance from lowest to highest notes playable by a given instrument or singable by a particular voice type.

Rank: in a pipe organ, a grouping of pipes of similar timbre.

Recapitulation: the third and final principal section of *sonata-form*, in which material from the first section (*exposition*) is repeated in different key relationships, mostly centering about the tonic.

Recitative: a style of narrative and/or conversational singing in which speech rhythms and inflections prevail over more formal musical considerations.

Refrain: in a song, a recurring thematic section, often involving a single text; by analogy, in instrumental music, a recurring section framing contrasting episodes. See *rondo*.

Register: a region of pitches, usually described as low, medium, or high, or associated with the range of

Glossary of Terms

pitches produceable by a given voice type or instrument.

Registration: the *stops* (i.e., timbres) used in the performance of an organ piece.

Relative Major, Relative Minor: a pair of major and minor keys with the same key signature. E.g., E minor is the *relative minor* of G major (key signature, one ♯). Correspondingly, G major is the *relative major* of E minor.

Renaissance: a period in music history extending from roughly 1400 to 1600.

Reprise: a repeated section, especially the final section of a *da capo aria* and similar A–B–A forms.

Requiem: the musical setting of a liturgical service for the dead.

Resolution: a note or chord which follows a dissonance, as when an ornamental note *resolves* to a more stable note, or a dissonant chord resolves to a consonant chord.

Rest: a (notated) silence occurring within a composition.

Retrograde: the presentation of the notes of a theme, or other musical material, in reverse order. See *twelve-tone system.*

Rhapsody: an instrumental piece in free form and flamboyant style, often associated with Gypsy music.

Ritard(ando): a gradual decrease in tempo (Ital.).

Rococo: the early Classical period (mid-18th century).

Romantic: a period in music history from roughly 1820 to 1900.

Rondo: a musical form consisting of a *refrain* which is restated after contrasting *episodes.* The simplest type of rondo is represented by the scheme A–B–A, but the term usually applies to longer chains, as in A–B–A–C–A and A–B–A–C–A–B–A.

Root: the fundamental note of a triad or other chord. A chord is said to be in *root position* when its root is in the bass part.

Round: a simple *canon* with imitation at the *unison.*

Row: see *tone row.*

Scale: an ordering of a collection of pitches from low to high (or the reverse).

Scale Degree: a numerically specified member of a scale, such as the fifth *scale degree* of a diatonic scale. Scale degrees are usually numbered from low to high, with octave equivalents counting as a single scale degree; thus, in C major the scale C–D–E–F–G–A–B–C is represented by the scale degrees 1–2–3–4–5–6–7–8 (with "8" as an alternate expression for "1").

Scena: an extended solo scene in a musical drama, involving a mixture of *recitative* and formal *aria* (Ital.).

Scherzando: in the style of a *scherzo* (Ital.).

Scherzo: a movement of a large instrumental work in brilliant fast tempo, usually in triple meter; replaces the *minuet* movement of early Classical symphonies in late Classical and Romantic works (Ital.—derived from *Scherz,* German for *joke*).

Secondary Tonic: a subsidiary key; in a tonal piece the principal note of a diatonic scale which temporarily replaces the principal scale of the composition.

Semi-Classical: combining characteristics of classical and popular musical styles within a single work.

Semi Tone: a half step.

Sequence: a passage in which an initial harmonic/thematic progression is imitated at different pitch levels.

Serialism: the arrangement of various musical elements—pitch, dynamics, durational values, timbres, etc.—into series as the structural basis of a composition. See *twelve-tone system, tone row.*

Seventh: an interval formed by two notes seven scale degrees apart; e.g., C–B, G–F.

Seventh Chord: a four-note chord consisting of a triad and a fourth note two scale degrees higher than the top note of the triad, e.g., C–E–G–B, G–B♭–D♭–F♭. In the tonal system there are several sizes of seventh chords—*major seventh, diminished seventh* (both illustrated above), *minor seventh,* and *half-diminished seventh,* the size depending both on the type of triad supporting the seventh and the size of the seventh itself (*diminished, minor, major*).

SF: abbreviation of *sforzando* (see below).

Sforzando: a loud accent (Ital.).

Sharp (♯): a symbol which raises a pitch a half step.

Sixteenth Note: a duration equivalent to one half an eighth note, or a quarter of a quarter note.

Sixth Chord: the first inversion of a *triad* or *seventh chord,* in which the second lowest note (of the root-position chord) is located in the bass.

Slow Introduction: the slow commencement of a fast movement (usually the first or last movement of a sonata or symphony).

Slur: a marking indicating the *legato* connection of one note to another.

Solo: a piece for a single performer; also, a passage within an ensemble work for a single performer, or

Glossary of Terms

featuring a single performer accompanied by other players. Since within a given work two or more performers may share the role of soloist, the term may connote *featured performer* rather than *individual*.

Sonata: an instrumental work, generally in several movements, for one or a few players.

Sonata-Allegro-Form: optional term for *sonata-form* in fast tempo.

Sonata-Form: the structure of a movement in an instrumental work, consisting essentially of three sections: (1) *exposition* (2) *development*, and (3) *recapitulation*, optionally preceded by a *slow introduction* and ending with a *coda*. The *exposition* presents fresh material, initially in the tonic, then in secondary keys; the *development* reworks the same material in numerous keys; and the *recapitulation* restates the exposition, but now mainly in the tonic.

Song Cycle: a collection of songs which form a single compositional entity, often based on a set of interrelated texts by one poet.

Song Symphony: a symphonic work based in part on previously composed songs—associated with symphonies of Gustav Mahler.

Soprano: a woman's high voice type; also the highest notes of a multi-voiced texture, as in the *soprano part* of a vocal or instrumental texture.

Sotto voce: literally "under the voice"; to play or sing very softly in the manner of an aside (Ital.).

Sprechstimme: a cross between speaking and singing, wherein the performer attacks notes on specified pitches but then allows the voice to assume a spoken inflection (Ger.).

Staccato: executing a note shorter than its notated duration; the opposite of *legato*. Indicated by small dots set above or below noteheads.

Staff: a set of lines (and spaces) for locating pitches (with the addition of a *clef* sign). During the past several hundred years the standardized staff has consisted of five lines.

Stop: a timbral setting on an organ.

Stretto: (1) a fast acceleration; (2) the overlapping of successive statements of a *fugue subject* (effected by accelerated entrances) (Ital.).

Strophic Form: repetition of the same music for the several verses of a song.

Subdominant: the fourth degree of a diatonic scale; the triad built on that degree as root.

Subject: a principal theme, as in a *fugue*.

Suite: a collection of instrumental pieces. See also *ballet suite*.

Suspension: the extension of a note into the time-span of a following chord, often resulting in a dissonance between the suspended note and the other members of the suspension chord.

Sustaining Pedal: on the piano, a foot device which allows all the strings to resonate, producing a rich, sometimes blurred effect that is one of the main characteristics of piano sound.

Symphonic Poem: a *tone poem* (for full orchestra).

Symphony: a large-scale work scored for orchestra; also an abbreviation for the term *symphony orchestra*. In the Baroque period, *symphony* more generally signified any instrumental work.

Syncopation: a rhythmic effect deriving from the accentuation of weak metrical beats, especially associated with a note commencing on a weak beat and continuing past the next strong beat.

Synthesizer: a versatile electronic instrument used in generating electronic music. It can imitate some of the acoustical effects of traditional instruments, as well as create novel effects through the manipulation of various acoustical parameters.

Tam-Tam: a tuned gong.

Tape Loop: in electronic music, the continuous repetition of a taped sound segment.

Tape Music: generally any electronic music produced through the manipulation of sound on tape recorders and related electronic instruments.

Te Deum: a musical setting of the Latin hymn of praise, "Te deum laudamus" (Latin).

Tempo: the general musical term for speed (Ital.).

Tempo I: return to the original tempo.

Tenor: a man's high voice type, and the second lowest part in a four-part vocal texture.

Tenor Clef: a symbol locating middle C on the second highest line of a five-line staff. Used primarily in violoncello and bassoon parts.

Ternary Form: three-part form in which the third part corresponds literally or approximately to the first part. Often represented as *A–B–A form*. See *da capo aria, minuet-and-trio*.

Theme: a melody, particularly an important one in a given composition. See also *theme and variations*.

Theme and Variations: the structural organization of a single movement or complete work in which the melody, chords, and metrical/rhythmic structure of an original or borrowed theme serve as the model for a series of varied imitations.

Glossary of Terms

Thirty-Second Note: a note duration lasting one eighth of a *quarter note*, or one thirty-second of a complete measure in ⁴⁄₄ meter.

Tie: a notational symbol (a brief curved line) which connects two notes of the same pitch, meaning not to reattack the note, but simply to extend it for the duration of the second note. Used when longer duration values or a *dot* are not employable, as when a note-duration extends past a *bar line*.

Timbre: the character of a pitch as produced by a voice or instrument, as in the contrasting *timbres* of the oboe and clarinet. Also, orchestrational color effected through the combination of various instruments. (See *overtone series*.)

Time Signature: the numerical indication at the beginning of a piece or section thereof, indicating the number and size of beats per measure. E.g., ⁴⁄₄ indicates four quarter note beats per measure.

Tonality: the organizational system of a piece in which one note serves as the principal note of a *triad* and *scale*, and in relation to which all other notes are subsidiary. See *key, tonic*.

Tone Poem: a descriptive work for orchestra or smaller ensemble, usually in one extended movement.

Tone Row: in serial music, an ordering of the twelve members of the *chromatic scale*, selected by a composer as the structural basis of a composition.

Tonic: the principal or first degree of a *diatonic scale*—thus, the main note of a tonal piece. Also the major or minor triad built on that degree as root.

Tonicization: the establishing of a temporary tonic within a tonal piece, as when chromatic chords are introduced which mildly or powerfully undermine the preeminence of the main tonic. See *modulation*.

Transcription: the arrangement of an original work for different voices and/or instrumentation.

Transposition: the repetition of a note configuration (chord, melody, mixture of both, etc.) retaining identical internal relationships but starting on a different note. E.g., the scale of D major represents a *transposition* of the scale of C major.

Treble Clef: a symbol locating G above middle C on the second lowest line of a five-line staff.

Tremolo (Tremolando): in instrumental music the extremely rapid repetition of a note or set of notes—on stringed instruments through quick short bow movements, on keyboard instruments through quick alternations of two notes. Also a vocal wavering (Ital.).

Triad: a three-note chord consisting of a root, a second note two scale degrees higher, and a third note two scale degrees above the second note. E.g., C–E–G, D♯–F♯–A, E♭–G–B.

Trill: rapid alternation between two pitches, one principal, the other ornamental (abbrev., *tr.*).

Trio: a work for three instruments, or a group of three performers of such a work. Also, the middle section of a minuet—see *minuet and trio*.

Trio Sonata: a Baroque genre for two solo instruments and *continuo*.

Triple Meter: the organization of rhythmic pulses (beats) in threes, producing successions of one strong beat followed by two weak beats (as in a *minuet* or *waltz*). Exemplified by time signatures of three or odd multiples of three beats per measure (³⁄₄, ⁹⁄₈, etc.).

Triplet: a durational value equivalent to one-third of some larger value. A triplet eighth note lasts one third of a quarter note; a triplet half note occupies one third of a complete measure in ⁴⁄₄ meter; etc.

Triplet Sign: a rhythmic notation indicating the division of a durational unit into three equal sub-beats.

Tritone: an augmented fourth, equivalent in size to three whole tones. Also, by *inversion*, a diminished fifth.

Tutti: *all*, referring mainly to the entire instrumental ensemble in orchestral works (Ital.).

Twelve-Tone System: a compositional approach in which each member of the chromatic scale is ostensibly structurally equal to each other member. See *tone row*. The twelve-tone system was conceived circa 1920 by Arnold Schoenberg as a replacement for the tonal principle of key relationships.

Unison: the interval formed by two notes of the same pitch.

Upbeat: a beat preceding the first beat of a measure.

Variation: a varied imitation. See *theme and variations*.

Vespers: an evening liturgical service; a musical setting of the Roman Catholic vespers.

Vibrato: a technique used on string instruments for effecting a warm tone, based on rapidly vibrating the fingers as they depress the strings on the fingerboard. Also a vocal tremor which (in excess) may spoil a singer's tone.

Vivace: very fast and lively (Ital.).

Vocal Range: the distance from lowest to highest pitches in a singer's voice or in a given vocal piece.

Voice: In instrumental music, a given line in a polyphonic texture, as in a *three-voice fugue* or *five-voice counterpoint*.

485

Glossary of Terms

Waltz: a fast dance in triple meter; a romantic instrumental piece in the character of this dance.

Whole Note: a note equivalent to the duration of four quarter notes or of one complete measure in ¢ meter.

Whole Step (Whole Tone): an interval equivalent to two half steps.

Whole-Tone Scale: a scale of successive whole steps, dividing the octave into six equal parts. Associated with *Impressionist* music.

Glossary of Terms

NOTES

INTRODUCTION

1. Romain Rolland, *Essays on Music*, New York, 1948, p. 5.

CHAPTER 1

1. See Peter G. Davis, "Ken Russell's Film Studies of Composers—Brilliance Gone Berserk," *The New York Times*, October 10, 1975, Sect. 2, p. 13.

2. André Gide, *Notes on Chopin*, trans. by Bernard Frechtman, New York, 1949, pp. 30, 54–55.

3. Edward Lockspeiser, *Debussy*, New York, 1972, p. 196.

4. From a letter written to André Messager in 1903, quoted by Lockspeiser in *Debussy: His Life and Mind*, Volume 2, New York, 1965, p. 26.

5. Lockspeiser, *Debussy*, p. 196.

6. Constant Lambert, *Music Ho!*, New York, 1934, pp. 30–31.

7. Quoted by Prof. Dr. Wilh. Altmann, Eulenburg Miniature Score, London, n.d., page i.

8. André Gide, *Two Symphonies*, trans. Dorothy Bussy, New York, 1968, p. 172 (originally published in 1919). The title of the novella ingeniously overlaps the pastor's "symphony"—concerning his illicit love for Gertrude—with Beethoven's.

9. From *The Letters of John Keats, 1814–1821*, Hyder Edward Rollins, ed., Vol. 2, Cambridge, Mass., 1958, p. 198.

10. Quoted in Calvin S. Brown, *Music and Literature—A Comparison of the Arts*, Athens, Georgia, 1948, p. 251.

11. Olive Cook, "Notes on the Plates," from *Scotland*, a book of photographs by Edwin Smith, New York, 1968, p. 212.

12. Brown, p. 252.

13. See Foreword to Mendelssohn's *Fingal's Cave Overture*, Eulenburg Miniature Score, London, n.d.

14. Brown, p. 251.

CHAPTER 5

1. Calvin S. Brown, *Music and Literature—A Comparison of the Arts*, Athens, Georgia, 1948, pp. 250–251.

2. Percy A. Sholes, *Oxford Companion to Music*, 10th ed., rev. John Owen Ward, London, 1970, p. 110. In an entertaining essay Scholes mentions a wide variety of works from different periods.

3. Nicolas Slonimsky, *Music Since 1900*, 4th ed., New York, 1971, p. 1067.

4. Hans W. Heinsheimer, *Fanfare for 2 Pidgeons*, New York, 1952, pp. 121–122.

5. Quoted in *Time*, November 3, 1975, p. 66.

6. From record jacket notes to Lythgoe's performance of MacDowell's piano music, Philips Recording 9500 095.

7. Quoted from a letter written by Debussy, in Edward Lockspeiser's *Debussy*, 3rd ed., New York, 1949, p. 32.

CHAPTER 6

1. Brian Large, *Smetana*, London, 1970, p. xiii.

2. Robert Layton, *Sibelius*, London, 1965, pp. 61–62. The first two sentences of this extract have been reversed. The term *symphonic poem* is synonymous with *tone poem* (for orchestra).

3. Sibelius's own words, quoted in Layton, p. 78.

4. Layton, pp. 79–80.

5. Halsey Stevens, *The Life and Music of Béla Bartók*, rev. ed., New York, 1964, p. xi.

6. See Gilbert Chase, *The Music of Spain*, 2nd rev. ed., New York, 1959, p. 188.

7. Chase, p. 188.

CHAPTER 7

1. Igor Stravinsky, *Autobiography*, New York, 1936, pp. 53–54.

2. See Igor Stravinsky and Robert Craft, *Expositions and Developments*, New York, 1962, pp. 132–134.

3. Igor Stravinsky and Robert Craft, *Conversations with Igor Stravinsky,* New York, 1959, p. 82. See Chapter 6 for more information on Bartók and Hungarian folk music.

4. Gilbert Chase, *The Music of Spain,* p. 155.

5. Quoted by Chase, p. 159.

CHAPTER 8

1. Virgil Thomson, *American Music Since 1910,* London, 1971, p. 2.

2. Thomson, p. 2.

3. *Aaron Copland, His Life and Times,* New York, 1967, pp. 160–161. At about this same time, Copland's Russian counterpart, Dmitri Shostakovich (1906–1976), composed the *Leningrad Symphony* (No. 7), honoring the heroic defense of that besieged Russian city at the height of the German invasion.

4. Arthur Berger, *Aaron Copland,* New York, 1953, p. 61.

5. Henry and Sidney Cowell, *Charles Ives and His Music*, New York, 1955, p. 11.

6. H. and S. Cowell, p. 12.

7. Vivian Perlis, *Charles Ives Remembered: An Oral History*, New Haven, Conn., 1974, p. 161.

8. See *Charles E. Ives—Memos*, John Kirkpatrick, ed., New York, 1972, pp. 96–101.

9. Kirkpatrick, p. 97.

CHAPTER 10
1. Hans Heinsheimer, *Best Regards to Aïda*, pp. 141–142.

2. David Ewen, *George Gershwin—His Journey to Greatness*, Englewood Cliffs, N.J., 1970, p. xx.

3. Ewen, pp. 86–87.

4. Foreword to Eulenburg Edition scores of Bach's *Brandenburg Concerti*, a set of six (Baroque) concertos scored for three or more soloists.

CHAPTER 11
1. Nicholas Slonimsky, *A Thing or Two About Music*, New York, 1948, p. 182.

2. Quoted from record jacket notes by Charles Burr, Columbia Recording CL-920.

3. Igor Stravinsky, *Autobiography*, New York, 1936, p. 69.

4. From record jacket notes by Vincent Sheehan, RCA Victor Recording LM-2323.

5. Hector Berlioz, *Memoirs*, David Cairns, trans. and ed., New York, 1969, p. 225. One commentator has suggested calling the piece "Hector in Italy."

6. James Harding, *The Ox on the Roof—Scenes from Musical Life in Paris in the Twenties*, New York, 1972, p. 68.

7. Harding, pp. 134–135.

CHAPTER 14
1. Peter Viereck, "Hitler and Richard Wagner," *Common Sense*, 8 (November 1939), 3.

2. A summary and interpretation of Shaw's monograph are offered by Martin Cooper in "Wagner's *Ring* as Political Myth," reprinted in Cooper's *Ideas and Music*, London, 1965, p. 109 ff.

3. From Elmer Davis, "The Imperfect Wagnerite," in *Not to Mention the War*, Indianapolis, 1940, p. 193.

4. Davis, pp. 193–197. Reprinted by permission of the publisher, The Bobbs-Merrill Company, Inc.

CHAPTER 15
1. Stanley Green, liner notes, MGM recording of *The Threepenny Opera*, MS-31210C.

2. Mosco Carner, *Alban Berg, The Man and the Work*, London, 1975, p. 11.

3. *Best Regards to Aïda*, New York, 1968, pp. 54–55. Copyright 1968 by Hans W. Heinsheimer. Reprinted with permission.

4. From "Beethoven," in H. L. Mencken, *Prejudices: Fifth Series,* New York, 1926, pp. 87–94.

5. Anthony Burgess, New York, 1974.

6. Burgess, pp. 304–305. Reprinted by permission.

CHAPTER 17

1. *Atlantic Monthly,* 186 (December 1950), 43–47, reprinted by permission of Hallie Burnett.

UNIT IV

1. See Friedrich Nietzsche, *The Case of Wagner,* Walter Kaufman, trans., New York, 1967, p. 158.

CHAPTER 18

1. Translation of excerpts from Schiller's *Ode to Joy* by Norman MacLeod, in *Friedrich Schiller—An Anthology for Our Time,* Frederick Ungar, ed., New York, 1959, pp. 42–43.

CHAPTER 19

1. See George Bernard Shaw, *The Perfect Wagnerite,* London, 1905, pp. 156–157.

2. Ernest Newman, *A Study of Wagner,* London, 1899, p. 250.

3. Herbert Reid, record jacket notes, Columbia Recording MS 6547.

4. Reid, record jacket notes.

5. William Mann, record jacket notes, Angel Recording 35994.

6. Original text drawn from *The Youth's Magic Horn* (1805), a collection of German folk poetry. English translation copyright 1963. Reprinted by permission.

7. Paul Stefan, *Gustav Mahler—A Study of His Personality and His Work,* T. E. Clark, trans., New York, 1913, p. 121.

8. Hermann Hesse, *Demian—The Story of a Youth,* New York, 1948, pp. 122–123.

9. Donald Jay Grout, *A History of Western Music,* rev. ed., New York, 1973, p. 540.

10. Igor Stravinsky, *Autobiography,* New York, 1936, pp. 53–54.

CHAPTER 20

1. Charles Ives, *Essays Before a Sonata,* Howard Boatwright, ed., New York, 1962, p. 3.

2. Frank R. Rossiter, *Charles Ives and His America,* New York, 1975, p. 135.

3. George Crumb, record jacket notes, Nonesuch Recording H-71255.

4. Crumb, record jacket notes.

5. Kenneth Clark, *Civilization,* New York, 1969, p. 243.

6. Aldous Huxley, "The Rest Is Silence," from *Music at Night,* New York, 1931, pp. 17 ff.

7. Fernand Ouellette, *Edgard Varèse,* Derek Coltman, trans., New York, 1968, pp. 16–18.

8. Gordon Mumma, *Live-Electronic Music,* in Jon H. Appelton and Ronald C. Perera, *The Development and Practice of Electronic Music*, Englewood Cliffs, N.J., 1975, p. 300. Note that Mumma himself designed the computer program and therefore retained responsibility for the music ultimately produced.

9. Berio's record jacket notes, Columbia Recording MS 7268.

CHAPTER 21

1. Reprinted in *Pleasures of Music*, Jacques Barzun, ed., New York, 1951, pp. 21–34. (Unfortunately, the story is omitted in the 1977 reprint of this volume.)

2. See *Either/Or*, Volume 1, "The Immediate Stages of the Erotic or the Musical Erotic," David F. Swenson and Lillian Marvin Swenson, trans., New York, 1959, pp. 43–134. The excerpted sentence is found on p. 46.

3. Modern Library Edition, copyright 1963, pp. 230–231. A musical composition based on Hesse's novel is *Music for the Magic Theatre,* by the contemporary American composer, George Rochberg. Rochberg combines his own atonal style with a mélange of excerpts from earlier composers and featuring a recomposed version of Mozart's *Divertimento in E♭*, K.287.

4. From Shaw's preface to *Man and Superman,* London, 1903, p. ix. "Shavio" and "Shavian" are adjectives derived from the pseudo-Latin version of Shaw's name, "Shavius."

5. George Bernard Shaw, "The *Don Giovanni* Centenary," *Pall Mall Gazette,* October 31, 1887. Permission for all Shaw excerpts granted by The Society of Authors on behalf of the Bernard Shaw estate.

CHAPTER 22

1. Thomas Mann, "The Making of *The Magic Mountain*," an autobiographical essay appended to the novel, New York, 1969, pp. 722–723.

2. See the English translation by H. T. Lowe-Porter, New York, 1948, pp. 51 ff.

3. Ibid., p. 58.

4. Thomas Mann, *The Story of a Novel — The Genesis of Doctor Faustus*, New York, 1961, p. 41.

5. Mann, *Doctor Faustus*, p. 191.

6. Mann, *The Story of a Novel*, p. 29.

7. Ibid., p. 30

8. Author's note, following p. 510 of *Doctor Faustus.*

9. *The Story of a Novel*, p. 36.

UNIT V

1. Igor Stravinsky and Robert Craft, *Conversations with Igor Stravinsky*, New York, 1959, p. 141.

CHAPTER 23

1. From a letter of August 17, 1782, quoted by Alfred Einstein, *Mozart, His Character, His Work,* Arthur Mendel and Nathan Broder, trans., New York, 1945, p. 79.

CHAPTER 25

1. Robert Manson Myers, *Handel's Messiah, A Touchstone of Taste,* New York, 1948, pp. 59–60.

2. Myers, pp. 71–72.

3. Frans Brueggen in George Gelles, "Breathing Life into the Recorder," *New York Times,* October 12, 1975, Sect. 2, p. 15.

4. Ned Rorem, *Pure Contraption, A Composer's Essays,* New York, 1974, p. 84.

5. Rorem. p. 85.

6. See Jacques Chailley, *The Magic Flute, Masonic Opera: an Interpretation of the Libretto and the Music,* Herbert Weinstock, trans., New York, 1971. A related literary work is D. H. Lawrence's novella, *The Man Who Died,* in which Jesus survives the crucifixion, escapes from the tomb, and wends his way to Egypt, where he discovers the temple of Isis and Osiris.

CHAPTER 26

1. Tony Heilbut, *The Gospel Sound,* New York, 1971, p. 10.

2. From *The Rolling Stone Illustrated History of Rock and Roll,* excerpted in *The Boston Globe,* August 21, 1977. The person quoted is the late Elvis Presley.

3. James H. Cone, *The Spirituals and the Blues: An Interpretation,* New York, 1972, p. 5.

4. John Updike, *A Month of Sundays,* New York, 1975.

5. Herbert Norman and H. John Norman, *The Organ Today,* New York, 1967, p. 16.

UNIT VI

1. *H. L. Mencken on Music,* selected by Louis Cheslock, New York, 1961, p. 35.

CHAPTER 27

1. John Reed, *Schubert, the Final Years,* New York, 1972, p. 123.

2. Quoted in Herbert Weinstock, *Tchaikovsky,* New York, 1946, p. 354.

3. J. W. N. Sullivan, *Beethoven, His Spiritual Development,* New York, 1936, p. 223.

4. Sullivan, p. 262.

5. From an introduction (unsigned) in the pocket score of the late quartets published by Wiener Philharmonischer Verlag, Vienna.

6. Sullivan, pp. 243–245.

7. Aldous Huxley, *Point Counter Point,* New York, 1928, p. 505. Reprinted by permission of Harper & Row and Chatto & Windus, Ltd.

8. Huxley, p. 508.

9. Huxley, *Music at Night*, "The Rest Is Silence," New York, 1931, pp. 17ff. Huxley's "three or four minutes of violin playing" is a reference to the sound of the entire quartet.

10. *The Kreutzer Sonata*, from *The Complete Works of Leo Tolstoy*, Volume 16, New York, 1899, p. 130. As well as being inspired by an earlier musical composition, Tolstoy's novella has also served as the inspirational source of a later composition, the *String Quartet No. 1* (1923) by the Czeck composer, Leoš Jánaček.

CHAPTER 28

1. Cited in Reed, *Schubert, The Final Years*, p. 112.

2. John N. Burk, Eulenburg Miniature Score of Berlioz's *Romeo and Juliet*, page XIII.

3. See Charles Baudelaire, "Richard Wagner and *Tannhäuser* in Paris," in Jonathan Mayne, trans. and ed., *The Painter of Modern Life and Other Essays*, p. 117. ©1964 Phaidon Press Ltd., London. Excerpted and reprinted by permission of Praeger Publishers, Inc., New York.

4. Quoted in Faubion Bowers, *The New Scriabin*, New York, 1973, p. 188.

5. Bowers, p. 188.

6. Bowers, p. 189.

CHAPTER 29

1. Quoted in the Eulenburg Miniature Score, page XIII.

2. Thomas Mann, *Stories of Three Decades*, H. T. Lowe-Porter, trans. New York, 1948, p. 310. Reprinted by permission of Alfred A. Knopf, Inc.

CHAPTER 30

1. Erika Ostrovsky, *Céline and His Vision*, New York, 1967, pp. 130–131. Ostrovsky's book is cited in Kurt Vonnegut's novel, *Slaughterhouse Five*, New York, 1969, pp. 12–13.

2. Robert Collet, "Works for Piano and Orchestra," in Alan Walker, ed., *Franz Liszt: The Man and His Music*, New York, 1970, p. 273.

3. Hans F. Redlich, Foreword to Mahler's *Symphony No. 4*, Eulenburg Miniature Score, London, 1966, p. xvi.

4. Harry Ellis Dickson, *Gentleman, More Dolce, Please!, An Irreverent Memoir of Thirty-five Years in the Boston Symphony Orchestra*, 2nd ed., Boston, 1974, p. 120.

5. Herbert Weinstock attributes this title to the noted nineteenth-century Russian pianist, Anton Rubenstein. See *Chopin, the Man and His Music*, New York, 1949, p. 241. Weinstock aptly describes the music as spectral.

6. Quoted from the composer's liner notes, Vanguard Recording VCS-10057.

7. Vanguard Recording VCS-10057.

8. Roman Vlad, *Stravinsky*, London, 1960, p. 29.

9. Igor Stravinsky and Robert Craft, *Themes and Episodes*, New York, 1966, p. 320.

CHAPTER 31

1. Ned Rorem, *Critical Affairs—A Composer's Journal*, New York, 1970, p. 117.
2. Rorem, p. 118.
3. Donald Jay Grout, *A History of Western Music*, rev. ed., New York, 1973, p. 657.

CHAPTER 32

1. The information on Dufay's anthem, including the English translation of the quoted lines, is borrowed from Alec Robertson's *Requiem, Music of Mourning and Consolation*, London, 1967, pp. 26–28. Reprinted by permission of Praeger Publishers, Inc.
2. Robertson, pp. 213ff.
3. Charles Koechlin, *Gabriel Fauré*, translated by Leslie Orrey, London, 1946, p. 28. Koechlin was another composer who studied with Fauré.
4. Nadia Boulanger writing in a special issue of *La Revue musicale*, October 1, 1922, as quoted by Koechlin. Boulanger also pointed out that it was against Fauré's nature to judge and condemn others.
5. Translation in Robertson, p. 12.
6. Quoted by Robertson, p. 19.
7. *The Letters of Mozart and His Family*, ed. and trans. by Emily Anderson, Vol. II, 2nd edition, New York, 1966, p. 907.
8. See Robertson, p. 227.

CHAPTER 33

1. Albert Schweitzer, *J. S. Bach*, Ernest Newman, trans., Volume 1, London, 1935, pp. 169–170.
2. "Über dieser Fuge, wo der Nahme B. A. C. H. im Contrapunkt angebracht worden, ist der Verfasser gestorben."
3. From *Epipsychidion* by Percy Bysse Shelley, cited in Samuel Chotzinoff, *Day's at the Morn*, New York, 1964, p. 71.
4. Samuel Chotzinoff, *A Lost Paradise*, New York, 1955, p. 316.
5. *Day's at the Morn*, p. 124. The performance described was the occasion of the Metropolitan Opera conducting debut of Gustav Mahler (1908).
6. Thomas Mann, *Stories of Three Decades*, H. T. Lowe-Porter, trans. New York, 1948, pp. 155–156. Reprinted by permission of Alfred A. Knopf, Inc.

GENERAL INDEX

GENERAL INDEX

An asterisk (*) indicates a composer listed in the Index of Composers and Compositions, pp. xiii ff. All compositions mentioned in the book are included (under *composer*) in that index. In addition, compositions identifiable exclusively or alternatively by unique names—such as Strauss's *Death and Transfiguration* and Beethoven's *Symphony No. 9 in D Minor*, known also as the *Choral Symphony*—are included below under those specific *titles*. For definitions of terms, in addition to those listed here, see the checklists following each unit, and consult the Glossary, pp. 476 ff.

Ewen, David, 105–106, 110
Exotic Birds (Messiaen), 45
exposition
    fugal, 188
    sonata-form, 133
expressionism, 20

*Falla, Manuel de
false reprise, 327
Falstaff (Verdi), 149n, 161
Fancy Free (Bernstein), 328
Fantasia (Disney), 412
Fantastic Symphony (Berlioz), *see*
    Symphonie fantastique
"Farewell" (Mahler), 239–41
*Fauré, Gabriel
Faust, 218, 268ff, 428
Faust (Goethe), 149n, 237, 264n,
    268ff
Faust (Gounod), 264, 268
Faust Overture, A (Wagner), 268
Faust Symphony (Liszt), 177, 268,
    397
Fell, Jesse, 83
Fellowship of the Ring, The
    (Tolkien), 153
Fêtes (Debussy), 5
Fiddler on the Roof (Bock), 152,
    286, 330
figured bass, 112
Fingal's Cave Overture
    (Mendelssohn), 11–14, 20,
    23–24, 57, 119–20
Finlandia (Sibelius), 61–63
Firebird (Stravinsky), 78, 427
First Hundred Years of Tristan,
    The (Zuckerman), 153n
Fisher, William Arms, 129
Five, The, 74, 78
Five Easy Pieces, 377
flamenco, 68
flat, 30
Flaubert, Gustave, 75
Fledermaus, Die (Strauss), 161
Florestan, 233

Flying Dutchman, The (Wagner),
    268
folk music, 286
Follia, La (Corelli), 302
Fonteyn, Margot, 382
"For He's a Jolly Good Fellow,"
    89
forms, musical, 23–24; *see also*
    genres, rondo, theme and
    variations, sonata-form
*Forrest and Wright
Four Etudes for Orchestra
    (Stravinsky), 120
Four Last Songs (Strauss), 461
Four Serious Songs (Brahms), 444
Four Slovak Songs (Bartók), 64
4' 33" (Cage), 249
Fourth of July (Ives), 88
*Franck, César
Franklin, Aretha, 336
Franklin, Benjamin, 18, 142
Fremstad, Olive, 462
French Revolution, 18
French Suites (Bach), 6
"Frère Jacques," 85–86, 237, 346,
    403
*Frescobaldi, Girolamo
Freud, Sigmund, 330n, 377
*Friml, Rudolf
From Bohemia's Meadows and
    Forests (Smetana), 57
"From Heaven Above I Come To
    Thee" (Luther–Bach), 337–38
From the Steppes of Russia
    (Borodin), 78
fugato, 122, 197, 224–25
fugue, 182, 186–97, 270, 448, 451,
    453
Fuller, Buckminster, 250
Funerailles (Liszt), 436
funeral march, 403–406, 446
"Funiculi' Funicula'," 120

*Gabrieli, Giovanni
Garcia Lorca, Federico, 250

*Gay, John
Genesis, 36, 54, 316
Genet, Jean, 405
genres, 42
    vocal, 42–43
Georg, Stefan, 215
George I, 14
George II, 318
George V, 436
George White's Scandals
    (Gershwin), 104
German Requiem, A (Brahms),
    198, 435, 443–53
*Gershwin, George
Gershwin, Ira, 106
Gertrude (Hesse), 241
Gettysburg Address (Lincoln), 84
Gide, André, 3, 10, 51
*Glinka, Mikhail
glissando, 180
Gloria, 288
*Gluck, Christoph Willibald von
"God Bless America" (Berlin), 117
"God Save the King," 117–18,
    226
Godspell (Schwartz), 286, 330,
    336
Goethe, Johann von, 18, 149n,
    232, 237–38, 264n, 268ff, 418
"Goin' Home," 129
Goldberg, Johann Gottlieb, 197n
Goldberg Variations (Bach),
    197–98
Gondoliers (Gilbert and Sullivan),
    150
Good Friday Music (Wagner),
    330n
"Goodnight, Ladies," 90
gospel music, 336
Götterdämmerung (Wagner), 157,
    432
*Gounod, Charles
Goya, Francisco, 18, 80
Goyescas (Granados), 80
*Granados, Enrique

Luke (apostle), 328
*Lully, Jean Baptiste de
Luther, Martin, 289, 303, 336–37
(see also Composers' Index)
*Lutoslawski, Witold
Lydian mode, 352–56
Lyric Suite (Berg), 463n
Lythgoe, Clive, 51

Macbeth (Verdi), 149n, 160
*MacDowell, Edward
*Machaut, Guillaume de
Madagascan Songs (Ravel), 123
Madame Butterfly (Puccini),
118n, 123
Maelzel, Johannes, 34
Magic Fire Music (Wagner),
157–58
Magic Flute, The (Mozart), 25, 30,
46, 148, 161, 259, 292, 330
Magic Mountain, The (Mann), 269
Magister Ludi (Hesse), 241
Mahagonny (Weill), 397
Mahler, Alma, 436n
*Mahler, Gustav
"Majority, The" (Ives), 247–48
major mode, scale, 47, 91,
345–47, 353–54, 359ff, 403
Mallarmé, Stefan, 50
Man and Superman (Shaw), 235,
263, 266, 268
mania, 372–76
Mann, Thomas, 153, 218, 268ff,
389–90, 464
Man of La Mancha (Leigh), 425,
432
manual, organ, 339–40
Man Who Died, The (Lawrence),
491
Marie Antoinette, 142
Marlowe, Christopher, 268
Marriage of Figaro, The (Beaumar-
chais), 141–42
Marriage of Figaro, The (Mozart),
141–46, 148–49, 153, 161,
164–65, 257

"Marseillaise," 118, 442–43
Marx, Karl, 19
Masonic Funeral Music (Mozart),
259
Masonry, 330
Mass, 287ff, 303–305, 330, 337
Master Raro, 233
Matins, 287
Ma Vlast (Smetana), 57, 59
Mavra (Stravinsky), 78
mazurka, 73
McLuhan, Marshall, 250
meaning, musical, 247
measure, 31
Medieval period, 23, 101, 287–78,
353–54
"Mee chomocho," 332
Meistersinger, Die (Wagner),
160–61, 389
melisma, 315
Melville, Herman, 19
memorial music, 434–51
Mencken, H. L., 173–74, 176,
330n, 492
*Mendelssohn, Felix
*Menotti, Gian-Carlo
Mephistopheles, 264, 268
Mer, La (Debussy), 3–5, 16–17,
20–21, 23–25, 28, 40, 50–54,
57, 63, 254
Merry Widow, The (Lehar), 67
Merry Wives of Windsor, The
(Shakespeare), 149n
Messe de Notre Dame (Machaut),
288, 354
*Messiaen, Olivier
Messiah (Handel), 42, 316,
318–23, 451
Metapolitics, The Roots of the
Nazi Mind (Viereck), 153n
metronome, 34
microtones, 251, 358
Mighty Fortress Is Our God, A
(Luther–Bach), 303, 306–307,
337n
Mighty Handful, The, 74

Mikado, The (Gilbert and
Sullivan), 123, 150
*Milhaud, Darius
Milne, A. A., 179
Milton, John, 36
minor mode, scale, 47, 91, 97,
345–57, 353–54, 359ff, 403
minuet, 23, 373
mirror inversion, 276–77
Missa Solemnis (Beethoven), 270,
291, 351, 444
Mitzvah for the Dead, A (Sahl),
406–407
mixolydian mode, 353–54
mixture, organ, 340
mode, 91, 353–55
cantorial, 331
modern music, 246
Modern period, 17, 20–21, 341,
407, 427
modulation, 98, 185
Moldau, The (Smetana), 57,
59–61, 125, 346
Molière, 265–66
Monet, Claude, 4–5
monody, 429
monophony, 287, 317, 434–35
*Monteverdi, Claudio
Month of Sundays, A (Updike),
336–37
"Moonlight" Sonata (Beethoven),
207, 242
motet, 288
Mother Goose (Ravel), 48
Mother of Us All, The (Thomson),
87n
motive, 187; see also Leitmotif
Mozart, Leopold, 84
*Mozart, Wolfgang Amadeus
Mudgett, Herman Webster, 423
Mudgett: Monologues of a Mass
Murderer (Randall), 423–24
Müller, Wilhelm, 359
*Mumma, Gordon
Münch, Charles, 383
Mürger, Henri, 383, 386n

504

General Index

505

Rhapsody in Blue (Gershwin), 58, 101, 104–112, 114, 122

Rhapsody on a Theme of Paganini (Rachmaninoff), 114, 198–99, 400–401, 406

Rheingold, Das (Wagner), 54, 154–58, 160, 165, 170, 234

rhythm, 409ff

Rhythm (Lardner), 101

Rigoletto (Verdi), 160

*Rimsky-Korsakov, Nicolai

Rinaldo (Handel), 47

Ring of the Nibelungen, The (Wagner), 152–54, 156–57, 160, 234, 386, 431

Rite of Spring, The, see Le Sacre du printemps

Ritter, Alexander, 459

Robertson, Alec, 435

*Rochberg, George

rock music, 330

rock opera, 328–29

Rococo, 18

Rodeo (Copland), 82, 320

*Rodgers, Richard

Rodin, Auguste, 19

Rolland, Romain, 71n

Romanticism, 350, 358, 370, 372, 380

Romantic period, 17–22, 24, 101, 184, 242ff, 301, 341, 349–50, 358, 436

*Romberg, Sigmund

Romeo and Juliet Symphony (Berlioz), 232, 380–82

Romeo and Juliet (Prokofiev), 382–83

Romeo and Juliet (Shakespeare), 141, 379–83, 385, 431

Romeo and Juliet (Tchaikovsky), 382

rondo, 327, 415–16

Roosevelt, Franklin Delano, 404, 436

Rorem, Ned, 328–29, 430

Rosamunde (Schubert), 209

Rosenkavalier, Der (Strauss), 161, 254

*Rossini, Gioacchino

row, *see* tone row

"Row, Row, Row Your Boat," 197

Royal Ballet, 382

Rubenstein, Anton, 493

"Rule Brittania" Variations (Beethoven), 118

Rumanian Folk Songs (Bartók), 64

Rumpert, Madame, 412

Ruslan and Ludmila (Glinka), 74

Russian music, 74–79, 407–408

Russian Revolution, 20

Sacre du printemps, Le (Stravinsky), 25, 27, 53, 78, 185, 254, 397, 407–17, 427

*Sahl, Michael

"Sailor's Hornpipe," 89

"Saint Anthony Preaches to the Fishes" (Mahler), 237–38

Saint Cecilia, or The Power of Music (Kleist), 303–305, 356

Saint Francis, 437

*Saint-Saëns, Camille

Salammbo (Flaubert), 75

Salome (Strauss), 161, 425

Salon Mexico, El (Copland), 120

Samson and Delilah (Saint-Saëns), 330

Sanctus, 288, 434

Sand, George, 404

Satan, 270–71

*Satie, Erik

Saudades do Brasil (Milhaud), 121

Saul (Handel), 317, 403

scales, 91–93, 353–54

*Scarlatti, Alessandro

Scenes from Faust (Schumann), 268

Schering, Arnold, 112

scherzo, 23, 373, 402

Schiller, Friedrich, 18, 217, 219ff, 232, 242

Schirmer, G., & Sons, 102

*Schoenberg, Arnold

Schöne Müllerin, Die (Schubert), 359

Schopenhauer, Arthur, 233, 241

*Schubert, Franz

Schumann, Clara, 444–45

*Schumann, Robert

*Schütz, Heinrich

*Schwartz, Stephen

Schweitzer, Albert, 453

Scottish Symphony (Mendelssohn), 11, 119

*Scriabin, Alexander

Sea Symphony (Vaughan Williams), 53

Seasons, The (Vivaldi), 5–7, 17, 20, 23–24, 44, 57, 112, 446

secondary tonic, 98–99

seguiriya gitana, 68

semi-classical, 53

sequence, 442

serialism, 20, 199, 251, 270, 407

Seven Last Words, The (Haydn), 327

Seven Last Words of Christ, The (Schütz), 327

Seven Spanish Folk Songs (Falla), 68–70, 80

Shakespeare, William, 17, 76, 141, 234, 256, 265, 379–83, 386n, 390, 431

sharp, 30

Shaw, George Bernard, 153, 156, 173, 218, 234–35, 263–68, 419n

Shearer, Norma, 379

Sheehan, Vincent, 120

Shéhérezade (Ravel), 122–23

Shelley, Percy Bysshe, 18, 494

Shentall, Susan, 379

"Sh'ma," 332–33

*Shostakovich, Dmitri

Showboat (Kern), 117, 164

*Sibelius, Jan

Siddhartha (Hesse), 241

Siegfried (Wagner), 46, 157

Siegfried's Rhine Journey (Wagner), 158
Silence (Cage), 249
"Simple Gifts," 82
Simpson, Henrietta, 370–71
Sinfonia (Berio), 238n, 254
Sirenes (Debussy), 5, 52
Sister Angelica (Puccini), 330
Sketch of a New Aesthetic of Music (Busoni), 251
Slaughter on Tenth Avenue (Rodgers), 328
Slonimsky, Nicolas, 45, 118
slur, 442
Smart, Christopher, 378
*Smetana, Bedřich
Society of David, 233
Society of Friends, 285
Socrate (Satie), 425, 429–30
Socrates, 263, 429–30
solfège, 254
Solomon (Handel), 317
Solti, Georg, 157n, 158
sonata allegro form, see sonata form
sonata form, 128, 133–34, 174–76, 327
song, 358
song cycle, 68, 358ff
Song of Norway (Forrest and Wright), 72
"Song of the Birds" (Jannequin), 44
Song of the Earth, The, see Das Lied von der Erde
"Song of the Volga Boatmen," 78
Songs and Dances of Death (Mussorgsky), 421
Songs of a Wayfarer (Mahler), 237
songs of death, 418–425
song symphony, 236–238
Sorcerer's Apprentice, The (Dukas), 375
Sound of Music (Rodgers), 106
"Sourwood Mountain," 103

South Pacific (Rodgers), 106, 164
souvenirs, musical, 119ff
Spanish Civil War, 20
Spanish Folk Songs, see Seven Spanish Folk Songs
Spanish music, 79–80
Spectator, The, 47
spirituals, 125
"Spring" Concerto (Vivaldi), 5–7, 23–24, 44, 112, 446
"Springfield Mountain," 83
Spring Rounds (Debussy), 52
staff, 29
Staffa (Keats), 12
*Stainer, John
"Star Spangled Banner, The," 118, 273
stasis, harmonic, 409–11
Stein, Gertrude, 87n
Steppenwolf (Hesse), 241, 263
Stevenson, Adlai, 83
St. Exupery, Antoine de, 179
*Stockhausen, Karlheinz
Stokowski, Leopold, 106
stop, see organ
Stradivari, Antonio, 213
*Strauss, Johann, Jr.
*Strauss, Richard
*Stravinsky, Igor
stream-of-consciousness, 377
stretto (fugal), 191–92
Strindberg, August, 19
string instruments, 15
string quartet, 200ff
strophic, 359
*Strouse, Charles
Student Prince, The (Romberg), 163
styles, compositional, 20–23
subheadings, movement, 25
subject, fugue, 186, 190–91, 195–97
suite, 274, 382–83
*Sullivan, Arthur
Sullivan, J. W. N., 352–53, 356

*Sulzer, Solomon
Sundgaard, Arnold, 103
Sunken Cathedral, The (Debussy), 48, 51
Superman, The, 233, 235, 263
"Surprise" Symphony (Haydn), 242
Survivor from Warsaw (Schoenberg), 333
suspension, 100
*Sussmayr, Franz
Swan of Tuonela, The (Sibelius), 63
"Swanee, How I Love Ya" (Gershwin), 104
Swift, Jonathan, 18
"Swing Low, Sweet Chariot," 125, 127, 132
symphonic poem, 23; see also tone poem
Symphonie fantastique (Berlioz), 121, 133, 177, 243, 370–77, 380, 397, 402, 439
symphony, 25–27, 111–112, 126ff
syncopation, 126, 131–33, 378, 414
synthesizer, 253, 340

Tale of Don Juan, A (Hoffmann), 262
Tales of Hoffmann, 262
Tapiola (Sibelius), 63
tape loop, 253
Tate, Nahum, 426
Tchaikovsky, Modest, 120
*Tchaikovsky, Peter Ilich
*Telemann, Georg Philipp
tempo, 34
Tennyson, Alfred Lord, 19
tenor clef, 30
texts, opera, 148–49
theme and variations, 182, 219–31, 296–302, 308, 400, 455–57
Thirty Years' War, 18

*Weber, Carl Maria von
Weber, Constanze, 292
*Weill, Kurt
Weinstock, Herbert, 493
Well-Tempered Clavier, The
(Bach), 93, 186–92, 347
"Were You There?" 286, 327
West Side Story (Bernstein), 164,
330, 333–34, 383, 425,
431–32
"When Johnny Comes Marching
Home," 86
*When Lilacs Last in the Door-Yard
Bloomed* (Hindemith), 436
Whistler, James, 19, 106
Whitaker, W. Gilles, 13

"White Cockade, The," 89
Whiteman, Paul, 106
White Peacock, The (Griffes), 52
Whiting, Leonard, 379
Whitman, Walt, 19, 83, 436
whole-tone scale, 47–51
"Whoopee ti yi yo," 425
Wilde, Oscar, 150–51
Winnie the Pooh (Milne), 179
Winterreise (Schubert), 345,
359–70
*Wolf, Hugo
Wonderful Town (Bernstein), 330
Woodland Sketches (MacDowell),
51
woodwind instruments, 15

World as Will and Idea, The
(Schopenhauer), 233
Woyzeck (Büchner), 169–70
Wozzeck (Berg), 165, 169–72,
234, 254, 334

"Yankee Doodle," 86
Year from Monday, A (Cage), 249
*Young Person's Guide to the Or-
chestra, The* (Britten), 179,
181–82, 272, 291, 341
Youth's Magic Horn, The, 421–22

Zeffirelli, Franco, 379, 383
Zeitoper, 167
Zuckerman, Elliott, 153n

DATE DUE

APR 4 '84			
MAY 2 '84			
MAR 25 '87			
APR 8 '87 4/21/17			